A PECULIAR
OCCUPATION
NEW PERSPECTIVES ON HITLER'S CHANNEL ISLANDS

A PECULIAR
OCCUPATION

NEW PERSPECTIVES ON HITLER'S CHANNEL ISLANDS

PETER TABB

Ian Allan
PUBLISHING

This book is dedicated to my wife Therese and my children Philippa and Matthew who have had to endure sharing their life with the ceaseless pounding of a keyboard

First published 2005

ISBN 0 7110 3113 4

© Peter Tabb 2005

Published by Ian Allan Publishing

an imprint of Ian Allan Publishing Ltd, Hersham, Surrey KT12 4RG.
Printed in England by Ian Allan Printing Ltd, Hersham, Surrey KT12 4RG.

Code: 0505/B

Contents

Chapter 14 – Aftermath   **217**

*The scars and the heritage — some reminiscences of those who lived
through Occupation — those for whom the Occupation is distant history —
the swords of war into the ploughshares of peace. How we remember —
was it victory or peace? A reconciliation*

*'The enduring achievement of historical study is an historical sense — an
intuitive understanding — of how things do not happen.'*
Sir Lewis B. Namier

Foreword

I was born in Jersey in 1944, on Saturday, 3 June, and my birth was announced in *The Evening Post*, then and now Jersey's only daily newspaper, on 6 June, sharing the front page with the news that the Allies had landed in Normandy.

A little over 11 months later, on 9 May 1945, I sat on my mother's shoulders and saw the Union flag being hoisted at the Harbour Office in place of the German ensign that had fluttered there for almost five years.

Although too young to retain any memories of the joys of the first Liberation Day, I grew up with the evidence of the German occupation all round me. Across the road from my parents' rented cottage was a meadow bisected by the ballast of an *Organisation Todt* (OT) railway built to bring coal to its power station nestling in a quarry just 100 metres away. The rails themselves had been taken up for scrap in 1946.

Further up the valley, and within five minutes' bicycle ride, lurked what was already a major tourist attraction — the German Underground Hospital (now known as the Jersey War Tunnels) — and in an adjacent valley lay a series of even bigger tunnels, made more enthralling by the fact that they were sealed and were reputed to be filled with guns, vehicles and other debris of war. The reality was that the tunnels, when eventually probed by schoolboys who could squeeze through gaps adults could not, were revealed to contain rusting field kitchens, gas-mask canisters, lots of helmets and precious little else. Tiger tanks and 88mm anti-tank guns there were not. However, these tunnels did have the ability to bite back: two contemporaries from my school suffocated when a fire they had lit consumed the available air with tragic consequences. Nevertheless, we wore German helmets and used gas-mask canisters to carry our school books and other juvenile paraphernalia.

The land above and adjacent to the German Underground Hospital (still looking much as it did in 1945) yielded more interesting finds including belts of live ammunition of up to 20mm calibre and, most exciting of all, a German anti-tank bazooka with one of its bombs still 'up the spout'. This last was sold to the curator of the German Underground Hospital for the princely sum of a half-crown (12½p), in those days sufficient to invest in two illicit packets of local Ching & Company's cigarettes!

Although it was in private ownership, access to the old power station was readily achieved by climbing through the furnace doors that once served the boiler. The principal contents of the power station — steam engines and huge generators with miles of copper wiring — had been taken for scrap within months of the Liberation, but there were still sufficient items of interest left behind to stimulate young imaginations — imaginations stirred to fever pitch when the body of a local man was found, having, apparently, fallen to his death from the first floor to the concrete ground floor.

All German fortifications were built with emergency exits. In the case of the German Underground Hospital, the emergency exit was an escape shaft extending nearly vertically from the boiler room some 33 metres below and emerging into a field. The shaft also served as the flue for the hospital's two Potterton coke-fired boilers and the exhaust pipes from diesel generators. It comprised a steep concrete staircase (without handrails!) and a vertical ladder of iron staples. The stair treads were narrow enough for it to be almost impossible for an adult to descend (although relatively easy to run up) which was, of course, an anti-invasion measure, although clearly the tunnel complex's builders had not anticipated that their attackers would be inquisitive schoolboys who had discovered the shaft in the field. Today the shaft is barred with a steel grille but in those days only the original steel gas-tight door jammed in the half-open position prevented the intrepid from entering once the ladder and steps had been negotiated. And if the intrepid was a slim schoolboy . . .

Once inside we played a game called 'winding up the air raid siren'. The siren (conveniently situated near the boiler-room door) was operated by a hand pump which forced air into the air-conditioning system past a reed, giving, as it was intended to, a passable impression of the London Blitz. The intention was to terrify any visitors and the usual result was a huffing and puffing curator who had had to abandon his post at the cash desk while the miscreants vanished up the escape shaft.

For many years, until it came into private ownership, the German Hospital was simply bare concrete tunnels, its contents having been stripped by souvenir hunters (starting with the liberating forces) who took everything that was not bolted down and much that was.

Between the power station and the sea and alongside the former railway track were also the remains of *Lager Schepke*, the camp where OT workers were once housed in Nissen-type huts. For many years just one hut remained where we played table tennis even as adults but as a child the enduring memory was that these remains were known as the 'German lavatories' because the foundations of the ablution block with its murky trenches and sluices were still recognisable and, with the wind in the wrong direction, wafted their own noisome memories.

While I was growing up, memories of the Occupation were omnipresent. Strangely (at least it seemed so to me) my parents never talked about their experiences except when asked direct questions. Indeed, almost as soon as the war was over, they 'emigrated' back to the United Kingdom, to live with my London-born mother's sister in Leicester. My father, Jersey-born and by trade a lorry driver, became a driver for the Midland Red Omnibus Company, his experience of driving lorries around Jersey's narrow lanes allowing him to pass the Public Service Vehicle driving test in a matter of days when others required weeks. Their sojourn lasted a mere 18 months for surprisingly my mother, who had not come to live in Jersey until 1937, felt homesick!

Despite growing up with the evidence of German occupation all around, the intent of all seemed to be to eradicate the memories and the artefacts that fed them. Indeed it was 30 years after the Liberation that the Channel Islands Occupation Society was formed and then by enthusiasts to whom the occupation was already part of their parents' lives rather then their own.

Around the Islands many fortifications were simply allowed to be returned to nature, although some — particularly the anti-tank walls along many of the Islands' bays — fulfilled a very useful postwar purpose of keeping back the sea that would have taken millions from the public purse. Others — bunkers in particular — were ground down until modern buildings and even car parks were created on their foundations. Some found a use — one tunnel is used to grow mushrooms, another stores the bits and pieces of Jersey's annual floral festival, the Battle of Flowers, and several rifle ranges. A bunker which once housed a 10.5cm coastal defence battery is now a café and the *Kriegsmarine's* MP2 tower, overlooking Jersey's famous Corbière lighthouse (the first in the world by bizarre coincidence to be built entirely of concrete, in 1874), until very recently housed a maritime radio station. In the 1960s, at the height of the Cold War, a telecommunications bunker in Jersey's capital, St Helier, was converted to be the Civil Defence Headquarters, its location supposedly secret provided invading Russians were not able to read 'Civil Defence HQ' on the dustbin outside the main entrance!

In an earlier career mode I served as a meteorological officer at the Civil Defence HQ and took part in Operation 'Dust Fall' which anticipated a Russian nuclear assault on Cherbourg. Since the Channel Islands are blessed with a prevailing south-westerly wind, it was anticipated that the nuclear fall-out from Cherbourg, some 50 miles or so to the north-east, would take several years to reach us. So we all went home.

I first became *really* interested in the German Occupation in the 1980s when, following a number of career changes, I was retained as a public relations consultant by the owners of the German Underground Hospital. I worked with that organisation until 2003 and in 22 years I must have conducted hundreds of press and television journalists from national and international media around the complex. I also saw what was a tourist attraction which still largely relied on a heavy dose of imagination transformed into a museum of international stature, a deserved award winner and now a definitive living history of the German occupation that both entertains and educates. Its change of name to the Jersey War Tunnels is, if anything, a more accurate description of the complex than 'underground hospital', which was a sobriquet acquired by common usage well after the Occupation.

As I grew older and the journalists I was talking to got younger, I found that not only did I need to explain why it was a *German* underground hospital rather than a British, French or even American one — the fact that the Channel Islands were the only part of Great Britain to be occupied by German forces seems somehow to have been missed off contemporary history curriculums — I also found that I was having to explain how the entire World War 2 came about before ultimately focusing on the part that the Channel Islands played in it.

In the 1980s my mother, along with many others, was interviewed by BBC Radio Jersey and invited to relate her wartime experiences. My mother told of what happened when Germans billeted in the same building where my parents lived stole her radio aerial. She told how she went to College House (the headquarters of *Feldkommandantur 515* — Field Command 515) and complained to the Commandant, *Oberst* (Colonel) Friedrich Schumacher. Within a day or two my mother had her aerial returned. Unfortunately my mother's memory, although as sharp as a tack on many things, mixed up the year and she confused 1940 (when the incident happened) with 1944 (which she told the BBC) when possession of the radio into which the aerial fed its signal was a serious offence punishable with a prison sentence!

In 1993 my mother died (my father had died seven years earlier) and I inherited a small cache of private papers, amongst them some Red Cross letters and a Southern Railway embarkation ticket. The embarkation ticket was dated 5 July 1940. Like so many others my parents had dithered about evacuating. My mother, a Cockney, wanted to return 'home' to her family, all of whom still lived in the East End of London. My father, a native-born Jerseyman with a large local family, preferred to stay. They probably bickered but eventually my mother's will prevailed. Unfortunately, the earliest sailing they could obtain was scheduled to depart Jersey on 5 July, four days after the Germans invaded! The sailing ticket today is framed and on the wall in my hall — a poignant reminder of the perils of prevarication.

Viewed from the perspective of half a century later, the Red Cross letters to and from my mother's sister in London are almost laughably banal. Text was limited to 20 words and thus one or two brief, very brief, sentences of trivia to pass the censor. For example: 'All well. Eric's father (my grandfather) died Christmas Day.'

A commiseration came nine months later.

More than one journalist, after a visit to the German Underground Hospital and weighed down with the notes and other ephemera I supplied, commented that I should 'write a book about it'.

Despite a professional involvement with the topic for more than 20 years I had no specific intention to 'write a book about it'. I had spoken (and written) long about the Occupation which was a period of extreme tedium, an extended period of deprivation of all those elements that, even in the 1940s, created a 'quality of life', under a rigorous regime that while it lacked the extremes of Nazism — in particular the *Gestapo* and the *SS* (except in

Alderney) — was nevertheless driven ultimately by the same leadership and had the same objectives. Although he never visited them, Adolf Hitler proved time and time again (as we shall see) that the Channel Islands, the only British possessions actually to fall under his hegemony, were never too far from his thoughts, almost a peculiar preoccupation. His Commander-in-Chief *Vizeadmiral* Hüffmeier's comment to Bailiff Coutanche that they would both be 'eating grass' before he surrendered was no idle boast.

Yet at the time the remark was made, in February 1945, the German Reich was already in ruins. Hitler's faith in his armed forces had diminished dramatically after the July 1944 bomb plot. With the Army distrusted and the Air Force discredited, only the Navy, whose loyalty to Germany was indivisible from its loyalty to Germany's leader, and had suffered appalling losses in the Battle of the Atlantic which for so long had looked like achieving its objective of strangling Britain, was deemed by the *Führer* to be loyal enough to be given command of strategic or otherwise valuable locations.

Thus it was that the Channel Islands came under naval command. That is why, along with the U-boat bases at Lorient and La Pallice and the port of Dunkirk, they celebrate their liberation the day after the rest of Europe, since the German Navy would not surrender until ordered to by its own Commander-in-Chief, Hitler's nominated successor, *Grossadmiral* Karl Dönitz.

Since the 50th anniversary of the Liberation in 1995, where my role as commentator was to keep the crowds milling about in Jersey's Liberation Square entertained until the arrival of HRH Prince Charles, I have read most if not all of the plethora of publications on the Occupation that appeared on the bookshelves at that time.

Thus I started out with no particular mission. I wanted to tell the story of the German occupation as I understood it and I wanted to tell it from my own perspective. But there was also a little more to it than that. History is littered with 'what ifs'. What if someone had taken a pot shot at the first German to land in the Channel Islands, *Hauptmann* Liebe-Pieteritz of the *Luftwaffe*, who touched down at Guernsey airport in his Dornier *Do17P* on Sunday, 30 June 1940? What if the Allies *had* decided to use the Channel Islands as stepping stones into continental Europe? What if the German raid on nearby Granville in March 1945 had succeeded in acquiring the fuel and food (destined for the US Third Army) that had been the objective? What if *Vizeadmiral* Hüffmeier had not agreed to surrender?

Throughout the narrative I have used the German titles since they serve to emphasise the alien nature of the Occupation.

And, while telling the story of the Channel Islands' invasion, occupation and ultimate liberation in my own way, I will also be looking at what might have happened if . . .

Acknowledgements

Initially this was a book that I didn't really want to write. I was much more taken with the 'factional' trilogy of Occupation novels I had embarked upon some months earlier and which, at the time of writing, is still incomplete. Like Harry Patterson (*The Night of the Fox*), Tim Binding (*Island Madness*), Guy Walters (*The Occupation*) and even historian Charles Cruickshank, whose *The German Occupation of the Channel Islands* has been for many years the definitive and official history, and who was tempted into fiction with *The V-Mann Papers,* I always perceived that a fictional story rooted in fact and historically accurate was likely to be more commercially successful than just another book about the history of the Occupation. Even the prospect of producing a work to coincide with the 60th anniversary of the Liberation of the Channel Islands offered little incentive, particularly since the Jersey Heritage Trust had very properly engaged its own established historian to do the same thing.

It was the eagerness of my friend and one-time near neighbour Howard Butlin Baker, with his own indefatigable enthusiasm for the project that, ultimately drove me on. No mean historian himself, he was able to convince me (as probably no one else could have done) that despite my own reservations and with his nose for research and insatiable curiosity feeding me, there was ample scope for such a publication.

No one attempting to record the Occupation of the Channel Islands (in whatever way he or she were to contemplate such a project) can do so without first reading Leslie Sinel's Occupation Diary. Leslie was a proof-reader at *The Evening Post* (the *Jersey* was added in the 1960s) throughout the Occupation and, in the forward to the diary which was printed and published by *The Evening Post*, the managing editor Arthur Harrison acknowledged the risks taken by Leslie, particularly when making notes at the *EP's* offices under the very noses of the German censors who were a daily feature of every edition. Many years later when Leslie was works manager at the *EP* and I was a very new member of the staff he invited me into his office and gave me a copy of *The Evening Post* of 6 June 1944 on whose front page was recorded my birth.

William Bell's *Guernsey Occupied but Never Conquered* is a seminal work and is a must for anyone attempting to understand just how things were in the Bailiwick of Guernsey in those extraordinary years.

It is a measure of the degree of how much Islanders wanted to forget that they had ever been occupied by an enemy (despite the decaying concrete evidence all around) that a Channel Islands Occupation Society (CIOS) was not formed until the 1960s and then by men who were little more than schoolboys. Michael Ginns is both president and honorary secretary of the

Jersey branch of the CIOS and was deservedly awarded the MBE for his comprehensive and meticulous chronicling of the Occupation although, as a schoolboy, he was one of those deported in September 1942 to Germany. Michael is inspirational and his published works under the CIOS imprint are the definitive guide to the fascinating minutiae of the five years of conflict. I am deeply indebted to him for taking the time and trouble to read the draft manuscript and pointing out my many initial errors. Any that remain are strictly my own.

I am especially indebted to my friend and fellow-collector Trevor du Feu who gave me unlimited access to his amazing collection of Occupation memorabilia. Trevor, like me, is an avid collector of many things but until he offered his collection I had no idea just what a goldmine of material he was storing in his loft.

I am privileged to be acquainted with Joe Mière, one-time political prisoner of the Germans, one-time curator of the German Underground Hospital and indefatigable fighter for formal recognition (not actually achieved until 2001) of the hundreds of individuals who fought back, many of whom paid for their defiance with their lives. Joe was a teenager who openly defied the German occupiers and suffered beatings and imprisonment at the hands of the *GFP*, the *Geheimefeldpolizei* or Secret Field Police, for what they described as acts of terrorism. It is possible to read between the lines of a report by *Polizeiinspektor* Richard Bode of his frustration at this particular Jerseyman who was determined not to 'come quietly'. Joe is a man of forthright views and he has recently published his own characteristically forthright record of the Occupation. I wonder how many other historical works include the words 'sods' and 'farts' to describe some of the protagonists!

The friendly help, advice and archives available from the Jersey Archive Service, the Société Jersiaise and the *Jersey Evening Post* are invaluable to any budding historian and are very much appreciated as are the various sources in the other Islands, all of whom are happy to share their accumulated knowledge and experiences.

Writing is a lonely profession, even with modern technology. I first started writing as a hobby more than 30 years ago when my tool of the trade was a vintage, stand-up Imperial typewriter. My first attempts at writing thrillers were very much a case of the journey being more interesting than the destination. Certainly those early efforts, as fulfilling as the journey was, rightly ended up as scrap paper. Later efforts, although running into millions of key strokes, were probably not much better and it was easier to earn a living writing advertisements and press releases. Nevertheless the beavering away in the corner over a hot keyboard has been a feature of my married life and my wife Therese has had to endure my intent of 'This is the one, this really is the one' so many times . . . I owe any success I may achieve in any of my endeavours to her because where other wives might have cavilled at sharing their lives with a word processor, she did not.

Chapter 1
Peculiars of the Crown

The Channel Islands' unique relationship with the Crown of England, how it came about and what it was to mean more than seven centuries later

Victor Hugo famously referred to the Channel Islands as pieces of France dropped into the sea and scooped up by England. Quite how this came about and how the Channel Islands came to be 'peculiar' can be a rather long story.

So this is the shorter version and although its relevance to the events of the first half of the 20th century may at first be a little obscure it is the special relationship enjoyed by the Bailiwicks of Jersey and Guernsey with the English Sovereign (that endures to this day) that both conditioned how the Islands reacted to enemy occupation and for some still fuels a long-standing resentment. Resentment because the Sovereign's most loyal possessions were abandoned by his government not so much without a fight — since a fight would have been a disaster for the Islands' tightly packed populations (see what might have happened in Chapter 4) — but without even a credible expression of regret from the British government although the King himself did write us a note on 24 June 1940, addressed to the Bailiffs of Jersey and Guernsey.

'For strategic reasons it has been found necessary to withdraw the armed forces from the Channel Islands. I deeply regret this necessity and I wish to assure my people in the Islands that, in taking this decision, my Government has not been unmindful of their position. It is in their interest that this step should de taken in present circumstances.

'The long association of the Islands with the Crown and the loyal service that the people of the Islands have rendered to my ancestors and myself are guarantees that the link between us will remain unbroken and I know that my people in the Islands will look forward with the same confidence as I do to the day when the resolute fortitude with which we face our present difficulties will reap the reward of victory.'

So just who were these ancestors to whom HM George VI referred?

In AD911 the Norse princeling Rollo or Rollon or even Rolfe made a deal with the French king Charles the Simple. Charles was prepared to cede to Rollo the province of Rouen if the Norseman became a Christian and married his daughter (probably in that order) and provided he pensioned off the longboat which had brought him from Norway on his campaign (presumably) of rape and pillage. Although Rollo was initially known as Count, within 20 years the province had become a duchy and Rollo's son William Longsword, now elevated to Duke of Normandy, in AD933 annexed the nearby (and virtually uninhabited) Channel Islands into his realm.

In 1066 Rollo's great-grandson, known as William the Bastard (although rarely to his face), took off from Normandy, fought the Battle of Hastings and wrested the crown of England from his relation Harold Godwinson, becoming William the Conqueror in the process. Channel Islanders went with him and their descendants still lay claim to England as their oldest possession!

In 1189 William's own great-grandson King Richard (he of the Lion Heart) succeeded his father Henry II to the throne of England and the Dukedom of Normandy. Almost immediately Richard was off to the Holy Land, in the company of King Philippe Auguste of France, to eject the Saracens from Jerusalem. He also created his youngest brother, Prince John, Lord of the Isles, with the Channel Islands falling into his *fief*. During the Crusades (which were somewhat unsuccessful) Richard and Philippe fell out over strategy and after many adventures (one allegedly involving Blondel, a wandering minstrel) Richard returned to Normandy and began building a magnificent castle on the banks of the Seine at Les Andelys in what Philippe now regarded as his France. In 1199 Richard was killed by an arrow while besieging a castle near Limoges and his brother John and nephew Arthur (son of his deceased elder brother Geoffrey) were rivals for his throne. The mischief-making Philippe seized his opportunity and in 1202 he invaded Normandy to support Arthur's claim. Arthur, invading Normandy from Brittany, was taken prisoner by John's defenders and, never being seen again, was presumably done to death. However, one after the other the great castles built all over Normandy by King John's brother, father and grandfather fell to Philippe's irresistible advance until by June 1204 John's last stronghold, Rouen, had surrendered. John was living up to his name, 'Lackland', acquired at his birth since his father, Henry II, had already decided how his lands were going to be divided up and John, the youngest son, was given none.

However, the Channel Islands, although nominally still part of Normandy and sharing the Norman language and culture, since they had been largely colonised by Normans who even in those days saw benefits in being 'offshore', chose to remain loyal to the English rather than the French crown. Quite what pressures John exerted on the Channel Island nobles present at his court in London can only be guessed at but whatever they were, the Islands' leaders decided that loyalty to John Lackland of England was preferable to fealty to Philippe Auguste of France. Since everybody who was anybody in England still spoke French at that time, becoming 'English' rather than 'French' was not quite the culture shock it would be today. As a reward for this loyalty John gave the Islands their status as 'peculiars of the Crown', which granted them many privileges, the most important of which was the right to govern themselves under the protection of the Crown without interference from any English parliament.

That situation pertains to this day.

* * *

The archipelago known as the Channel Islands comprises nine separate islands and islets, in descending order of size: Jersey, Guernsey, Alderney, Sark, Herm, Jethou, Brecqhou, Burhou and Lihou. The suffix *–ey* is Old Norse for an island and the suffix *–hou* for an islet. In addition there are several reefs, the principal of which are Les Minquiers and Les Ecréhous, both between Jersey and France. Although being as close to France as they are to Jersey, both reefs were deemed to be British by a decision of the International Court in The Hague in 1954. While the rocks support just a few cottages which Jersey residents use as summer residences, the seas around them teem with fish and thus in whose fishing grounds they are is crucially important. The extremities of the Minquiers reef (which stretches between Jersey and France to the south) are French owned: the Roches d'Ouevres to the west and the Chausey islets to the east. The main island of Chausey is just eight miles from Granville and supports a small community whose principal activities are either fishing or catering for summer visitors. At one time the island was owned by the Renault family and its mansion is still a major feature of the bleak landscape. Chausey was also the source of much of the pink granite seen in Jersey, particularly that used to build Fort Regent, a fortification begun during the Napoleonic Wars but not finished until well afterwards.

Although comprising nine islands, the Channel Islands are actually just two Bailiwicks, each presided over by the Sovereign's appointed Bailiff whose original role was exactly that of a steward acting on behalf of the lord of the manor. The Bailiwick of Jersey comprises Jersey and the Minquiers and Ecréhous reefs while the Bailiwick of Guernsey comprises everything else. Notwithstanding the Bailiwicks, each island is essentially self-governing with Jersey, Guernsey, Alderney and Sark each having its own 'parliament' while the others are either privately owned or on leases from the Crown. Although each has accommodation, Jethou, Burhou and Lihou are not inhabited on a year-round basis while Brecqhou now has a castellated mansion which was built as the occasional home of media moguls, the Barclay brothers.

Having English islands sitting in the Bay of St Malo was a continuing provocation to the French and the Islands' loyalty was to be tested many times. Jersey, being just 14 miles from France and visible as a desirable gem set in a silver sea on all but the murkiest days, was invaded by France many times, the invaders staying, in the Middle Ages, sometimes for years, although the last successful incursion, in 1781, actually lasted for less than 12 hours. Great castles were built; in 1204 work commenced on building Castle Cornet to guard Guernsey's capital St Peter Port's deep water harbour and less than a decade later Mont Orgueil (Mount Pride) was commenced on Jersey's east

coast. Both were erected for much more than show although Mont Orgueil
became more or less obsolete when the cannon replaced the bow and arrow
and trebuchet (a device that threw large stones). It was superseded by a castle
on an islet off the south coast built around an ancient abbey at the instigation
of Governor Sir Walter Ralegh during the reign of Elizabeth I. It was actually
named by him as Fort Isabella Bellissima in a serious bit of brown-nosing.
Both trembled to gunfire given and received.

Although the Islands had opted jointly for fealty to the Crown of England
in 1204, during the Civil War more than 400 years later, the Islands actually
backed opposing sides. Jersey was staunchly Royalist while Guernsey, whose
geographical location a bit further out into the bleak and breezy Western
approaches was more suited to a puritan Calvinism than the flamboyance of
the King's Court favoured by many Jerseymen, favoured the
Parliamentarians. The ramifications for the Islands of this fratricidal conflict
will be examined in more detail in Chapter 2.

Although formally divorced from France in 1204, the Islands maintained a
distinct French personality, so much so that their present legal system owes
much more to the *Code Napoléon* than it does to English jurisprudence and
French only ceased being the official language in the late 1940s and is still
widely used in legal documentation. In both Islands an ancient Norman
French language or *patois* is still spoken (although differing to the extent that
neither can be understood by the other, as a matter of course!) and indeed is
encouraged in Jersey with junior schools now running classes in the language
which did not even have its own dictionary until the 1960s.

During the Occupation news sheets with news gleaned clandestinely from
the BBC were typed out in the *patois* and were widely circulated on both
Islands. Many were intercepted by the Germans who sent the documents to
Paris for translation, from whence they were returned in consternation
because they could not be translated. Since neither language had actually
advanced much since the 16th century and both lacked several of the letters
of the modern alphabet and were not even pronounced, let alone written, in
the same way in different parts of the same Island, it is no wonder that the
occupiers and their French helpmeets were confounded. Unfortunately, since
those who could actually read the texts were relatively few and far between,
these news sheets were more of an irritant to the Germans than a valuable
source of news to the beleaguered civilian population as a whole.

Although the Islands, even to this day, are keen to point out that their
loyalty to Britain is to its Sovereign (still toasted as *Nôt' Duc* — Our Duke) in
practice it is the British government that has always been responsible for the
Islands' foreign policy and defence. Guernseyman Professor J. H. Le Patourel
wrote, in an essay for *La Société Guernesiaise* in 1946, that prior to the
German Occupation of 1940 'the Channel Islands had achieved a high degree
of self-government' and 'their constitutions have not been given them at any
time by an Act of the Crown or by an Act of Parliament. These constitutions

are both home-made and unique.' He went on to say that, although having enjoyed the protection of the English armed forces down the centuries and a relationship with Parliament where the latter, recognising the Islands' strategic importance (for 900 of the Islands' thousand-year history, France was almost always a hostile neighbour), was 'generous, tolerant and helpful', the Islands' autonomous status had been largely achieved by their own efforts. Asking for help from London was not in their nature even though all local legislation had to be (and still has to be) approved by the Sovereign's Privy Council.

With their proximity to France the Channel Islands provided a haven for privateers to prey on French shipping. Privateers were essentially armed ships under private ownership carrying a Letter of Marque, a licence from the King to pillage his enemies in time of war so long as he had a share of the spoils. Jersey's famous Old Court House Inn at St Aubin was the site of the Admiralty prize court where the loot was shared out. Privateers were particularly active during the American War of Independence (France being America's ally) and cargoes destined for the West Indies or the Americas from ports such as Brest, Nantes and Bordeaux frequently ended up in St Helier or St Peter Port where the value of their captured cargoes were divided between the King and his privateer captains.

On 28 September 1769 the overthrow of a despotic government and the pursuit of basic democratic rights occurred in Jersey almost 20 years before it did in France.

'We are here more slaves than our neighbours the French,' wrote one Jersey resident in the *Middlesex Journal*.

The revolution arose because of the 'cruel tyranny' of Charles and Philip Lemprière, as Lieutenant-Bailiff and Attorney-General, and their domination of the Royal Court over many years. In fact, Jersey had only a Lieutenant-Bailiff throughout the 18th century because the descendants of the Carteret family (who we will meet in the next chapter) inherited the appointment as Bailiff like a monarchy but never even visited the Island. One such, Lord Granville, the absentee Bailiff at the time, was described by one historian as a drunken nitwit.

Thomas Gruchy was just one of many arrested after 28 September and the Lemprières were keen that he be hanged or transported for daring to publish a manifesto which intended '. . . to suppress all revolts and to establish a union in the Island. That the Jurats, Connétables, Centeniers and all other elective officers be annually chosen by ballot. When persons are elected but for a certain time, that keeps them subject to the people and the people by those whom they elect.'

Gruchy was pardoned along with all the others by the King.

English and British soldiers have been garrisoned in the Islands since the 13th century, and although there never was a successful invasion by French forces of Guernsey, on two occasions in the late 18th century French soldiers actually successfully invaded Jersey. In May 1779 the Prince of Nassau attempted to lance one of 'the postules on Albion's backside' (Napoléon Bonaparte's irritation at the depredations of the Guernsey and Jersey privateers manifesting itself in his language) with a very brief invasion of Jersey's St Ouen's Bay, the French scurrying back to their boats at the first sign of English redcoats and local militia. The Admiralty sent some frigates and sloops to defend the Islands but just two years later, on 6 January 1781, a Baron de Rullecourt, scalpel at the ready, with 800 French mercenaries and guided by a renegade Jerseyman, Pierre Journeaux, landed on Jersey's south-eastern tip and marched on St Helier, where they convinced Lieutenant-Governor Moise (or Moses) Corbet to surrender.

Fortunately the 24-year-old Major Francis Peirson, officer commanding the 95th Regiment of Foot in barracks at St Peter, decided that the surrender did not apply to him and marched on St Helier where a pitched battle was fought in the Royal Square. Anticipating Nelson, Peirson fell at the moment of victory (de Rullecourt was killed, too), the whole event being captured on canvas by the Bostonian artist John Singleton Copley, although the artist came no closer to the Royal Square than London, creating his masterpiece on the basis of newspaper and eye-witness reports. The original painting is in the Tate Gallery, a copy is in Jersey's Royal Court and the image is on the Jersey £10 note.

The last units of the British Army left the Channel Islands in June 1940 when a confrontation with the German armies racing across France was a looming prospect, and without any doubt the most significant invasion in the Channel Islands' long and often turbulent history was that by the German forces in July 1940. They stayed for five long years, not leaving until the day after VE-Day. The Channel Islands were the only pieces of British soil to fall under German occupation and for the Germans the uncontested capture of the Islands was deemed to be a significant propaganda coup, although very quickly it was abundantly clear that they were the only ones who thought so. No attempt was made to reclaim the Islands by the Allies, and the German forces, armed to the teeth and a division in strength, surrendered on 9 May 1945 without ever having taking more than a few, albeit mostly accurate, potshots at Allied shipping and overflying aircraft.

Since the 1960s, the Channel Islands' autonomy within the British Isles (the Islands are not part of the United Kingdom and neither Bailiwick is a member of the European Union) and the freedom to decide their own fiscal policies (and the awareness that an interest rate above 5% need no longer be perceived as usury) have led to their still burgeoning role as one of the world's most important offshore financial centres.

When the United Kingdom joined the then Common Market in the early 1970s the Channel Islands' 'peculiarity' obtained for them a form of associate membership governed by Protocol 3 of the Treaty of Rome, which meant that while free movement of goods into and out of the Channel Islands was assured, little else dented the Islands' autonomy to do things their way. Indeed, Jersey and Guernsey were among the last places in Europe to abolish capital punishment although the ultimate sanction was last used in the 1950s, Britain's official executioner travelling to Jersey to carry out his grisly function. Sark's parliament — the Chief Pleas — actually voted on the subject as recently as 2003 and, bizarrely for an island whose lock-up is not much bigger than a telephone box, retained it.

In the 10th century a citizen of Normandy could call on his Duke to intervene in disputes with his neighbours. Today Channel Islanders still have the right to call on their Duke of Normandy (currently Queen Elizabeth II) for regal intervention in a procedure known as the *clameur de haro* (the 'ro' bit refers to Duke Rollo). To 'raise the *clameur*' the appellant must fall on his or her knees outside the Royal Court and invoke the Sovereign by calling out: '*Haro, haro, haro, à l'aide, mon Prince, on m'a fait tort!*' ('Ha Rollo, help me, my Prince, someone is doing me wrong!') and then (and this is the difficult bit) reciting the Lord's Prayer in French followed by the complaint (also in French). If properly raised, the Royal Court (acting for the Sovereign) must sit immediately and consider the case. Raising the *clameur* frivolously is not recommended since the penalties are severe although failed appellants no longer need fear having their ears cut off!

The *clameur de haro* has lasted for more than a thousand years. Like much of what can be discovered about the Channel Islands, it is very peculiar . . .

Chapter 2
Civil War

How Jersey and Guernsey found themselves on opposite sides in the English Civil War with consequences that reached into the 20th century

The English Civil War began in the autumn of 1642 and lasted for nine years. Despite the sternly puritan image of Cromwell's Ironsides, the armies on both sides were led by aristocrats and, indeed, in the view of King Charles I, it was the nobility, tired of forking out for Charles' excesses, who had instigated the Civil War.

Although Jersey and Guernsey were both 'peculiars of the Crown', their attitudes to the personage whose flowing locks filled that crown differed markedly. In fact, to put it simply, during the Civil War, the Islands were on opposing sides although, despite being separated by only 20 miles of sea, never actually went to war with each other. The people of Guernsey, further out into the grey Atlantic Ocean, had developed a bleak lifestyle much more akin to the teachings of John Calvin, eschewing the spurious pleasures and the 'cavalier' antics of the Royalist supporters to be found in Jersey.

In fact, the population of Jersey as a whole was itself broadly Calvinist and more liable to favour the Roundheads than the Cavaliers, but one family in particular — the Carterets (who had emigrated from the Norman town of the same name in the 11th century) — decided it was for the King and since it had the wealth and the arms and ammunition, it dragged a largely indifferent population with it.

And in the early days the Carterets' choice seemed to be the right one as Charles defeated the Earl of Essex, 'the rebel in chief', at the Battle of Edgehill in October 1642 and the Royalists enjoyed a number of victories in 1643 until fighting a draw with Essex at the Battle of Newbury in September. Indeed, that first year of the war saw the Parliamentarians at their nadir and a growing popular demand for a cessation of hostilities.

The Channel Islands were far enough apart to prevent open war between them. Nevertheless in 1644 a Captain Lane of the Jersey Militia attempted to recapture Sark which, being part of the Bailiwick of Guernsey, had followed its 'parent' into the Parliamentary camp. The raid was repulsed but the States of Guernsey ordered that there be a permanent garrison to prevent any future incursions.

Many historians today view the English Civil War as one of Europe's last wars of religion with Parliament upholding the Protestant Anglicanism introduced by Henry VIII (although his purposes seemed to be concentrated below the belt) and the Royalists supporting the King who many perceived as a crypto-papist (his wife Henrietta Maria was Catholic). Nevertheless, in 1639 and again in 1640 Charles had tried to force Anglicanism on to the Presbyterian Scots — the Bishops' Wars — and failed, and when Parliament promised to uphold the Presbyterian form of church government and impose it on a largely compliant England, a Scots army of 20,000 came charging over the Tweed early in 1644. The ensuing Battle of Marston Moor was a crushing defeat for Charles' army despite the dashing leadership of his nephew Prince Rupert.

Although Parliament was now winning more battles than it was losing, Sir Henry Vane and Oliver Cromwell purged their armies of their leadership and formed the New Model Army, fortified by constant pay and religious indoctrination. This army inflicted defeat after defeat upon the King's forces and by May 1646 most Royalist forces had surrendered and Charles had handed himself over to the Scots (he was, after all, a Stuart).

Charles was executed on 30 January 1649 and it was in Jersey's aptly named Royal Square that on 17 February Prince Charles was proclaimed Charles II (although it would be another 11 years before his throne was restored to him). As Prince of Wales Charles had visited Jersey in 1646 and he had charmed the Islanders, so much so that diarist Jean Chevalier wrote of him: '*C'étoit un Prince grandement bénin*' ('Here was a Prince greatly blessed') and he returned, fleeing from England, in September 1649, with his brother, James, Duke of York, and 300 followers, seeking refuge in Elizabeth Castle, where they could be protected if the populace decided it was Calvinist after all.

Charles and his substantial retinue stayed in Jersey for nine months, living in the King's House on Elizabeth Castle, visiting with the Carterets at their family seats of St Ouen's and Trinity Manors and joining in their shooting parties, the game in those days consisting of hares, rabbits and red-legged partridges, a species which is now extinct.

In the meantime the Civil War was coming to its conclusion and Parliament decided to do something about pestilential Jersey, whose small fleet was harassing Parliament's shipping in the English Channel. It was also keeping Castle Cornet and its Royalist Governor Sir Peter Osborne supplied to defy the Guernsey population who had been besieging the 'impregnable fortress' (where will we read that phrase again?) for nine long years. During the siege Sir Peter and his successors Sir Baldwin Wake and Colonel Burgess got their own back by shelling the town with some 30,000 cannon balls.

In October 1651, long after the King and his entourage had left for France, a force of 80 ships under the command of the redoubtable Admiral Robert Blake attacked Jersey. Within a week St Aubin's Fort and Mont Orgueil Castle had surrendered. Seven weeks later Elizabeth Castle, commanded by Sir George Carteret, besieged by land and blockaded by sea, and under a bombardment which eventually caused the magazine holding Carteret's ammunition to explode and blow the ancient abbey to smithereens, also surrendered, although on terms which allowed the defenders to march out with colours flying, drums beating and the honours of war. Within days Castle Cornet, finally cut off from its source of supplies, also surrendered in similar fashion, the last bastion of the Royalist cause to do so. For the next nine years all the Channel Islands lived under the stern rule of Lord Protector Oliver Cromwell's Commonwealth.

Sir George joined the King in France and did not return to England until he rode with his monarch on his triumphal entry into London in May 1660.

So thankful was Charles to the people of Jersey (especially those, it is said, of the distaff side) that he gave to Jersey his Royal Mace and the one in the Houses of Parliament in London is actually a replacement.

At the Restoration the still grateful King both ennobled the Carterets and gave them significant tracts of North America, particularly New Jersey. At Sir George's death in 1679 his American possessions were sold to William Penn and his Quaker associates for £3,400. Guernsey, of course, did not warrant such generosity and although the King ordered a general pardon of the people of Guernsey, they were not properly forgiven (by being permitted to have the Sovereign's features on their banknotes and coinage) for several hundred years!

* * *

So, almost four centuries later, how did the fact that Jersey and Guernsey found themselves on opposite sides in the English Civil War impact on the events of the 20th century?

Visitors to the Islands often remark that, despite their obvious similarities, there are marked differences between the Islands, particularly Jersey and Guernsey. We have already seen that during the Civil War the Islands had divided loyalties. In many ways it was almost inevitable that this would be so, for, despite a joint fealty to the Crown of England and an economic dependence on Britain for foodstuffs and most manufactured goods, the Islands have never been dependent on each other and although they are just 20 miles from each other, they have grown apart like twins separated at birth. Almost everything about the Islands is different. They have a different form of government, although both are known as the States (*les Etats*). They have a different way of maintaining law and order, for in Jersey, as well as a uniformed force which is run on the same lines as any constabulary in the United Kingdom, each of the 12 parishes has its own 'honorary' police force whose function pre-dates that of the uniformed force by several hundred years. These worthies wield real policing powers (unlike the specials in the UK) to the extent of presenting cases in court, the uniformed bobbies acting as their aides. Guernsey just has the Island-wide uniformed force.

The Islands have a different language; Jersey-French and Guernsey-French have a common root but a different bloom. Their residents speak with different accents. The way a true Jerseyman speaks English is reminiscent of how English is spoken in South Africa, Australia or even North America, a derivation of how 17th century English sounded with flat vowels and curious inflections. A true Guernseyman has an accent much more akin to the West Country with rounded vowels and a distinct burr. The same names in Jersey and Guernsey are often pronounced differently too. A Le Cocq in Jersey would call himself 'Le Cock', in Guernsey he would call himself 'Le Coke'; similarly Mr Langlois in Jersey pronounces himself 'Longwah', while in Guernsey he would call himself 'Langlay'. There are dozens of other examples.

Islanders also have their own personalities, typified in the names they give each other. People from Jersey are *crapeaux,* toads. The common toad (*bufo bufo*), along with other reptiles and amphibians, still inhabits Jersey (although the agile green frog is only clinging on by his fingertips). Due to the manner in which the English Channel flooded the Bay of St Malo several thousand years ago, Guernsey has no reptiles at all. Instead, its inhabitants are known as donkeys. Neither expression is intended to be complimentary.

The Islands are famous far beyond their shores for similar things: a cow, a knitted sweater and a crop. But there is a world of difference between the Jersey cow and the Guernsey cow. One has a black nose and is very pretty, the other has a pink nose and isn't. The oiled wool sweaters both serve the same purpose of keeping seafarers warm and dry but they do it with different stitches in different patterns and while Jersey is famous for the Jersey Royal potato grown in the open air, Guernsey is just as famous for the Guernsey Tom, mostly grown under glass.

In recent times the Islands have often sought to draw closer together, for, as far as the ubiquitous European Union is concerned, the Islands do not exist as separate entities. Indeed, there are times when Islanders might perceive that the panjandrums of Brussels might prefer them not to exist at all! When Britain negotiated the Channel Islands' associated status under the Treaty of Rome, it did so in the knowledge that while Jersey wanted to stay out of what was then known as the Common Market to maintain its offshore finance industry, Guernsey wanted to go in because of the benefits to its horticulture industry.

Is it any wonder that when it came to dealing with an imminent German invasion, the Islands behaved differently?

Nevertheless, they had one thing in common: both Islands were headed by lawyers and both men, the Islands' Bailiffs, had a profound respect for the rule of law, as did their respective Attorney-Generals, although in Guernsey the title is actually *Procureur du Roi. . .*

The role of Bailiff in the Channel Islands is a unique one for nowhere else does the 'chief citizen' combine the role of the head of the judiciary with being the head of the legislature. The Bailiff is each Bailiwick's chief executive. He presides over the States (the Islands' parliaments, although the States of Guernsey is more accurately described as the States of Deliberation) as well as the Royal Court. Thus, for the benefit of readers more used to the way other jurisdictions function, the Bailiff can be described as someone who fulfils the role of prime minister, Speaker of the House and Lord Chief Justice. Bailiffs are appointed by the Sovereign but the Sovereign also appoints a Lieutenant-Governor (the role of Governor was effective phased out in the 19th century) as his or her personal representative and, in particular, as Commander-in-Chief of the military forces in the Islands however significant, or otherwise, they may be.

The protagonists we shall meet in due course, Messrs Alexander Coutanche and Charles Duret-Aubin in Jersey and Victor Carey and Ambrose Sherwill in Guernsey, were distinguished lawyers and each one held a Crown appointment whose prime role was the upholding of the law of the land. All four recognised that the German Occupation was legal and the laws laid down by the occupiers, while some may have been repulsive (for instance, the Order brought before both Royal Courts in October 1940, 'Relating to Measures against the Jews'), had the force of law. Only one member of the Royal Court of Guernsey, Jurat Sir Abraham Lainé, spoke out against the Order but his eloquence, honed by years of colonial service, fell on deaf ears.

The lawyers at the head of the Islands' administration had a very difficult furrow to hoe. Nevertheless, Alexander Coutanche, Bailiff of Jersey, though recognising the legality of what the Germans had undertaken, used the law, particularly the Hague Convention, to protest and protest again to the discomfiture of the occupiers who, in the person of Baron von Aufsess, the head of the German Civilian Administration, referred to the Bailiff as 'vulpine'. It was not intended as a compliment, but his diary (*The von Aufsess Occupation Diary*, edited and translated by K. J. Nowlan, Phillimore, 1985) records his annoyance at being bested by the foxy Coutanche time and time again. Adherence to the Hague Convention was a two-way street — for instance, it allowed a local fire brigade to pump out a flooded bunker to render it safe for human habitation but not enough to save stored ammunition.

Sadly, the olde-worlde courtesy of Guernsey Bailiff Victor Carey and his respect for the rule of law led to many accusations of too ready compliance with the German diktats. To expect a man who had spent his entire life upholding the law (he was 69 when the Germans invaded) to seek ways to subvert it, was asking a lot.

Chapter 3
The Great War

The Channel Islands' role in the Great War — the war to end all wars — and how events in World War 2 stemmed from it

This chapter will, of necessity, be a brief one for in any history of World War 1 the role of the Channel Islands is not writ large.

Unlike in World War 2, when the Western Front came to them, in the Great War the front stayed quite firmly far to the east of the Channel Islands in a broad strip of mud, shell-holes, ruins and corpses stretching from the Belgian coast to the Swiss border.

Nevertheless, 2,298 young men of the Islands gave their lives in the conflict from the 12,460 (6,292 from the Bailiwick of Jersey and 6,168 from the Bailiwick of Guernsey) who rallied to the colours. Traditionally Channel Islanders have not been subject to conscription, although in both wars, they volunteered to defend their Sovereign in a significantly greater proportion relative to the population of the Islands than any community in Britain, even when conscription replaced Lord Kitchener's plea that '*Your Country Needs You!*' Both Islands maintained Royal Militias, and it was this early version of the Territorial Army that provided young men already trained in the use of firearms and basic military drills.

The term 'militia' is defined as a 'body of citizens enrolled as regular military forces for periodical instruction, discipline and drill but not called upon for active service except in an emergency'. In 1337 King Edward III sent a commission to levy and train the men of Jersey, Guernsey, Alderney and Sark into 'militias'. In 1814 the Jersey and Guernsey Militias were designated 'Light Infantry', the Royal Jersey having six regiments (later battalions) and the Royal Guernsey four. In 1831, on the 50th anniversary of the Battle of Jersey, the entire Channel Island Militias were granted the 'Royal' prefix by King William IV and by General Order of 1881 Queen Victoria granted the Battle Honour 'Jersey 1781' to the 1st (West), 2nd (East) and 3rd (South) Regiments.

By 1902 these battalions had been reduced to three in Jersey and two in Guernsey although by the outbreak of war in August 1914 these had been augmented by artillery, engineer and medical units as well as garrison battalions. Uniforms, arms and equipment were supplied by the British government and, curiously, the Channel Islands were the only pieces of the British Empire where there was compulsory Militia service. Following the Militia Act of 1906 all males between the ages of 16 and 45 years were obliged to serve, the 16 to 18 year olds carrying out 40 days of compulsory drill per year.

The Jersey Militia consisted of 1,800 men plus their commissioned officers.

On Saturday, 1 August 1914, following the general mobilisation in France, a steady stream of French residents left the Channel Islands to answer their country's call.

The *Evening Post* of Monday, 3 August, duly recorded sorrowfully: '. . . hotels are very badly hit by the French mobilisation order. In one instance the chef has already left the Island, and the remainder of the staff are due to leave this week. Practically all the German waiters have gone. The position in which proprietors of such establishments are placed is indeed awkward.'

By the end of 1914, 2,000 Frenchmen from Jersey and 300 from Guernsey had rallied to the colours, although the number of Germans who did so is not recorded. However, one German did not have the opportunity to leave. The tenant of Herm, Prince Blücher, was arrested and interned as an enemy alien despite the fact that his two sons were both officers in the Guernsey Militia.

In March 1915 the Jersey Overseas Contingent of the Royal Jersey Militia, consisting of six officers and 224 other ranks commanded by Captain, later Lieutenant-Colonel, Stocker was absorbed into active service with the 7th (Service) Battalion, Royal Irish Rifles, while a contingent of the Guernsey Militia was detached and joined the 6th (Service) Battalion of the Royal Irish Regiment. Both contingents were sent to Ireland to join their regiments for training.

The men of the Jersey Overseas Contingent took part in the Battle of the Somme and the third battle of Ypres at the end of July 1917. They were withdrawn after four days, having suffered heavy casualties. In November 1917 the remnants fought at Cambrai in the same action as the Royal Guernsey Light Infantry.

While the remainder of the Royal Militia in Jersey formed the Royal Jersey Garrison Battalion and remained in Jersey, in December 1916 the Royal Guernsey Light Infantry was formed so that Guernsey would have a fighting unit bearing its name rather than let Islanders fight under the names of the Irish regiments they had been joining up to then. At this time the RGLI consisted of two full battalions. The 2nd (Reserve) Battalion remained in Guernsey on garrison duty (although, as in Jersey, supplying drafts to the 1st Battalion) and the 1st (Service) Battalion moved to England and joined the 202nd (2nd Kent) Brigade, 67th (2nd Home Counties) Division. In September 1917 the 1st Battalion left the division and moved to France, and on 2 October was attached to the 86th Brigade, 29th Division.

At the end of November 1917 the RGLI suffered heavy casualties in hand-to-hand fighting at Cambrai, with 156 men simply listed as missing. The commander of the 29th Division, General de Lisle, wrote to the Bailiff of Guernsey commending the RGLI, stating that: 'Guernsey has every reason to feel the greatest pride in her sons . . . Many officers and men greatly distinguished themselves . . .'

In April 1918, after sustaining heavy casualties, the 1st Battalion was transferred to Sir Douglas Haig's headquarters, where the men were employed as guards until the end of hostilities.

In 1883 the Lieutenant-Governor of Jersey had formed a Militia Cadet Corps which was attached to the South Regiment of the Royal Jersey Militia but it does not seem to have been a success and the Cadet Corps was re-established at Victoria College (Jersey's boys' public school) in 1903, attached to the East Battalion of the Royal Jersey Militia. Two years earlier the Elizabeth College Cadet Company was formed in Guernsey, parading for the first time in January 1902. Like Victoria College in Jersey, Elizabeth College was (and still is) the boys' public school. The Elizabeth College Cadet Company was originally attached to the Royal Guernsey Artillery and Engineers but in 1908 was separated from the RGA&E to become an Officer Training Corps. The Victoria College Cadet Corps also included a band of bugles and drums, and shooting practice was undertaken with the Jersey Militia. There were annual shooting competitions between the Victoria College and Elizabeth College cadets and they regularly represented the Islands at Bisley. In 1908 the Victoria College Cadet Corps also became an Officer Training Corps and was no longer attached to the East Battalion of the Royal Jersey Militia.

During the Great War the OTC was on active service assisting with the manning of the Islands' coastal defences and by 1917 the Victoria College OTC provided guards for the Albert Pier (the Island's principal harbour) and Government House. No fewer than 631 former members of the Victoria College OTC served in the Great War, of whom 126 were killed. They served with distinction throughout the war and the Victoria Cross was awarded to former cadets Lieutenant W. A. M. Bruce and Temporary Lieutenant (Acting Captain) A. M. C. McReady-Diarmid.

Lieutenant William Arthur McCrae Bruce (24) of the 59th Scinde Rifles, Indian Army, was killed on 19 December 1914 near Givenchy, France, after leading a night attack which captured one of the enemy trenches. In spite of being wounded in the neck he walked up and down the trench encouraging his men to hold out all the next day against several counter attacks until he was killed by enemy rifle fire.

On 30 November/1 December 1917 at the Moeuvres Sector, France, Acting Captain Allastair Malcolm Cluny McReady-Diarmid (29) of the Middlesex Regiment (Duke of Cambridge's Own) led his company through a heavy barrage, immediately engaging Germans who had penetrated the British position and drove them back at least 300 metres, causing numerous casualties and taking 27 prisoners. The following day the Germans attacked again and drove back another company which had lost all its officers. The captain called for volunteers and, leading the attack, again drove the enemy back and it was entirely due to his skill at throwing grenades that the ground was regained before he himself was killed by a German grenade.

Altogether 212 decorations for gallantry were awarded to Islanders.

For the Islands themselves the Great War had little direct impact, although for more than 2,000 families the arrival of a telegram from the Minister of War would bring the horrors of the Somme and Passchendaele devastatingly home.

Initially the garrisons on the Islands were substantially increased, with men of the 2nd Battalion of the Yorkshire Regiment being posted to Guernsey to boost the local Militia and men of the 1st Battalion of the Devonshire Regiment being posted to Jersey. The troops were brought by the steamers of the Great Western and London & South Western Railways and billeted in barracks, many of which had been built at the time of the wars against Napoleon. However it was soon realised that these soldiers would better serve the cause fighting at the front rather than guarding communities where the likelihood of attack or invasion was negligible and a little over three weeks later they were all taken away again, the defence of the Islands entrusted to the men of the Militias and, in Jersey's case, a special reserve unit, the 4th Battalion of the South Staffordshire Regiment.

The sea services were maintained between the Islands and the United Kingdom (although the services to France disappeared) throughout the war, albeit with much reduced passenger numbers, which was just as well since many of the railway companies' vessels had been requisitioned for war service. Those that remained performed their principal duty, as in peacetime, of carrying the Royal Mail.

However, within days of the declaration of war there had been naval activity around the Channel Islands for on 6 August 1914 a French warship had captured a German steamer scurrying for home off Sark, 12 days later another French vessel captured an Austrian cargo vessel near the Casquets reef and a week later French cruisers intercepted a neutral vessel, the Dutch SS *Orange*, with a number of German reservists on board.

Although just 11 years since the Wright Brothers flew the first aircraft a few metres, by 1914 the potential of aircraft and airships as weapons of war was already recognised and the possibility of aerial bombardment — even on targets as far away from the front as the Channel Islands — could not be discounted. The Militias were consequently issued with airship recognition cards.

In August 1914 the War Office ordered the immediate construction of a temporary prisoner-of-war camp in Jersey. Within a month the Royal Engineers had converted the Royal Jersey Agricultural and Horticultural Society's showground at Springfield, St Helier, for the purpose. However it was never used as a POW cage and instead housed the South Staffords before becoming the Army Service Corps Supply Depot, a role it was also to fulfil for a different army in a different conflict. Many, many years later, still in the ownership of the RJA&HS, Springfield stadium was the venue for the annual inter-Island football battles for the solid silver Muratti Vase, named after a long-forgotten brand of cigarettes. And it is still the venue today, albeit now in public ownership, and they still compete for the same vase.

In December 1914 the War Office ordered the building of a permanent prisoner-of-war camp in Jersey capable of housing 1,000 inmates in rows of huts. The site chosen was Blanches Banques, an area of sand dunes in the parish of St Brelade, on land already owned by the British government. The camp thus created was about 300 metres square and surrounded by a 3-metre-high barbed-wire fence with buildings for the guards outside the perimeter.

The first prisoners from the Western Front arrived in March 1915 and despite being planned for 1,000 inmates by July the camp contained 1,500 of them. It remained in being until October 1919 and during the time it was open there were a number of escape attempts including at least two tunnels, which were defeated by the soft sand on which the camp was built. Several inmates died during their incarceration and were buried in a corner of St Brelade's church cemetery. In World War 2, the occupying forces requisitioned much of the cemetery so that the fallen of that conflict could lie alongside their *Kamaraden* of World War 1.

During World War 1 the power to make Defence Regulations was the exclusive preserve of His Majesty's Government in London. These Regulations were sent to the Islands by post which, of course, came by sea for although the newfangled aeroplanes were already being employed to carry the mails, no such services existed to the Channel Islands and it would be the late 1930s before proper aerodromes (other than the beaches and the sea) were created. Thus the mail came by the 'mailboat', either from Southampton or Weymouth, depending upon which railway company the Royal Mail was using on any particular day. There was an ever-present threat of an attack by German U-boats but in practice submarines, although they haunted coasts and harbours much more than they would in World War 2, were still very vulnerable in the comparatively shallow waters around the Channel Islands. The Royal and French Navies maintained a presence in the Islands throughout the Great War, but for most of the time they had comparatively little to shoot at. Nevertheless a detachment of the South Staffords was stationed on Herm to prevent the landing of spies and saboteurs by submarine. Quite what a spy would have found on Herm worthy of reporting upon or what a saboteur found to blow up is not recorded!

In fact German U-boats were occasionally spotted in the English Channel near the Islands and to counter this threat the French government established a seaplane base in the shadow of Castle Cornet in St Peter Port harbour in May 1917. A seaplane base was also considered for St Catherine's Bay on Jersey's east coast. Before radios were fitted as a matter of course, patrolling seaplanes sent messages of sightings to their base by carrier pigeon, although the aircraft often arrived back before their messengers.

Altogether 110 men of the *Aviation Maritime Française* were stationed in Guernsey and one *Légion d'Honneur* and several *Croix de Guerre* were awarded to these aviators. In January 1918 a U-boat was sunk by two seaplanes while lurking off Guernsey's Les Hanois reef, in April another

U-boat was attacked off St Martin's Point, Guernsey, and on 31 May a U-boat was destroyed 30 miles west of Guernsey while it was attempting to sink the sailing ship *Dundee* by gunfire.

Alongside the seaplanes was a flotilla of French torpedo boats. These too earned the *Croix de Guerre* in the autumn of 1918 in recognition of no fewer than 25 attacks on submarines and the discovery of three minefields between August 1917 and August 1918.

Altogether 179 Jerseymen served in the Royal Flying Corps or the Royal Naval Air Service, of whom eight died. One of these was Lieutenant Stanley Mossop DSO who, in August 1918, landed his seaplane in St Helier Harbour in order to pay an unofficial visit to his parents' home in nearby Commercial Buildings. Two days later he was killed while landing his damaged craft near Bayeux.

In the course of the Great War Jersey contributed £100,000 to the war effort but in 1923 the government suggested that Jersey might like to make an annual contribution of £275,000 towards the running costs of the British Empire. This suggestion was declined and instead the States of Jersey offered a single payment of £300,000 towards the cost of the Great War which was eventually paid in 1927. Guernsey too contributed £100,000 to the war effort and in 1927 the States also made a single payment of £220,000 towards the cost of the war to end all wars.

Many years later the Channel Islands made generous donations to the Falklands Islands as an expression of fellow-feeling with British islanders who had suffered an enemy occupation. Once again the British government suggested that the Islands might like to make this an annual contribution only this time the government of Margaret Thatcher wasn't going to take no for an answer! Jersey's gift of £5 million to the Falklands became an annual contribution to the British government to fund a Territorial Army unit while Guernsey's one-off gift of £250,000 became an annual commitment to maintaining several British government installations in the Bailiwick including Alderney's continually crumbling breakwater.

Chapter 4
Prelude

The Channel Islands were still exporting their potatoes and tomatoes and advertising themselves as 'ideal places to escape the war' even as the Germans marched into the Low Countries and Adolf Hitler and Albert Speer posed beneath the Eiffel Tower

In June 1940, William Joyce, Lord Haw Haw, in one of his broadcasts from Hamburg proclaimed: 'We are coming very soon, you Channel Islanders, to get those potatoes and tomatoes. And when we're finished with you, there'll be nothing left.'

Depending on your point of view (albeit the matter is now rather academic), Joyce was either a Briton, an Irishman or an American but, by bizarre circumstance, a German might have already been in power in Guernsey almost six years before Joyce's prophetic outburst had the Guernsey States of Deliberation approved the application of a certain Herr Johann Rolling of Oberursel in the Taunus Mountains of Germany for the position of His Majesty's Procureur du Roi. Herr Rolling had been tempted to apply for the post by the wide media coverage given to the fact that Guernsey had been unable to find someone to take on the role of the Island's senior Law Officer because the pay was so much less than any local lawyer could earn in private practice.

Quite what his qualifications were for such a role Herr Rolling's application did not specify, and it was politely rejected by the Bailiff's Secretary on the grounds that the post was open only to British subjects anyway. Thus Guernsey was spared a German legislator — at least for a few years . . .

Guernsey's Bailiff of the day, Arthur Bell, convinced the States that the salary offered should be raised from £1,200 per annum to £1,400 (worth perhaps 50 times as much today), a significant increase in those days before inflation, and after much deliberation (and guarantees about his pension rights) Advocate Ambrose Sherwill, who currently held the part-time post of HM Comptroller (the rank below Procureur and similarly a Crown appointment) and who should have been the natural successor to the role of Procureur anyway, was appointed His Majesty's Procureur in April 1935.

A month later Bailiff Bell died suddenly. The natural progression in the Channel Islands (this was before the role of Deputy Bailiff was created) would have been for Sherwill to have succeeded but, having been in his new office for just weeks, the 64-year-old Receiver-General Victor Carey, who had held that particular office since 1912, was appointed Guernsey's new Bailiff with the view that he would probably serve in that capacity for a few years until Sherwill could accede to the role.

The Careys are to Guernsey what the Lowells and the Cabots are to Boston and Victor Carey's father had also been a general in the British Army. Victor Carey was perceived by all to be a gentleman of the old school, a staunch traditionalist, conservative yet kindly and charming and almost excessively courteous, inevitably signing letters to all and sundry 'your obedient servant', a practice that would not go down well in hindsight when such sentiments were offered to the German occupiers. He is also described as being of generous proportions and, in common with many Channel Islanders, certainly enjoyed his food.

Barely a year after taking up office, Victor Carey's wife Adelaide died and thus, unlike Ambrose Sherwill and, in Jersey, Alexander Coutanche, the Bailiff of Guernsey was denied the spiritual and connubial partnership that both found so valuable in the trying times to come.

In Jersey the situation was somewhat different.

Alexander Coutanche had been called to the Jersey Bar in 1913 and, after military service, returned to Jersey in 1920 and a legal practice. In December 1922 he followed many others of his profession into the States, being elected a Deputy for the Parish of St Helier. Although the salaries offered for Crown Officers were as meagre in Jersey as they were in Guernsey, Coutanche was invited to apply for the position of Solicitor-General, despite being a relatively junior member of the Bar. Such appointments were made by the King, acting on advice from the Home Secretary, which he received from the Lieutenant-Governor, who might, or might not, confer with the Bailiff.

Alexander Coutanche was duly sworn in as HM Solicitor-General on 24 October 1925. In May 1931 he succeeded Charles de Carteret as Attorney-General (de Carteret having been appointed Bailiff) with his old friend Charles Duret-Aubin becoming Solicitor-General, and on 27 August 1935, following the resignation of Charles de Carteret through ill-health, and at the age of 43, he took the Oath of Office as Bailiff.

In between the wars the Channel Islands became more and more popular with the people of Britain as places of 'popular resort' and they developed their tourism industries accordingly, building hotels and guesthouses to cater for a growing number of Britons (and a few enterprising Continentals) who enjoyed the beaches and, in those far-off halcyon days, the very low prices for drinks and cigarettes. Customs duties were low, as was income tax, and many other taxes commonplace in Britain, such as purchase tax, simply did not exist.

The Islands enjoyed the reputation with British holidaymakers much as Spain or the South of France does today. Taking a holiday in the Islands was an adventure at the end of at least an eight-hour sea voyage. Both Islands boasted wide, clean beaches, the sort of climate that prompted palm trees to grow, dramatic cliffs, unspoilt countryside and enough castles, forts and towers to hint at a belligerent yet romantic history. Nevertheless Guernsey, calling itself 'the Central Channel Island', was also touting for the retired to come and settle, claiming that retirees would find that there were many of their friends from all over the Empire already there.

Today, the Islands thrive on their offshore finance industries — a version where the people don't come but their money does — but before the war finance was represented solely by the high street banks and the Guernsey and Jersey Savings Banks. In both Islands the largest consumer of labour was the land although, typically, the Islands majored on different crops for export — Jersey Royal new potatoes, almost always the first on the market and with a very distinctive taste, and Guernsey tomatoes and grapes grown in 9,000 glasshouses which were, and are, known as vineries. Both Islands had their own breeds of cattle noted for the rich butter-fat content of their milk which, in those days, was deemed to be a *good* thing. Both breeds were vigorously protected by a total ban on the import of any other stock but since both breeds were adaptable to a wide variety of climates and conditions they were exported worldwide. Alderney had also once had its own breed but that had died out and the cattle on Alderney at the outbreak of war were Guernseys.

However, the market for the Channel Islands' goods was almost exclusively the United Kingdom and it was also the UK that supplied the Islands with all their daily needs, particularly fuel and food, for the Islands, whose principal exports were agricultural and horticultural, had been incapable of feeding themselves for a century or more.

Jersey's airport did not open until 1937 and Guernsey's until 1939, although surprisingly Alderney's airport pre-dated both of them by having been opened in 1935. Aircraft did land on the beach of Jersey's St Aubin's Bay but services to Britain were subject to the state of the tides! The vast majority of visitors travelled to the Islands by mailsteamer, the Great Western Railway in the 1930s operating the popular *St Helier* and *St Julien* on daily services from the Islands to Weymouth while the Southern Railway (the successor of the London & South Western Railway) had the well-loved trio of the *Isle of Jersey*, *Isle of Guernsey* and *Isle of Sark* running to and from Southampton. Although the railway companies no longer raced each other, the vessels left Jersey and Guernsey barely half an hour apart before making their separate ways to the 'mainland'. The numbers of travellers carried during the summer months made up for the few that were carried (on reduced services) during the winter.

Islanders themselves travelled little. Indeed for some in the outlying country areas, none of which can ever be more than six or seven miles from the town centre, a visit to town was often an annual treat, planned much as we would today a visit to London or Paris. Not only that, when these intrepids arrived in town they found that few of the shopkeepers they spoke to, or attempted to speak to, actually spoke or understood their language!

Party politics as such were almost unknown in the Islands, the means of governance being largely the same as had pertained for a century or more with members being elected on their own merits rather than because of any party label.

However, that is not to say that there were no political parties. On 18 August 1934 a Mr W. Brasier, titling himself Branch Organiser Jersey, British Union of Fascists — Overseas Department, wrote to the Bailiff reassuring him that 'Jersey is guaranteed its full measure of liberty and freedom as at present enjoyed when a Blackshirt administration is in power in Britain in the very near future'. He asked for his letter to be read out to the States Assembly. There is no record that it ever was. Later the British Union of Fascists added 'and National Socialists' to the name of the party which could still count Channel Islanders amongst its membership. The Blackshirts had been joined by the Brownshirts. To maintain this colourful theme there was even a party of Greenshirts, forerunners of the later environmentalists.

The head of each Bailiwick was the Bailiff. His seat in the States Assembly was several inches higher than that of the Sovereign's representative and the medium by which the Island authorities conferred with the Home Office, the Lieutenant-Governor. By tradition, and because of the nature of his role as Commander-in-Chief, the Lieutenant-Governor was always a military man, usually not far from retirement. In 1939 the Lieutenant-Governor of Jersey was Major-General J. M. R. Harrison and his Guernsey counterpart was Major-General A. P. D. Telfer-Smollett.

The Crown Officers were, like the Bailiffs, Crown appointments and, as we have seen, there was usually a natural progression up the ladder from HM Comptroller to HM Procureur to Bailiff in Guernsey and from HM Solicitor-General, via HM Attorney-General to Bailiff in Jersey. Both Islands also maintained the roles of Receiver-General and *Vicomte* in Jersey and *Prevôt* in Guernsey although neither of these were, in normal circumstances, rungs on the ladder to being chief citizen.

In Guernsey the Bailiff presided over the States of Deliberation which comprised 18 People's Deputies, 12 Jurats, the Rectors of the Island's 10 parishes and 15 *Douzaine* (parish council) representatives (one each from nine of the parishes and six from St Peter Port) as well as the two Crown Officers who could both speak in the States and vote. Since the Bailiff, Crown Officers and the Rectors were all Crown appointments, a sizeable proportion of the 'government' was unelected.

Similarly in Jersey, the Bailiff and Crown Officers were joined by the 12 Jurats (elected for life by the ratepayers of each parish), 12 parish *Connétables* (Constables) who were elected by the parishes and whose role was similar to that of Mayor but with rather more executive authority, 12 parish Rectors, 17 Deputies and the *Vicomte* who, although he sat in the States as the chief executive of the Court, could neither speak nor vote. Presumably he watched! Also unlike Guernsey, the Crown Officers could speak but they could not vote. But, as with Guernsey, a popular democracy Jersey was not!

The role of Jurat is one peculiar to the Channel Islands, dating back several hundred years when they formed, with the Bailiff, the Islands' first parliaments. In the 1930s, the role, like that of the Bailiff, straddled the legislature and the judiciary, Jurats being 'judges of fact'. These worthies, and in those days they were always men, were elected for life, in Guernsey by an electoral college of their peers but in Jersey by parish ratepayers.

In Jersey, much of the government was conducted at parish level, the instrument being an assembly of parish ratepayers presided over by the *Connétable*. Other parish officers were the *Procureurs du Bien Public* (public trustees whose principal role was to oversee the parish accounts), the Rector, the Churchwardens and the Almoners. The parish's honorary (unpaid) police comprised *Centeniers*, who were responsible for charging miscreants and prosecuting them at the Police Court (Magistrates' Court), *Vingteniers*, who also had the role of collecting the parish rate, and Constable's Officers. As their names imply, *Centeniers* and *Vingteniers* originally had responsibility for 100 and for 20 households respectively. The rank of Constable's Officer was introduced when the Island's burgeoning population decreed that the number of *Centeniers* and *Vingteniers* would have become unwieldy. Only St Helier, the town parish, could boast a police force that outsiders would recognise, the St Helier Paid Police, a uniformed body of men typical of the English bobby except even in the town these had to defer to their honorary colleagues. What's more the Paid Police could not venture beyond the borders of the town parish because to do so would incur the wrath of whichever parish *Connétable's* territory was so violated!

In Guernsey parish administration was in the hands of the Senior and Junior Constables, plus 12 *Douzeniers*, except for St Peter Port where there were 20 and the Vale which had 16. Since the *Douzaines* were represented in the States, there was a direct link between the parish assemblies and the States of Deliberation. In Jersey that link was provided by the *Connétables* who were automatically members of the States by virtue of their office.

The Guernsey police force was much more typical of what pertained elsewhere in Britain: a paid, uniformed force with an Island-wide responsibility for maintaining law and order. How these forces would function when the Germans occupied the Islands would sow the seeds of much later controversy.

Not only did the parishes exert considerable influence over the Islanders' daily lives, they also, in those simpler days, exerted a much stronger influence over their spiritual lives or, more specifically, each parish's Anglican church did and parochial ecclesiastical assemblies, presided over by the Rector rather than the Constable, were as well attended as the general parish assemblies.

Much of the law in the Channel Islands derives from the *Code Napoléon* of the early 19th century. Local custom and usage has modified it down the ages but it has developed almost entirely independently of Common Law in Britain as much because of difficulties of communication as the self-determining disposition of the Islanders who have always preferred to do things their way.

Then, as is the case today, the Royal Courts of Jersey and Guernsey had all the judicial authority necessary to determine civil and criminal causes. They could, and did, impose extreme penalties and, in common with French practice, tended to carry the sentences out in a matter of hours or days rather than weeks although they did use the halter rather than the blade. The Royal Courts also constituted the court of appeal, although, in certain circumstances, leave might be granted to appeal to the Judicial Committee of the Privy Council. However this was a lengthy and often very expensive process and was seldom invoked. Even Alderney and Sark had their own courts, with the Royal Court of Guernsey fulfilling the role of court of appeal. It will be no surprise for the reader to discover that even when it came to how their Royal Courts functioned, the Islands differed.

In Jersey the Royal Court with jurisdiction in both civil and criminal matters sat as either the Superior Number (the Bailiff and at least seven Jurats) or the Inferior Number (the Bailiff and two Jurats). The Inferior Number registered Orders in Council (the Island's laws) and also comprised the Divorce Court while the Superior Number also acted as the court of appeal. There were also two lower courts, the Police Court (for trying criminal cases although if these were perceived to be particularly serious — such as homicide — these were referred upwards to the Royal Court) and the Petty Debts Court. These courts were presided over by a Magistrate and occasionally a Jurat with the appropriate legal qualification. In the 1930s the Debtors' Prison was still a reality where for just a shilling a day a creditor could keep a debtor incarcerated for a year and a day or until the debt was repaid, whichever was the sooner. Four times a year the Assize Court sat where the Bailiff presided with at least seven Jurats and a jury comprising 24 good men and true. Majority verdicts were always acceptable.

The Royal Court in Guernsey had three divisions: the Full Court where the Bailiff sat with at least seven Jurats, the Ordinary Court where the Bailiff sat with two Jurats (sounds familiar?) and the Matrimonial Causes Division where the Bailiff sat with four Jurats. The Full Court dealt with all indictable offences as well as registering Orders in Council, while the Ordinary Court had jurisdiction in all civil matters and acted as an appeal court for the Magistrates' Court which ruled on criminal matters and in minor civil cases. Trial by jury did not exist in Guernsey; instead, the 12 good men and true were the 12 Jurats.

But in the 1930s the events of the first five years of the next decade were a long way away, not just in time but also in mind.

In general terms the Channel Islands had little reason to be concerned about world events and while many in Jersey would recall the German prisoners once kept behind the wire at Blanches Banques, few would have been worried that one day the new German Chancellor, whose National Socialist Workers Party had been elected democratically to power, would wreak a terrible revenge for the humiliation of the Versailles Treaty and that revenge would involve the Islands that had once confined his Great War contemporaries. There were occasional reminders of the big world outside when, for instance, members of the Peace Pledge Movement and British conscientious objectors came to the Islands to work in the fields and glasshouses to escape the gathering clouds of war — not, in the event, an inspired choice. However, most Channel Islands residents believed the rhetoric that the Great War had been the war to end wars and surely Adolf Hitler, like his role model in Italy, Benito Mussolini, would be more concerned about getting the trains running on time and putting his people back to work than starting another blasted war! And the mainland of Europe was no nearer in 1933 than it was in 1914 or 1918.

Nevertheless those redoubtable expressions of public opinion, the Letters to the Editor in the local newspapers, did make frequent references to what was happening on the Continent. There were, surprisingly, frequent pro-German sentiments expressed and admiration for the way Germany had fought its way back to (apparent) economic success, the Nazis' stance on law and order and even their theories on racial improvement (eugenics).

When Alexander Coutanche became Bailiff in 1935 he had already established links with the British Home Office, having, in 1926, to the amusement of Attorney-General de Carteret who claimed he did not even know where the Home Office was, travelled to London and met the man with whom he would have much more contact in 1940, Charles Markbreiter. Markbreiter had been the Home Office official in charge of Channel Islands affairs for several years (although he had never actually visited the Islands) and he arranged for Coutanche to meet Sir John Anderson, the Permanent Under Secretary of State and who, as Lord Waverley, would be Home Secretary in Winston Churchill's War Cabinet. Coutanche and Markbreiter would become firm friends but that visit was something of a two-edged sword since Anderson used the opportunity to sound out the then Solicitor-General Coutanche on the possibility of an annual Imperial Contribution, a suggestion that had been made three years earlier and to which the Islands had yet to give an answer. In the event the British government, in the person of Chancellor of the Exchequer Winston Churchill, accepted the £300,000 referred to in the previous chapter as a one-off payment and the concept of a regular payment was not mentioned again. Coutanche got the credit from the Bailiff of the day, Sir William Vernon, for brokering the deal.

The 1930s were generally good times for the Islands. They were peaceful, thriving and slow to change. The United Kingdom provided a lucrative market for the products of their fields and glasshouses and a growing source of tourism income. The Seymour family in Jersey who had started with a modest town guesthouse in the 1920s was already the owner of three hotels. There was little or no political agitation for reform (a local branch of the British Union of Fascists and trade unions notwithstanding) and little fear that events in Europe, despite the headlines in the national newspapers which were still sold only in relatively small numbers, the news on the BBC and news items in *The Evening Post* in Jersey and *Evening Press* and *The Star* in Guernsey (which were inevitably relegated to minor pages), would one day engulf the Islands themselves.

There were warnings on the rise of fascism, Nazism and even the prospect of another global war (including leaders in the local press) but in the main it would seem that the Islanders preferred the view of Neville Chamberlain that war with Germany could be averted rather than the view of the maverick Winston Churchill that war with Germany was inevitable. Certainly if there was a war the young men would rally to the colours as they had always done but the likelihood was that should the unthinkable happen once again trenches would stretch across Europe and the stalemates of 1914 to 1918 would be repeated. Besides, had not premier Neville Chamberlain returned from a meeting with Herr Hitler in Munich waving a piece of paper and claiming that he had brought back from Germany to Downing Street, 'peace with honour' which he believed would guarantee 'peace for our time'?

The Lieutenant-Governor of Jersey prepared a report on the threat of war for the War Office but it will come as no surprise that, given everything else that was exercising the British government, little attention was paid to it, the decision having already been taken that the Islands had no strategic value to Britain and probably, therefore, had none to anyone else.

Nevertheless some Islanders, particularly those who were Jewish, were not unaware that within three months of Adolf Hitler being appointed Chancellor of Germany on 30 January 1933, and within a week of his assuming dictatorial powers, the Nazi Party was organising boycotts of Jewish-owned shops and a month later was making bonfires of banned books, particularly those by Jewish authors.

There had been a Jewish community in Jersey since the early 19th century and Jews were recorded in Guernsey in the late 18th. Although a synagogue had been built in St Helier in the 1840s, no such formal building was ever known to have existed in Guernsey. There were also at least two Jewish cemeteries in St Helier.

It is most likely that the Jewish families in the Channel Islands were well aware of what was happening in Germany. In September 1935, the annual Nazi Party rally saw the first public display of the resurgent armed forces — the *Wehrmacht* already comprised 36 divisions and conscription had been announced in March of that year, the new *Fahnengesetz*, the Flag Law which replaced the Kaiser's black, red and white striped ensign with the swastika as the nation's official symbol, and the announcement of the anti-Semitic Nuremberg Laws on Citizenship and Race. Article 4 (1) of the Nuremberg

Laws stated that 'a Jew cannot be a citizen of the Reich. He cannot exercise the right to vote; he cannot hold public office'. Article 4 (2) decreed that 'Jewish officials will be retired as of 31 December 1935' although such officials who had served at the front in the Great War would continue to receive any pension to which they were due. Article 5 defined precisely what a Jew was, principally an individual who was descended from at least three grandparents who were, racially, full Jews. Article 6 allowed that there could be requirements for the purity of German blood beyond the provisions and sub-provisions of Article 5, and Article 7 authorised the *Führer* and Chancellor of the Reich to 'release anyone from the provision of these administrative decrees'.

The laws were adopted by unanimous vote of the Reichstag, promulgated on 16 September 1935 and in force a fortnight later.

Like their fellow-Islanders, the Jews in the community would not have felt particularly threatened. There were already bizarre examples of anti-Semitism in some local legislation. For instance, in Jersey, Jews (along with Roman Catholics and Freethinkers) were barred from the office of Jurat. In Guernsey, similar restrictions to the office applied although these were confined to Roman Catholics, brewers and publicans! It is not likely that such historical exclusions were perceived by anyone, even those excluded, as being especially racially motivated or even particularly distasteful.

However, when he was still Attorney-General, Alexander Coutanche was instrumental in introducing an amendment to a 1933 law that ensured the painless killing of animals to allow for ritual slaughter according to Jewish custom.

There would be accusations made — and the controversy continues to this day — that the Islands' authorities were far too compliant when it came to enacting 'Nazi' anti-Semitic Laws through their Royal Courts. An excuse still trotted out is that it was perceived by the authorities that since all the Jewish residents had actually left the Islands before June 1940 — and indeed the vast majority had — introducing rules that actually didn't apply to anyone would do little harm, however repellent their ethos might be, and it would avoid a confrontation with the occupiers.

In 1938 and 1939 a number of Jews living in Germany applied to reside in Jersey in order to escape Nazi persecution which several applications described in considerable detail. At that time there were strict rules governing the immigration of 'aliens' (broadly speaking an alien was anyone who was not a citizen of the British Empire) which dated back to the 1920s. An elaborate process was invoked involving the Bailiff, Chief Aliens Officer Clifford Orange and the States of Jersey Defence Committee who, while they actually had no responsibility for defence (that was the liability of the British government), controlled the police and immigration services.

The Defence Committee rejected almost all of the applications — which included a group of 'refugee' children already in Britain — and communicated its decision to the Bailiff. Why such applications were rejected still arouses considerable argument and recent commentators have castigated the people responsible for the decision, most notably local historian Joe Mière. In his 2004 book *Never To Be Forgotten* he referred to them as 'mean old sods'. This author believes that the Islands' exaggerated fear of being overrun by immigrants, of whatever race or hue, (and still manifest today) was as much the reason as it might have been that they were Germans. It is easy, with the benefit of hindsight and today's knowledge of the Holocaust, to underestimate just how little credibility was given to the stories of atrocities against the Jews emanating from Germany and the little understanding of just how much the German Jewish community was already marginalised. After all, not too many years before, the man with the *Pickelhaube* shooting at you from a German trench could well have been a German Jew.

Some European Jews *were* admitted, the Guernsey authorities granting immigration permits to four Austrian-born women and a Pole to live and work in the Island.

On 30 January 1939, Adolf Hitler, in a speech to the Reichstag on the sixth anniversary of his coming to power, declared: 'In the course of my life I have very often been a prophet, and have usually been ridiculed for it. During the time of my struggle for power, it was in the first instance only the Jewish race that received my prophecies with laughter when I said that I would one day take over the leadership of the State and with it that of the whole nation and that I would then, among other things, settle the Jewish problem . . . but I think that for some time now they have been laughing on the other side of their face. Today I will once more be a prophet: if the international Jewish financiers in and outside Europe should succeed in plunging the nations once more into a world war, then the result will not be the Bolshevising of the earth and thus the victory of Jewry, but the annihilation of the Jewish race in Europe.'

Prophetic words indeed and just a week earlier Hermann Göring had ordered rising *SS* star Reinhard Heydrich to speed up Jewish emigration.

At 11.15am on Sunday, 3 September 1939, Prime Minister Neville Chamberlain broadcast to the nation in the following terms: 'This morning the British Ambassador in Berlin handed the German government a final note stating that unless we heard from them by 11 o'clock that they were prepared at once to withdraw their troops from Poland, a state of war would exist between us. I have to tell you that no such undertaking has been received and that consequently this country is at war with Germany.' Later he told Parliament: 'This is a sad day for all of us, and to none is it sadder than to me. Everything that I have worked for, everything that I have believed in during my public life, has crashed into ruins. There is only one thing left for me to do: that is, to devote what strength and powers I have to forwarding the victory of the cause for which we have to sacrifice so much . . . I trust I may live to see the day when Hitlerism has been destroyed and a liberated Europe has been established.'

In London air raid sirens sounded immediately and in Guernsey an immediate blackout was ordered and a German national known to have Nazi sympathies was carted off to HM Prison.

Two days earlier the Lieutenant-Governors of Guernsey and Jersey, eager to play their part in Hitler's downfall, ordered the call-up of the Militias. Strictly they should have waited for positive instructions from London but both felt that there was no time to lose even though, by invading Poland, the German armies were actually moving further away from the Islands rather than towards them.

However this eagerness to rally round the flag was not mirrored in Whitehall. In fact the War Office, faced with carrying out the British government's obligation to defend the Channel Islands, actually had no idea how this would be carried out, nor indeed whether they were allowed (by the Home Office) to communicate with the Islands' Commanders-in-Chief at all!

By 11 September the situation was clarified. The Home Office had no objection to the War Office talking directly to the Lieutenant-Governors and since these gentlemen were both serving Army officers, it was actually their duty to do so.

Since time immemorial the menfolk of the Channel Islands had been exempt from conscription into Britain's armed services unless required to rescue the Sovereign him or herself from attack by an enemy. Nevertheless, as we have read, 12,460 young Islanders volunteered for service in the Great War and when the United Kingdom introduced conscription, the Islands followed suit, although not obliged to do so.

On 16 September the States of Jersey approved a resolution assuring His Majesty of its loyalty and devotion and on 27 September the States of Guernsey agreed that 'for a period of the duration of the present war, in which the liberties of mankind are at stake, our constitutional rights and privileges in respect of military service overseas, while being formally preserved in perpetuity, should be waived'. Thus the young men of the Channel Islands would be placed at His Majesty's disposal for military service, subject only to the Islands' own requirements to maintain essential services and defence.

The States of Jersey actually approved the National Service Law on 20 January 1940 which directed British subjects in Jersey aged between 18 and 41 into HM Forces. The Guernsey National Service Law followed the sending of a somewhat equivocal loyal address to the King which reminded His Majesty that 'for centuries past by authority of Princely Writ we have been exempt from military service out of the Islands, unless it be to accompany Your Majesty in person for the recovery of England, or that the person of Your Majesty should be taken prisoner by the enemy. Your Majesty's Norman subjects earnestly trust that their services may never be needed by reason of the happening of either of these calamitous events which render them obligatory.'

There were already men from the Bailiwicks serving in HM Forces — many had joined up even before the formal declaration of war so certain were they that war was coming — and the Island governments were prepared to give up their rights to exemption 'for the duration of the struggle'.

There had been a few administrative problems with the legislation, inevitable perhaps when two separate administrations sought the same objectives but did not confer as to how these objectives were to be achieved, and they were dealing with a War Office which itself was dealing with a situation unique in its experience.

Earlier, in 1939, when war clouds were gathering, the Islands' Commanders-in-Chief had examined the Bailiwicks' defences and, not surprisingly, had found them wanting. However, reports to Whitehall were received with little enthusiasm. The Channel Islands were not strategic and Britain had bigger things to worry about than their defences. When a formal application for some coastal defence guns, anti-aircraft Bofors guns and a dozen Bren guns was made from Jersey, a Whitehall warrior's response was to wonder whether or not the Jersey authorities really wanted to spend £40,000 on such armaments and in any case the 4.7in coastal guns could not be delivered before August 1940 and the others might follow in due course. In fact the War Office told the Home Office that it considered the prospect of an attack on the Islands 'somewhat remote' and suggested that a few Lewis guns to defend the airports (Guernsey's had only opened in June 1939) from low-flying, attacking aircraft would be a sensible precaution and the Militias should be trained in defence, although the War Office couldn't actually spare anyone to do that.

Thus the Islands' attempts to defend themselves achieved little but what they could do was boost their Sovereign's government's war chest and in the summer of 1939 the States of Guernsey voted the sum of £180,000 (which caused the rate of income tax, at that time 9d [3.75p] in the pound to be doubled). Jersey, with perhaps greater experience of the perils of offering money to the British government, took a little longer but agreed in March 1940 to raise a loan of £100,000 to be given to Britain as a first instalment.

In fact the Home Office, even before Neville Chamberlain's ill-starred Munich declaration, had given thought to how the Islands might be put on a war footing. In the Great War the power to make Defence Regulations was the exclusive prerogative of Whitehall but, in April 1939, the Home Office took the decision to delegate to the Jersey States and the Guernsey Royal Court the power to make their own defence regulations, although many UK Regulations would be extended to the Islands as a matter of course. After all, the British government was still responsible for the Islands' defence, although there were times when this responsibility seemed to be somewhat haphazard, and the Islands themselves still found that centuries of separation often meant that what was understood by one was misunderstood by the other.

Nevertheless plans were made to ensure supplies of essential commodities, new emergency legislation was enacted and, despite some glitches such as discovering that the special code to alert the Air Raid Precautions services to the imminence of war did not actually extend to the Channel Islands, the Islands were as prepared for war as they were ever likely to be, except, of course, that no one was contemplating the type of war they would actually have to endure. However, sand bags were filled and piled high around the entrances to important buildings and potential air raid shelters. Men of uncertain age (that today we would probably regard as the precursors of 'Dad's Army') wore armbands and white helmets and drilled with shovels and stirrup pumps. In Jersey enemy aliens were interned in the former Oxenden's Holiday Camp at Grouville in the east of the Island. These were German and Austrian nationals who had been working in the hotel industry and they would be joined, in June 1940, by Italians when their country declared war. Intended only for summertime occupation, the chalets had no heating facilities and would have been rather chilly in winter. Bizarrely the existence of the camp was advertised with a sign on which were written the two words 'Concentration Camp'. Later in the war this would cause a very different chill but was a reminder, perhaps, that 'concentration camps' had been a British invention first used in the Boer War and were seen, at that time, as a legitimate contrivance of war. After the invasion, from November 1941 to February 1942, the camp became *Lager Franco*, a camp for Spanish workers of the *Organisation Todt*.

The 'phoney war' was as phoney for the Channel Islands as it was for the rest of Britain. No one in the Islands is recorded as saying that 'Hitler has missed the bus' but there was the distinct feeling that although the conflict had started with the *Blitzkrieg* into Poland, somehow things had ground to a halt and quite what Germany would do next was something of a mystery.

Within days of the declaration of war, nine divisions of the French Army began a tentative move into the Saarland and a week later the first elements of the British Expeditionary Force began to arrive in France. Wiseacres predicted 1914 all over again and indeed by 25 September artillery duels were flaring up along the Western Front.

Barely a month into the war Hitler declared the victorious end of the Polish campaign and called upon Britain and France to cease hostilities and talk terms. His suggestion was rejected.

Many Jerseymen and Guernseymen who had joined the Regular Army at the outbreak of war found themselves posted to places with names like Bapaume and Peronne which would have been very familiar to their fathers.

Life for the Islanders went on much as before. Initial knee-jerk reactions such as the blackout were changed so that cinemas could stay open later and the business of earning a living continued to be pursued in earnest. Guernsey was rightly proud of its new airport and wanted to see people using it. Jersey's tourism industry was already larger than that of its sister and advertisements in the national press offered holidays in an Island 'far removed from the theatre of war'. In justification (in case anyone should think going on holiday was rather a frivolous thing to be doing in wartime) the Jersey tourism committee claimed that holidays meant that those taking them would return refreshed mentally and physically and 'ready to give of his best in the national war effort'.

Stirring stuff. And it worked since a regular flow of visitors disgorged themselves from the mailboats of the Southern and Great Western Railways during the spring of 1940. As late as 22 June 1940 the London *Times* was publishing the names of hotels in Jersey recommended by Ashley Courtney, and the St Brelade's Bay Hotel proclaimed itself the 'safest place on earth'! Within a year it would be a *Soldatenheim* (the German version of the NAAFI) providing recreations for *Wehrmacht* officers and other ranks alike. Obviously the wrong people had been reading the advertisements!

As long ago as October 1939, with his non-aggression pact with Russia protecting his eastern flank, Hitler was issuing orders for the invasion of France and the Low Countries. This time there would be no messing about with regard to Dutch neutrality since a sweep through Holland and Belgium would render France's Maginot Line so much scrap metal. He had hoped that the exercise would start in November but the weather and his generals decreed that such a move should be postponed to early in 1940.

On 9 April 1940 the Germans invaded Denmark and Norway. Denmark, taken completely by surprise, surrendered the next day. Norway took a little longer but by 7 June King Haakon VII and his government were evacuated to England and three days later Norway had surrendered unconditionally. By September government was in the hands of Vidkun Quisling and his pro-Nazi National Union Party and a new word was finding its way into the English dictionary.

In the event, the attack on France and the Low Countries, *Unternehmung 'Gelb'* (Operation 'Yellow'), commenced at 5.35am on Friday, 10 May 1940. The plan, devised by *Generalfeldmarschall* Gerd von Rundstedt and his former chief of staff, *Generaloberst* Erich von Manstein, involved the invasion of Holland, Belgium and Luxembourg and a thrust through the heavily wooded Ardennes which the Allies would not expect. Hitler sent the troops on their way with typical rhetoric: 'Soldiers of the Western Front! The battle which is beginning today will decide the fate of the German nation for the next thousand years. Go forward now and do your duty!' And Army Group A commanded by von Rundstedt and Army Group B commanded by *Generalfeldmarschall* Fedor von Bock did exactly that. And many in the Channel Islands began to feel decidedly uneasy.

In their view the Channel Islands were like choice plums ready to fall from an easily accessible tree. It was just a case of how long the tree would need to be shaken before the plums dropped.

Chapter 5
The road to the Isles opens

Following the British and French armies' escape at Dunkirk, German forces march into Paris. The Islands' Lieutenant-Governors and garrisons are withdrawn, the Islands are inhabited with 'rabbits and rats', Alderney is evacuated and the Islands are declared 'open towns' but the German forces, now on the Cotentin peninsula, are not informed and the harbours at St Helier and St Peter Port are bombed

Despite the Channel Islands' long history as thorns in the side of the traditional enemy, the *Entente Cordiale* brokered by King Edward VII and their role in the Great War had convinced Whitehall that the Islands had little or no strategic value any more. Although wide open to attack from France by sea and air, unless something went terribly wrong with the *Entente*, there was little chance that France would be the aggressor. That someone else might use France as a springboard for invasion seems not to have occurred to anyone. What's more, in 1928, the Imperial Defence Committee had accepted a recommendation from a parsimonious War Office that funding for the local Militias should be withdrawn since for Britain to pay for something which had no value, namely the Islands' defence, did not make economic sense.

On 14 May 1940 the Germans took Rotterdam and the Dutch government was evacuated to London. The following day Holland capitulated and thousands fled from Paris after reports that the Germans had broken through at Sedan. The refugees clogged the roads, making themselves and the British and French units struggling to go the other way tempting targets for *Luftwaffe Stuka* dive-bombers.

On 18 May Antwerp fell to the Germans and the Allied front was seriously split as tanks of Guderian's 19th Panzer Corps reached Peronne and Rommel's 7th Panzer Division reached Cambrai during their rapid advance to the Channel coast. What the German armies of the Great War had failed to achieve in four years, Hitler's new virtuosos achieved in a matter of days. By 25 May, just a week later, the remnants of the British, French and Belgian armies had retreated to Dunkirk and the next day Operation 'Dynamo' began: the evacuation of the troops from the beaches to the east of the town by virtually anything that would float. By 31 May, King Leopold of the Belgians surrendered and more than 194,000 troops had been evacuated from Dunkirk, although losses were heavy, particularly amongst the ships taking the men off the beaches.

Eventually, by 3 June, 224,686 British and 121,445 French and Belgian troops had been evacuated and when the Germans entered Dunkirk the following day they took 40,000 French prisoners and vast quantities of abandoned equipment including 84,000 vehicles, 2,500 guns and 650,000 tons of supplies and ammunition.

On the day the Germans began *Unternehmung 'Rote'* (Operation 'Red') — the 'Battle of France' — with 119 divisions on the move, the Chief of the Imperial General Staff (CIGS), Sir John Dill, submitted a memorandum to the Chiefs of Staff Committee of the War Cabinet that implied that the possible loss of the Channel Islands might be a *bad* thing after all, since, apart from any other consideration, the Islands were guardians of the all-important telephone cable to France. On 10 June Major-General Harrison, Jersey's Lieutenant-Governor, wrote to Charles Markbreiter 'in an awful hurry to catch the post' suggesting that since the Germans were already bombarding Cherbourg, the Islands could well come under attack and unless the Germans were sporting enough to attack in very small numbers he simply did not have the men or equipment to repulse them. He had discussed with Bailiff Coutanche what would happen if a German invasion of Jersey were successful. Coutanche was concerned that if he were to be required to carry on his role but under German orders he would be betraying his oath of allegiance to the Sovereign. Harrison had disagreed — better for the Islanders that the Bailiff remained in office — and he ended his letter to Markbreiter by complaining that when it came to dealing with an invasion, Whitehall had kept the Island authorities very much in the dark.

There is still considerable resentment in the Islands at what, at the time, was perceived as the Islands being abandoned to a rapacious foe. Britain clearly did not know what to do to protect the Islands but there was also a feeling that it didn't much care either.

The CIGS reported to the War Cabinet that the Chiefs of Staff had decided that, despite having no strategic value, two battalions were to be dispatched to the Islands to defend them but almost immediately the orders were cancelled since it was assumed that the adjacent French coast was now in enemy hands and those British troops that were already there were to be withdrawn. If the Germans landed, the Lieutenant-Governors should be instructed to surrender to avoid useless sacrifice.

The decision that the Islands should be left undefended was finally taken on Saturday, 15 June (the day after the fall of Paris), although the Alderney-based Machine Gun Training Centre was given the task of defending Jersey and Guernsey airports since they might still be of use to the Royal Air Force in support of any land operations in nearby France. 'Thereafter the policy of demilitarisation will rule.'

A meeting took place at the Home Office to discuss this demilitarisation. The Islands were represented by Jurat E. A. Dorey of Jersey who returned with letters for the Lieutenant-Governors which read: 'I am directed by the Secretary of State to say that in the event of your recall it is desired by His Majesty's Government that the Bailiff should discharge the duties of the

Lieutenant-Governor, which would then be confined to civil duties, and that he should stay at his post and administer the government of the Island to the best of his abilities in the interests of the inhabitants, whether or not he is in a position to receive instructions from His Majesty's Government. The Crown Officers should also remain at their posts.'

Meanwhile a mini-Dunkirk was happening on Jersey's doorstep with a gathering of British troops at St Malo needing to be evacuated. Jersey soldier Maurice Buesnel, who had joined the Army in 1938, escaped from the beaches of Dunkirk only to find himself wading ashore a few miles down the coast when his transport sank beneath him. With hundreds of his colleagues he marched across France ahead of the advancing Germans, eventually arriving, very footsore, in St Malo, wondering how he was going to get home. Although there were ships to take off most of the troops, Bailiff Coutanche asked the Commodore of the St Helier Yacht Club to send as many of his members with their craft to St Malo as soon as possible to help.

Altogether 18 vessels of varying sizes went within 24 hours and brought out the demolition parties and stragglers. All returned safely to Jersey despite strong winds and heavy seas.

Private Buesnel had time to call on his mother who lived in Halkett Place, St Helier, before embarking on a mailsteamer to rejoin his unit. He was to see action in North Africa, Italy and Greece and would not return to Jersey, with a new wife, until some time after the Liberation.

The Islanders would have not been at all reassured to have learned that on 20 June 1940, with France subdued, Germany's architects of *Blitzkrieg* gave the order to their forward commanders: 'The capture of the British Channel Islands is necessary and urgent.' To these German commanders their capture was 'necessary and urgent' since, unless taken, the Islands could pose a threat to German plans to create U-boat bases on France's Atlantic coast as they dominated the Western Approaches to the English Channel. That same day the steamship *Malines* arrived to embark the last of the remaining British troops while the SS *Biarritz* had fulfilled the same function in Guernsey. After 'consultation with the Post Office' orders were given to cut the telephone cable that linked Jersey's east coast to France.

The abandonment of the Islands was finally confirmed when the Lieutenant-Governors left the Islands on HMS *Philante* on 21 June and the Bailiffs acceded to their title and assumed their new roles.

At that point the Foreign Office should have informed the Germans that the Islands were demilitarised but they chose not to do so since, they reasoned, such information was tantamount to an invitation to invade. That this piece of reasoning might lead to unnecessary deaths if the Germans then decided to attack did not, perhaps, occur to them.

In the meantime discussions had taken place about evacuating the civilian population of the Islands. At first early evacuation was considered for military reasons since 'we cannot contemplate the evacuation of large numbers of civilians under heavy air attack'. By mid-June the Home Office began a serious consideration of evacuation. Jurat Dorey at his meeting with the Home Office had estimated that up to 30,000 women and children should be evacuated. The Home Office agreed, although the Islands' authorities would have to make the necessary arrangements. And bear the cost.

The news that the Islands were not to be defended (although Prime Minister Winston Churchill felt that the Royal Navy should be up to the task but was dissuaded from putting this particular Gallipolian theory into practice) caused something of a panic. In the States of Jersey, Jurat Dorey, whose mission to the Home Office had started the fuss, declared that he could understand why English residents should want to leave but not why those of old Norman stock would want to pull up their roots. The House, he said, should show its utter contempt of them. Men of military age should go to England because they had an 'honourable mission' and they should not be mixed up with the rabbits and the rats.

The Bailiff, Crown Officers and Jurats announced that they would stay at their posts and Coutanche went on to address a huge, anxious crowd in the Royal Square. They had one duty — to keep calm. Many wanted to leave and it was up to everyone to act according to his own conscience. 'I will never leave,' he said, 'and my wife will be by my side.' He intended to do his duty, as did the Crown Officers and the States. He then led the crowd in singing the National Anthem. In his journal he would write: 'All that could be done was to show a good example.'

Jersey's daily newspaper *The Evening Post* of 19 June announced that the British government was providing ships to evacuate women and children, men who wanted to join up, and, if there was room, other men. Minds had to be made up rapidly — by 10 o'clock the following day — by which time almost 9,000 had registered including 434 volunteers for the forces. The situation had all the necessary ingredients to generate panic, which it duly did. Long queues formed outside the railway companies' offices. Homes were abandoned, often with food left on the table. Several thousand pets were abandoned too.

But gradually a sort of calm descended. Coutanche's resolve was an example many decided to follow. Better the devil you know and all that.

Ultimately the number of registrations was more than 23,000 but a large number, impressed by Coutanche's resolution, changed their minds and the number who did leave was around 5,000, about a 10th of Jersey's population. Unfortunately many changed their minds after they had packed and actually left their homes only to find that when they returned, their homes had already been ransacked by neighbours. One justified the looting, for that was what indeed it was, by claiming that 'better I have it than the Germans!'.

In Guernsey plans were made to evacuate schoolchildren but the announcements published in the *Evening Press* and *The Star* also suggested that men of military age should register for evacuation too. To add to the despair of parents facing separation from their children was added the prohibition of waving goodbye to them at the harbour since congregations of tearful parents might present too tempting a target for enemy aircraft. Goodbyes had to be made at home or school. Except for the evacuees the harbour would be out of bounds. Unlike Jersey, where Coutanche had been able to inspire the greater majority of Island residents to stay, the messages coming from the Guernsey authorities were mixed and a new Lieutenant-Governor had barely had time to put his feet under the desk before he was withdrawing them — even Sherwill whose judgement and reasoning were usually so sound vacillated as he received differing advice — and the result was that the ships sent by the British government left crammed with evacuees on a daily basis until almost half the population from Guernsey had opted for the unknown of a new life in war-torn Britain. In August 1940, after the dust of invasion had settled, the Guernsey States Education Department estimated that six and a half thousand children had left for England, leaving around a thousand in the Island. This mass evacuation (not compulsory, although it must be said that the authorities made it seem so) created a postwar breach in Guernsey society which has taken two generations to heal. Children who were 10 years old when they were evacuated were 15 when they returned after five years' growing up in a completely different culture. Many just couldn't wait to get back to mainland Britain.

Also evacuated were the Islands' stocks of gold coinage — mostly sovereigns — and the evacuees were limited to withdrawing just £20 in cash from their bank accounts. Although today almost a paltry sum, for many that was several weeks' wages.

At least Jersey and Guernsey had been able to communicate with London and could feel that at last they were being told what was going on. However, things were different in Alderney.

Alderney was just seven miles from the coast of France and palls of smoke from the bombardment of Cherbourg were quite visible, as were the boatloads of refugees suddenly appearing on the Island's rocky foreshore. As part of the Bailiwick of Guernsey, Alderney should have been able to look to that Island's authorities for guidance but poor communications (in every sense for no telephone link existed) meant that almost no one, particularly Alderney's titular head, Judge F. G. French, knew what was going on. Rumours abounded and the Islanders watched amazed as what little military defence forces the Island had were withdrawn to defend the Jersey and Guernsey airports, their own being deemed to be of little use to anybody! Understandably people began to panic.

A meeting was called and almost the entire population of around a thousand souls turned up and agreed to evacuate. Not only did the Guernsey authorities agree but they decided that evacuation should mean just that and arranged for not only the people to be taken off but also all the animals as well. Domestic animals too old or diseased to be moved were shot and residents who decided to stay where they were found themselves being ordered to leave at gunpoint! Victor Carey, now acting as the Lieutenant-Governor, decreed that anyone left 'in the Island of Alderney is to be removed, by force if necessary, to Guernsey'.

The situation in Sark was different again. There the Island's hereditary feudal ruler, the Dame, Mrs Sybil Hathaway, decided that not only was she staying (as would her husband Robert) but that the population of around five hundred should stay as well. She told a packed meeting at the Island Hall on 23 June that it was useless to run away to England and if the Germans came she would deal with them (and she spoke German fluently) as best she could. The Islanders agreed although a dozen or more English residents did leave, including the Island's relatively newly appointed Medical Officer of Health, Dr Fisher. Mrs Hathaway was not best pleased and she wrote to Jersey's Attorney General asking if Jersey could provide a replacement. It might seem that Mrs Hathaway's action was a little odd, given that Sark was part of the Bailiwick of Guernsey. However, the Island had in fact been colonised from Jersey in 1565 when Seigneur Helier de Carteret had settled 40 families on the Island and the shrewd Mrs Hathaway also realised that Alexander Coutanche was a man much more of her ilk than the vacillators in Guernsey. A Dr E. C. Ibotson, who had been in practice in Jersey since 1934, took up his new position in Sark almost three weeks after the Germans arrived to find 471 new potential patients on his books.

On the French mainland plans to invade the Islands had already been hatched.

Being sea-girt, the capture of the Channel Islands began as the responsibility of the *Kriegsmarine,* the German Navy. On 18 June the Admiral Commanding in France, *Admiral* Karlgeorg Schuster, discussed the situation with the operations staff of *Luftflotte 2* (Air Fleet 2). Whether the Islands were defended or not was unknown and thus aerial photographic reconnaissance was initiated that same day. Two days later, when the order came that the capture of the Islands was necessary and urgent, Schuster was able to report that the reconnaissance he had already ordered appeared to show little of significance although, of course, this could mean that the defences were well concealed! Moreover, when the photographs were analysed in detail, the Flag Officer Northern France, *Vizeadmiral* Eugen Lindau, reported to Schuster that there were harbour and coastal fortifications, and long columns of lorries in the port areas suggested the presence of military *matériel* and troops, indications that the garrisons had been strengthened. Of course the reverse was actually the case and the vehicles were loaded with produce for export waiting vainly for ships to take away their perishable cargoes. Nevertheless Lindau decided that it was more than likely that a full-scale assault from the sea, with air support, would be required to dislodge the defenders. The invasion, he felt and his superiors agreed with him, was not likely to be a walkover. The Royal Navy might well intervene for, although the German armies were very nearly invulnerable on land, the *Kriegsmarine* was very much a junior partner when it came to sharing the sea with the British navy. What's more, the invasion forces may well come under air attack from bases on England's south coast. All these factors needed to be taken into account since neither Schuster nor Lindau wanted to make a mess of what would be the German forces' first direct assault on British soil. Both men were cautious by nature so, in any event, the prelude to the assault would be softening-up bombing raids on the ports. The operation would be known as *'Grüne Pfeile'* ('Green Arrows').

It had become obvious to the authorities in both Islands that they were facing a situation unique in their history — an enemy invasion that would not be contested — and that their traditional States Assemblies were not fitted, with their penchant for debate, argument and delay, to cope with what would clearly often have to be instant decision making. In Jersey Bailiff Coutanche established the Superior Council which consisted of the presidents of all the various committees of The States. The Council comprised Coutanche as president, Attorney General Duret-Aubin as vice-president and 25 members whose portfolios covered essential commodities, transport and communications, finance and economy, agriculture and public health, essential services, education and labour, each portfolio having its own president supported by two other States members.

In Guernsey a similar decision had already been taken when its States met at short notice and created the Controlling Committee of the States of Guernsey with offices at the recently abandoned Elizabeth College. Procureur Ambrose Sherwill was appointed president with the power to appoint the other members, seven in all, with portfolios similar to their Jersey counterparts dealing with agriculture, horticulture, unemployment, re-employment and public assistance, economics, medical and nursing services, information and essential commodities.

These committees had much with which to concern themselves.

At 12.25pm on Friday, 28 June, the Southern Railway steamer *Isle of Sark* arrived in Guernsey from Jersey carrying 484 passengers. Although evacuation was continuing it had slowed right down and the *Isle* had the capacity to carry at least a thousand more passengers than were already aboard. Nor were there any longer panicking evacuees on the harbourside, although there was a forlorn queue of lorries loaded with tomatoes for export. The *Isle* would usually have sailed within the hour but Captain Golding decided to delay his departure until dark. Although a passenger vessel, the *Isle* was armed with a three-pounder and four Lewis guns and men who knew how to fire them.

Just before 7.00pm, six Heinkel *He111* medium bombers appeared over the Islands, strafing the dock areas of St Helier and St Peter Port and dropping bombs. Workers on the docks dived for cover behind the flimsiest of shelters. Elsewhere Islanders, tempted from their homes out of curiosity, were killed and injured by bombs and bullets. Although the ports were the prime targets, the aircraft roamed over the Islands, dropping bombs and firing their guns indiscriminately.

Altogether 44 civilians were killed and many more wounded. There were no military casualties since there were no military personnel left. The only opposition came from the light machine guns on the *Isle of Sark*. Casualties were random although one Jersey chronicler of the time, in St Helier, made careful note of how many licensed premises had either been bombed or machine-gunned. Perhaps this was inevitable since the docks area abounded with public houses. Mr Ferrand, landlord of 'Daley's Bunch of Grapes' in St Helier, was shot down and killed in the roadway outside his premises. The pub is still there, in Mulcaster Street, although today it is called 'The Lamplighter'.

Their bombs dropped, the Heinkels machine-gunned at random including, inexplicably, an attack on the St Peter Port relief lifeboat which was on passage to Jersey, killing one of the crew, Harold Hobbs, son of the coxswain. Along the White Rock in St Peter Port harbour the line of lorries loaded with tomatoes intended for shipment to Britain burned, their drivers dead and injured alongside their vehicles.

By coincidence Ambrose Sherwill was in his office at Elizabeth College in St Peter Port and on the telephone to Charles Markbreiter when the attack came. He held the telephone to the window to let the Home Office official hear for himself what enemy aircraft bombing and machine-gunning sounded like.

The *Isle of Sark* was undamaged although a passenger and a seaman were injured and taken to the local hospital. The ship sailed at just before 10.00pm with just 651 passengers, well below its complement. She was the last mailboat Islanders were to see until after the Liberation.

Islanders were shocked, appalled and fearful. Many were also outraged. The Islands were demilitarised. They were 'open towns' and the attack was thus wholly unjustified. There would have been no comfort in knowing that the officer responsible, commanding the *8e Fliegerkorps* of *Luftflotte 3*, was *Generaloberst der Flieger* Dr Wolfram Freiherr von Richthofen, cousin of the famous 'Red Baron', who had honed his bombing skills with the Condor Legion in Spain where he was responsible for the bombing of Guernica. There was even less comfort in discovering that the British government had actually failed to advise the Germans of the Channel Islands' demilitarised status.

In London *The Times* was to make much of the fact that the dastardly Germans had bombed 'open towns' and even the BBC, by broadcasting at 9.00pm on the Friday evening (some time after the raids commenced) that the Channel Islands had been demilitarised (although formal notification to the German government was not made until 30 June), sought to imply, without actually telling an untruth, that once again the Germans had broken the rules. Jersey historian Bob Le Sueur, committing his thoughts many years later to the Imperial War Museum's Sound Archive, commented: 'It didn't really happen that way . . .'

Although so little resistance had been encountered, the Germans decided that further armed reconnaissance was required before landings were attempted.

But why did the British government not inform the Germans of the Islands' 'open town' status and thus spare the lives of innocent non-combatants?

All sorts of theories have been advanced from forgetfulness to malice but the answer is probably quite simple, for the Government, like the Island authorities, was facing a situation unique in Britain's history — the potential loss of sovereign territory without a fight or even the threat of one. The British government was damned if it did and damned if it didn't. Declaring that the Islands were 'open towns' would be tantamount to an invitation to the Germans to invade. Not to, meant that the Germans might just change their minds if they thought they had a fight on their hands. Some hopes!

Whatever the reasons, the way was now open for uncontested occupation. It was not long in coming.

Chapter 6
Invasion

The Luftwaffe *and the* Kriegsmarine *vie for the privilege of invading and occupying the Channel Islands but what could have happened had things not turned out quite as they had planned?*

Unlike the impression frequently gained since (for instance, that the Germans merely walked into Islands handed to them on a plate), there really existed an elaborate plan to take the Channel Islands. The responsibility belonged to the *Kriegsmarine* who tended to claim the right to anything that was on the sea and islands fitted that particular bill. The man in charge of devising *Unternehmung 'Grüne Pfeile'* (Operation 'Green Arrows') was *Vizeadmiral* Eugen Lindau, Flag Officer Northern France (in the rather more colourful German, *Marinebefehlshaber Nordfrankreich*), reporting to the *Kommandierender Admiral Frankreich* (Commanding Admiral France) *Admiral* Karlgeorg Schuster.

It was planned for *'Grüne Pfeile'* to employ six battalions of assault troops — three for Jersey, two for Guernsey and one for Alderney. These would be supported by a *Marinestosstruppabteilung* (the *Kriegsmarine's* version of the Marines) and two engineer companies. A dearth of suitable landing craft meant that the assault on the Islands would take place over two days — Guernsey and Alderney would be the objectives for Day 1 and Jersey for Day 2. The troops would be conveyed to the Islands in motley craft, many of which had been requisitioned in the harbours along the Cotentin peninsula. *Schnellboote* (fast motor torpedo boats) would be held in reserve to beat off any attack by the Royal Navy and *Stuka* dive-bombers would attack the noted defensive positions. In addition strong fighter protection would be needed over the embarkation areas.

Admiral Schuster reported to *Oberkommando der Kriegsmarine* (*OKM* — Naval High Command) in Berlin on the progress of *Unternehmung 'Grüne Pfeile'* on Saturday, 29 June, and on the following day attended a conference with Lindau in Paris to finalise the details.

Despite the admirals' concerns (as much for their future careers as for the success of the operation) the decision was taken to scale down the attack. After all, the reaction to the air raid the day before had been very slight so it was deemed that the invasion force should be just one battalion each for Jersey and Guernsey and a single infantry company could take on Alderney. The troops would be drawn from 216 Infantry Division already stationed in the Cherbourg area, supported by the *Kriegsmarine Abteilung 'Gotenhafen'*

(Naval Assault Group 'Gotenhafen') and a *Luftwaffe* anti-aircraft detachment. The *Luftwaffe* would also maintain suitable air cover.

The conference broke up with the decision taken to carry out further armed reconnaissance the following day. If the incursions provoked any real opposition then the full-scale assault would take place as planned. If there was no opposition then the army and navy units would be flown into the Islands' airports.

However, as the delegates were returning their notes to their briefcases the news came that a *Hauptmann* Liebe-Pieteritz had landed his Dornier *Do17P* at Guernsey airport. He had been leading a flight of four reconnaissance aircraft and decided, in view of the lack of opposition, without orders, to land and take a look around. With his three colleagues circling protectively above, the captain landed and taxied over to the newly opened airport buildings. They were deserted and he had to break a window to enter. However, his audacious personal reconnaissance was interrupted by the untimely arrival of three RAF Blenheims. Reports differ as to what happened next. The Germans claimed that in the ensuing dogfight, two Blenheims were shot down, although RAF records throw doubt on that. Another report says that Liebe-Pieteritz was in such a hurry to rejoin his aircraft that he dropped his Luger pistol in the rush. Other reports, including one eye-witness, claimed that not one, but three Dorniers actually landed. Whichever way it was, very soon the *Hauptmann* and his comrades were reporting to their *Luftflotte 3* superiors in Cherbourg that the island seemed to be undefended. His arrival too was reported on the Island and Sherwill notified the Home Office, and the Bailiff of Jersey, that the Germans had landed. At 3.00pm Mrs Hathaway telephoned the Guernsey police asking what was going on since she had heard a rumour that the Germans had landed. The Station Sergeant extemporised. 'We have heard nothing official,' he replied.

While the naval officers with the responsibility for the invasion of the Islands were driving back to Cherbourg, a second landing took place at Guernsey airport when a party of *Luftwaffe* personnel from *Aufklärungsgruppe 123* (Reconnaissance Group 123) under the overall command of *Major* Hessel and led by *Hauptmann* von Obernitz arrived in the ubiquitous Junkers Ju52 transports and took control of the airport. They encountered one unexpected obstacle since cattle from Alderney had been allowed to roam over the grass field (since no one else was using it) and two cows were injured by the incoming aircraft and had to be shot.

Whether *Generaloberst* von Richthofen had intended cocking a snook at his naval counterparts we may never know but *Admirale* Schuster and Lindau can hardly have been delighted to learn that all their careful planning appeared to have been unnecessary and to see the victor's laurels snatched from their grasp. As von Obernitz secured his conquest, he had a visitor. Inspector William Sculpher, head of Guernsey's police force, arrived bearing a letter which had been written three days before, in English, by Bailiff Carey. The inspector had already been to the airport that day when a report was received that a German aircraft had landed but by the time he got there *Hauptmann* Liebe-Pieteritz had flown away. This time the Germans were not leaving and Sculpher handed over the letter, addressed to 'The Officer Commanding German Troops in Guernsey' which read:

'This Island has been declared an Open Island by His Majesty's Government of the United Kingdom. There are in it no armed forces of any description. The bearer has been instructed to hand this communication to you. He does not understand the German language.'

While he was doing that, Sherwill was once again calling the Home Office and the Bailiff of Jersey telling them what was happening and bidding them 'au revoir'. Communication with the Home Office was maintained until 10.30pm when the lines were finally cut. Like so many other things they would not be re-established until after the Liberation.

In the meantime Inspector Sculpher had driven *Major* Hessel, who spoke little English but enough to demand to meet the 'Chief Man', into St Peter Port to the Royal Hotel to meet the Bailiff, other Island dignitaries and holders of key offices. Sherwill and Bailiff Carey were collected from their homes and the Acting-Postmaster, the Telephone Manager and the Harbourmaster were summoned. A Mr Isler of the Hotel de Normandie was brought in as an interpreter.

That evening, until 11.30pm, *Major* Hessel told the assembled company how things were going to be.

In Cherbourg *Admiral* Lindau was distinctly rattled. Operation *'Grüne Pfeile'* was supposed to be a *Kriegsmarine* operation and those upstarts from the *Luftwaffe* had hijacked it. Early on Monday, 1 July, he ordered that the invasion take place immediately with troops of 216 Infantry Division being flown to Guernsey and Alderney as planned and then on to Jersey.

There were several other things to upset the admiral that morning. Fog in the Paris area had caused delays for the transport aircraft he had been promised for most of the day and he was informed that Guernsey had already surrendered to the *Luftwaffe* and the occupation had begun! What was even more annoying was that the *Luftwaffe* was now set to bring about Jersey's surrender for no less a personality than *Generaloberst* Hugo Sperrle had arrived at Cherbourg West airport at Querqueville. The fearsomely monocled Commander-in-Chief of *Luftflotte 3* (who would be promoted by Hitler to *Generalfeldmarschall* less than three weeks later on 19 July) immediately took charge. A message addressed to the Chief of the Military and Civilian Authorities was dropped in linen bags on the airfield and on the town of St Helier, in which *Generaloberst* von Richthofen spelled out the terms of surrender to the Jersey authorities which included the display of white crosses in a number of prominent locations and the flying of white flags. His terms concluded with the threat that every hostile action against his representatives would be followed by bombardment but the pledge that in the event of a peaceful surrender the lives, property and liberty of peaceful inhabitants were to be solemnly guaranteed. The message was in German and someone had to be found (eventually it was an Alsatian priest) who could translate it and that took a little time.

Since there was no immediate response, aircraft were dispatched to Jersey and thus it was that *Leutnant* Richard Kern, overflying Jersey airport and seeing all quiet, decided to emulate his colleague's Guernsey experience and land. Quite what happened next varies slightly depending upon whose report you read but the upshot was that Richard Kern was the first German who learned that the States had just met and taken the formal decision to surrender and the white crosses and flags were being displayed as requested. Met by the German-speaking airport commandant, Charles Roche, *Leutnant* Kern was able to have the Bailiff advised by telephone that he should now assume that Jersey was under German military occupation. And with that the *Leutnant* flew off to Guernsey to report the situation and his success to his superiors.

A detachment of naval assault troops from *Kriegsmarine Abteilung 'Gotenhafen'* (Admiral Lindau was determined not to be left out) and a company from 396 Infantry Division were flown in, accompanied by a *Luftwaffe* light anti-aircraft unit. At around 4.30pm more troop carriers arrived, bringing with them more troops, motorcycles and 20mm anti-aircraft guns. Bailiff Coutanche was instructed to go to the airport to meet them. He had just completed a task that he had promised only he would carry out — the lowering of the Union Flag at Fort Regent overlooking St Helier which had daily fluttered protectively over the town.

Coutanche was accompanied by Attorney General Duret-Aubin and the Government Secretary, Lieutenant-Colonel H. H. Hulton. He was met by *Hauptmann* von Obernitz (who had fulfilled the same role in Guernsey) and half a dozen other *Luftwaffe* officers including (in the photograph which crops up in almost every publication recording the event) a grinning *Leutnant* Kern.

Very soon German soldiers were occupying the Town Hall and Post Office in St Helier, while in Guernsey they had taken over Government House, although the Royal Hotel on the Glategny Esplanade had been chosen as their temporary headquarters.

In that island the invasion was well advanced. *The Star* had published a special edition (distributed free of charge) early on the morning of 1 July, the front page of which was devoted to the orders of the new German Commandant. *Major* Hessel had dictated a long list of orders which were given to Sherwill through an interpreter with instructions to put them into correct English so that they could be published in the morning newspaper early the next day. *The Star's* editor, William Taylor, had been summoned and given the most devastating piece of copy of his journalistic career (see Appendix I).

Alongside the orders was a notice from the Controlling Committee of the States of Guernsey addressed 'to every Islander' in which he or she was notified that no resistance whatsoever was to be offered to those in military occupation of the Island. The public were asked to stay calm, to carry on their lives and work in the usual way, and to obey the orders of the German Commandant printed on that page.

Some would argue later that even on the first day of enemy occupation, the authorities were being too co-operative but while the Superior Council in Jersey did not emulate its Guernsey counterparts when they were forced to have published similar instructions the following day, the Controlling Committee's actions have to be considered in the light of what was known then, not what we know to be so today. The Germans had already proved their deadly intent with 23 Guernsey Islanders killed and a similar number injured in what had been a comparatively minor air raid. That the casualties might have been greater had the attacking Heinkels not had to maintain sufficient height to avoid the Lewis gunners on the *Isle of Sark* had probably not been lost on Sherwill and his colleagues. In the light of an enemy they could not yet know, their action in publishing the notice seems realistic given their desire not to see more lives lost.

Amongst the instructions was an order for all British sailors, airmen and soldiers on leave in the Island to report to the police station and 41 men did so. They were transferred to Castle Cornet although Aircraftsman Jack Robert was allowed to attend the funeral of two sisters killed in the air raid.

Major Dr Albrecht Lanz (he was a Doctor of Law), commanding officer of the 2nd Battalion of Regiment 396, had been designated to carry out the occupation of Guernsey. He flew in to Guernsey at 2.45pm where he was met by *Major* Hessel who reported that all was quiet at the airport and in the town.

Hessel had been busy. As well as taking over the front page of *The Star* he had also organised the making of a German war flag since none was otherwise available. A sketch was provided and the flag was made by Creasey's, Guernsey's principal department store, in five hours (and remember this was a Sunday!) with Victor Creasey himself cutting out the swastikas and iron crosses. A few days later Creasey's submitted a bill for £3 0s 4d (£3.02). The bill was settled a few days later.

Major Lanz reported: 'A few minutes after 15.00hrs the first German Imperial War Flag, sewn by English hands, was hauled up the mast of the airport building to float over British territory.'

Within the hour more Junkers Ju52s arrived bringing with them *Generalleutnant* Hermann Böttcher, divisional commander of 216 Infantry Division, and *Admiral* Lindau, the man whose show this was supposed to have been and who was still anxious to share in the glory.

As the brass hats admired the new ensign flying above the airport buildings, *Major* Hessel handed over command of the island to *Major* Lanz and they were both driven in a police car to the Royal Hotel where they were joined by *Major* Dr Maass, the English-speaking medical officer of '*Gotenhafen*' (he had a diploma in tropical medicine gained at Liverpool University in 1931) and saw hundreds of anxious Islanders thronging around the hotel. They then drove to meet the Bailiff, Victor Carey, at his home. Their driver was probably Inspector Sculpher who no doubt made the most of the journey along narrow thoroughfares with nervous passengers unused to travelling on the wrong side of the road! Lanz recorded how they had been driven into the park surrounding the Bailiff's house, Le Vallon, had rung the bell and been ushered into a 'large richly furnished living room' where they met 'an old gentleman of 68, in a dark suit'. It was explained by Dr Maass that *Major* Hessel had handed over his command to Lanz, at which the Bailiff, his arms folded, bowed deeply. Lanz, clearly moved by the old world courtesy, recorded that it was 'the first time in the history of England a Governor and direct representative of His Britannic Majesty has ever bowed to the German Army'. The Bailiff thanked the German officers 'repeatedly' for the correct behaviour of the German troops and promised to make all the necessary arrangements for the Germans' wishes and regulations to be carried out 'in the smallest detail'. Everything we needed, Lanz reported with evident satisfaction, was at our disposal.

He might have been pleased — indeed he described the occasion as his proudest moment of the war — but Victor Carey, who would celebrate his 69th birthday the following day, was already sowing the seeds of the accusations of too fulsome co-operation that would be levelled at him both during and after the Occupation.

It is easy, from our perspective so many years on, and amid the powerful and constant images of British defiance — Churchill's speeches, the Battle of Britain, Dad's Army, et al — to be critical of Carey's almost craven compliance after just one day's military occupation. Certainly his words were ill-chosen but Carey was a man from an earlier era where elaborate courtesy was a norm and where phrases such as 'your humble and obedient servant' were used in an intricate gavotte of manners where form was greater than substance.

Glowing with pride (we can assume) *Major* Lanz returned to the airport where more Ju52s had landed. Now he turned his attention to Jersey.

The flight to the largest Channel Island took 20 minutes in the three-engined Junkers Ju52. This aircraft, with its characteristic 'corrugated iron' fuselage, was the workhorse of the *Luftwaffe* and was known affectionately as *Tante Ju* (Auntie Ju). Lanz reported a smooth landing and, on emerging from the aircraft, was greeted by von Obernitz who stated that everything was quiet and under control and that the Bailiff would formally surrender the Island at 6pm. Using the airport's radio, Cherbourg was informed and not long after more *Tante Ju* aircraft arrived from Querqueville carrying men of Lanz's battalion.

Before leaving Guernsey, Lanz had appropriated the ensign Hessel had gone to so much trouble to have made, offering his own head as security for its safe return (he had promised it to Hessel for his mess). With appropriate pomp (one gets the impression that Lanz would have liked to have had the services of a brass band) *Kapitänleutnant* Koch of *Kriegsmarine Abteilung 'Gotenhafen'* was tasked with hoisting the flag above the roof of the airport building. Lanz reported that 'with arms at the slope and eyes right, over the airfield rang the command "Hoist Flag!" and slowly and ceremonially over this British territory, also for the first time in history, rose the German War Flag high upon the mast. Now Jersey too was under German overlordship.'

Major Lanz appointed *Hauptmann* Erich Gussek, the commanding officer of No 1 Company, 216 Infantry Division, as the Commandant of Jersey. He gave the captain detailed instructions about the most important measures to be put into immediate operation as well as tactical instructions for the garrisoning of the Island. These instructions included publishing in *The Evening Post* the following day similar instructions that had already been published in *The Star* in Guernsey (see Appendix II).

Gussek was an interesting choice since he already knew Jersey well, having been a prisoner of war in the Blanches Banques camp during the Great War. One wonders what his thoughts were as he took up residence in Government House and availed himself of the Wolseley taxi made available to him (under the terms of the Hague Convention) by Mr John Curwood whose company still provides limousines for weddings and funerals to this day. Gussek took over the Town Hall as his operational headquarters and an official notice advised that the building was now *das Rathaus*. Few disagreed.

In his report Lanz waxed lyrical. Leaving Gussek to his new command to fly back to Guernsey, Lanz wrote:

'Back we went over the sea to Guernsey where I intended to make my stay, for although this Island is the smaller, it is on the other hand of more tactical importance. An unforgettable flight in the glorious evening sunshine, under a cloudless sky, the deep blue sea beneath us and on the horizon glowing red, the jagged cliffs of the rocky Guernsey coast. And above all, the proud consciousness on this historic day of having taken the Channel Islands into German possession.'

Major Lanz returned to the Royal Hotel and worked late dealing with a mass of administrative matters including making arrangements for the reglazing of windows in the Royal Hotel which had been shattered during the bombing of 28 June. His report says it all: 'It was long past midnight before the day's work was done and this first great day drew to a close.'

A great day it might well have been for Lanz but as far as the British media were concerned it was something of a non-event. At 7.20pm, amongst a host of national and regional announcements on the BBC, was broadcast a warning from the Postmaster-General that 'all communication with the Channel Islands has been suspended'. The 9 o'clock news made no mention of the invasion of British soil at all. Okay, so it wasn't Brighton or Eastbourne, but the Channel Islands were British . . .

For the Germans, busy adding to their empire, Alderney posed different problems, although they were relatively easily solved. Since there were currently no civilians on Alderney (although there were a few chafing to return) there was no one to surrender and the Germans' earliest attempts to land at the airport were thwarted by heavy trucks and wire entanglements scattered over the landing area. On 2 July two Fieseler *Storch* spotting aircraft, needing just a few metres of runway, landed and their crews cleared the obstructions.

On 4 July *Majore* Lanz and Maass visited Sark where they were greeted in the tiny Creux Harbour by the Sénechal (the Island's policeman) who also comprised the Island's entire police authority. He escorted them to the Seigneurie to meet the Dame of Sark.

Sybil Mary Beaumont had inherited the title (Dame is the title of a female holder of the Seigneurie) from her father, William Frederick Collings, in June 1927, and acquired the name Hathaway when she married her second husband in 1929. Until the German occupation she was noted for two things: in 1938 she designed Sark's flag and it was her decision to ban cars from the Island, a situation that pertains to this day (although in later life she did allow herself a motorised wheelchair).

Mrs Hathaway, a German speaker, found Lanz to be 'tall, alert and quick spoken'. Maass, she thought to be 'too smooth'. The Germans produced a poster printed in German and English which laid down similar conditions to those which had been published in Guernsey and Jersey. Sark's residents were allowed to keep their cameras and wireless sets, even when the latter were banned in Guernsey for the first time towards the end of 1940 as a result of the Nicolle/Symes affair of which we will learn a lot more anon.

In her autobiography, Mrs Hathaway wrote that she had advised the German officers, in German, that their orders would be obeyed. Dr Maass was impressed and surprised that Mrs Hathaway did not seem in the least afraid. The Dame, who was a lady of considerable courage and formidable intellect, turned wide eyes on the 'too smooth' Maass and asked innocently, 'Is there any reason why I should be afraid of German officers?'

An immediate rapport was achieved, although the redoubtable Dame continued to treat the officers as unexpected, uninvited and hopefully very temporary guests. Many publications purportedly show a photograph of Mrs Hathaway greeting the German officers that first time outside the Seigneurie but a close look at the photograph reveals that the Dame is almost skeletally thin, a physical state she would achieve only much later in the Occupation.

A section of just 10 men, under the command of *Obergefreiter* (Senior Corporal) Obenhauf, comprised Sark's occupying force and they worked with the civil authority to maintain the German hegemony but one suspects, despite her undertaking to *Major* Lanz, in the manner devised by the Dame herself. Lanz had invited her to communicate directly with the Commandant in Guernsey if she ever experienced difficulties and on several occasions she was to remind the Guernsey authorities 'to put a stop to any petty tyranny by local officers in Sark'.

Sybil Hathaway's husband, Robert, was an American. This was, he was later to remark, a hell of a way to celebrate the Fourth of July!

The occupation of the Channel Islands was completed. Despite the civilian deaths (for which both sides of the conflict, inevitably, blamed the other), the German occupation had been achieved without a single German casualty.

With the benefit of the hindsight that is a feature of every history of the German occupation of the Channel Islands, it can be argued that, by his curiosity and nerve, *Hauptmann* Liebe-Pieteritz rendered the people of the Islands a significant service. By establishing that the Islands were indeed undefended (since his superiors clearly had doubts about the veracity of the BBC), he spared the inhabitants the death and destruction of an armed invasion where the attackers would have been more inclined (as they often proved elsewhere) to shoot first and ask questions later. *Generaloberst* von Richthofen had been a pioneer in the use of concentrated air operations against a single target. He had built up a formidable reputation for the ferocity with which he deployed his dive-bombers and ground attack aircraft, a reputation that was so appreciated by his *Führer* that in February 1943 Hitler made him the youngest field-marshal in the *Wehrmacht*.

But it might not have been so.

The following is a fictionalised account of what might have happened had things occurred differently when *Hauptmann* Liebe-Pieteritz first landed in Guernsey but the consequences are based on plans known to have been in place had the German forces encountered opposition . . .

* * *

The airfield was deserted when *Hauptmann* Liebe-Pieteritz landed his Dornier *Do17P* at Guernsey airport. He had been leading a flight of four reconnaissance aircraft and decided, in view of the lack of opposition and without orders, to land and take a look around.

With his three colleagues circling protectively above, the captain landed and taxied the twin-engined 'Flying Pencil' over to the newly opened airport buildings. The Dornier carried a crew of four, the pilot, a bomb aimer/gunner and two more gunners.

The *Hauptmann* left the engines ticking over with propellers turning slowly and ordered his crew to man the aircraft's seven 7.92mm *MG15* machine guns and to keep them pointed at the windows of the airport building. He had swapped his leather flying helmet for his peaked cap (a decision with potentially fatal consequences) and took his Luger from its holster, releasing the safety catch. Finding the doors to the airport building locked, he broke a window to enter.

As he had suspected, the building was empty although there were abundant signs of a hurried evacuation. He was rifling through the desks in the first floor air traffic control office when he heard the sound of aero engines and saw the shadow of an RAF Blenheim flit across the window. Hurriedly he thrust some souvenirs into the pockets of his *Fliegerbluse* — sheets of States of Guernsey headed notepaper, several rubber stamps and a bottle of Stephens ink — and hurried out of the building towards his waiting aircraft.

There were no witnesses for what happened next for even Liebe-Pieteritz's crew who were nearest the action did not see the shot that caused their pilot to stagger and fall just a few metres from the aircraft.

The airport at La Villiaize had been built on green fields and at places, particularly near the terminal buildings and although inside the airport perimeter fence, there was still extensive gorse and other vegetation which, amongst other things, gave cover to rabbits and other wildlife.

Reuben Le Tocq was 17 years old, almost 18. Like Bailiff Carey he would celebrate his birthday in two days' time on 2 July. That morning he and his parents had attended the service at La Villiaize Congregational Chapel, just 200 metres from the airport's perimeter fence, where pastor Ernest Le Prevost had urged calm, patience and trust in God on his flock. Like many in the Islands, Reuben and his father were keen rifle shooters and members of a local gun club. The Controlling Committee had ordered all firearms to be handed in, but the Le Tocq father and son had yet to comply and, indeed, had no intention of doing so. Reuben's prized possession was a new BSA .22 sports rifle (an early 18th birthday gift) with which he had yet to compete and now, probably, never would. Thus, clutching resentment against the high-handed action of the authorities, and the BSA, to his bosom, having consumed his Sunday dinner (dinner in Guernsey is taken at lunchtime) Reuben Le Tocq decided to go shooting rabbits near the airport terminal which, he knew, had already been abandoned.

From the concealment of a thick clump of gorse, Reuben watched as the Dornier landed and, a few moments later, saw the German pilot break a window with the butt of his pistol to gain access to the control tower.

He was still staring at the parked Dornier with its windmilling propellers when the earth shook as a Bristol Blenheim flew low over the airport buildings. A muffled cheer was emerging from his throat when the German pilot appeared in a doorway and ran towards his aircraft. Instinctively Reuben pushed the BSA into his shoulder, took quick aim and fired. The range was a little over 50 metres. A subsequent post mortem examination would show that the .22 bullet entered the back of Liebe-Pieteritz's head just below his capband.

Oberfeldwebel Julius Schreiner, Liebe-Pieteritz's bomb aimer, watched in amazement as his captain stumbled and fell, his Luger falling from his hand and his cap tumbling from his head into the grass. He had heard no shot (the sharp crack of the BSA would have been lost in the roar of the Blenheim's engines and the rumble of the Dornier's own Bramo radials). Above him the other *Do17s* were engaged in a dogfight with at least three RAF Blenheims. He peered through the perspex of the aircraft's nose and cocked the *MG15* but there was nothing to shoot at. Apart from the still body of the fallen *Hauptmann*, the airfield was deserted. Nevertheless he fired a short burst at the windows of the terminal building, shouting to his colleagues to do likewise while he investigated what had happened to his captain.

A few moments later, the Blenheims beaten off, two of the overflying Dorniers landed beside their stricken comrade. *Oberleutnant* Büchs, the flight's second-in-command, had Liebe-Pieteritz's inert body loaded aboard his aircraft. At first Büchs was puzzled by a vivid blue stain that had spread across the captain's shirt and then realised that a bottle of ink in the captain's pocket had broken as he fell. Then, with the other members of Liebe-Pieteritz's crew aboard, he took off, leaving Liebe-Pieteritz's aircraft abandoned on the ground.

At his headquarters at Querqueville, *Generaloberst* Dr Wolfram Freiherr von Richthofen called a crisis conference. The general was almost incoherent with anger. In November 1944 he would be transferred into the Reserve suffering from a brain tumour and would die in an Allied prison camp in Austria in July 1945. Even now, five years earlier, he was already prone to sudden rages.

'These Islanders will be taught a terrible lesson!' And his tone brooked no argument. *Vizeadmiral* Lindau assured him that the assault craft were already assembled in the Grande Rade at Cherbourg, the invasion force of assault troops and marines waiting for the order to embark.

But the General had other ideas.

Exacting retribution for the death of *Hauptmann* Liebe-Pieteritz would be reserved for the *Luftwaffe*. A squadron, *Staffel III*, of twin-engined Heinkel *He111* bombers of *Kampfgeschwader 28* based at Dinard on the Rance estuary facing St Malo would bombard the population centres of St Peter Port and St Sampson at dawn the following day.

Each *He111* had a crew of five and carried eight 500lb high-explosive bombs. In addition each aircraft was equipped with one 20mm cannon, one 13mm *MG131* and seven 7.92mm *MG15* machine guns. The *Staffel* would separate into two flights on the approach to Guernsey, one attacking St Peter Port, the other St Sampson. The bombers would drop their bombs in sequence, each *He111* on its bomb run protected from any intrusion by the

RAF by its colleagues circling overhead. Many of the pilots, having flown with the Condor Legion in the Spanish Civil War, were experienced in low-level precision bombing, the techniques perfected by von Richthofen himself and used with devastating effect on Guernica and more recently Warsaw and Rotterdam.

The 12 Heinkels of *III/KG28* took off from Dinard's Pleurtuit aerodrome at 06.15hrs local time (05.15hrs in Guernsey). Their powerful Junkers Jumo engines would enable them to cover the 61 miles to Guernsey in just 15 minutes.

The attacks on St Peter Port and St Sampson lasted less than 10 minutes. The *He111s* came in low from the south, flying at less than 150 metres, out of the sunrise. The sky was cloudless and the visibility excellent.

The residents of St Peter Port were woken by the roar of engines only seconds before the first bombs fell on St Peter Port's St Julian's Pier, destroying the granite buildings and killing three dockers and the two women serving them with tea and sandwiches in the White Rock Café. The bombs continued to fall along St Julian's Avenue and Candie Gardens, fortunately with few casualties — one was the statue of Victor Hugo (who spent many years in exile in Guernsey) which was toppled from its plinth — since many of the houses and offices were empty, although there was considerable damage to property, in particular to the Priaulx Library which housed more than 25,000 volumes, most of which were destroyed in the subsequent fire. The Victoria Tower, a 19th century folly that dominated the St Peter Port skyline, and the fire station situated in the old town arsenal were both reduced to rubble.

There were however many more casualties in Brock Road, St Jacques and La Fosse André, residential streets where many householders were killed as they were startled awake either by exploding bombs or their homes collapsing around them.

One Heinkel swooped low over Castle Cornet firing its guns and releasing its bombs. The castle's ancient walls withstood the onslaught but the buildings inside the castle, mostly built in the 18th and 19th centuries, collapsed and burned. The Gardien and his family, who lived in the former officers' quarters, were killed when the building caught fire. The following bombers released their deadly cargoes along Hauteville Street, Charroterie and Prince Albert's Road, all residential streets and still densely populated. Human casualties were high and Victor Hugo's house, one of Guernsey's principal tourist attractions, was also destroyed by explosions and fire.

There were few people about and the Heinkels' gunners contented themselves with shooting at the parked vehicles that flashed beneath them. The last stick of bombs fell along Les Rohais, a major road leading out from St Peter Port, demolishing more houses, a garage and a Roman Catholic seminary whose residents, a French Jesuit order, had already returned to France.

The Heinkels that had wheeled off to attack St Sampson dropped their first bombs on Vale Castle, a fortification dominating the harbour but already a roofless ruin. Houses and shops along The Bridge which bordered St Sampson's harbour and the parish church which had, by tradition, been built in 1111, had their roofs blown off and windows blown out. Fortunately once again casualties were few although the Rector and his family in the Rectory alongside the church were injured by splinters and flying glass.

The trail of destruction swept across the Island to Grand Havre Bay, the clutch of houses around Vale Church attracting the attention of the bomb aimers and gunners.

The bombers made their rendezvous over Les Hanois lighthouse to the south-west of Guernsey before returning south to their airfield at Dinard. They left behind towering palls of dense smoke rising in the windless air. There had been no opposition.

The total number of helpless civilians killed was three hundred and six and the number seriously injured and requiring hospitalisation (with which Guernsey's limited facilities could barely cope) more than double that. It was estimated that as many as a thousand men, women and children suffered slight injuries.

Hauptmann Liebe-Pieteritz had been avenged.

Later that day, as Junkers Ju52 transport aircraft landed at Guernsey airport and disgorged troops in full battle order, motorcycle combinations and anti-aircraft guns, *Generaloberst* von Richthofen himself flew over the Island to assess the damage his bombers had caused.

* * *

But it was not so. Reuben Le Tocq, if he ever existed, fired no fatal shot that day.

Instead, in a matter of just three days, 150 square miles of British territory had been successfully invaded and occupied for the first time since the Middle Ages, without the loss of a single man.

Chapter 7
Occupation

An unfortunate broadcast — orders and instructions, the 'civil servants' arrive — law and order and the Nuremberg Laws come to the Channel Islands– driving on the right and German lessons in schools — postage stamps and insults

For many of the occupiers, exploring, wide-eyed, islands that only a matter of days before had still been welcoming summer visitors, the well-stocked shops, the comfortable hotels and the wary but polite local population implied that a similar invasion of mainland Britain (where not a few already thought they were) could well be a similar walkover.

It did not take the occupiers long to consolidate their conquest.

By 2 July radio communications had been established with France and regular air services (primarily for carrying mails but also for shuttling important personnel) began operating.

In Guernsey, from his temporary headquarters in the Royal Hotel, *Major* Lanz issued more instructions (see Appendix III). Judging by the language, Lanz was exerting his legal skills, or someone else was doing it for him, since words like 'heretofore' do not appear in contemporary German/English dictionaries. Nevertheless the new orders, in some respects, were little different from what Islanders were already familiar with although the intent of the new order was very clear — everything will be all right if you follow instructions.

Tuesday, 2 July, was also Victor Carey's 69th birthday.

With the benefit of hindsight (a phrase that is likely to become all too familiar, I'm afraid), the invasion, planned in such detail and approached by the *Kriegsmarine* with such caution, had been a relatively easy and simple military exercise, so much so that some historians have opined that this had been the Germans' intention all the time. A gentlemanly invasion carried out with nothing more hostile than a dubious handshake. However this hypothesis doesn't really hold water since an objective that was 'urgent and important' would have required much, if not all, of the planning that Schuster and Lindau devoted to it. In 1940 the German *Wehrmacht* was the world's most ruthlessly efficient military machine, led by generals who (certainly in their own minds) had been undefeated in the Great War. Without financial constraints the German military had been able to embrace new technology and new techniques. Commanders were encouraged (to use a dreadfully modern but somewhat apt phrase) to think 'out of the box'. *Blitzkrieg* was one such technique — rapidly moving mobile columns supported by screaming *Stuka* dive-bombers that terrified soldiers and civilians alike. These ideas had weaknesses — rapidly moving columns easily out-ran their supply chains and frequently ground to a halt waiting for their petrol to catch up with them. For all their howling fury, *Stukas* were slow and vulnerable to attack from fighters, their only self-defence a single *MG15* machine gun facing backwards. But in 1940 no army in Europe was the *Wehrmacht's* match and it would be two years or more before any could be.

What did this mean as far as the Channel Islands were concerned? Was the Island officials' apparent acceptance without demur of the occupiers' intrusive presence indicative of a recognition of helplessness in the face of overwhelming force? Or was it a craven unjustified surrender? After all, the Islands were taken by a little more than a handful of men, albeit men who were armed with guns, but they were, initially at least, outnumbered by the Islands' football teams. We know today of the plans devised by *Admirale* Schuster and Lindau which visualised an armed invasion by hundreds of troops prepared to shoot at anything that looked remotely hostile. Indeed we have examined a scenario whereby the death of a single airman might well have precipitated a harvest of death and destruction ordered by a man whose actions were already being conditioned by the early evidence of a brain tumour. But thanks to the curiosity (and undoubted courage) of *Hauptmann* Liebe-Pieteritz, just what a full-scale invasion would have been like we shall never know.

There was plenty of evidence that the German armies were prepared to wage war on civilians; the harrowing newsreels shown in local cinemas of their advance across the Low Countries and France were ample proof that this was an implacable and even bloodthirsty enemy, the same 'beastly Hun' of World War 1.

When the Germans arrived, without horns and forked tails, in the manner in which they did, the overwhelming emotion in the breasts of authorities and people alike would almost certainly have been relief.

Commentators would remark, long after the Germans had been ejected, that when they arrived, *Major* Lanz and his cohorts behaved like perfect gentlemen and that those first few weeks of occupation would have seemed unreal to both occupier and occupied alike. Islanders were gratified to discover that the invaders were invariably polite, well disciplined and were even prepared to take their place in the inevitable queues that formed at the local shops and paid cash for the goods they required. Many of the occupiers spoke good English and clearly intended to prove that they were not at all the barbarians who had been reported as having rampaged across Europe.

For the invaders there were surprises too. Hitherto they had been used to authorities fleeing and leaving just chaos behind. In the Islands the infrastructure survived, the Islands' governments remained intact, the local police forces — Jersey had two, uniformed and elected 'honoraries' in each parish while Guernsey had just the one island-wide constabulary — still controlled the traffic and investigated domestic crime, and the civilian heads of population made it clear that their people would look only to them and not the Germans, despite the daily flurry of instructions, for governance.

Comparisons with France, which some would later make, are well wide of the mark and any similarity drawn between the behaviour of the Vichy government of Marshal Pétain and Pierre Laval and what happened in the Islands is also ludicrous. From the German point of view, although the Channel Islands had a strategic value of their own, the invasion of the Islands was merely a step along the way to the ultimate goal — the invasion of Britain itself, which was planned to take place within three months. The concept that the invasion and subsequent occupation of the Islands was practice for the real thing — both in terms of the military operation and the establishment of a German 'overlordship' — given the timescale the Germans were working to, is nonsensical. Britain was not, and would never be, demilitarised and the likelihood of Churchill swallowing his rhetoric about fighting them on the beaches, nil.

Meanwhile the occupiers were busy settling themselves in.

In Jersey the Germans took over Villa Millbrook, the home of Lord and Lady Trent (Lord Trent was otherwise Jesse Boot, the founder of Boots the Chemists), and on 5 November 1940, George Seymour, owner of the Merton Hotel, received a States of Jersey notice of requisition (No R727) advising that, on the order of the German Army of Occupation, he was required to supply to Villa Millbrook one full-sized billiard table complete with ten cues, one cue rack, one long cue, one long and two short rests, one marking board, one set of billiard balls and box, one set of snooker balls and box, one triangle, one shadowless shade and one billiard table iron. Right away, please. And no argument.

The Channel Islands were designated as being in the military area of X Army Corps, the garrison coming under the command of 216 Infantry Division. Many of the assault troops, their specialist skills having been rendered unnecessary, were returned to France and for the time being just a detachment of harbour defence troops was posted to Alderney.

A detailed review of the castles and other fortifications scattered over the Channel Islands revealed just how pessimistic had been the admirals' reading of the intelligence reports. Most of these 'defences' were crumbling ruins and what armaments they mounted were rusty relics of the Napoleonic era or even earlier, incapable of any offensive intent for more than a hundred years. The relationship between the *Kriegsmarine* and the *Luftwaffe* was always cool, and often ice-cold, and the admirals were still smarting that their grandiose plans had been upstaged by a handful of flyers taking stupid risks. Their irritation would have been exacerbated had they read in *The Times* of 2 July that 'On 30 June the British Island of Guernsey was captured in a daring *coup de main* of the *Luftwaffe*. On 1 July the Island of Jersey was occupied by surprise in the same manner.' This text was distilled from a German broadcast but was confirmed in the same issue with a brief statement from the Ministry of Information. In celebration Berlin Radio triumphantly played *Wir fahren gegen England* (We're marching against England) and the Nazi Party-controlled press proclaimed that Britain's last continental bulwark had fallen and before long Britain itself would be finished.

From Berlin *Oberkommando der Wehrmacht* (*OKW*) directed that the Islands should be made secure from attack although none was expected. In the convoluted workings of the *Wehrmacht*, only the *Kriegsmarine* was allowed to shoot at ships so *Oberkommando der Kriegsmarine* (*OKM*) was given the task of protecting the coasts. The *Luftwaffe* had already established a number of anti-aircraft defences, particularly around the airport perimeters (since, they, of course, were the only ones allowed to shoot at aircraft), and, for the brief period of the Battle of Britain, fighters would be based at Guernsey airport.

Transport between the Islands and the nearby French coast posed a number of problems since, as *Admiral* Lindau discovered when he was assembling his invasion fleet, the *Kriegsmarine* possessed few, if any, suitable vessels to move personnel and matériel in any military quantity and, because of the evacuations, no vessels of any size had been caught in port when the landings occurred. Nevertheless shipping would have to be found from somewhere since the requirements of the garrison — initially arms and ammunition but also personnel, vehicles (including tanks) and military supplies — would need to be met. Cherbourg was ruled out as a supply port since shipping operating from there would be liable to attack from coastal forces and even submarines of the Royal Navy. St Malo was a better choice since the sea routes between that French port and the Islands were at the limit of the range of the Royal Navy's motor torpedo boats and the shallowness of the Bay of St Malo ruled out submarine operations.

The Germans had plans too for the produce that had been on the docks waiting for export. France would be the market for the Islands' potatoes and tomatoes in future, although the growers were unlikely to reap their usual financial rewards. Lord Haw Haw had not been joking.

When Guernsey's Controlling Committee met on 5 July, Ambrose Sherwill advised that *Major* Lanz had offered the members the opportunity to compose a message to be broadcast over German radio on behalf of the people of Guernsey. The Committee decided to take advantage of what was seen to be a generous offer to reassure the 20,000 and more evacuees that those they had left behind were safe and well.

The message (see Appendix IV), signed by Victor Carey as Civil Lieutenant-Governor and Bailiff, Sherwill as Attorney-General and G. J. P. Ridgway as Solicitor-General (these last two, curiously, using the titles more appropriate to Jersey), has a clear intent, and although the motivation is obvious, clearly the signatories were unaware of the potential for propaganda in their words. Phrases such as 'The German occupation took place without a single person being harmed' rather overlooked the casualties of 28 June and 'it is the fact that we are being treated with courtesy and consideration' and 'not a single civilian has been deprived of his or her liberty and the utmost correctness characterises the relations between the German Forces and the Civil Population' were somewhat sweeping statements to make, however reassuring, after less than a week of occupation.

However, whatever *Major* Lanz's motivation was (and it is not unlikely that it was entirely humanitarian), there is no evidence that this message was ever actually broadcast.

Nevertheless, as we shall see shortly, another, similar, message to the outside world would have rather different consequences.

The first German garrisons were relatively small: around 2,000 men in Jersey and Guernsey and smaller detachments in Alderney and Sark. Initially the invaders took over empty hotels and houses for their accommodation and most Islanders were actually little disturbed by their presence although, with the Germans' love of marching everywhere behind oompah-ing bands, nobody could actually ignore them.

Every day notices detailing new restrictions appeared in the local press, particularly as supplies in the shops dwindled. The invaders' gleeful buying up of shop goods that they had not seen for months or even years (like talcum powder, scented soap, silk stockings and underwear for their wives and girlfriends at home) meant that many shops ran out of stock very quickly with no hope of resupply. This buying became so frenzied that the authorities decreed that nothing could be purchased without an appropriate order which while it cooled the frenzy also caused their own administration almost to grind to a halt. In the meantime Woolworth's, always one of Jersey's largest and busiest town centre stores, moved into much smaller premises across the street and closed after a year, not to reopen until after the Liberation.

The German propaganda machine was busy too; pictures of German soldiers conversing with 'British' policemen and a German soldier buying a 'Smiths Jersey London Diploma ice cream' were sent home and published as proof that parts of Britain itself had already fallen under German hegemony.

However, within a few weeks the Germans were to achieve an even bigger propaganda coup, one which, even today, still arouses controversy.

From the German point of view, the loss of the Channel Islands was a major humiliation for Britain, a loss of face to be ruthlessly exploited even though it was merely a prelude to the real effort, the subjugation of Britain itself.

Winston Churchill, it will be recalled, was talked out of sending the Royal Navy to prevent the German invasion but on 2 July, just as *Major* Lanz was beginning his blitz of orders and instructions, the Prime Minister sent a minute to his Chief of Staff, General Hastings 'Pug' Ismay, asking for a plan to send commandos to 'kill or capture' the invaders. Ismay's response might well have been, 'What, all of them?' but a plan was hatched and only four days later Operation 'Anger' was mounted and Second Lieutenant Hubert Nicolle, late of the Royal Guernsey Militia, embarked on a submarine with the intention of making a two-day reconnaissance of his home Island, presumably to find out where the Germans were so that a subsequent raid by commandos could go in and 'kill or capture' them. If this is already sounding a little farcical, it was to get worse. Nicolle was supposed to land by canoe but his craft was taken aboard still in its box (it had been bought in Gamages, the London department store best known for its huge toy department) and when assembled it was too big to pass through the submarine's torpedo loading hatch. What's more, Nicolle had to confess that when it came to navigating even the few hundred metres to the coast he was likely to get lost, so it was decided that he should be accompanied by the submarine's navigating officer in the canoe that had only been partially assembled so that it could pass through the hatch.

Nicolle landed near Icart Point on the Island's south coast just after midnight on Monday, 8 July, and after clambering up the steep cliffs moved inland towards his home while the navigator put to sea and almost missed finding his submarine.

Hubert's father was Frank Nicolle, the Deputy Harbourmaster, who had access to all sorts of information useful to his son. What's more, his next door neighbour was the managing director of the Island's largest grocery company and was able to tell Hubert exactly how many Germans his company was having to supply. A farmer friend, whom Hubert had called in to see on his way home, lived near the airport and agreed to give Hubert details of German aircraft movements.

After just three days' spying (for that is what it was since he had been landed wearing civilian clothes and had been advised that, if caught, he could be shot) Hubert had all the information he required; how many Germans there were (469) and where they were (by virtue of where their groceries were being delivered). Thanks to his grocery friend he was also able to report that there were already shortages of certain commodities.

He was safely embarked on the submarine and two more former Militia subalterns, Philip Martel and Desmond Mulholland, were landed, their task to prepare the way for a commando landing planned for a few days later.

That too had all the elements of farce. On 15 July three landing parties comprising 140 commandos under the overall command of Lieutenant-Colonel J. Durnford Slater disembarked from two Royal Navy destroyers (which had had difficulty finding Guernsey). After clambering up the cliffs they spread out to find some Germans. And couldn't. They left behind a road block (by using stones from someone's rockery) which was discovered by the Germans some days later. Eventually after more farce — Colonel Durnford Slater tripped running down the steps at Jerbourg to the beach and nearly shot himself — the force was re-embarked. Later from evidence of the landing, abandoned equipment at the water's edge and the aforementioned road block, the Germans deduced that they had been subject to a raid and they told Sherwill, in no uncertain terms, that this type of thing had got to stop. It wouldn't but the pinprick raids that were carried out on the Islands in the early months of the Occupation achieved very little and one or two, of which more a little later, were to have consequences well out of proportion to their intent.

Churchill, despite the raids being his idea, was scathing and referred to them as 'silly fiascos'. And so say all of us, despite the undoubted courage of those who took part.

It is often said that Hitler did not really want to wage war with Britain and that he would have much preferred to have a negotiated peace that would leave him as undisputed emperor of Europe (and free to pursue his ambitions for *Lebensraum* — living space — in the East) while Britain maintained her empire. His reading of Winston Churchill as an old-fashioned imperialist — an opinion shared by many leading American politicians who were determined that their country would not enter a European war simply to maintain the British Empire — led him to believe that hostilities between the two empires need not be prolonged and that sooner or later Churchill — aided and abetted by the 'peace party' he and other Nazi leaders believed existed — would come to his senses.

Whether it was similar considerations or, rather more likely, an opportunity to assure those 20,000 and more Guernsey residents who had evacuated so hurriedly, that their friends and relatives left behind were safe (the message of 6 July not having been delivered) we shall never know, but Ambrose Sherwill was motivated to broadcast himself that news on the German station Radio Bremen.

The message was recorded on 1 August at the German military headquarters which had been established in the Channel Islands Hotel, just down the road from the Royal Hotel which was now used to cater for visiting VIPs. Unlike the message composed on 6 July, this was Sherwill himself speaking and the text of his address, even today, makes uncomfortable reading.

'This is His Britannic Majesty's Procureur in Guernsey, Channel Islands, speaking to the people of the United Kingdom and in particular to those who left Guernsey and Alderney during the evacuation which preceded the German Occupation.

'I imagine that many of you must be greatly worried as to how we are getting on. Well, let me tell you. Some will fear, I imagine, that I am making this record with a revolver pointed at my head and speaking from a typescript thrust into my hand by a German officer. The actual case is very different.

'The Lieutenant-Governor and Bailiff, Mr Victor Carey, and every other Island official has been and is being treated with every consideration and with the greatest courtesy by the German Military Authorities. The Island

Government is functioning, churches and chapels are open for public worship, banks, shops and places of entertainment are open as usual.

'Naturally, the sudden and entire severance of communications with the United Kingdom created innumerable problems with which we have wrestled and are still wrestling. Perhaps the best indication of the measure of our success will be shown by the latest figures of unemployment which are as follows, males unemployed, of whom hardly any are fit for manual labour, 186, females unemployed, 191. Relief by way of public assistance is not above the normal figure.

'The States have set up a Controlling Committee to speed up public business. My friends Sir Abraham Lainé, A. M. Drake, R. O. Falla, R. H. Johns, John Leale, Stamford Raffles and Dr A. N. Symons are collaborating with me on this Committee and are working like Trojans.

'The conduct of the German troops is exemplary.

'We have been in German Occupation for 4½ weeks and I am proud of the way my fellow Islanders have behaved and grateful for the correct and kindly attitude towards them, by the German soldiers.

'We have always been and we remain intensely loyal subjects of His Majesty and this has been made clear to and is respected by the German Commandant and his staff. On that staff is an officer (Dr Maass) speaking perfect English, a man of wide experience, with whom I am in daily contact. To him I express my grateful thanks for his courtesy and patience.

'And now let me end on a more personal note. To Elizabeth College, the Guernsey Ladies College, the Guernsey Intermediate School, the Guernsey Primary and Voluntary schools, to both teachers and scholars, all our love and good wishes.

'To all men of military age who left here to join His Majesty's forces, God speed. To all wives and mothers and sweethearts, God bless you. To all Guernsey children in England, God keep you safe. God bless you all till we meet again.

'And to Mary Rose, to John and Dick, Mummy and I send our fondest love and best wishes. Tell Diana Raffles that her parents are well and send her their love.

'Will the BBC please re-transmit this message and will the daily papers please publish it.'

When Islanders read in the local press what Ambrose Sherwill had said, reactions were mixed. Feelings varied from outrage that the President of the Controlling Committee had allowed himself to become a willing tool of German propaganda, to praise for his good intentions but coupled more often than not with a feeling that the way they were expressed bordered on naivety. Certainly for a German radio station to be able to broadcast to Britain, while the RAF and the *Luftwaffe* were dogfighting all over the skies above southern England, that this Guernseyman thought that the Germans were really quite a nice bunch of chaps, kind, considerate and patient, could not have gone down well in Whitehall just as Winston Churchill was telling the world that, were Britain to be defeated, the world would be entering a 'new, dark age'.

What Sherwill did not know (although perhaps he might have guessed) was how his broadcast would be introduced. He had presented German propagandists with a golden opportunity to illustrate just how benign German occupation could be, that the horror stories that were bolstering British resolve to resist as the Germans were poised to launch themselves across the English Channel were themselves so much lies and propaganda. What's more, when broadcast, they left off his personal messages.

Over the years Sherwill's broadcast has come to be regarded as a serious error of judgement. That verdict may be a little harsh, given that even a lawyer as astute as Sherwill often proved himself to be, in the circumstances that he found himself, and unschooled in the ways of propaganda in which German broadcasters were masters, genuinely felt that he was doing the right thing for, in his own words, 'I was deeply concerned to let thousands of Guernsey people who had gone and who, I surmised, were gravely worried about the fate of their relations, know that all was well in Guernsey.' However, his choice of reciting the current unemployment figures and the rather unfortunate phraseology used to describe how the members of the Controlling Committee were 'collaborating with me' indicate that he should have been more careful in composing his words. He also revealed that the offer to broadcast had been made by Dr Maass, whom the Dame of Sark had already assessed as being 'too smooth' and there is little doubt that Maass did exploit Sherwill's evident high opinion of him. The memoirs of Lord Coutanche, the Bailiff in Jersey, do not record whether or not a similar offer was made to him but if it ever was, it was certainly not taken up and no one in Jersey made any such broadcast.

The broadcast could be compared with those made by author and humorist P. G. Wodehouse from Berlin in June 1941 which were greeted with similar opprobrium and criticism. Wodehouse had agreed to make the broadcasts to secure the release of himself and his wife from the prison camp where they had been interned when the Germans overran his home at Le Touquet in France. He subsequently spent most of the war in the Adlon Hotel in Berlin. Like Wodehouse, Sherwill exhibited naivety rather than treachery.

At the time of the invasion in July 1940 the population of Jersey was around 45,000 people and that of Guernsey around 20,000. The population of Sark was 471 and that of Alderney nil. The islands of Herm, Jethou and Brecqhou, although each had been inhabited (albeit by only a very few families) before the war, had all been evacuated. Thus the Islands' population represented 0.1% of that of the British Isles.

We don't know precisely at what moment in time the Germans decided on their special plans for Alderney but a short time after the invasion farmer

Frank Oselton (who had been forcibly ejected from Alderney with his herd of cows) applied to *Major* Lanz to return. Lanz, recognising the value of fresh milk to his troops, agreed and even arranged for him to be given some cows since the ones brought to Guernsey could not be found (we last saw at least two of them playing with the traffic on Guernsey's airport runways). Some time later, Oselton was joined by George Pope and his family. The Popes had arrived in Alderney in 1939 and lived for a time on a converted lifeboat in Braye harbour. They were evacuated with everyone else but a few weeks later they were back, George Pope offering his services as a local pilot, particularly for the relief vessels serving the lighthouse on the nearby Casquets reef and also taking up farming on one of the deserted holdings. Mrs Daphne Pope gave birth twice during the Occupation, these being the only births recorded in Alderney during those five years.

The Casquets were (and still are) a notorious ships' graveyard and although the light had been extinguished along with all other navigation lights prior to the invasion (presumably in the hope that the *Kriegsmarine* would find the rocks rather than avoid them) the Germans maintained a garrison on the reef. As well as maintaining the light, it provided useful information on the movement of Allied ships and aircraft. In September 1942 the reef was raided — Operation 'Dryad' — and the German garrison of seven men, their code books and diaries were spirited away. However, due to the importance of the lighthouse to the German Navy the garrison was replaced, strengthened and eventually numbered up to 35 men.

A salvage party of local men was also sent to Alderney in order to clear up the mess left after the panic withdrawal, clear the shops and harvest the barley crop. The party found the decaying corpses of animals that had been shot and left unburied, other animals running loose (a pig had given birth in the Post Office) and the refuse of the hurried evacuation everywhere including cancelled cheques from the banks fluttering like fallen leaves in the breeze. Alderney residents would later claim that the salvage party did more looting of private properties than the Germans ever did and, indeed, some of the party were arrested on their return, tried and convicted of pilfering and given prison terms.

Initially the administration of the Islands was in the hands of the *Wehrmacht*, the German military, although the industrious *Major* Lanz and his subordinate in Jersey, *Hauptmann* Gussek, had proved themselves bureaucrats of the first order with their blizzard of orders and instructions, announcements and diktats.

But in practice the governance of the Islands was largely unchanged except that orders which had previously required the Royal Assent now needed the assent of the Commandant and alongside the Islands' courts was now a *Kanalinselnmilitärischegericht* — the Channel Islands Military Tribunal — and although no German could be tried in a civil court, the reverse was not so.

Nevertheless relations between occupier and occupied were remarkably genial and Islanders were actually encouraged to contact the Commandants with their concerns, even when the occupying forces were involved. Dr Charles Cruickshank, in the official history, *The German Occupation of the Channel Islands* (Alan Sutton & Guernsey Press, 1975), cites an instance of someone who reported that his bicycle had been stolen by a German soldier being assured that every effort would be expended to recover it. And it was. However, a woman who requested permission to write to her bank in London received a very polite reply to the effect that it would not be possible in the current circumstances.

In Jersey Bailiff Coutanche found that *Hauptmann* Gussek had little interest in civil affairs and let him and the Superior Council get on with it.

From the outset the occupation of the Channel Islands was to be more than a simple military exercise run by soldiers. Within two months the Germans set up a new command structure with the Islands being administered by *Feldkommandantur 515* (Field Command 515) established in Jersey, responsible for all civilian affairs and itself being subject to the overall control of the Islands' military command who would direct matters were the Islands ever to be invaded. The men and women who comprised *FK515* were mostly civilians in uniform, civil servants and bureaucrats drafted to the Islands from Germany. Many spoke good English.

The first *Feldkommandant*, *Oberst* Friedrich Schumacher, arrived in Jersey on 9 August and a civilian/military bureaucracy was created that, with its complexity, could have run an entire country rather than a group of small islands. He announced his presence with an advertisement in *The Evening Post* (see Appendix IV). At the same time *Major Prinz* zu Waldeck replaced Gussek as *Festungkommandant*.

Schumacher set up three subordinate posts — a *Nebenstelle* (branch) in Guernsey, an *Aussenstelle* (outpost) in Marais Square in Alderney and a *Zufuhrstelle* (stores assembly point) in Granville in Normandy. Sark would be administered from Guernsey.

After the war Bailiff Coutanche, when asked how he coped with the constant stream of orders and instructions (which often countermanded each other) that emanated from *Feldkommandantur 515,* replied simply, 'I protested.' And he kept protesting to the very last day of the war. It is perhaps to the credit of the men and women of *FK515*, many of whom had legalistic backgrounds, that because they believed they were acting within international law and wanted to create 'a model occupation', many of his protests were actually taken note of and acted upon.

Somehow Hitler (who, no doubt because of the psychological boost now being overlord of a part of Britain gave him, took a significant interest in the Channel Islands) seemed to think that the Islands were unwilling British colonies and dispatched a lawyer from Berlin to study the Islands' constitutions. Not surprisingly the lawyer discovered that his

Führer had got hold of the wrong end of the stick and any thoughts that the Germans might have been regarded as liberators from a British yoke were quickly dispelled.

The German command structure was complicated and led all the way to the Paris headquarters of Army Group A which itself was divided into the *Verwaltungsstab* (administration staff) which dealt with civilian affairs and the *Kommandostab* (command staff) which dealt with the armed forces. That situation was replicated in the Channel Islands where *FK515* had a military branch (*militärische Führung*) and a branch dealing with civil affairs lorded over by an *Oberkriegsverwaltungsrat* (senior war administrator). This official had four departments to deal with every aspect of Island life including general administration, price control, policing, propaganda, education (teaching the German language would become mandatory in schools), health, postal services and the rationing of food and essential supplies and doing things very much in the German way. The military branch, which liaised closely with the *Festungkommandant* and his staff, was headed by a major with three captains and two lieutenants and they looked after quarters, transport, victualling, weapons, recreation and defence. The personnel included court martial staff, a paymaster, a medical officer and a vet. Also responsible to the *Feldkommandant* was the *Geheimefeldpolizei* (Secret Field Police, despite the title an adjunct of the *Wehrmacht* rather than the *Reichssicherheitshauptamt* [State Central Security Office] and whose speciality was detecting sabotage and dissidents), and the *Feldgendarmerie* (the Field Police with the responsibility of dealing with the saboteurs and dissidents, guarding installations, directing traffic, etc.), each with their own particular role in maintaining law and order. All these services existed in Guernsey although on a smaller scale. There was no civil administration as such in Alderney since there was only the handful of civilians to administer.

In addition to the police forces of *FK515*, both the *Kriegsmarine* and *Luftwaffe* maintained their own police forces whose primary role (and one jealously guarded) was to maintain the security of their own installations.

While the maintenance of law and order was still largely in the hands of the civilian police and the Islands' courts, alongside them there was the sinister presence of the *Geheimefeldpolizei (GFP)* whose role was also to quell any political opposition to its version of good order. The *GFP* had originally been part of the *Abwehr*, the military intelligence service under the control of the *Wehrmacht*, but during the first years of the war it became part of *Reichsführer-SS* Heinrich Himmler's security services, the most notorious of which was the *Geheimestaatspolizei*, the *Gestapo*, and although Islanders frequently referred to the *GFP* by that name, the Channel Islands were spared the excesses of the security apparatus created and operated by the Nazi Party. Moreover, in the Channel Islands, the *GFP* had reverted to being controlled by the *Wehrmacht*.

The *GFP*, who favoured trilby hats, long leather overcoats and even black

Citroën *Onze Légère*s, but rarely had more than half a dozen operatives in each Island, was augmented by the *Feldgendarmerie*. The latter was a uniformed organisation whose presence was almost always betrayed by the clanking of their gun metal breastplates (the Germans' own derogatory name for them was *Kettenhunde*, chained dogs). Nevertheless their combined activities gave Islanders something of an insight into the kind of ruthless suppression of opposition practised by the truly dreaded *Gestapo* throughout the rest of occupied Europe and within Germany itself.

When he took up his post, *Oberst* Schumacher, who outranked his military colleagues, made it clear that he was concerned only with civilian affairs — that the soldiering was going to be left to the soldiers — and he reaffirmed the terms and conditions of the occupation that had been laid down by *Major* Lanz. Everything would be all right as long as one followed instructions, etc.

The establishment of *FK515* in the Islands followed the pattern of what had already occurred in other occupied countries. The 'fighting' *Wehrmacht* was expected to move on, particularly to England, leaving Schumacher and his bureaucrats in charge. Although there was no love lost between the various branches of the *Wehrmacht*, they did have one thing in common: they all despised the crypto-military bureaucrats of *FK515* who, although they postured in military uniforms, were really just civilians in disguise.

The relationship between the military and *FK515* was a curious one. While the military had the responsibility for the defence of the Islands, *FK515* was responsible for their security. In Jersey the secret policemen of the *GFP* first set themselves up in a private house near the *Feldkommandantur* before, in March 1943, moving to Silvertide Guest House in Havre des Pas on the outskirts of St Helier. In Guernsey they occupied a private house at the foot of the Val de Terres, the long twisting hill that runs south out of St Peter Port and today is used for speed hill-climbing on several occasions each year.

Silvertide was a solid Victorian structure (it still stands) more used to catering for visitors of a very different hue. The *Feldkommandantur* itself was established in College House, the boarding house of the Jersey boys' public school, Victoria College, a mock Gothic pile built in the 19th century that still overlooks St Helier and was commandeered between October 1941 and April 1942 by the *Reichsarbeitsdienst*, the State Labour Service, while the *Feldgendarmerie* moved into Tudor Lodge, a large detached mock-Tudor villa across the playing fields from College House (on which has now been built the car park for the Jersey College for Girls).

In Guernsey the *Nebenstelle* was presided over by *Kriegsverwaltungsrat* Dr Wilhelm Reffler with Dr Richard Brosch, a Doctor of Jurisprudence (and with an even longer German title), as his deputy. They took over the Grange Lodge Hotel as their headquarters. There was no place for Dr Maass in the new set-up and he was posted in mid-August. Before he left he opined to Ambrose Sherwill that Guernsey's troubles were about to begin since the civil servants had arrived!

Moreover, after September 1940, the Islanders glumly realised that their invaders, their grandiose plans for invading Britain having been so effectively thwarted by the Royal Air Force, were now likely to cling even more tenaciously to the few pieces of British soil they already had.

Nevertheless the Germans were keen to maintain good relations with the Islands' authorities for they recognised that they did not have the manpower to run the Bailiwicks themselves. For their part the Superior Council in Jersey and the Controlling Committee in Guernsey wished to retain as much of the control of Islanders' welfare as they could. However, it was made clear that if the governance of the Islands was to be a 'partnership', then there was only one senior partner and that was *FK515*. Despite the need to maintain co-operation, the German authorities were instructed by their own masters in France not to show 'unnecessary mildness' in their dealings, nor should they be lulled into any false sense of security by the amenability of the Islanders.

Both sides chose to follow the Hague Convention although Germany had not been a signatory to it. The Convention laid down a series of markers by which daily life could be ordered. Both sides were concerned with maintaining law and order, the Germans because their numbers were insufficient to control civilian unrest resulting from the flouting of regulations, and the Island authorities because of the ease with which a local crime wave might be attributed to 'having a poke at the Germans'.

Another aspect of the Occupation which is often overlooked is that the Islands had to pay for it! There were continual differences between the local and German authorities as to who should pay for what, the local authorities arguing forcefully (and winning the argument) that they could not be expected to pay for the heavy concentration of troops that Hitler's directive was demanding. In fact in 1942 three-quarters of the sums levied on the Bailiwicks were waived. The Dame of Sark asked that her Island receive a similar consideration but it was pointed out to her that since she had not actually ever paid anything, a refund of nothing equalled nothing! By March 1944 the cost to the Channel Islands of the enemy occupation was in excess of 10 million *Reichsmark*, three-fifths of which was owed by Guernsey. These were large sums that the Islands manifestly could not afford and they survived on credit extended by the local banks and the French government. In the opinion of the Reich Minister of Finance the British Empire, rather than the Islands, should bear the liability.

There was, however, a third element in the relationship between the Islands' authorities and the new administration — the German military. For five weeks or so, *Oberst* Schumacher outranked his military counterparts — *Major* Lanz in Guernsey and *Hauptmann* Gussek in Jersey. Then, on 19 September 1940, *Oberst* Rudolf Graf von Schmettow was appointed *Befehlshaber der britischen Kanalinseln* (*BdbK*), Commander-in-Chief of the Channel Islands, Schumacher's equal in rank. Graf von Schmettow was a professional soldier, a former cavalry officer, holder of the German Cross in

Gold and a nephew of von Rundstedt. Ambrose Sherwill described him as 'a man of great charm and humanity' and while Alexander Coutanche was not given to such fulsome comments, he found von Schmettow to be a man who was reasonable and fair.

The new Commander-in-Chief established his headquarters in Jersey, first in a private dwelling, Monaco in St Saviour's Road in St Helier, before moving to the more spacious Metropole Hotel in April 1941. While *FK515* had a clear role, that role would be subsidiary to the military in the event of an attack. But in the absence of any enemy action von Schmettow and Schumacher established an accord which, given how watchful and suspicious each arm of the occupying forces was of the other, was something of an achievement.

Life began to develop a bleak pattern, one categorised mostly by boredom as pre-war pursuits became more and more difficult to follow. Until the United States joined in the war, local cinemas could still show Hollywood 'B' movies from Paris as well as German feature films (often in colour) which were of excellent quality. Photographs illustrating 'Victory in the West' showing at the Forum Cinema in Jersey and the Gaumont in Guernsey (long after such a victory had become an illusion) implied that cinema-goers had little else to watch but in fact the feature was shown only twice, once without and once with English subtitles. Lending libraries received no stocks of new books and those they had were subject to rigorous censorship, with numerous titles being withdrawn because they offended Nazi sensibilities.

The States in both Islands continued to pass 'statutes' although the number issued was limited by the circumstances. The Superior Council and the Controlling Committee issued orders which were sanctioned by the German authorities and were obliged to enact edicts from the military government in Paris when the terms were applicable to the Channel Islands. From time to time the *Wehrmacht* also issued instructions affecting the civil population, the justification being military necessity and the authority that they had the armed might to enforce them.

FK515 required orders originating from Paris to be registered and published. Some, however, were impossible to comply with, for instance the order that all civilians had to be evacuated to at least ten kilometres inland from coastal regions. With the largest Channel Island, Jersey, measuring just fifteen kilometres by eight, there is nowhere in the Channel Islands that is more than ten kilometres from the coast!

However, the same did not apply when, in October 1940, it came to registering those orders which were the result of Nazi philosophy concerning the Jews.

It was widely believed that all the Jews in the Islands had evacuated in advance of the invasion and enacting anti-Jewish legislation, while it would be repugnant, would also be meaningless. Thus both Island governments complied, although Jurat Sir Abraham Lainé, a member of Guernsey's Controlling Committee with the Control of Essential Commodities portfolio, openly and categorically refused his assent, believing a vital principle to be at stake.

However there *were* still Jews in the Islands, at least four in Guernsey and 12 in Jersey, who were duly registered as demanded by the German authorities. In both Islands a significant number did not register and managed to avoid detection or denunciation.

With our present-day knowledge of the Holocaust, it might be difficult to understand the seemingly ready acceptance by the States of both Islands (with the notable exception of Sir Abraham Lainé) of anti-Jewish legislation but so far there had been little or no evidence of the 'beastly Hun' nor of overt Nazi ideology and it is tempting to think that the local authorities, having registered their Jews, thought that would be an end to it. A later order, the Eighth, that Jews should wear the yellow six-pointed Star of David, caused the Jersey authorities to protest and the Germans appeared to back down although *Oberkriegsverwaltungsrat* Dr Casper ordered the appropriate number of stars anyway. On 30 June 1942, 15 days after Jersey's Bailiff refused to do so, Guernsey's Royal Court registered the Eighth Order. On 23 August Dr Casper noted peevishly that the stars (ordered from Paris) had not yet arrived and four months later, on 28 December, they still had not been delivered. In a note to Guernsey's *Nebenstelle* on 5 January 1943 Dr Casper again noted the non-arrival of the stars but added ominously that the matter was no longer of importance since 'the deportation of the Jews is in sight'.

However, some months earlier, on 21 April 1942, Austrian-born Therese Steiner and Auguste Spitz, and Marianne Grunfeld, a Pole, three of Guernsey's registered Jews, were deported to France. They were among the first Jews to be deported from a German-occupied area of Western Europe and sadly their ultimate destination was Auschwitz where they arrived on 23 July and perished.

In Jersey Albert Bedane, French-born but a naturalised British subject since 1921, was a chartered masseur (today we would call him a physiotherapist) with a clinic in Roseville Street, St Helier, where he successfully hid the Dutch-born Jew, Mary Erica Richardson, for nearly two years from June 1943. He also managed to conceal several others including an escaped French prisoner of war and a number of escaped Russian slave labourers. He did none of this for any reward, obtaining the food for his guests from his farmer patients in return for his massage services.

Albert Bedane was presented with a gold watch by the Russian government in 1965 for his efforts to help Russian labourers and in January 2000, 20 years after his death, he was recognised as 'Righteous among the Nations', Israel's highest Holocaust honour, for his selfless action in protecting Mary Richardson.

Jewish-owned undertakings carried notices with black print on a yellow background advising they were a 'Jewish Undertaking', while some, like the premises of men's outfitters Montague Burton, were arbitrarily taken over. In

Jersey, the branch of this particular Jewish-owned British chain was first the Forces' Book Shop (*Frontbuchhandlung*), a prime site for German propaganda, and in 1943 it became the Soldiers' Shop (*Soldatenkaufhäuser*), the bookshop moving to the nearby Fifty Shilling Tailors. The role of the *Soldatenkaufhäuser* was to enable members of the garrison to buy the same goods as were available to the troops in France. Although operated by the *Feldkommandantur*, the shops were staffed by Islanders, mostly young women. The goods on sale included toiletries (shaving soap, razor blades, etc) as well as gifts for the wives and girlfriends back home in Germany such as perfumes, handbags, silk stockings and lingerie. The *Soldatenkaufhäuser* in Jersey and Guernsey closed in 1944 when they ran out of stock.

Later, when the *Organisation Todt* imported a number of Alsatian Jews to work on the fortifications, the 'meaningless' anti-Jewish legislation became rather less so. But more of that anon.

While the German authorities were content to allow the local magistrates and Royal Courts to continue to function and deal with most of the matters they would normally have dealt with in peacetime, more courts were established. *Kanalinselnmilitärischegerichte* — Channel Islands Military Tribunals — were *FK515's* courts dealing with offences investigated by the *GFP* or *Feldgendarmerie*. In addition each arm of the *Wehrmacht* had its own court to judge offences perceived to have been carried out against it or on its premises. In fact it was possible for an offender to appear before three or even four courts for the same offence depending how many of the authorities thought it had been sinned against!

The first Jersey resident to be arrested and tried by the Germans was, somewhat bizarrely, an Advocate of the Royal Court who was sentenced to two months' incarceration on a charge of using insulting language about the German occupiers to a client who reported him to the *Feldgendarmerie*! So much for client/advocate confidentiality! The Advocate, for health reasons, served his sentence in the Public Prison and was spared deportation to France.

The local authorities had ordered that all weapons be surrendered before the invasion and the German authorities issued the same injunction — all firearms and other weapons to be surrendered within 24 hours. However, they did allow Islanders to keep some weapons as souvenirs and issued licences for all sorts of exotic weaponry that reflected many Islanders' colonial service or private collections of historical armaments. For a while sporting airguns were also permitted but it was realised that this might be a liberal step too far.

Although the Channel Islands had long been famous for their exports of potatoes, tomatoes and vegetables, the Islands had never, in recent times, actually been capable of feeding their own populations from their own resources. Moreover, the crops (principally potatoes and outdoor tomatoes in Jersey and glasshouse tomatoes and flowers in Guernsey) had been produced for profitable export. Now farmers would have to learn how to grow food to feed the Islanders and the occupiers, and to do it with constant interference from so-called German specialists who were constantly endeavouring to teach their grandmothers to suck eggs and whose priority anyway was to provide sustenance for the *Wehrmacht*. The idea was that surplus potatoes and tomatoes would be sent to France and in return the Islands would receive those goods they had traditionally obtained from 'Britain and the colonies'.

Milk was essential for nourishment and the Islands possessed herds of the finest dairy cattle in the world, capable of producing copious quantities of high-quality, creamy milk. Nevertheless rationing was introduced as early as October 1940: in Jersey a half pint of whole milk per day for everyone aged 16 or over and in Guernsey a half pint of skimmed milk for everyone aged over 14. Children, nursing mothers and invalids enjoyed more generous rations. Inevitably there were debates as to whether or not the herds were more valuable as producers of milk or beef. Traditionalists (and the Jersey and Guernsey herds had been unadulterated for more than a century) insisted that the breed was a dairy breed and thus the milk output should be maintained and cattle preserved for that purpose. In Guernsey, doctors objected, observing that a healthy, well-nourished human being was more desirable than a well-nourished, healthy cow. Nevertheless 'foreign' cattle were imported to provide both milk and beef, and were kept strictly apart from the local herds. Despite constant German supervision there were numerous instances of bogus registration of cows and falsification of milk records. As the Occupation progressed and rations diminished, theft of milk (by clandestine milking while cows grazed) became commonplace and even cows themselves were sometimes stolen, often for their meat but just as often for their milk.

Bodies were set up in both Islands to control and monitor agricultural output (with inevitable German interference) and the Islands' traditional industries underwent major changes as new crops displaced the cash crops that had brought the farming communities considerable wealth. In Jersey, cereals replaced potatoes and old water mills were reactivated — fortunately there were still alive millers who could work them and show others how to do so — while in Guernsey the glasshouses grew vegetables rather than tomatoes, grapes and flowers. One glasshouse grower, Dutchman Gerrit J. Timmer, who had arrived in Guernsey in 1927, offered to supply the occupying forces with fruit and flowers. The Germans appointed him an 'official contractor' and so began a lucrative association. The Controlling Committee were disturbed that Timmer was making undue profits at the expense of the people of Guernsey since his bills to the Germans were submitted to the States as part of the costs of the occupation. The activities of Timmer Ltd continued to be a source of concern and in June 1944, the Controlling Committee was advised (after a complaint had been lodged concerning some aspect of the company's activities) that 'Mr Timmer is a servant of the German Reich'. With regard to the complaint no action was taken. Following the Liberation, Gerrit Timmer was accused of collaboration but more of that anon.

The seas around the Channel Islands were rich in fish (although between the wars the fishing industry had declined) but, not unnaturally, the Germans were not keen to let fishing boats wander around the Channel looking for catches. Immediately after the invasion fishing boats were restricted to a mile offshore unescorted and two miles with an escort. In September 1940, following a successful escape from Guernsey (whereby a fishing boat just kept going until it reached England), all fishing was banned and the boats were taken into St Peter Port and St Helier's harbours where they were confined for a time. Later, fishing was resumed under escort provided the fishermen had an appropriate permit.

Since all manufactured goods had always been imported (mostly from Britain) new ways had to be found to sustain the Islands' populations which ultimately included another 30,000 mouths and more needing to be fed, clothed and sustained. A Purchasing Commission was set up to trade with France, headed by the bilingual John Jouault for Jersey and Raymond Falla for Guernsey with a full-time agent in Granville.

While many of their purchases were foodstuffs, Messrs Jouault and Falla had to learn to deal in such bizarre items as G-strings (for violins), billhooks, underwear (winter weight, ankle length) and even medical supplies such as insulin and X-ray films.

In October, just four months after the invasion, the *Feldkommandantur* limited the use of motor vehicles to essential purposes, the principal reason being shortage of fuel. A month earlier it had started requisitioning vehicles up to five years old, a process that would continue until August 1941. For the time being, the British rule of the road was maintained, although accidents involving military personnel were daily occurrences.

The petrol shortage would become acute at the beginning of 1941 and more vehicles were taken off the road and either stored in 'motor pools' with their tyres removed to aid the Reich's war effort, or shipped to France.

The Germans imported more than 600 horses for their own use — the German military (despite the sophisticated mechanisation of the Panzers that drove the *Blitzkrieg*) was still largely reliant on the horse as a prime mover — and for it, as well as Islanders, horses-drawn vehicles became commonplace, with, by 1944, mechanised vehicles having their engines removed and shafts put in their place.

Under Article 53 of the Hague Convention bicycles were also requisitioned despite the protests of the Island authorities, most of which were ignored. Indeed, in Guernsey, when the number required was not forthcoming, the Island authorities were accused of 'intolerable sabotage' and threatened with dire consequences.

In Guernsey, on the first anniversary of the declaration of war, two Guernseymen, Lieutenants Hubert Nicolle and James Symes, were landed on

Guernsey from a Royal Navy motor torpedo boat. Nicolle had already been to Guernsey since the beginning of the occupation, a two-day reconnoitre at the specific instigation of Winston Churchill just a matter of days after the German invasion. On this occasion Nicolle was instructed to make contact with Ambrose Sherwill and although he did not do so (his father acted instead as an intermediary) he was made aware that the presence of him and his colleague was regarded as a nuisance and that in essence Sherwill's message was 'don't bother us, go and fight your war somewhere else'.

Nevertheless Nicolle and Symes, by contacting family and friends, managed to glean enough information to make their mission potentially a success, provided they could get off the Island again but that was where the operation fell apart. The two men were out of uniform and thus could be liable to be shot as spies and, despite making the rendezvous for several nights in succession, when no craft arrived to take them off they realised they were stranded.

On 30 September a Captain Parker (in uniform) was landed by MTB at Corbière (there is one in Guernsey too) on a rescue mission but, having scaled the cliffs, fell into a German trench and was promptly taken prisoner.

The presence of two British soldiers was becoming common knowledge and they realised that it would not be too long before the Germans were also in on the secret. Ambrose Sherwill advised Frank Nicolle that they should surrender, recognising that were the men to be captured, there would be problems for his administration if it became known (as it almost certainly would) that he and others of it had been aware of the existence of British spies in the Island.

What happened next provided a chilling insight into the realities of enemy occupation. Sherwill was summoned by an *Oberleutnant* Schnadt, *aide-de-camp* to the Military Commandant *Major* Fritz Bandelow, and advised that the Germans were aware of the two British spies and that they should surrender themselves immediately. Should they not do so and were discovered, they would be shot and those who had sheltered them would suffer the same fate. If they were caught and it could not be established who had hidden them, then 20 prominent residents would be shot instead. However, Sherwill would have to wait for three more days before he could discuss the situation with *Major* Bandelow himself (who was usually charming) although he did advise the Controlling Committee that he had offered the Germans the members of the Town *Douzaine* (who numbered 20) as potential volunteers for the firing squad, a somewhat gruesome joke with an ability to backfire.

Between Sherwill and Bandelow a formula was devised that would allow the British soldiers to surrender and be treated as prisoners of war and on 18 October a notice appeared in the *Evening Press* giving a deadline for the surrender of any fugitive British military personnel and an undertaking that no action would be taken against those who had given them shelter.

To maintain the fiction that these were soldiers and not spies, British uniforms were found for them.

Later Ambrose Sherwill, in his unpublished memoirs, admitted that, being in the throes of the negotiations with the Germans regarding the predicament of Nicolle and Symes, he felt ashamed that he had not objected to the introduction of the anti-Jewish Orders which were being promulgated at the same time and that he 'had no premonition of the appalling atrocities which were to be perpetrated on the Jews by the Nazi regime'. He was also aware that the Germans suspected that he was rather more involved in the Nicolle/Symes affair than he had let on and, to his horror, when the two soldiers gave themselves up, they were tried separately by a court martial, found guilty of spying and sentenced to be shot. Furthermore, despite *Major* Bandelow's promises, their relatives and friends who had sheltered them were also arrested. Sherwill protested and was advised that despite what he had been assured, the final decision rested with higher authority, perhaps even Hitler himself. Sherwill became even more despondent when he heard on the wireless that two German spies had been executed in the Tower of London. In his memoirs, he recalled: 'I fully anticipated that the two officers and some at least of the 16 persons implicated would be court-martialled and shot and the remainder would receive sentences of imprisonment.' Finally he himself was accused by the *Geheimefeldpolizei* of 'being head of the British espionage service in Guernsey', arrested and flown to Paris where he was imprisoned at Versailles and subsequently at the infamous Cherche Midi prison where he was joined by the States Supervisor H. E. Marquand, Nicolle and Symes (still under sentence of death) and most of those who had been arrested. With Sherwill's incarceration, Jurat the Rev John Leale became acting president of the Controlling Committee. As a further reprisal, on 12 November, a notice was published in the *Evening Press* that for 'favouring espionage in the Island of Guernsey' all wireless sets were to be confiscated and subsequently nearly 13,000 sets were handed in, including 171 from Sark. The punishment for not handing over a wireless was six weeks in prison or a fine of 30,000 *Reichsmark* (around £3,125).

As it happened, Berlin decided that Nicolle and Symes should not be shot and instead be treated as prisoners of war. On Christmas Eve the Channel Islands' *Feldkommandant Oberst* Schumacher published a notice in the press to the effect that not only were those in prison in the Cherche Midi to be released, but wireless sets would also be returned to their owners (an amazing feat actually achieved in most cases by lunchtime on Christmas Day!). Nevertheless, while Mr Marquand was allowed to resume his position as States Supervisor, Sherwill was 'released from his office as further co-operation with the German Authorities is no longer possible'. The Bailiff wrote to the *Feldkommandant* expressing the people's relief that despite the fact that Guernsey citizens had been found guilty of 'grave offences under German military law' they would be exempted from punishment.

The Nicolle/Symes affair had certainly soured relations between the occupiers and the occupied in Guernsey and, while no similar event occurred in Jersey, it began to dawn on the Islanders that, despite the rebuff of the Battle of Britain, Germany was still victorious throughout Europe and North Africa and that their lives were now liable to change for ever, since the Germans were no longer a temporary phenomenon and their grip on Islanders' lives was complete. No lives had been sacrificed in the Nicolle/Symes affair (although sadly James Symes' father had died in prison on 22 December) but it was feared that the initial draconian punishments laid down by the courts martial might not be waived again. It may not be surprising that Sherwill was not returned to office (Jurat Leale was elected to the presidency of the Controlling Committee in January 1941, although his appointment had to be approved by the German authorities — as it was) but what is perhaps more significant was that it was made clear that, despite acceding to his office from a Crown appointment, the Germans were now the ones who decided who did what. And ultimately who lived and died.

In January 1941 a group of 16 paroled French soldiers escaped from Brittany by boat in an attempt to get to England to join de Gaulle's Free French forces. Their 20-year-old leader was François Scornet. Tragically, their navigational skills did not match their enthusiasm and on sighting Guernsey believed it to be the Isle of Wight. They landed at Vazon on the west coast where a German sentry was as surprised to see them as they were appalled to see him.

Scornet was brought to Jersey where he was tried and, as leader of the group, sentenced to death. He was shot by firing squad in the grounds of St Ouen's Manor on Monday, 17 March, for 'favouring the actions of the enemy by wilfully supporting England in the war against the German Empire'. The justification was that, as a paroled prisoner of war, François Scornet had broken that parole and forfeited his life by so doing. Theoretically, all 16 could have been shot but the Germans chose to execute only the leader '*pour encourager les autres*'. The execution sent a chill through the Islanders when it became common knowledge.

Daily life was changing in other ways too. There were already food shortages (despite the evacuation of so many Islanders, particularly from Guernsey, actually boosting existing food stocks) and the curfew (10pm to 6am) meant that visiting friends became more and more a limited daylight activity.

Organisations like the Salvation Army, the Oddfellows, the Buffaloes, the Rotary Club, the Boy Scouts and Girl Guides and even the Girls Friendly Society were banned. Strangely enough the Germans did not proscribe the uniformed St John Ambulance Brigade, even allowing it to keep its black uniforms. The Islands' Freemasons took comfort from the initial German proclamation that the 'lives, property and liberty of peaceful inhabitants is solemnly guaranteed'. Nevertheless, advice was taken and meetings were suspended and the Masonic Temples, in Jersey in St Helier's Stopford Road, and in Guernsey in St Peter Port's Le Marchant Street, were locked up. However, with the Nazi paranoia about Freemasonry, it is not surprising that there was soon a change of heart. In November 1940, the *GFP* in Jersey demanded the keys to the Temple and in January 1941 a special group arrived from France and systematically looted the building, the contents eventually being used for an anti-Masonic exhibition in Potsdam. The building was taken over by the occupying forces and used as a liquor store and also provided storage for the wireless sets confiscated in 1942. In Guernsey the regalia and other articles were confiscated and the building also used as a temporary store for confiscated wireless sets.

The Island authorities also had to cope with what, for them, was something of a new social phenomenon: unemployment. In Jersey, at the end of 1940, there were 2,300 men unemployed. The German occupation had deprived many of their daily occupations, particularly those in the tourism industry, and although the evacuations created many job opportunities, the Superior Council and the Controlling Committee had also to devise means to prevent the unemployed being lured to work for the Germans. The Hague Convention specifically prohibited the occupiers from forcing Islanders to work for them or their contractors (and sometimes where this line was to be drawn led to protracted arguments) but it did not prevent Islanders working for the Germans if they freely chose to do so. Many did, particularly those who felt no special allegiance to the Crown, ie the Islands' Irish citizens whose own country's neutrality (and not too distant history) did not impose any fealty to Britain upon them. Other Islanders, particularly tradesmen, were tempted by offers of wages three and four times what they were used to and even extra rations.

Like Germany itself in the 1930s, the States embarked upon programmes of public works to absorb the unemployed. In Jersey the scenic North Marine Drive (*La Route du Nord*) stands to this day as a memorial to the Islanders of 1939–1945.

Following the evacuation some schools found themselves without pupils and teachers. In Jersey and Guernsey, the prestigious Victoria and Elizabeth Colleges (both public schools for boys and both originally endowed by the Monarchs after whom they were named) were closed and taken over by the occupiers. While the pupils remaining at Victoria College moved into the premises of Halkett Place School in St Helier, *Feldkommandantur 515* set up its headquarters in the College boarding house.

To cope with the lack of teachers, classes became bigger and because of the dearth of job opportunities the school leaving age was raised from 15 to 16 in 1941. Shortages of paper and books led to exercise books being used over and over again while any usable space remained and slates were reintroduced. Learning German became compulsory in schools in September 1942 and English lessons were reduced to allow for five 45-minute sessions of German per week. In Guernsey the Education Council protested that, under international law, the occupying power had no right to make such a ruling. The protest was ignored and some time later *Oberst* Knackfuss attended a presentation where prizes of books (paid for with the proceeds from German band concerts) were presented to pupils and their teachers. In Sark the Dame offered to teach the language, reporting that 22 children were willing to learn it. Her offer was accepted. In Jersey schoolgirl Audrey Anquetil remembers a schools' inspector, a German officer, being very unimpressed with the progress that she and her schoolmates were making: 'I can only assume he must have considered Jersey schoolchildren a very ignorant lot.'

Everyday items like tobacco became in short supply. Islanders began experimenting by putting matches to such substitutes as dried blackberry leaves, dock leaves and even used tea leaves. Tobacco plants brought in from France took their place alongside potatoes and tomatoes as a cash crop and, in Jersey in 1943, the States imposed a tax on the tobacco plants to help pay for the costs of the Occupation.

Prices, and wages, were fixed and in the Islands barter became a common currency — a set of bicycle tyres being exchanged for five pounds of flour, for instance — and inevitably the black market reared its ugly head. At one time two pounds of raw coffee beans commanded £24, a pound of tea was selling for £30 or about three months' wages for a labourer, and a pound of tobacco for around £100. A tablet of Sunlight soap was offered in exchange for 100lb of wheat, a small tin of sardines cost a guinea (£1 1s — £1.05) and meat dripping was selling for 25s (£1.25) per lb. A packet of Vim (the abrasive cleanser) whose normal retail price was 9d (4p) was selling for 17s 11d (90p). A box of 50 matches usually sold for a penny (0.5p) was fetching 7s 6d (38p). These prices must be put into the context whereby £100 was a year's wages for many of the population.

Although a general fuel shortage meant that there were actually few vehicles on the Islands' roads (the even fewer vehicles fuelled by gas derived from charcoal were largely ineffectual since the undulating nature of the Islands' roads imposed loads the Heath-Robinson outfits could not cope with), in June 1941 the Germans decided to change the rule of the road to driving on the right with the inevitable consequences. However, it was now the few local drivers who were having the accidents rather than the Germans, and bus passengers had to exit in the middle of the road!

The banks functioned much as usual for the first 18 months or so of occupation. However, English money gradually disappeared (although bank accounts were maintained in sterling) to be replaced by the Occupation *Reichsmark*, worth a little over two shillings (10p) but whose rate was fixed and remained so until after the Liberation. French francs were also in common usage, so for some time no fewer than three different currencies were in use and Channel Islanders were the first Britons to experience decimal currency.

As small change became scarce (more so as the Germans found the local coinage to be suitable souvenirs to send home) local banknotes were designed and although this was an opportunity for some significant 'Germanisation', they were printed in sterling values. In Jersey notes with a value of 2s (10p) were issued in June 1941 to a total value of £5,000. Signed by States Treasurer Herbert Ereaut (later Bailiff of Jersey) these notes, printed by *The Evening Post,* were on pinkish paper with details and values printed in blue. The paper was very poor quality and the notes not only became grubby very quickly (earning themselves the sobriquet 'Dirty Berties' — presumably in Mr Ereaut's honour although no doubt not to his pleasure), they also fell apart. They were withdrawn and replaced in April 1942 by new notes designed by the Jersey-born and distinguished Royal Academician Edmund Blampied. These notes were issued in values of 6d, 1s, 2s, 10s and £1 (2½p, 5p, 10p, 50p and £1) to a total value of £65,000. They were printed in Paris and remained legal tender until 30 November 1946. Although no longer legal tender, they could be bought from Jersey's States Treasury, at face value, until 1960.

Similarly, local postage stamps (so far the Islands had always used the standard UK issue from the General Post Office) needed to be produced. In Guernsey existing twopenny stamps were cut in half to create two penny ones until new penny ones could be printed. In Jersey designer Major N. V. L. Rybot initially refused the commission (believing it to be assisting the enemy) but then used the opportunity to include in his design a minute **A** in each corner standing for *Ad Avernum Adolfé Atrox* or, to put it another way, *To Hell with you, Atrocious Adolf.* The stamps were printed on newsprint by *The Evening Post.* In a later set of pictorial stamps printed in Paris, artist Edmund Blampied managed to work the royal cipher **GR** into his designs.

Mail to destinations outside the Islands, with the exception of Germany itself and its allies, was, as far as the local populations were concerned, restricted to Red Cross letters. These letters were limited to just 25 words and subject, if necessary, to rigorous censorship if anything military was hinted at. Red Cross letters could also take months to reach their destination. However, Islanders could write letters to relatives in prisoner-of-war camps and, once the deportations had taken place, to friends and relatives in internment camps who in turn could correspond with relatives in Britain. In this way news from the Islands could be in Britain in as little as three weeks.

Then, in October 1941, Adolf Hitler, who had always taken a particular interest in the Islands, decided that they should become 'impregnable fortresses' and be German for all time.

Chapter 8
Fortification and daily life

Organisation Todt, forced labourers, slave workers and civilians — building, manning, guarding and living in impregnable fortresses. Living with shortages, boredom, the curfew, GUNS, epidemics, deportations, the 'Gestapo' and the enemy not only on the doorstep but also in the house. Policemen breaking and entering, the 'Island of Death', Charybdis, denunciations and Jerrybags

Just why on 20 October 1941 Adolf Hitler commanded in a directive that the Islands be turned into 'impregnable fortresses' has never been fully explained. And neither will it be here although, as ever, a theory or two will be examined.

On 22 June 1941 Hitler launched *Unternehmung 'Barbarossa'* (Operation 'Barbarossa'), the long-awaited invasion of Russia in the quest for *Lebensraum* in the East, living space for the German people. Three weeks earlier he had demanded maps of the Channel Islands and to know how well they were defended. Gerd von Rundstedt, *Oberbefehlshaber West* and Commander of Army Group D in whose *fief* the Channel Islands sat, ordered measures to strengthen the Islands' defences (the garrisons between them still numbered less than 6,000 men) straight away. Plans for coastal guns were initiated as were plans to provide tanks and the crews (*Panzertruppen*) to man them. In fact plans were already afoot to strengthen the garrison, and men of *319 Infanterie Division* were beginning to replace the invaders of *216ID* (who were destined for the Eastern Front). So far the defences that had been constructed consisted mostly of slit trenches and flak (anti-aircraft) positions.

It has been argued that Hitler did not want Britain interfering while his principal attention was elsewhere. The mission of his deputy, Rudolf Hess, to England, it is now believed by some, was a doomed attempt to contact a 'peace party' that would take power in Britain and leave Germany alone to pursue her adventure in the East. That mission (whatever it really was) obviously failed, but Hitler wanted to ensure that Britain would not take the opportunity of his temporary but overwhelming preoccupation with Russia to reclaim the Channel Islands and restore the prestige he assumed that Britain had lost by their occupation. Hence the decree that they become 'impregnable fortresses'.

Another theory is that, since Britain had a Gibraltar, Hitler had decided that he wanted one too, and having abandoned Operation 'Felix', the invasion of Gibraltar itself, the Channel Islands would fit the bill as an outpost of the German Empire on the edge of Europe to be retained by the new owners in perpetuity (although it had already been agreed that Alderney would be 'returned' to France in the event of a German victory). Yet another theory is that, having observed how Malta had survived intensive bombing and provided a haven for the forces harrying the *Afrika Korps* by air and sea, Hitler was insistent that the Channel Islands must not be retaken so that they could fulfil a similar harrying role amongst shipping in the British-dominated English Channel. Long-range guns must be installed on the Islands and at suitable locations on the adjacent coast of France to give absolute mastery over the Bay of St Malo and guard the western approaches to the English Channel. In short, Hitler believed the Islands to have strategic value when no one else did. Take your pick.

Within weeks the German garrison in the Islands had swelled almost tenfold and consisted of the full *319 Infanterie Division*, comprising a headquarters company, three infantry regiments, one artillery regiment, an anti-tank battalion, an engineer and pioneer battalion, a reconnaissance company and a signal company, in all in excess of 15,000 men. One unit which had been in the Islands, and latterly in Guernsey, since the invasion, *Maschinengewehr Bataillon 16* (Machine Gun Battalion 16) was moved to Jersey and stayed there until the Liberation. In time, *319ID* would become the largest division in the German army yet it would never fight in any major engagement.

The division was formed in Germany at Gera in *Wehrkreis IX* (Defence Area 9) in November 1940 with troops drawn from divisions who had already seen action in Poland and France. In April 1941 the division moved to France where it took up garrison duties in the St Lô/Carentan area of Normandy despite being below strength particularly with regard to artillery.

In his entry for 20 June 1941, Jersey diarist Leslie Sinel noted that 'German troops arrive in very large numbers, the figure mentioned being 3,000; many more houses have been requisitioned including West Park Pavilion (a local dance hall), Highlands College (a former Jesuit seminary) and Springfield (a theatre and banqueting hall adjacent to the Island's main football ground); some soldiers are billeted with private families.' Despite the fact that the topography of the Islands was unsuited to tank warfare, at the *Führer's* insistence, *Panzer Abteilung 213* (Tank Battalion 213) was posted to the Islands. The battalion was equipped with Renault *Char de Bataille B1* tanks, inter-war vehicles captured during the *Blitzkrieg*. The tankers' black uniforms with the Death's Head insignia on the collar led many to believe that there were members of the dreaded *SS* in the Islands, but the *Waffen-SS* ceased to wear black uniforms after 1939. During its lifetime *PA213* was probably the only armoured unit of the German army never to fire a shot in anger!

In addition to the army personnel, the numbers of *Luftwaffe* and *Kriegsmarine* were also significantly increased although the Islands' location, perceived by Adolf Hitler to have such strategic value, meant that neither of these forces were ever able to use the Islands as bases of any significance. None the less, St Catherine's Bay in Jersey was suggested as an E-boat base, while servicing and refuelling facilities were considered for St Peter Port. Although an underground fuel store was built for the U-boats in Havelet Bay behind Castle Cornet, the facilities (which elsewhere had occasioned the building of huge bomb-proof pens) were never developed and very rarely used, the seas around the Channel Islands being too shallow for U-boat operations.

The German garrison in Jersey was also augmented by the 643rd Battalion of the *Russkaya Osvoboditelnaya Armiya*, the Russian Liberation Army, uneasy allies against the Soviets, who were made responsible for the defence of much of the Island's north and north-east coast, from Archirondel on the east coast to Sorel Point half-way along the north. It is perhaps a measure of the Germans' faith in their allies that the area given them to defend was already well-endowed with the natural defences of high cliffs and narrow, steeply shelving beaches. The Liberation Army had been founded by General Andrei Vlasov in 1943. A hero of the defence of Moscow when commanding the 2nd Shock Army at the end of 1941, he was captured by the Germans in 1942 and changed sides, having become disillusioned by the Soviet brand of Communism and the way in which his command had been abandoned. He also became convinced that 'the interests of the Russian people have always been similar to the interests of the German people and all other European nations . . . Bolshevism has separated the Russian people from Europe by an impenetrable wall.'

More hotels were requisitioned and private houses, even many still lived in by their owners, found new and unwelcome occupants. The Island authorities did pay home owners a rental amounting to a few shillings a day for their German guests although they werc not expected to wash their linen!

Soon the Germans were building defences in earnest, digging trenches and knocking down buildings, most notably the Abergeldie Hotel in St Clement's Road in Jersey which was demolished in April 1943 to make way for an *OT* railway and three 18th and 19th century Conway and Martello towers were also reduced to rubble to create clear fields of fire. Oddly enough, when about to demolish the tower at Bel Royal, the Germans suggested to Bailiff Coutanche that, since the tower was of historical interest, the Department of Labour could have the stones so that they could rebuild the tower somewhere else! Defence zones were created which effectively banned Islanders from huge tracts of their own islands, particular along the coasts.

Railways had been established in Jersey in the 1870s, a standard gauge running from St Helier (Snow Hill) to Gorey Pier, and a narrow gauge (3ft 6in) from St Helier (Weighbridge) to Corbière, and a standard gauge tramway had been established from St Peter Port to St Sampson in Guernsey in the 1890s. These railways and tramways, closed for many years, having been driven out of business by the motor bus and private car, were reactivated by the *Organisation Todt* (on a variety of narrow gauges varying from one metre to 60cm) to move building materials — sand, gravel and cement — rapidly to those areas where strongpoints and resistance nests were to be created. In this instance railways made economic sense because they saved scarce motor fuel for more important military purposes. Spurs were opened to link quarries, sand pits and docks with the new fortifications, to carry the construction materials, the tracks often being laid across fields, farmyards and even front gardens.

The railways' motive power was either diesel or wood-burning locomotives and Islanders and their animals were often injured by an *OT* train careering along the unballasted tracks. Jersey schoolgirl Audrey Anquetil remembered seeing the blanket-clad body of a German soldier who had cycled head-on into a train crossing a main road. The German, Otto Fettig, survived the collision but lost a foot. On 10 June 1943 a Mr Coutanche, a farmer at St John in Jersey, was killed by a train when, moving his cows and being stone-deaf, he did not hear the train's approach although it is said that, in bizarre acts of defiance, he would often deliberately stand on the track and defy the *OT* drivers to run him down!

Alderney was unique in the Channel Islands in already having a standard gauge railway linking Mannez Quarry with the ever-crumbling breakwater. Today these railways (except in Alderney) have largely disappeared and only the discerning can recognise the traces of their erstwhile busy existence.

Otherwise, haulage for the *OT* was entrusted to the *Nationalsozialistische Kraftfahrerkorps (NSKK)* — the National Socialist Motor Transport Corps — who were equipped with a range of vehicles, some dating back to 1914! The *OT* also brought in many of its own specialist vehicles, many of them really far too large for the Islands' narrow roads (particularly in Guernsey) with consequent trails of damage to road surfaces and roadside walls.

The first defences were designed and built by the division's own pioneers and men of the *Reichsarbeitsdienst* (State Labour Service) billeted at Victoria College, but it was soon evident that they would never be able to accomplish the mass of construction and excavation work that Hitler's vision involved. That was when the labourers of the *Organisation Todt* began making an appearance, shortly followed, in November, by *Dr Ing* Fritz Todt to see for himself the scope of what was being proposed, which was nothing less than an eight-year programme of fortification and consolidation. For the *OT's* convenience (although no one seems to know why it was more convenient) the Islands were known by the code names *Julius* (Jersey), *Gustav* (Guernsey) and *Adolf* (Alderney).

The eponymous *Organisation Todt (OT)* had been founded and headed by civil engineer Dr Todt in the early 1930s as a means devised by the Nazi Party to absorb Germany's mass of unemployed. Its first civil engineering projects had been the *Autobahnen* (motorways) linking Nuremberg and Munich with Berlin. Within a year of the outbreak of war, the numbers 'employed' by the *OT* had grown to almost two million men, the ranks swelled by nationals (men and a few women) from the countries occupied by the Germans.

France's new Vichy government had introduced *Le Service du Travail Obligatoire* (Compulsory Work Service) by which means young Frenchmen were called up for work in factories in Germany but could avoid this fate by opting to join the *OT*. These men were essentially volunteers and there were also many Belgians and Dutchmen amongst their ranks who were attracted by the high wages and good rations that volunteer tradesmen, in particular, could command.

For its headquarters in Jersey the *OT* took over the Portland Hotel (*Bauleitung Julius*) and in Guernsey *Bauleitung Gustav* occupied an imposing mansion in Saumarez Park.

Initially the workers were Frenchmen and Spaniards (former Republicans who had fled to France only to be handed over to the Germans by the pliant Vichy government). They were employed by German civilian building contractors brought to the Islands to turn Hitler's order into concrete reality. In Jersey they lived in 10 camps, most commonly named after the war heroes of the Great War and the current conflict. For instance, *Lager Immelmann* was named after the Great War air ace Max Immelmann while *Lager Schepke* (where the workers on the Jersey War Tunnels complex were housed) commemorated the U-boat ace Joachim Schepke who in *U-100* would be responsible for sinking 146,000 tons of Allied shipping in this war. In Guernsey there were just five camps, three with German girls' names (*Ute*, *Ursula* and *Liesel*) in the north of the Island and two, *Ostmark* and *Westmark*, in the south. These 'forced labourers' were augmented by North African French colonial prisoners of war who were mostly Algerians, Tunisians or Moroccans. The North Africans were not part of the *OT* (nor were they forced labourers) and were employed in stores and ammunition dumps. Large numbers of North Africans were accommodated in requisitioned houses in what is known as St Peter Port's 'Old Quarter' and in his book *One Man's War* (Guernsey Press, 1967) Frank Stroobant describes the area as 'the Kasbar'. Despite the German attitude towards those races they considered inferior, 115 North Africans arrived in the Islands in August 1943 and the same number left in June 1945.

Although 'forced', the workers in the *OT* camps were fed and paid and the Germans also tried to recruit local tradesmen by offering wages well in excess of those they could earn from Island employers.

However, the States of Jersey, having begun a series of public works of its own, in particular creating the North Marine Drive along the north coast and repairing and erecting granite walls, substantially reduced the labour pool and less than 600 worked for the new masters despite the lure of high wages and better rations.

As early as October 1940 the States Textile Delegation decided to reopen Jersey's Summerland Factory of the Channel Islands Knitwear Company with the objective of providing employment for women and girls making clothing and footwear, not only for Jersey but also for Guernsey. Eventually

250 were employed who made a whole range of utility clothing and footwear for both Islands including the Summerland slipper, the Jersey boot, the Jersey shoe, a winter clog (more than 45,000 pairs were made using over 500 tonnes of beechwood) as well as carrying out thousands of textile repairs. Nevertheless, the Germans did find a ready pool of labour amongst those Irishmen (almost 500 of them) who, neutrals, had been caught in the Islands by the rapidity of the invasion.

The *OT's* chain of command, emanating from *OT-Einsatzgruppe West* in Paris under the command of *Oberbaudirektor* Karl Weis, was, not surprisingly, bureaucratic, cumbersome and ultimately inefficient. This situation was exacerbated by the rivalry between the three armed services of the *Wehrmacht* who, despite Hitler's directives, frequently did not confer with each other with regard to the siting of batteries and fortifications. *OT* overseers and foremen were Germans mostly drawn from the *Reichsarbeitsdienst* although as the Occupation progressed they were joined by Hungarians and Bulgarians. The latter were best noted for the harsh treatment they meted out to the labourers from Russia and Poland for, in the spring of 1942, prisoners of war from the Eastern Front began to arrive to swell the ranks of the volunteer and forced labourers.

Having been transported right across Europe in cattle trucks they were in a pitiful condition. In his *Occupation Diary* Leslie Sinel noted, on 13 August 1942, that: '. . . hundreds of Russians arrive for work in the western part of the Island; they make a pathetic sight, and many of them were mere boys, the majority of them with no footwear and many with bleeding feet; they were under the escort of the Todt Organisation and were very badly treated, being hit with truncheons.'

Being Slavs, the Germans regarded them as *Untermenschen*, 'sub-humans', and treated them worse than domestic animals, literally slaves to be worked till they dropped, although accusations made after the Occupation that these unfortunates were deliberately worked to death were wide of the mark. Certainly they were savagely treated and many died as a result of malnutrition, injury and disease, but there is no evidence that the Germans or their *OT* overseeing allies were pursuing any specific policy of extermination. Indeed the German civilian building contractors responsible for delivering the fortifications often sought to ensure that their workforce was always capable of working since replacing workers who dropped dead was never easy. Similarly tales told that exhausted workers who died on the job were tipped into the wet concrete of the fortifications are nonsense since a body in the fabric would significantly weaken the structure and because most were constructed of reinforced concrete with iron rods and meshes only centimetres apart, bodies would not have fitted anyway. It is possible that bodies might have been tipped into foundations but there is no actual evidence of this nor have stories that bodies were buried in Alderney's breakwater ever been substantiated.

By mid-1942 there were more than 3,000 skilled German workers and 10,000 foreign workers, mostly labourers, in the Islands as the occupiers embarked upon their defensive projects which would involve the removal of a staggering 244,000 cubic metres of rock to defend less than a hundred miles of coastline. To put this into a wider context, the entire length of the Atlantic Wall (stretching from the North Cape of Norway to the Pyrenees and some 4,000 miles in length) involved the removal of just 11,000 cubic metres more! Civilian building contractors were brought in mostly from Germany and a few from France although two Irishmen, a Mr Macnamara and a Mr O'Sullivan, set themselves up as contractors in Jersey. The most active of the Jersey contractors was Theodor Elsche of Cologne who became a regular advertiser in *The Evening Post* seeking tradesmen and general labour despite the workers provided for him by the *OT*. In Guernsey the largest contractor was Räbel-Werke of Bremen. Details of the contractors working in Alderney are sketchy but that Island owes many of its now well-surfaced roads to work carried out by Strassenbahn AG.

Not all the foreign workers came under the control of the *OT* since several hundred were employed directly by the Navy and Airforce's clumsily titled *Marinehafenbauamt Kanalinseln* (Naval Harbourworks Office Channel Islands) and *Luftwaffe Feldbauamt Kanalinseln* (Air Force Field Works Office Channel Islands) respectively.

What made the *OT* special in the wary eyes of the Islanders was the manner in which it treated its workforce, particularly those they regarded as little more than beasts of burden. The working day began at 7.00am and lasted for at least 11 hours with only a short break at midday. In the winter months the working day was from dawn to dusk (the Islands were on Central European Time, ie Double British Summer Time) and in winter the dawn did not come up until 9.00am. However, because of the nature of the materials they used, particularly the concrete which had to set as a single homogeneous mass if it was not to be weakened, labour gangs often worked long into the night under floodlights despite the risk of attracting marauding enemy aircraft. However, air attacks were relatively few and far between and those that did happen tended to be directed at the harbour installations although nearby houses and other buildings often suffered damage.

Not all the workers were harshly treated. Volunteers and forced labourers were actually quite well paid (albeit in Occupation *Reichsmark*) and were not physically assaulted, the overseers reserving their encouragement with truncheons, pickaxe handles and carpet beaters for the Russians, Poles and North Africans. Civilians who attempted to intervene were given short shrift and could be hauled off to the *Feldkommandantur* where they were told very firmly to mind their own business. Residents of St Brelade in Jersey (where there were three camps) petitioned the *Feldkommandant*, protesting at the way the workers were treated. They were told that if they interfered, access to St Brelade's Bay would be closed off to them. German soldiers tended to avert their eyes from the treatment being meted out in their cause and when, on one occasion, a soldier did intervene and stopped an *OT* overseer beating two Russians with a pickaxe handle by threatening him with his rifle, his superiors forced him to apologise to the overseer for his actions and then posted him to the Eastern Front!

The death rate amongst the Russians in the first few months after their arrival was horrendous, 63 dying and being interred in Jersey's Strangers' Cemetery between August 1942 and March 1943. Nevertheless, the fact that they were given formal burials in a cemetery is indicative of a tiny spark of humanity in those who bore the responsibility for their deaths, although the Superintendent of the cemeteries was disturbed to discover that bodies were being buried without his knowledge and thus were not being recorded. In fact these burials numbered no more than half a dozen. Who they probably were we shall discover shortly.

The living conditions of these workers were not conducive to cleanliness or hygiene and infestations of lice and fleas were so commonplace that the *OT* had to establish delousing units. Despite these measures there were inevitable outbreaks of typhus although it was thought that the Russians might have brought the disease with them. The outbreaks in Jersey were relatively mild; none the less Leslie Sinel confided to his diary that dead Russians were often buried in lime, a consequence of the infection. In Guernsey a typhus epidemic broke out amongst the North African workers, killing nine of them and causing 700 *OT* workers to be quarantined for three weeks.

Not all the forced and slave labourers were male and in Jersey on 27 March 1943 the *OT* published an advertisement in *The Evening Post* asking 'any kind person who has unrequired baby clothes' to write or bring them to the *OT* headquarters in Midvale Road for 'pregnant Russian working women' who were shortly to be in need of them. The baby clothes were duly delivered. And, one assumes, so were the babies.

It is easy to gain the impression that the life of an *OT* worker was all work and no play, seven days a week. Although their working lives were undoubtedly hard (and for the Russians, Poles and North Africans extremely harsh and unremitting), unless working on a specific and urgent project they worked six days a week with Sunday off. On their day off *OT* workers could visit the cinema, go to a café (if they could find one open with something on offer), visit an *OT* brothel where their physical needs might be met by French prostitutes brought to the Islands for the purpose (most *OT*s were well paid and could often afford luxuries not available to many Islanders surviving on much lower incomes) or even go to church, although few in the congregation wanted to sit or kneel too close to them. Nevertheless they did mingle with the local population and sometimes this mingling became quite intimate and marriages between local girls and Belgian, Dutch, French and Spanish workers did take place after permission was obtained from the *Feldkommandantur* (which was always granted). Entertainers were even brought to the Islands and the *Kraft durch Freude* (*KdF* — Strength through Joy) movement staged concerts for the *OT* workers to which the general public were also invited. In Guernsey there were even plans for a charity football match between 'Occupation Champions' Les Vauxbelets Old Boys (Les Vauxbelets was a Catholic boys' college whose most memorable artefact is the Little Chapel) and a 'Continental XI' of *OT* workers. The match was scheduled for 7.45pm on 8 June 1943 but the *Evening Press* of the following day reported that the Continental XI had failed to show and had been replaced by a scratch Island eleven. Perhaps, being a Tuesday and a working day, the Continentals had simply been too tired to play football! On 28 August 1943 the *Evening Press* announced the return visit of 'the dextrous Effie with his conjuring tricks, sly humour and glamorous companion Halima'. This was another entertainment organised for the *OT* workers by the Strength through Joy movement. In an interview with the magazine *Jersey Topic* in the 1960s, Graf von Schmettow (who had requested and received permission to visit the Islands he had once commanded) confided that had the war gone differently, the Channel Islands would have become Strength through Joy holiday centres for German workers.

May Day was a German holiday and Leslie Sinel noted, somewhat acerbically: 'The Germans are celebrating May Day today, and all work on the various fortification schemes is stopped, with the result that there is a noticeable lack of motor traffic on the roads; the town was crowded with foreign workers who apparently have plenty of money but nothing to buy with it; in the afternoon a German band plays in the Royal Square — but that cannot fill empty stomachs!'

As Leslie noted, food was a major preoccupation for the labour force.

Throughout their period in the Islands the labourers were constantly hungry. Their rations, despite the workload demanded of them, were less than the troops and those were subject to *OT* distributive inefficiency and massive pilfering, food destined for the workers often being diverted to the *OT* overseers, many of whom added to their income by operating in the black market. Theft of foodstuffs from civilian farms by Russians and Poles who were at the bottom of the food chain became commonplace (vegetables and chickens were prime targets for larceny) and although sympathetic Islanders did offer the starving workers food scraps they did so at considerable risk since such humanitarian gestures were forbidden. Some, it must be said, were not above selling food to the workers but this too was a criminal offence and could earn fines and even imprisonment.

Security at the *OT* camps was not strict — it being perceived that the Islands themselves were sufficient prisons — and there were many escapes, the *OT*s often mingling with the locals and surviving by raiding farms and German stores for food and clothing. Many found sympathetic Islanders prepared to hide them. This was an extremely risky undertaking since the Germans viewed such actions very seriously and for several Islanders harbouring escaped slave workers was literally a death sentence. Early in 1942 a Russian prisoner of war, Feodor Burriy, escaped from a working party in Jersey and was hidden for 18 months by Mrs Louisa Gould at her home in St Ouen, the sparsely populated north-western corner of the Island. Her motive, she said, was that having just lost her eldest son (an officer in the Royal Navy) she had to help 'another mother's son'. Burriy (who came to be known as Bill) was a Red Army officer, a member of the Communist Party and by profession a photographer. While being hidden by Louisa Gould he learned to speak English, wore her dead son's clothing and became so assimilated into the community that he ran errands for her, did her shopping and even attended church with her. But an anonymous informer reported her to the *GFP* and she was arrested on 25 May 1944 despite being tipped off to 'get rid of Bill and destroy all traces of him'. Unfortunately a search of Mrs Gould's chicken house revealed a concealed wireless set, a Russian-English dictionary, her son's shotgun and, most telling of all, the same photograph of 'Bill' that was hanging up in the *GFP* headquarters on a 'Wanted' poster. Bill himself avoided capture and was passed to other 'safe' houses, including being boarded by two English conscientious objectors who had avoided deportation and with whom he stayed until the Liberation, supplied with identity papers by Dr Noel McKinstry, Jersey's Medical Officer of Health. Thanks to well-established contacts at the Town Hall from where identity cards were issued and access to the photographer who took the photographs for them, the papers the ingenious Dr McKinstry supplied were the real thing.

Louisa Gould was charged with failing to surrender the wireless set and harbouring an escaped POW, both potentially capital offences. And so it proved. Louisa Gould was deported first to Rennes prison in France and then to Ravensbrück, the concentration camp for women, where she died in the gas chamber in February 1945. Her brother Harold Le Druillenec and sister Mrs Ivy Forster were arrested with her. Mrs Forster managed to avoid deportation by being falsely diagnosed by staff at the General Hospital as suffering with tuberculosis (a condition for which the Germans seemed to have a particular apprehension). Harold Le Druillenec survived incarceration in Neuengamme concentration camp and was sent to the typhus-ridden Belsen camp a matter of just nine days before its liberation by British forces. He was the only known British survivor of that particular living hell and afterwards described it as 'the foulest and vilest spot that ever soiled the surface of this earth'.

Escapes continued and at one time there were as many as 15 escaped Russians on the run, most evading capture and still free at the Liberation. The Germans placed notices in *The Evening Post* threatening dire consequences for those harbouring the escapees.

The escapees lived rough and survived by thieving (a risky business since they were as likely to be speared by a farmer's pitchfork if caught as being detained by the *Feldgendarmerie*) or were given shelter by Islanders who, like Louisa Gould, were prepared to risk their lives and freedom to shelter them.

However, the thefts by marauding foreign workers could also have tragic consequences. On 1 December 1942 Ernest Le Gresley, who with his sister kept a shop near St Peter's Windmill in Jersey, disturbed intruders who were raiding his henhouse. Both Mr Le Gresley and his sister were stabbed and Mr Le Gresley succumbed to his injuries and died. The Germans blamed escaped Russians for the tragedy and gave dire warnings to the local population about the hazards involved in sheltering the murderers.

Escaping Russians were almost exclusively a Jersey phenomenon; because of the small number in Guernsey the situation seems never to have arisen there. Escape from Alderney, itself almost entirely a large camp, was impossible.

However, Islanders did work for the Germans, some for the money and other benefits (since employment by the *OT* gave access to all sorts of commodities otherwise out of their reach), others from higher motives, particularly since working for the *OT* also gave access to sites which were meticulously sketched. These images were ultimately passed to British Intelligence by escapers later in the Occupation.

Some men brought before the German courts for a variety of misdemeanours (most commonly breaking the curfew) were given the choice of working for the occupiers or being imprisoned. Not surprisingly they frequently chose the former but their contribution to the Reich's war effort was often minimal since the opportunities offered frequently led them to commit various acts of sabotage.

At their most active, during 1942, there were some 15,000 *OT* workers in the Channel Islands, circa 7,000 in Guernsey, 6,000 in Jersey and 2,000 in Alderney. These numbers do not include political prisoners in Alderney who numbered more than a thousand at one time.

There has been some controversy — and even a falling out — amongst local historians as to whether or not there were Jews amongst the *OT* (or any other) workforce. One late historian's view was that since the Nazis' intent for the Jews was extermination, letting them lose themselves amongst the *OT* workforce (of which the vast majority survived the war) was most unlikely. He went so far as to offer a £100 reward to anyone who could provide evidence to the contrary. In this he clashed with the redoubtable Joe Mière who promptly provided such evidence, albeit second-hand but nevertheless convincing, and did not, he claims, receive the £100! Knowing Joe's knowledge of these things, and having seen the evidence, I am inclined to believe him. Although the number seems small, probably no more than a couple of dozen, the evidence that there were Alsatian Jews amongst the workers brought over by the Fortress Engineers as early as April 1941 is compelling. They were part of that well-documented group recorded by Leslie Sinel as being 'nationals from countries subject to Germany'. The group consisted of Alsatians, 'half-Jews' and some Poles, their masters in this instance requiring the sweat of their brow rather than the blood in their veins.

They were shipped out in April 1942, leaving a half dozen or so behind in the Strangers' Cemetery. Several hundred Jews were incarcerated for a time in *Lager Sylt* in Alderney and treated extremely harshly by their *SS* guards but their treatment was no worse than that meted out to the other unfortunates who struggled to build the massive fortifications that exist to this day. *Lager Sylt* was operated from March 1943, and then, from February 1944, the *SS* also took over *Lager Norderney* on the island, which were the only Nazi concentration camps ever established on British soil. Both were shut down in July 1944.

In concept the German defensive plan for the Channel Islands was simple but effective and deadly. Each island would become a self-contained fortress, ringed with impregnable bunkers and anti-tank seawalls. Inland batteries would support the coastal defences and provide overlapping fire up to 20 miles out to sea, effectively sealing off the Bay of St Malo. A series of resistance nests would be created, each one capable of stalling an invader, all over the islands but particularly on the approaches to the airports, and anti-aircraft batteries and searchlights would provide a lethal welcome for any airborne intruder. Above-ground huge command bunkers were created in Jersey and Guernsey, linked to all the defensive positions by miles of telephone wires laid mostly below ground level — the Fortress Cable Network (*Festungkabelnetz*).

In the Islands' steep-sided valleys would be created a network of deep tunnels into which the entire garrison could descend in the event of an invasion. Just how effective this 'underground' concept was would be discovered at enormous cost in Allied lives at Monte Cassino, St Malo, Cherbourg, Caen and dozens of other strongpoints in Europe as the defences of the Third Reich crumbled.

In Guernsey 29 deep tunnels were planned while 25 were intended for Jersey and nine in Alderney. The Islands' topography was ideally suited for such tunnelling with short, steep sided valleys, and despite much of Jersey's bedrock being granite the engineers found seams of Brioverian shale and conglomerate which were easier to work. Where the rock was granite the tunnels, once excavated, needed neither lining nor propping since granite was self supporting. These tunnels were designed to be large enough to house the entire garrison (up to 20,000 men and less than 100 women on each Island), their guns, ammunition, vehicles, fuel, food and medications. They were described as *Höhlgangsanlagen (Ho)* or 'cave passage installations' and were all to be deep enough to survive intense bombing and shellfire. In World War 1, German bunkers (many constructed of earth and timber) just 12 metres underground survived the week-long artillery barrage that preceded the Battle of the Somme, the greatest barrage of all time. The average depth of the tunnels in the Channel Islands was more than twice that, although the development of the Tallboy and Earthquake bombs used by the RAF towards the end of the war to smash the massive U-boat pens on the Biscay coast (with little success) may well have rendered the tunnels death-traps rather than shelters.

After the Occupation all sorts of fanciful theories were advanced as to the real purposes of the tunnels, from being the beginnings of an underground railway system to gas chambers for exterminating Britain's Jewish population (despite the fact that the tunnels were commenced long after all German plans to invade Britain had been shelved) and even as launch sites for V-weapons. Indeed this last theory has been explored in *The Occupation* (Guy Walters — Headline, 2004), wherein Alderney is chosen as a site for the V-3, a 'super' gun theoretically capable of hurling a shell all the way to London. V-weapon theories tend to fall rather flat when you consider that all the hardware would have had to be brought to the Islands by sea, by that stage of the war not notable for the amount of German shipping on it.

The reality is that the tunnels were intended primarily as secure, bomb-proof storage and ultimately shelter in the event of attack. Rock removed from the tunnels was crushed for aggregate and used to make more concrete. *Ho8* became better known as Jersey's 'German Underground Hospital', having been converted from a half-finished ammunition store and artillery workshop by Italian *Hilfswillige* (auxiliaries). Who these people were calls for a little explanation.

Following Italy's surrender in September 1943 many Italians remained willing to co-operate with the Germans but not fight for them. It was these *Hilfswillige* who arrived in the Islands in October 1943 (even bringing a band with them) to carry out fatigues for the German forces. When tradesmen were needed to carry out the conversion of *Ho8*, the Italians fitted the bill, changing the former store and workshop to a bomb-proof casualty clearing station early in 1944 when invasion seemed to be a real possibility.

Beaches were sealed off with concrete anti-tank walls more than three metres high and up to 2 metres thick, in places extending for up to three miles. Where there were gaps in the walls, huge steel gates were covered by bunkers mounting anti-tank guns, machine guns and flame-throwers. Along Jersey's St Ouen's Bay deep ditches were dug behind the defences to trap any tank that might, somehow, have scaled the walls.

Existing fortifications, Martello and Conway towers, castles and forts, were pressed into service as observation posts, gun positions and 'resistance nests'. Ancient Mont Orgueil Castle in Jersey, built in the 13th century and outmoded once cannon were invented in the 15th, received three new watchtowers which the architects managed to blend very successfully with the medieval architecture, having asked advice on how to achieve this objective from the redoubtable Major Rybot (he of *Ad Avernum* fame). It is perhaps a little cynical to suggest that their concern had less to do with sympathy for the Island's heritage than the need to disguise the towers against air attack.

Altogether there were approximately 1,500 new military constructions on the Channel Islands and what must be remembered is that the occupiers were at work for little more than two of the eight years' programme they had intended.

Observation towers (*Marine Peilstände und Messstellen*) of a design unique to the Channel Islands, and 17 metres high, designed for ranging and directing the sea-defence guns, were planned on prominent headlands around the Islands. Twenty-two were intended although only nine — five in Guernsey, three in Jersey and one in Alderney — were actually completed in two years. Massive blockhouses, designed to be regimental and battalion command posts (*Kernwerken*), were built amongst the fields and farms in St Peter in Jersey in what is now The Living Legend Jersey Village. Similar structures were built along the Oberlands Road in Guernsey near what is now the Princess Elizabeth Hospital. The *Kriegsmarine* tower at Les Landes in Jersey (*MP3*) was fitted with a *Gema Seetakt* radar array while at Guernsey's Fort George two *Freya* arrays kept watch over the St Peter Port harbour approaches. Altogether there were three *Freya* arrays in Jersey, five in Guernsey and one in Alderney. These *Freya* were on constant alert. Radar units known as *Würzburg* units were in use by anti-aircraft batteries in all three Islands and there were also three radar arrays in Guernsey known as *riese* (giant) *Würzburgen*, one to track targets for *Batterie Mirus*, the other two operated by the *Luftwaffe* at Fort George. Unlike *Freya*, *Würzburg* was only in use when there was something to shoot at.

The Islands' fine sandy beaches were made hazardous with anti-tank and anti-personnel mines and sewn with a variety of obstacles including iron structures known as *Igel* (hedgehogs) designed to rip the hulls of landing craft apart and posts topped with anti-personnel mines designed to shower invaders with something akin to grapeshot. Fields were scattered with obstacles to deter landings with gliders, and 'spiders webs', cables strung across open spaces with a high-explosive shells at their centre, promised a lethal welcome to any paratrooper. Sites were established for searchlights and flame-throwers. Roll-bombs (highly explosive Great War howitzer shells on the end of cables which could be activated by cutting them) were suspended over anti-tank walls, harbour walls and other structures and buried along the Islands' airport runways. Rusting roll-bombs were found secreted by the walls of Jersey's Mont Orgueil Castle (where they had been buried by the British in 1945) as recently as the 1980s. Such ordnance (and barely a month goes by without some rusting explosive device still being found) is today either made safe or more often detonated by police bomb disposal teams.

Approaches to harbours and potential landing sites were sewn with ground-lying sea mines designed to be detonated electrically from control panels (*Zundtischen*) inside concrete blockhouses.

Few German fortifications were identical since each contractor employed his own architects who all had their own ideas of what the edifices, although built to meet strict military specifications, should look like. However, many features, such as the Tobruk machine gun stand, were standardised.

Miles of coiled barbed-wire were strung around the harbours, beaches and defence installations and more than 165,000 mines were sown in coastal areas, harbour approaches and all potential landing sites.

The *OT* built a coal-fired power station in an abandoned quarry in St Peter's Valley in Jersey and an underground one beside Jersey's harbour at La Folie which was never completed. A similar plant in Guernsey was under construction but never completed so the island relied on existing power resources. It built huge stone crushers, workshops, ration stores and even bakeries. In Jersey the OT also had its own farm in Grands Vaux valley. It had its own hospital in each Island: in Jersey in the former Jersey College for Girls (the Red Crosses can still be seen) and in Guernsey it took over a large house at Ruette Braye. It established *OT Heime*, clubs where *OT* officers could relax and visiting engineers and other specialists could stay, in Jersey the Beaufort Hotel and in Guernsey the Red Lion, and its own brothels for the lower ranks with imported French women providing the appropriate services.

The *OT* brothel in Jersey was at the Abergeldie Hotel (the same one that was to be demolished to make way for an *OT* railway) and then at Norman House Hotel at First Tower although where the Guernsey one was (and there must have been one) remains a mystery. The *OT* also maintained punishment camps: at Les Vauxbelets in Guernsey, where a camp complete with barbed-wire, watchtowers and searchlights was established in a meadow, and on Elizabeth Castle on an islet in Jersey's St Aubin's Bay, from where escape was deemed impossible because of the surging tides which isolated the islet for all but four easily guarded hours a day (the Channel Islands have one of the greatest tidal ranges in the world). There was no special *OT* punishment camp in Alderney but errant workers were punished by being incarcerated in *Lager Sylt*, where the appalling conditions of the concentration camps of eastern Europe had been carefully re-created by the same *SS* units who managed the concentration camp at Neuengamme near Hamburg. The depth of cruelty against the inmates of *Lager Sylt* was unique in the Channel Islands, more of which we shall explore later.

Of the many coastal defence batteries created by the occupiers by far the most impressive was *Batterie Mirus* at La Frie Baton in the centre of Guernsey. The four guns of the battery were 30.5cm naval guns from a World War 1 Russian battleship. It took contractors Räbel-Werke more than a year and a half to build the gun emplacements and excavate the underground barracks for up to 400 men which utilised 45,000 cubic metres of concrete. The *Mirus* building programme diverted so many resources that other planned defences, particularly tunnels, were delayed or abandoned. The first gun was fired in April 1942 and the completed battery was handed over to the *Kriegsmarine* in November that year. The guns' range of more than thirty miles enabled them to dominate much of the Gulf of St Malo.

In Jersey, in the space of just two years, the occupiers and their reluctant workforce had turned thousands of tonnes of reinforced concrete into

59 infantry and naval coastal defence strongpoints and bunkers, with another 31 batteries inland.

The German chiefs of staff in Berlin were alarmed at what they perceived to be the profligate waste of resources but no one dare defy Hitler's instructions based on his belief that sovereignty in perpetuity of Britain's oldest possessions constituted an on-going major propaganda benefit. Almost a tenth of all the materials used on the 4,000-mile Atlantic Wall from the North Cape of Norway to the Pyrenees were expended on the non-strategic Channel Islands.

Many planned fortifications were incomplete and actually unusable by the time the *OT* labourers began to be withdrawn late in 1943 to work on the defences of mainland Europe, repairing bomb damage and strengthening the defences along the Atlantic Wall (some also finding themselves in the South of France), although local construction received another boost after D-Day when Jersey's east coast defences were strengthened. On 30 September 1943 Leslie Sinel noted: '. . . large numbers of Todts are leaving almost every day, together with quantities of building materials, concrete mixers, and even railway engines which have only been in the Island a couple of weeks'.

The Islands had other, unwelcome, visitors during the German occupation. Infectious diseases, many now eradicated, made their unpleasant presence felt. In Jersey the Medical Officer of Health, Dr McKinstry, reported that an epidemic of chicken pox in January 1941 caused the General Hospital to be closed and, in 1943, diphtheria brought to the Island by foreign workers in 1942 was diagnosed in 277 cases leading to 15 deaths, of which nine were children. By coincidence there was an outbreak in Paris at the same time with 279 cases leading to 34 deaths. The reason for the lesser death rate in Jersey was that children in the Channel Islands were better nourished. The diphtheria epidemic led to 7,600 people being inoculated and of these 7,000 were children. Drugs to combat this and other diseases, particularly tuberculosis and venereal diseases, were supplied from 1941 to 1944 by the International Red Cross, although stocks of such vital substances as insulin ran out leading to several deaths before the arrival of more regular Red Cross supplies from the beginning of 1945.

As the Occupation itself wore on and restrictions — such as the banning of radios — became tighter and tighter and foodstuffs bought by the buying commissions in France became less and less nourishing, Islanders began to manifest their objection to occupation in different ways. 'V' signs scrawled in tar appeared on walls, telephone wires laid between military installations were cut and military vehicles were found to have all sorts of strange substances in their fuel tanks.

On 2 July 1941 'V' signs were found daubed on various German signposts along the west coast of Guernsey. A little while earlier, in a broadcast to Europe received in the Islands, the BBC — in the person of one Colonel Brittain — had encouraged the people of occupied lands to put up the 'V' for victory and some Guernsey residents had taken the BBC at its word. The Germans were not amused and *Rittmeister Furst* (Prince) Eugen von Oettingen-Wallenstein, who had been appointed Military Commandant of the *Nebenstelle*, wrote to the Bailiff stating that such provocation would not be tolerated and demanding that an advertisement be inserted in the press to this effect. On 9 and 10 July notice was published in the *Gazette Officielle* of the Guernsey *Evening Press* offering a reward of £25 for giving information leading to the conviction of anyone for committing the offence of marking a 'V' or any other sign calculated to offend the German authorities or soldiery. The notice was signed by Victor Carey and caused widespread resentment. Suffice it to say that no reward was ever paid out. Instead 'V' signs proliferated but the Germans decided to join in and daubed up 'V' signs of their own claiming that it stood for the inevitable *German* victory. Nevertheless, after 'V' signs were chalked up at Guernsey's Beaulieu Hotel, all wireless sets belonging to locals within a thousand metres were confiscated. In Jersey two young women, one married with a baby, were caught putting a 'V' on a German sign. They were immediately arrested and sent to imprisonment in France without even being allowed to return home, a response the brutality of which was out of all proportion to the seriousness of the offence. They returned to the Island at the end of their sentence. One Islander noted in his diary that putting up 'V' signs appeared to achieve nothing other than to give the Germans the 'opportunity to pounce down on a defenceless people'.

Dire punishments were promised for the perpetrators of what the Germans defined as sabotage, including a well-publicised warning that 'saboteurs would be shot', likewise anyone trying to escape. One intrepid Jerseyman, Denis Vibert, actually escaped by boat to Britain early in 1941 and, despite his vessel being flooded which ruined his food and water supplies and the two outboard motors with which he had equipped his craft both failing, he rowed until picked up a Royal Navy destroyer, HMS *Brocklesby*, off Portland Bill. When he was landed HM Customs charged him 10s (50p) import duty on his dinghy *Ragamuffin*. The German headquarters in Paris initially responded to Denis Vibert's escape by allowing no one within ten kilometres of the coast. Except, as we have already seen, there is nowhere in the Islands that is *not* within ten kilometres of the coast! Incidentally, Denis, who died in September 2004, joined the RAF and became a Wellington pilot with Coastal Command. He emigrated to the USA after the war and died in Maine.

However the *Geheimefeldpolizei* were assiduous in hunting down 'saboteurs' and many Islanders found themselves incarcerated in their own Public Prison for a variety of offences or, much worse, condemned by a military court to be sent to France and, in a number of unfortunate instances, to horrific imprisonment and death in concentration camps. In Jersey 20 Islanders were imprisoned in France and were swept up by the notorious *Nacht und Nebel* (Night and Fog) decree issued on 7 December 1941 whereby prisoners became the property of the German state and could be made to disappear, usually to a death camp, at the state's whim. The crimes committed by these unfortunates, in the hazy light of history, seem comparatively trivial (attempting to escape the Island, concealing a radio set, sheltering escaped slave workers, etc) since none was a murderer or rapist but their actions were deemed to be prejudicial to the well-being of the German state. And death was the price paid. We will look at some of these acts of resistance in greater detail in the next chapter.

In October 1941 *Oberst* Schumacher resigned as *Feldkommandantur* due to ill-health and was replaced by *Oberst* Friedrich Knackfuss. Knackfuss, a 54-year-old Prussian given to wearing a monocle, was the son of the court painter to Kaiser Wilhelm II and possessed a much more aggressive personality than his predecessor, not only towards the Island authorities but also towards his own military colleagues.

On 8 June 1942 the *Feldkommandantur* announced that wireless sets were to be banned (even in Sark) although this time for strategic rather than punitive reasons. A high-level conference held the previous year in St Lô had deemed that since wireless receiving sets could be converted into transmitters by any competent radio mechanic, Islanders were likely to communicate to Britain the Germans' intentions with regard to their 'impregnable fortresses'. Such information could not be allowed to be 'escape'. What's more the BBC had been broadcasting (somewhat prematurely) that invasion of Continental Europe was imminent and encouraging those in occupied countries to offer every assistance to the liberators when they arrived. Seeing how enthusiastically Islanders had responded to the BBC's last good idea — the 'V' sign — the ban on wireless sets exhorting them to even greater anti-German efforts was not unreasonable. Although it was pointed out by Bailiff Coutanche that such a ban was against the Hague Convention, the orders to the *Feldkommandantur* had come from higher authority and had to be obeyed, even if the local authorities were uneasy about it. Fortunately the BBC anticipated this and told all its listeners how to make crystal sets which could be much more easily concealed.

Hopes for an early liberation were raised briefly, and just as rapidly dashed, when Islanders learned that British and Canadian troops had landed at Dieppe on the Normandy coast in August 1942. The battle lasted less than 12 hours and ended disastrously with almost 3,000 killed or wounded and a further 2,000 taken prisoner. Newsreels showing the British soldiers being taken into captivity were shown at the Islands' cinemas. Frank Keiller, a Jersey youth who would defy the Germans himself and pay the inevitable price of beatings and imprisonment, watching a German newsreel showing long columns of British prisoners on their way to Germany wondered if there were any young men of military age left in Britain. The rout at Dieppe caused many to think that the Germans were indeed invincible.

Vital items such as medicines began to be in short supply and in February 1942 requests from the Islands were made to the Joint War Organisation of the International Red Cross. A large consignment of medicines, drugs and medical stores was dispatched via the Red Cross, reaching the Islands in June and September 1942, with a further consignment in 1943. Further supplies of Vitamin D and insulin (much of the existing stock had been pilfered) were dispatched in 1943 and 1944.

In those pre-television days disseminating news in the Channel Islands was the prerogative of the wireless (the BBC) and the local press. In Jersey *The Evening Post* and *Les Chroniques de Jersey* catered for the English and French speaking populations while in Guernsey the news came via *The Star* in the morning and the *Evening Press* later in the day. Due to the pressures on newsprint supplies, these two newspapers were urged to merge. They didn't (not then anyway) but from 26 January 1942 they published on alternate days, the *Evening Press* on Mondays, Wednesdays and Fridays and *The Star* on Tuesdays, Thursdays and Saturdays.

However, the news they could print was heavily censored (particularly when the BBC was still a permitted prime news source). Many books about the Occupation publish a picture of a German censor, *Sonderführer* Hohl of *FK515*, bending over the *Evening Post's* stone (the heavy table upon which type is laid out and so called because it used to be made of stone) while a sceptical *EP* compositor, the late Henry Grube, looks on. The reality was a little more complex and is encapsulated in another photograph taken at the *Evening Post* which shows editor Arthur Harrison in the company of no fewer than three censors — the same aforesaid *Sonderführer* and a colleague from the Army and another from the Air Force for, as in Germany itself, the various arms of the *Wehrmacht* distrusted each other intensely even when it came to news management.

The newspapers adopted a simple strategy. News that the editors believed to be factual was printed impeccably, news passed to them by the Germans was printed exactly as it was presented and despite the evident fluency of many of the Germans when it came to speaking English, that same fluency rarely extended to the written word with sometimes hilarious results, eg, the use of the word 'backside' instead of 'reverse', the Censor being unable to tell the difference. Very soon the readers could.

Censorship was everywhere. Red Cross letters were censored. Mail within the Islands could be intercepted (and often was) and any reference to military matters could lead to a late night or early morning knock on the door.

The Islands were the occasional targets for Allied leaflet drops although just as often by accident rather than design when the wind blew propaganda leaflets intended for France on to their shores. The Germans rounded up these leaflets as quickly as they could and possession by an Islander of such 'enemy' propaganda was yet another offence against the German state. However, even they might have been amused to note that, in the absence of the real thing, many of these flimsy propaganda sheets ended up in Island toilets!

The Germans made use of the media themselves, producing local newspapers for their own troops. The *Deutsche Inselzeitung* (the German Island Newspaper) was printed as an integral part (usually the back page) of *The Evening Post* and the *Evening Press* (where it was called the *Deutsche Guernsey Zeitung*) two or three times a week. The news was essentially the same as that carried on the other pages except, of course, it was printed in German and their backsides were all reverses! Their other reading was usually *Signal!* — a very well-produced magazine (not dissimilar to *Picture Post*) that was printed in German and the languages of the countries that Germany had overrun and even English so that it could be circulated in the United States (until December 1941) and Eire.

In May 1942 the established media in Guernsey were joined by another: *GUNS*, the Guernsey Underground News Service. *GUNS* was the creation of Charles Machon, a linotype operator at *The Star*, and its name was devised by Frank Falla whose book *The Silent War* (Leslie Frewin, 1967) tells the story in detail. *GUNS* was printed daily (except Sundays) for almost two years on foolscap-sized sheets of tomato packing paper. Each edition reproduced the BBC 9.00pm news of the previous day with an update from the 8.00am news on the day of publication and consisted of around 800 words. Each edition was typed and carbon copies made and passed on so that more copies could be made. That way some 300 copies a day were printed and distributed, one copy finding its way, each day, to Victor Carey's desk.

The five men involved were Machon, Falla, Cecil Duquemin, Ernest Legg and Joseph Gillingham and with the widespread distribution of GUNS, it was inevitable that the Germans would try to discover who was publishing it and put a stop to their activities. In this they were helped by an Irish national, supposedly a friend of Charles Machon, who, given a copy of *GUNS* in February 1944, promptly handed it over to the *GFP* and told them where he had obtained it.

The five were arrested and tried before a military court. They were sentenced to varying terms of imprisonment from two years and four months for Charles Machon down to ten months for Joseph Gillingham. In April Machon was deported to Germany where he died five months later. He is buried in Hamelin.

On 4 June, just two days before D-Day, the other four were transported to France and thence to a prison in Frankfurt am Main where, Falla reports, there were 30 executions by guillotine a week. In August they, and seven other Channel Islanders, were moved to a prison in Naumburg in the centre of Germany where five of the Channel Islanders died. Frank Falla was liberated on 13 April 1945 and returned to Guernsey on 27 July. Like Joe Mière he has constantly sought recognition for those who suffered and died for their acts of resistance. Joseph Gillingham served a year in prison but died very soon after his release.

In September 1942 it was announced that Jersey residents born in England,

and their families, would be evacuated to Germany in retaliation, it is understood at Hitler's personal insistence, for the internment of German civilians in Persia (now Iran). The British government had asked the Persian government (ostensibly neutral) to 'hand over' German citizens in the country who were working against the Allied cause (and, of course, who were rather close to one of the Allies' principal sources of oil). Hitler was incensed and demanded reprisals against any British citizens the Foreign Ministry could conjure up. So guess where they looked?

Initially Hitler had insisted that the deportations should be to the Pripet Marshes in Russia (quite why he picked that God-forsaken wetland on the Eastern Front is not known) and that for every German deported from Persia, 10 prominent Islanders should be deported from the Channel Islands.

In practice the number of *Prominente* fell very short of Hitler's intentions. In all, 1,200 men, women and children from Jersey, 825 from Guernsey and 11 from Sark were to be deported to internment camps in Germany. Amongst them were several of the Islands' Jewish population including not only those who had registered as Jewish but others who had not but were either born in Britain or married to men who were. In Jersey the first 280 of these unfortunates were given barely 24 hours to prepare themselves for their forthcoming ordeal although the remainder had between four days' and two weeks' notice. In fact the German authorities in the Islands resisted complying with this order for as long as possible (for partly humanitarian but mostly logistic reasons, not the least of which was that neither the German High Command nor the Foreign Ministry could decide whose responsibility moving the Islanders would be) since the original order from Berlin had been received almost a year before, when the *Feldkommandantur* in Jersey and the *Nebenstelle* in Guernsey had demanded the appropriate details of potential deportees. They had also asked for the names and addresses of any resident Persians and, possibly to their surprise, were advised that there was one, a 69-year-old man. He was somehow overlooked when it came to making up the lists of those to be sent away.

That a direct order from the *Führer* should not be acted upon for almost a year speaks volumes for the bureaucratic muddle that was the German administration. However, at one of his interminable conferences Hitler suddenly demanded to know what had happened to the Channel Islanders he had ordered deported and was enraged to be told that they were still there. Despite the fact that the Persian problems had long been overtaken by world events, Hitler demanded that immediate steps be taken to remedy the situation.

Both Island authorities protested vigorously, reminding the Germans that they had promised that the lives and liberties of Islanders would be preserved. What the Germans were proposing was a shameful breach of faith. It is said that *Oberst* Knackfuss pointed to the signature on the document and advised that its owner's wishes overrode all other considerations. Bailiff Coutanche and the members of the Superior Council threatened to resign but recognised that since the Germans were clearly not going to go against the orders of their *Führer*, little purpose would be served and stayed at their posts. In Guernsey the Bailiff, Sherwill and Leale met with Dr Brosch of the *Nebenstelle* but received the same answer.

The Germans, many of whom obviously felt that their personal honour had been impugned, assured the Island authorities that the deportees would be well looked after in the internment camps.

The Germans demanded that the Island authorities select those to be deported and then deliver the notices of deportation. In Jersey, Bailiff Coutanche refused to allow the Constables to make the selection, although he did reluctantly agree to them delivering the notices. After the Liberation the police (in this case the Honorary Police) would be criticised for being too prepared to do the Germans' bidding and comparisons were even made with the French police who mainly did the Germans' job for them, particularly when it came to rounding up Jews. But such accusations are unfair and unrealistic. In agreeing to allow the Constables to deliver the notices Coutanche recognised that the deportees would be treated with a greater degree of sensitivity than had the activity been undertaken by the *Feldgendarmerie* who, had Coutanche refused, would certainly have carried out the task. In Sark a Major Shelton and his wife, two of the 11 to be deported, cut their wrists. The Major died but his wife survived.

The deportees were told to take with them warm clothes, solid boots, some provisions and luggage no heavier than they could carry. They were given little time to prepare and friends and neighbours helped by supplying clothes and even food. It was reported that, in Guernsey, when a can of soup was accidentally knocked over on the dockside, nearby North African prisoners of war were crawling in the gutter to lick up the contents.

Within 24 hours thousands of Islanders were turning out to see the unfortunates off at the quayside. The crowds were so large that the routes to the harbours were guarded by lines of German troops, many of whom, Islanders were glad to note, looked shamefaced at what was going on. In Jersey four youths — Frank Le Pennec, Hugh La Cloche, Frank Killer and Joe Mière — sang 'There'll always be an England' so lustily that they were arrested and given a beating by the naval police for their patriotic fervour.

The first deportees from Jersey, just 280 of them, left on 16 September on the steamer *La France* bound for St Malo and who knew what. Two days later a further 460 left on *La France* although another 300 returned home when a Dr Shone representing the Red Cross complained about the conditions on the freighter *Robert Müller* which had only just discharged a cargo of coal and *Oberst* Knackfuss agreed. Some of those returning home found their houses stripped by neighbours who had clearly thought they were never coming back!

However, all the deportees had left the Islands by 28 September and after some had a brief sojourn at Dorsten in the Ruhr, were dispersed amongst three camps in southern Germany — at Laufen, Bad Wurzach and Biberach — near the Swiss and Austrian borders.

There were more deportations in January and February 1943, this time as a reprisal for a commando raid on Sark (of which more a little later). This time the Germans wanted a whole range of 'undesirables' to be deported and these included anyone who had offended against the regime, Communists and others politically suspect, the work-shy, young men without important work (in the German sense), former officers, Jews and Freemasons, people prominent in public life, rich men known to be anti-German and, oddly enough, anyone on Sark not involved in agriculture or who lived in the centre of the Island! Around a thousand would be involved, plus their families. In the event, by 30 January, for all sorts of reasons, only 115 men and 86 women and children were deported but these included Ambrose Sherwill who was deported on the grounds that he was a former British officer and not a native Guernseyman (although Sherwill himself believed that it was also for his role in the Symes/Nicolle affair) and Robert Hathaway, husband of the Dame of Sark, who was actually an American. Among the number were three Jews from Guernsey (plus the husband of one of them who was deported because his wife was a Jew) and five Jews (three from one family) from Jersey. Many of these deportees went to the same camps as their predecessors (Sherwill becoming Camp Senior at Laufen) but others were sent to a former lunatic asylum in Kreuzberg in Silesia. There were exemptions but whatever were the rules the Germans applied they did not apply them to those two worthies, Sherwill and Hathaway.

On 8 March, to the evident relief of Germans and Islanders alike, it was announced that 'as far as can be judged, the evacuation is over'.

The claim by the Germans prior to the deportations that the deportees would be well looked after in the internment camps turned out to be largely true, despite the camps coming under the blanket jurisdiction of *Reichsführer-SS* Heinrich Himmler. In practice the camps were administered by the Württemburg Interior Ministry and guarded by the *Schutzpolizei* (civilian police), largely old soldiers from the Great War who were mostly benign, kind to children and respectful to ladies!

The camp at Laufen, which housed unattached men, was in a converted *Schloss* just over the Austrian border from the village of Obendorf where the Christmas carol 'Silent Night' had been composed. The camp produced its own memorial book, *The Bird Cage*, compiled in 1944 and published a year later.

Bad Wurzach and Biberach were family camps where the regime was comparatively relaxed. The camp at Bad Wurzach had not long been evacuated by Corsican prisoners of war whose concept of personal hygiene was somewhat primitive and they left behind a legacy of fleas and one room (58) infested with rats. The Swiss YMCA provided delousing powder but it seemed to send the fleas to sleep rather than kill them and when they awoke they were ravenous! Biberach, a former 'Strength through Joy' centre, was bitterly cold but clean and tidy. The internees were kept under almost continuous observation by the International Red Cross who also provided prisoner-of-war food parcels. The camps were in an agricultural region largely ignored by Allied bombers and thus the inmates did not suffer any reprisals from local inhabitants and relations with the local townspeople were often cordial.

Once in the camps the deportees were expected to organise themselves and appoint a 'Camp Senior' as liaison with the local authorities. There were few guards to keep watch over them and some internees volunteered to work on farms and would mingle with the local population. Those who did were not at all popular since Hitler had once proclaimed, in one of his interminable speeches, that 'every worker, even the humblest farm labourer, is a soldier of the Reich'!

Nevertheless life in the camps was bleak and boring, particularly for the children and teenagers, despite almost constant activities including concerts, sports and education classes. With regular Red Cross parcels the internees fared much better than those Channel Islanders who had been deported to penal institutions and better even than those they had left behind, so much so that in March 1944 the internees at Biberach (who mostly came from Guernsey) were able to send 300 pieces of soap and 500 tins of cocoa to children at home! Likewise the internees at Bad Wurzach decided that each family should send one complete, unopened, Canadian Red Cross parcel to a friend or relative in Jersey. They were all delivered safely.

Like their counterparts in the Islands, the internees were starved of news until in Laufen Jerseyman Bill Williams constructed a clandestine radio set (known as The Forbidden Whisper) able to receive BBC bulletins.

It was only towards the war's end that conditions deteriorated but this was a reflection of what was going on all around them rather than any deliberate policy.

There were frequent suggestions that the internees might be exchanged or repatriated and, indeed, 150 sick and elderly internees were repatriated from Biberach and Bad Wurzach in September 1944 and more in March 1945. However, the majority were still there (other than those who had died — mostly through natural causes) when their camps were liberated in April 1945 by the Allied advance into southern Germany.

* * *

Despite the fact that Jersey is at least 90 miles south of the nearest point of the English mainland, escapes by boat from the Islands were contemplated and the success of Denis Vibert emulated.

One such escape attempt took place on 3 May 1942 when three Jersey teenagers, Peter Hassall, Dennis Audrain and Maurice Gould, carrying photographs of the Island's fortifications (mostly copies of snapshots taken by soldiers and developed by Peter's father who ran a film processing workshop licensed by the Germans), attempted the hazardous journey across the English Channel. However, still just a few hundred metres from their starting point at Green Island on Jersey's south coast, swells caused their 4-metre dinghy to capsize and Dennis, a non-swimmer, was drowned. His two companions were captured and after interrogation by the Navy police and the *GFP* (the incriminating photographs having been discovered) they were deported to France where they underwent interrogation by the real *Gestapo* and then ultimately to Wittlich prison in Germany where Maurice Gould died of tuberculosis and was buried in a local cemetery. Peter Hassall survived but was not to be liberated from his German prison until 9 May 1945. On 3 May 1997, 55 years to the day after the escape attempt, Maurice Gould's remains were interred in the Allied War Cemetery in St Helier's Howard Davis Park.

In April 1943 barges carrying supplies to Jersey from France were attacked by the RAF and one barge was sunk. Without any consultation with the local authorities, *Oberst* Knackfuss published a notice in *The Evening Post* to the effect that the whole of the English civilian population was to have its rations reduced because of the RAF attack. The Superior Council decided not only to protest to the *Feldkommandantur* but also, for the first time, to Switzerland, the Protecting Power, through the Swiss Ambassador in Berlin. The next day Bailiff Coutanche was invited to confer, for the first time, by telephone with Bailiff Carey in Guernsey where the restrictions were also to apply. Coutanche advised Carey that he intended to protest since the Germans' action was a reprisal and against the Hague Convention. As soon as he mentioned the word 'reprisal', the telephone connection was cut.

An acrimonious meeting with Knackfuss followed at which Coutanche delivered the formal letter to the Protecting Power. The *Feldkommandant* refuted that the act of cutting the rations was a reprisal (since the RAF was to blame for sending supplies to the bottom of the Channel in the first place) and demanded that Coutanche withdraw the letter since such a course of action was a very serious matter indeed. Coutanche refused but, as a result, he believed, of a meeting between Knackfuss and *Befehlshaber* von Schmettow, the *Feldkommandant* eventually agreed to limit the restriction to bread which was in short supply anyway (and thus the cut was justified) and accept the principle that without any such shortage cuts in rations to the civilian population were contrary to the Hague Convention. Such a victory did little to improve relations between Coutanche and Knackfuss (and even the Guernsey authorities protested that Coutanche had been too intransigent until Knackfuss backed down) but Coutanche had long recognised that, except when the *Führer's* signature was on an order, his German antagonists preferred to obey the rules.

Early in 1943 those with concealed radios could tell their friends that the tide of war was gradually changing. Where there had been only German victories there were now defeats and retreats.

For one Channel Island, however, the changes in the occupiers' fortunes had little impact.

Alone of the Channel Islands, Alderney, just three miles by one, was to witness genuine Nazi brutality and little but.

The Island, deserted except by its handful of stubborn civilians, was already the most defended of the Islands, being ringed by sturdy 18th and 19th century forts built to defend the Island and a major British fleet anchorage against the French, who were just six miles away. These crumbling fortifications were reinforced and new strongpoints constructed. In October 1940 George Pope (who had returned with his wife in July to act as a harbour pilot for the Germans) was quoted in a German radio broadcast, denying a statement broadcast by the BBC that Alderney had been completely abandoned, stating that 'we have been and are being treated with the greatest respect and kindness by the forces occupying the Channel Islands'. He even added that he was thankful to the German authorities for allowing him to say so!

The original German intent for Alderney was to provide foodstuffs — cereals and vegetables — for Guernsey but this scheme became secondary when Hitler's order to make the Channel Islands impregnable fortresses began to take effect. In November 1941 there were 2,426 men in Alderney (and one woman, Mrs Pope). Of these, 1,104 were from the army, 1,100 from the *Luftwaffe* and 179 from the *Kriegsmarine*. There were also 43 civilians and 31 horses. To comply with Hitler's order almost 500 more workers were expected, 40 civilian craftsmen labourers and 455 prisoners of war. Concern was expressed by the *Kommandant, Hauptmann* Carl Hoffmann, that although the Island's foodstocks were supposed to be able to feed 3,000 men for 60 days, the reality was that due to shipping difficulties — the principal port of supply for Alderney was Cherbourg — and bad management in Guernsey, there was actually less than half the amount required. Angry radio messages were sent, particularly when mail for the Alderney garrison failed to arrive. *Rittmeister* von Oettingen was quick to respond, not only accusing his colleague of a lack of 'comradely spirit' but also threatening to take the matter to a higher authority if Hoffmann complained again!

Most of the civilian workers came from Guernsey and were either involved in exploiting Alderney's soil to grow food or maintenance work on the breakwater but when, late in 1941, the forced and slave labourers of the *Organisation Todt* arrived in considerable numbers to begin building real fortifications, the civilians were returned to Guernsey. However, tradesmen from both Jersey and Guernsey were sent to Alderney in 1943 to carry out repairs to houses and other buildings.

The *OT* workers were housed in four camps of wooden huts behind barbed-wire fences which had been built by French and Belgian volunteer workers who were well paid for the work. The camps were named after islands in the North Sea, *Helgoland*, *Norderney*, *Bokum* and *Sylt* and between them could house as many as 5,000 inmates. Initially the camps housed European and Russian labourers although German and volunteer specialists were housed in *Bokum* camp.

In March 1943 *Lager Sylt* was handed over by the *OT* to the *SS*. The guards and administrators were drawn from Neuengamme while the thousand inmates were transferred from Sachsenhausen concentration camp to the north of Berlin. Half the inmates were Russian prisoners of war or partisans, 200 or so were German political prisoners, criminals, the 'work-shy' and conscientious objectors and the remainder were political prisoners from all over Europe. They formed *SS Baubrigade 1* (SS Work Brigade No 1). Security at *Lager Sylt* was significantly greater than at the other camps, with a densely wired inner compound to house the prisoners and an outer wire perimeter with concrete sentry boxes. The camp commandant was *SS Hauptsturmführer* Maximilian List (who lived in a bungalow outside the perimeter fence which was joined to the camp itself by a tunnel) and his deputies *SS Obersturmführer* Klebeck and Braun. The regime in the camps (*Norderney* was taken over by the *SS* in February 1944) was extremely harsh with prisoners being beaten for the most trivial of reasons or no reason at all and often beaten to death.

One former inmate of another Alderney camp, Spanish Republican Francisco Font, recalled: 'While doing jobs in Alderney we were near Sylt one day where we saw a Russian strung up on the main gate. On his chest he had a sign on which was written "for stealing bread". His body was left hanging like that for four days.'

Not only did the *SS* and the *OT* overseers beat and mistreat their charges, they also stole their meagre rations and sold them so the inmates rapidly became seriously undernourished. *Lager Norderney* was used as a punishment camp for workers from the other Islands and even Channel Islanders who had offended the authorities were incarcerated there as were 300 French Jews. After the war one inmate, Gordon Prigent from Jersey, reported that within a month of his arrival at *Norderney* the average death rate was two or three a day. At the time of his arrival, he and his colleagues had been in normal health but a starvation diet and constant beatings soon reduced them to an extremely feeble condition. No clothing was issued and the prisoners had to make do with whatever they were wearing when they were conscripted although they were supplied with wooden clogs when their shoes wore out.

The number of deaths amongst the Alderney workforce was the highest of all the Channel Islands, earning for itself the sobriquet 'The Island of Death'. Despite the somewhat sensational stories to emerge from the Island after the Liberation that thousands had died, many of whom, it was claimed, had been tossed over the cliffs or tipped off the end of the breakwater, the number of deaths recorded was actually less than 400 (397) compared with 96 in Guernsey and 116 in Jersey. The most common recorded causes of death were exhaustion and heart failure, followed by dysentery and tuberculosis, although a surprisingly large number died of poisoning caused by eating deadly nightshade berries and hemlock mistakenly believing them to be edible.

Although the number of deaths were almost certainly fewer than postwar sensation-seeking journalists might have surmised, for the unfortunates confined behind the wire there is no doubt that Alderney was a true hell on earth. The camps were run by *Kapos,* German prisoners who were often more brutal than their *SS* guards. What's more, List and his staff were not responsible to the Island Commandant since, being *SS,* they reported directly to their masters in Berlin. *Lager Sylt* has since become notorious as being the only German concentration camp to exist on British soil. After the Liberation British War Crimes personnel investigated the goings-on at the Alderney camps and although there were plenty of witnesses to the brutality of the regime and the sadism of the guards, none was around to be prosecuted, Maximilian List dying in his bed in Hamburg many years later.

At the beginning of 1942, Operation 'Blazing' was among a number of operations conceived to launch an attack on Alderney. To date the commando raids on the Islands had yielded little of value but in this instance the Chief of Combined Operations, Vice-Admiral Lord Louis Mountbatten, approved the concept, believing it to be good for morale and prestige. 'Blazing' would be (if successful) a propaganda triumph and would even open up the second front constantly being demanded by Joseph Stalin, who himself had suggested that the Channel Islands would be suitable for such an assault on German occupied territory. Furthermore the occupation of Alderney would provide a naval base for attacking the German convoys linking the Channel and Biscay ports and it could be a site for a radar station, extending the RAF's coverage, and provide an emergency air strip. There were even strategic advantages since Alderney back in British hands would divert *Luftwaffe* squadrons from other fronts and pull land forces into the Cherbourg peninsula which would be better employed elsewhere.

This was the theory. And, to Mountbatten, it was a good one. The lack of British civilians meant that the casualties (the ones that caused critical headlines) from aerial and naval bombardments were bound to be small in number although quite what effect the planned low-level 65-minute softening-up bombing attack on the Island's defences at dawn would have had on the thousands of forced and slave labourers on their work projects and in their camps has not been recorded. The plan visualised an ensuing infantry assault from the air and sea that would put almost 5,000 troops ashore and be concluded by lunchtime. Once established the garrison would be supplied on a weekly basis with 400 tons of food, ammunition and general supplies.

Air Chief Marshal Sir Arthur Harris, head of Bomber Command, was scornful. He was not prepared to risk his precious bomber crews on a target where they would be so vulnerable to flak and enemy fighters. There were major enemy airfields within 20 miles and the nearest RAF airfield was 70 miles away. Major-General F. A. M. (Boy) Browning, he of subsequent Arnhem fame, and chief of the newly formed Airborne Division, was also opposed to the scheme. Casualties would be too high and for what real purpose? It was not on. And it wasn't going to be.

Mountbatten, used to getting his own way, persisted and resurrected 'Blazing' again in the summer. But since he quoted the same tenuous benefits, he got the same result.

Nevertheless the Royal Navy did have some successes attacking shipping plying between Alderney and Cherbourg, sinking several coasters carrying supplies to the Island and on occasion causing the loss of personnel going on leave.

The sinking of two coasters in February 1943 caused the Flag Officer, Sea Defences, West to consider court-martialling whoever it was who had allowed the vessels to sail without a naval escort but since that was the *Hafenkommandant* and he had gone down with one of the ships, all that happened was that a more experienced *Hafenkommandant* was appointed, radio communications and escort services were improved and faster ships were used in future.

SS Hauptsturmführer List was posted from Alderney to Oslo in the spring of 1944 and was succeeded by *SS Obersturmführer* Braun who, if anything, was even worse than his predecessor, particularly with regard to misappropriating the camp inmates' already meagre rations.

Lager Sylt was progressively evacuated by the *SS* between December 1943 and February 1944, the workers being sent to the Cherbourg area. However, following objections from *General der Artillerie* Erich Marcks, General Officer Commanding LXXXIV Corps in north-western France (not noted for his tolerance of the manner in which the *SS* treated its charges), they were returned to Alderney. *Sylt* was eventually evacuated in July 1944 and the *SS* took with them all the surviving prisoners who were dispersed to other concentration camps in Germany including Buchenwald. *Sylt* remained unused thereafter, its huts being progressively broken up for firewood for use in the other camps during the harsh winter of 1944/5.

At Mountbatten's instigation, in 1943 a series of plans were drawn up for combined operations offensives against all three of the Channel Islands under the overall banner of Operation 'Constellation' which incorporated Operation 'Concertina', an offensive against Alderney; Operation 'Coverlet', an offensive against Guernsey; and Operation 'Condor', an offensive against Jersey. In the event, none of these was ever put into effect, the larger objective of Europe itself taking up all the planners' resources.

However, although all plans for any invasions of the Channel Islands had been shelved indefinitely, the Islands were subject to attacks by the Royal Air Force and Royal Navy including a bombardment of Alderney by the 16in guns of HMS *Rodney*. *Rodney* managed to score several direct hits on bunkers but to little effect although two soldiers were killed.

German transports were bombed in the Islands' harbours and attacks on ships on passage between the Islands and the nearby French ports were carried out to such good effect that voyages were authorised only during the hours of darkness. Escorts were increased to deter sneak attacks. The Royal Navy too was active in the Bay of St Malo, rendering the operation of convoys between the Islands and around the French coast a hazardous and costly business despite the threat posed by the 30.5cm guns of *Batterie Mirus*.

However, the Royal Navy did not always have its own way for on the night of 23/24 October 1943, the Dido Class light cruiser HMS *Charybdis* with six accompanying destroyers was carrying out Operation 'Tunnel' to the west of the Channel Islands, hoping to intercept SS *Münsterland*, a German freighter carrying vital war supplies from Brest. The RN ships were detected by the *Gema* radar on the *Kriegsmarine* tower at Les Landes in Jersey and *Münsterland's* escorts, which included five *Elbing* Class T (torpedo)-boats, were alerted. In an action which began at 01.30hrs (the moon had risen at 01.25) HMS *Charybdis* was torpedoed by *T23* and sank and a destroyer, HMS *Limbourne,* was torpedoed by *T22* and disabled, eventually being sunk by her own consorts. More than 500 officers and ratings lost their lives and over the next few days the bodies of British sailors were washed up on the Channel Islands: 29 on Jersey, 21 on Guernsey and one on Sark. Many more were washed up on the coast of France and were buried near Dinard. In Jersey and Guernsey the seamen were buried with full military honours and the funerals were attended by thousands of Islanders. At the graveside, *Befehlshaber* Graf von Schmettow paid tribute to the dead sailors. 'We honour them as soldiers. They did their duty for their country.' The London *Daily Mail* published a photograph of the funeral on 27 January 1944.

Nevertheless, the outpourings of such pro-British sentiment made the Germans nervous and although they continued to bury Allied servicemen with full military honours, the public was barred from the events. In Guernsey, *Charybdis* Day, the anniversary of the funeral, is still commemorated.

Despite reverses throughout Europe in 1943, the German forces in the Channel Islands continued their fortification programme, albeit on a reduced scale. By January 1944, 1,555 acres of Jersey's rich arable land (circa 10% of the total) had been lost to military constructions leaving the Island littered with building materials, often disused railway tracks and stark edifices in concrete and steel. Because of the loss of usable land for growing foodstuffs, it was suggested that all remaining private lawns that had not already been dug up, be turned over and planted. The Islands' cattle, pure breeds for two centuries, came under threat as other breeds were imported to boost milk and beef production. Farmers, jealous of the local cows' uniqueness, kept the breeds well apart. Animals had to be registered with the German authorities but since it was almost always only the farmer who was present when his cows

Above:
In June 1940, with their market in the United Kingdom no longer available to them, Jersey farmers gave away their potatoes to an eager crowd of young consumers. *Jersey Evening Post*

Below:
Potential evacuees wait patiently on St Helier's quayside for the ships that will take them to England. *Jersey Evening Post*

Above:
Tragically mistaken for military vehicles, these lorries loaded only with tomatoes are now the mangled and bloody aftermath along St Peter Port harbour of the German bombing of 28 June 1940. *Channel Islands Occupation Society*

Above:
Hauptmann Erich Gussek, Jersey's first commandant, prepares to leave Government House in his requisitioned limousine with John Curwood, its requisitioned driver. The bonnet mascot hints at the Wolseley's peacetime role. Note the distinctive 'J' plate carried by all vehicles in Jersey.
Michael Ginns collection

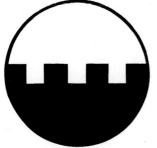

Left:
The insignia of *Infanterie Division 319.*
The device is now used by the Channel Islands Occupation Society.

or pigs gave birth, the numbers given to the inspectors were often fictitious and sooner or later roast beef, veal or pork would make a welcome appearance in the family's diet. However, cows and their milk were targets for thieves — civilians, troops and labourers — and farmers had to be constantly on their guard to protect these valuable assets.

Not everyone regarded the Germans with fear and trepidation. There were some, just a few, who, for reasons of their own, looked forward to a German victory, convinced that life under the Nazis would be an improvement on their pre-war lot. There were others who regarded the Occupation as an opportunity to settle old scores, expose jealousies and repay slights. This phenomenon most commonly manifested itself in the stream of anonymous denunciations delivered (usually by post) to the *Feldkommandantur* and the *Geheimefeldpolizei*. Fortunately, employees at the Islands' General Post Offices, at great risk to themselves because they were under almost constant German scrutiny, were often able to intercept these letters and while not all could be destroyed (and, indeed, most were not) those being denounced could be forewarned (as was Louisa Gould) that they should expect a late-night hammering on their front door and anything incriminating (usually a concealed wireless set) should be moved. It is sad to record that of the 20 from Jersey who died in concentration camps, a quarter of them were denounced by fellow Islanders.

While this is perhaps the least agreeable aspect of the German occupation of the Channel Islands (and defies any form of justification) because there were occasionally deadly consequences of their actions, since the writers of these letters were mostly anonymous and thus could not be identified after the war, the young women and men (and occasionally the not so young) who consorted with the Germans had reserved for them the most opprobrium, that persists even to this day.

Between the outbreak of war and the invasion of July 1940, several thousand young men left the Islands to join HM Forces leaving a huge void in the social, marital and sexual aspirations of the equal or even greater number of young women left behind. It is not surprising, therefore, that when these young men were replaced by several thousand other young men liaisons should develop. The state of war that actually existed between the countries of the participants was largely illusory since the occupying army took its place in queues for the buses (while they were running) and in the shops (while they were open), and except when on duty rarely wore side arms, and an awful lot of them were blond and good looking, and many spoke very good English and took every opportunity during that first hot summer to disport themselves on the beaches with very little on.

Women who consorted with the Germans were called 'Jerrybags' and even today there is probably no greater insult. Some were well known, such as 'Ginger Lou' (Alexandrine Baudains, who was also known as Mimi the Spy) who flaunted her liaisons with German officers in Jersey. Jerrybags often found swastikas daubed on their front doors although when two girls working at Boots the Chemists in Jersey were perceived to be over-friendly with the occupiers and someone scrawled 'Boots for Bags' on the premises, the perpetrators were caught and imprisoned.

There *were* some genuine love matches although those that survived the Liberation could be counted on the fingers of two hands, perhaps even one. In these instances the people of Guernsey tended to be more tolerant than their neighbours in Jersey. Many women and girls, perhaps in naivety, really did believe that the war and the occupation had changed the established order of things for ever. It is difficult to believe otherwise when gazing on the photographs of these ladies and their German admirers, for why else would they have allowed themselves to provide such readily available evidence of their fraternisation with an enemy? There were, of course, women and girls who recognised that they were sitting on an asset that could yield them extra rations and privileges and above all relieve the tedium and deprivation of a life without radio, Hollywood films, lively dance halls open to the small hours and cafés with more than one stodgy menu. The German authorities provided brothels for their troops but not all Germans wanted to avail themselves of the paid for and oft-used charms of the resident French prostitutes even though they were subject to regular medical examinations (despite the protests of the local doctors who were instructed to carry them out) and were classified by the *Feldkommandantur* as 'heavy workers' and thus qualified for extra rations. Liaisons with local girls, themselves denied male company, were inevitable although military regulations prohibited such relationships.

At the Liberation some of the local girls who had consorted with the Germans were abused and physically assaulted although the police or the military managed to intervene before anyone was seriously injured or worse. However, the shaving of heads, tarring and feathering and other humiliations piled on the girls in France who had been too friendly with the occupiers were largely missing.

Published estimates of as many as 900 births in Jersey to local girls and German fathers are a gross exaggeration, the true number, according to Dr John Lewis who delivered most of them, being less than a tenth of that. Between 1941 and 1945 there were 471 illegitimate births in the Channel Islands but it must be remembered that it was not just Germans who were impregnating the local womenfolk, since there were liaisons between Islanders not married to each other, with forced and even slave labourers and even those young Jerseymen who came to puberty during the Occupation years. The best estimate is that some 120 of the illegitimate births were to German fathers. This did not stop a unit of the German *Rasse- und Siedlungshauptamt* (Race and Settlement Head Office) visiting the Islands in May 1944 with a view to transporting the babies born of German fathers to *SS Lebensborn* (Fountain of Life) homes in France and even Germany should they prove racially suitable to perpetuate the Master Race. Fortunately D-Day intervened.

The Associated Life Offices Central Fund (Jersey)

On behalf of The Pearl Assurance Co.

Fire and General and Accident Cover Note.

No. P.E.938F.   18th May   194 4.

Mr. Eric H. Tabb   of   4 Malakoff Place, First Tower,

Jersey.   having this day proposed an Insurance

against Fire only.

with the said Company/Society for   Two Hundred

pounds on   Household Goods & Personal Effects as

described on proposal.

and having paid the premium stated below, the said property will be held insured hereby

until the   17th   day of   May   194 5 : or until notice be

previously given that the proposal is declined, pending the issue of the duly stamped

policy.   It is also expressly understood and agreed that :—

(a) The Cover Note is issued subject to the Memorandum governing the activities of the Associated Life Offices Central Fund Scheme (Jersey) and to any amendment that may be deemed necessary by the Committee of Management of the said Central Fund Scheme.

(b) No liability shall attach to the Company under this insurance for any consequence whether direct or indirect, of War, Invasion, Act of Foreign Enemy, Hostilities (whether war be declared or not), Civil War, Rebellion, Revolution, Insurrection or Military or Usurped Power.

(c) The insurance risk described herein is subject to and governed by all the current terms and conditions of the usual policy, notwithstanding the non-issue of same, during the period of this Cover Note, as from the above date.

Sum Assured £ 200. 0. 0d.   Premium £   4/-.

Signature for the Company/Society

Signature for Committee of Management

(left margin, rotated:) All claims of any description must be registered at District office within 7 days of occurrence.

Left:
Life goes on. However, this cover note points out that no liability shall attach to the Company for any consequence of war, invasion, hostilities or the act of a foreign enemy! Perhaps that's why the premium was only 4s (20p). *Author's collection*

Above:
The identity card of Alexander Coutanche, Bailiff of Jersey throughout the German Occupation. What other head of state would be obliged to carry an identity card?
The Hon John Coutanche

Above:
The German plan of the Channel Islands.
Channel Islands Occupation Society

Area Chief Wardens and Post Leaders.

AIR RAID ACTION.

I wish to thank you for your loyal services in the past and, particularly, in the recent troubles, and there is no doubt that the whole Island appreciates your services.

Since I have been put in charge of A.R.P., I have come to several decisions which I hope will meet with your approval.

WARDENS. Should the Alarm sound, or an unexpected raid take place, Wardens, like every one else, should take cover at once, and so avoid becoming a casualty. When the All Clear sounds, if there has been firing and Bombs dropping, Wardens must patrol their Districts, and report damage, where necessary, to St. John's Ambulance for casualties, the Fire Station for fire, and for other damage of less urgent nature either to yourself or A.R.P. Headquarters, 'Phone 1721, as before. The telephone messages should be given to the Exchange as Air Raid Damage for casualties, etc., and, otherwise, as A.R.P. Service Message.

UNEXPLODED SHELLS & BOMBS. When any such are found the Warden must stand by it, so as to prevent anyone approaching, and obtain any available assistance in this guard duty until such time as it is taken over by the Police or German Authorities. Reports concerning unexploded Shells and Bombs should be communicated to the Police Station.

All Wardens are particularly requested to carry their Whistles and Armbands with them continually, because the Armband is recognised by the German Authorities at all times, and when actually on Air Raid Duty will, naturally, wear their White Helmets. These latter orders are instructions from the German Commandant, and should be strictly adhered to for the safety and efficiency of A.R.P. Personnel.

FIRST-AID POSTS. A skeleton staff of two living near the Post should go there as soon as the All Clear sounds, and if nothing untoward has happened should remain there till they get the White Signal by 'Phone, or if in doubt should communicate with A.R.P. Headquarters.

Should Firing or Bombing have taken place, all First Aid Workers will go to the Posts and remain there until instructed to leave. Any First Aiders who find themselves a great distance from their Posts at the time should communicate with their Posts after the All Clear for instructions from their leaders by means of an A.R.P. Service message. First Aiders, like Wardens, should carry their Armbands with them always, and wear their White Helmets when going on duty. They should also have their White Helmets with them when they are turning out for practice.

In the event of Transport being required, other than the Island Ambulance, it will be in order to requisition any suitable Petrol-Driven or other vehicle obtainable.

PLEASE NOTE.—THE FOREST DRESSING STATION has now been abolished.

W. L. HENDERSON,

15th August, 1940. Chief A R.P. Organiser,

TOWN ARSENAL.

BANKS, BROWNSEY & CO., LTD., GUERNSEY 400/8/40

Above:

The Islands had been bombed by the RAF two weeks before this notice was issued on 15 August 1940 but other than pinprick raids would not be bombed again. None the less, in Guernsey the ARWs were ready. *Trevor du Feu collection*

Right:
The German artillery curtain around the Channel Islands did not, as intended, seal off the Bay of St Malo and with the Kriegsmarine largely ineffective due to lack of fuel, Allied access to Granville and eventually St Malo was virtually unhindered. *Channel Islands Occupation Society*

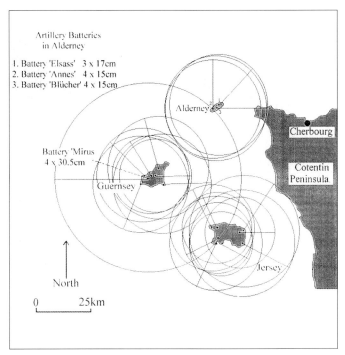

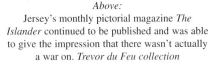

Above:
Jersey's monthly pictorial magazine *The Islander* continued to be published and was able to give the impression that there wasn't actually a war on. *Trevor du Feu collection*

Above:
The centre page of this edition of *The Islander* featured an attractive street-scene drawing — the only indication of the Occupation being the swastika flying above the town hall. *Trevor du Feu collection*

Above:

This country cottage was in reality part of the massively fortified *Kernwerk*, the Germans' battle headquarters in Jersey. *Channel Islands Occupation Society*

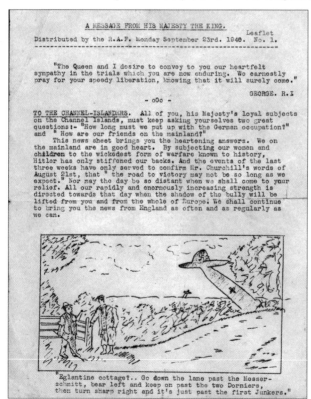

```
                A MESSAGE FROM HIS MAJESTY THE KING.
                                              Leaflet
     Distributed by the R.A.F. Monday September 23rd. 1940.   No. 1.
     -------------------------------------------------------------

          "The Queen and I desire to convey to you our heartfelt
     sympathy in the trials which you are now enduring.  We earnestly
     pray for your speedy liberation, knowing that it will surely come."

                                                    GEORGE. R.I

                         - oOo -

     TO THE CHANNEL-ISLANDERS.  All of you, his Majesty's loyal subjects
     on the Channel Islands, must keep asking yourselves two great
     questions:- "How long must we put up with the German occupation?"
     and  " How are our friends on the mainland?"
          This news sheet brings you the heartening answers.  We on
     the mainland are in good heart.  By subjecting our women and
     children to the wickedest form of warfare known to history,
     Hitler has only stiffened our backs.  And the events of the last
     three weeks have only served to confirm Mr. Churchill's words of
     August 21st, that " the road to victory may not be so long as we
     expect."  Nor may the day be so distant when we shall come to your
     relief. All our rapidly and enormously increasing strength is
     directed towards that day when the shadow of the bully will be
     lifted from you and from the whole of Europe.  We shall continue
     to bring you the news from England as often and as regularly as
     we can.
```

```
     "Eglantine cottage?.. Go down the lane past the Messer-
     schmitt, bear left and keep on past the two Dorniers,
     then turn sharp right and it's just past the first Junkers."
```

Above:

A typed and hand-drawn message from His Majesty the King distributed by the Royal Air Force on Monday, 23 September 1940.

Trevor du Feu collection

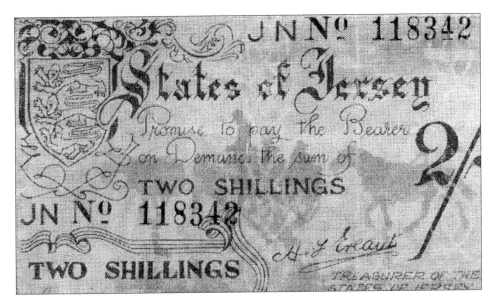

Above:
The successor to the 'Dirty Bertie'. A States of Jersey 2s (10p) note designed by Jersey artist Edmund Blampied RA.
Trevor du Feu collection

Left:
Guernsey workers in Alderney. The foremen are the ones in uniform!
Carel Toms collection

Opposite:
Designer Edmund Blampied RA incorporated 'GR' into the design of the Jersey 3d stamp (on either side of the figure 3). The illustration is of La Rocco Tower in Jersey's St Ouen's Bay which was used by the Germans for target practice.
Author's collection

Datum_____19

AUSWEIS.

D_____

ist berechtigt die Stadt und die Verkehrswege der Insel während der Sperrstunden und bei Nacht zu betreten.

_____
Feldkommandantur

Above:
A pass that allowed a doctor to be out on the roads after curfew.
Trevor du Feu collection

Left:
Berlin is that way.
Pictures like this were
valuable propaganda
tools. *Author's collection*

Right:
Jersey's unofficial
anthem, *'Beautiful
Jersey'*, with some new
and appropriate words.
Trevor du Feu collection

Order Your
WIRELESS SET
from
W.H.COLE
61 HALKETT PLACE,
who has NOT worked for the
enemy during the Occupation
Sole Agent for MURPHY RADIO Sets

Left:
A trader is keen to
announce that he didn't
collaborate.
Trevor du Feu collection

Right:
The author's father's
identity card.
Author's collection

Beautiful Jersey. 1941.

Beautiful Jersey, Isle of the free.
Happy indeed were the dwellers in thee,'
Beautiful Jersey, Set is Thy Sun.
Now must thy name be writ, Isle of the Hun.

Beautiful Jersey in happier days.
Hoardes of wild trippers invested thy bays.
Now, thro the lanes of thy green countryside.
Cartloads of steel hatted enemies ride.
And in the streets of thy ransacked town
Pleased with their purchases stroll up and down.

Eandmines and wire encompass thy shore.
In place of the trippers who lay there before.
Baking and browning themselves in the sun.
Little they thought they'd be chased by the Hun.

Ye Statesmen of Jersey, Ye Jurats beware'
Your prestige is threatened, you'd best have a care.
The people are wak'ning, they'll not forget soon
How badly you handled that panic last June.
Nor the way that you crumpled, when faced by the Hun.
Oh Statesmen of Jersey' Your end has begun.

Never mind Jersey, All will come right.
You've one consolation you hadint to fight
The Germans just walked in ...demanded and got,
Your motor cars, lorries, and cycles , the lot,
Your wireless and clothing,& foddstuffs the while,
All that you did was to look on and smile.
Occupied Jersey' once proud and free'
Humbled indeed are the dwellers in thee.

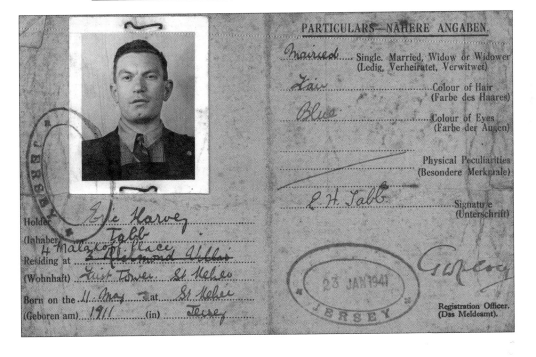

Programmfolge

I. TEIL :

FEST- UND OPERNMAERSCHE.

1.) Einzug der Gäste auf Wartburg aus der Oper „Tannhäuser " ... ... *R. Wagner*

2.) „Feierlicher Marsch " aus der Suite Nr. 1 d-moll *F. Lachner*

3.) Huldigungsmarsch aus „Sigurd Jorsalfar " *E. Grieg*

4.) Hymne und Triumphmarsch aus der Oper „Aida " *G. Verdi*

II. TEIL :

WIENER NOTENREGEN.

5.) Flieger-Marsch ... ... *H. Dostal.*

6.) Ouvertüre zu „Die schöne Galathé " ... *F.v.Suppé*

7.) „Die Schönbrunner " Walzer ... ... *J. Lanner*

8.) Johann Strauss, der Walzerkönig. Fantasie über Themen aus seinen Werken ... ... *J. Strauss*

9.) Tritsch-Tratsch-Polka ... ... *J. Strauss*

10.) Hoch- und Deutschmeister-Regimentsmarsch *K. Jurek*

Programme

FIRST PART.

FESTIVAL AND OPERA MARCHES.

1.—Entrance of Guests on Wartbourg from "Tannhäuser " ... ... *R. Wagner*

2.—Solemn March, from the Suite No. 1 in D Minor *F. Lachner*

3.—March of Allegiance from "Sigurd Jorsalfar " *E. Grieg*

4.—Hymn and Triumph March from the Opera "Aida " *G. Verdi*

SECOND PART.

MELODIES FROM VIENNA.

5.—Flying March ... ... *H. Dostal*

6.—Overture from "Galatea " ... ... *F.v.Suppé*

7.—" The Schönbrunner " Waltz ... ... *J. Lanner*

8.—Johann Strauss, the Waltz King. Fantasia on Themes from his works ... ... *J. Strauss*

9.—Tritsch-Tratsch Polka ... ... *J. Strauss*

10.—Regimental March ... ... *K. Jurek*

This Week—Tuesday, Thursday and Saturday—

The Rogues

Return of this Popular Concert Party.

Above:
A military concert — *'Merry Notes for a Sunday Evening'* — at Candie Gardens, Sunday, 25 July 1943, with music by a regimental band under the conductorship (sic) of *Obermusikmeister* Gerhard Anders. *Trevor du Feu collection*

Above:
Listening to the band in Guernsey's Candie Gardens. *Guernsey Ancient Monuments Committee*

| JERSEY | | GUERNSE |

THE
CHANNEL ISLANDS
MONTHLY REVIEW

Journal of Channel Islands Refugees in Great Britain

PUBLISHED BY THE STOCKPORT AND DISTRICT
CHANNEL ISLANDS SOCIETY

| ALDERNEY | AT 24, ST. PETERSGATE, STOCKPORT | SARK |

Vol. 3. No. 6.   32 Pages   DECEMBER, 1942.   Price 4d.

A HAPPY CHRISTMAS?

WITHOUT a question mark it would seem insincere. This morning, passing along the street, I remembered that this message had yet to be written. At that moment I confronted two khaki-clad men and saw they were Polish soldiers. I asked myself whether they would think I was mocking them if I wished them a " Happy Christmas." And then I wished I had never promised to write this to you. The third Christmas of separation ! Thirty slow-moving months of weary anxiety—no man knowing how many more are yet to follow ! Disquieting news of deportations ! Homeland and home being disfigured with the mark of the beast ! A Happy Christmas indeed !

And yet there are those messages. You must have seen hundreds of them, as I have, besides those you have received yourself. How many of them were depressed and sad ? You could count them on one hand. How many were cries of lost hope ? Never one ! I marvel at those messages. The folk who write them are brave. They are keeping the faith. Imagine it ! They have the sorrows of separation to bear as well as we—with added hardships to which we are strangers. The enemy is a living daily reality of brutal strength to them, and the possibility of deliverance must sometimes seem remote. Yet even at times when discomforts have multiplied, when food has not been too plentiful and the house has been fireless and shivery in the winter—there has been a message to send (to you) and they have gone down to the appointed place to write it, with love and courage in their hearts, telling themselves to be sure to say something cheerful for your sake ! They write it so, and when at last it comes you read " hoping to see you soon ! "

If they can do that surely we can still wish one another—and them—a Happy Christmas !

It springs from deep sources. Too deep to be invaded by Germans, or destroyed by separation.

Then, I remembered another Polish soldier. Ten days ago he told me he had not seen his wife, his mother, his father, all the others, since August, 1939. He had heard nothing since. One doesn't discuss that kind of situation over much. But I know he had found the secret of peace. His speech was courteous and his smile was kind (yes, he could still smile). If I run across him again within the next few days I shall wish him a " Happy Christmas." It will be all right !

Of course, the " Good Tidings " were to men of " Good Will." I suppose it is in the " goodwill " itself that the " happiness " of Christmas (or any other day) becomes possible. Then may your inner mind, and mine, be undisturbed by discontent, cleansed of self-love and self-interest, undismayed by circumstances, willing if needs be to serve and suffer and endure.

A " good will " does not look for happiness where happiness never was. Indeed, a " good will " does not *look* for happiness at all. It finds it by accident—by the inevitable accident of God's contriving. For He built this into the foundations of life and the ground-plan of the Universe—that there shall forever be good tidings of great joy to men of good will.

So my greeting then may ring true, happy and confident—may you and all your loved ones everywhere have the one essential ingredient of a Happy Christmas ! And, if it be possible, may your next one be together !   R. D. Moore.

Right:
A pamphlet produced on a regular basis for Channel Island evacuees. This is the December 1942 edition, published by the Stockport and District Channel Islands Society. *Trevor du Feu collection*

Right:
German officers relax outside a typically 'British' pub. However, the lack of glasses in hand suggest that the objective of the photograph was to show where they were rather than what they were doing. *Channel Islands Occupation Society*

Left:
Behaving like country squires — German officers on a hack overlook Jersey's Gorey harbour. *Carel Toms collection*

Above:
The occupiers in pristine marching order along Guernsey's Glategny Esplanade.
Channel Islands Occupation Society

Left:
Batterie Mirus shows its teeth. *The Priaulx Library Council*

KOMMANDANTUR DER INSEL JERSEY.

JERSEY, DEN 27.1.42.

Requisition order for articles removed from Merton Hotel.

The following articles have been requisitioned from the Merton Hotel by the German forces and removed to the following places:

a) General Hospital: 16 small 1 door wardrobes, 12 chairs, 13 single beds & mattresses, 20 pillows, 11 night tables, 27 pieces bed linen, 46 pillow cases.

b) Easton, Bagatelle Lane: 1 carpet, 1 large armchair, 2 double beds & mattresses, 1 bedside table, 1 small round table, 1 bedside lamp.

Proprietor: Mr. Seymour.

STANDORTKOMMANDANTUR

Standortoffizier.

Above:
Mr George Seymour's Merton Hotel was a ready source of supply for the German forces.
Author's collection

Right:
The Merton Hotel, from which so much was requisitioned, was eventually requisitioned itself to become a military hospital for the *Luftwaffe. Author's collection*

Left:
Organisation Todt workers march to their labours on Guernsey's west coast. The armed guard and the scraps of uniform imply that these men might be prisoners of war. *Channel Islands Occupation Society*

Below:
Self-explanatory leaflet — the shortage of shillings for gas meters. *Trevor du Feu collection*

GUERNSEY GAS LIGHT CO. LTD.

Shortage of Shillings

OWING TO THE SHORTAGE OF SHILLINGS, WHICH ARE INSUFFICIENT TO MEET THE REQUIREMENTS OF AUTOMATIC METER CONSUMERS, A NEW PROCEDURE WILL BE ADOPTED TO OVERCOME THE DIFFICULTY AS FROM THE NEXT COLLECTION OF THE METERS COMMENCING ON THE 2ND JANUARY, 1943.

OUR COLLECTORS WILL THEN IN THE PRESENCE OF CONSUMERS PREPAY GAS UP TO THE AMOUNT OF THE RATION ALLOWED, IN EXCHANGE FOR MARKS TENDERED BY THE CONSUMER, BY PASSING A SHILLING THROUGH THE MECHANISM A GIVEN NUMBER OF TIMES, WHICH WILL BE INDICATED ON THE PREPAID DIAL OF THE METER.

CONSUMERS WHOSE METERS HAVE BEEN COLLECTED BETWEEN THE 16TH NOVEMBER, 1942, AND THE 31ST DECEMBER, 1942, CAN COLLECT SHILLINGS UP TO THE BALANCE OF RATION AMOUNT AT THE GAS OFFICE, SMITH STREET, FROM THE 2ND TO 10TH JANUARY, 1943, AFTER WHICH DATE NO FURTHER SHILLINGS WILL BE SUPPLIED FROM THESE OFFICES.

CONSUMERS ARE THEREFORE ADVISED TO HAVE MARKS IN THEIR POSSESSION TO TENDER TO OUR COLLECTORS WHEN THEY NEXT CALL.

4343)

R. G. LUXON,
Engineer and Manager.

Right:
Unless you knew there was an enemy occupation in being, this programme of sports events would be entirely unremarkable.
Trevor du Feu collection

Below left:
Leaflets dropped by the Royal Air Force intended for France often fell on the Channel Islands. This one, dated 7 October 1943, tells its audience that Corsica has been liberated. *Trevor du Feu collection*

Below right:
News from England: For the Channel Islands was a regular publication dropped by the RAF. This particular edition, dated 30 September 1940, highlights the successful escape of eight men from Guernsey. It was to be the last successful escape for several years.
Author's collection

NUMBER ....

Island Sports Meeting

AUGUST BANK HOLIDAY, 1941

AT THE

King George V. Playing Fields

AT 2.30 P.M.

DISTRIBUTION OF PRIZES by
Sir ABRAHAM J. LAINÉ, K.C.I.E. (Jurat)
Chairman: Deputy W. J. CORBET.

OFFICIALS:—

Referee: Major R. G. Davies.
Judges: Messrs. H. W. Prins, W. Green, E. P. Rault, H. Snell, L. Purdy and R. de Garis.
Timekeepers: Messrs. G. Snell, E. W. Laker and A. Foster.
Starter: Major E. M. Langlois.
Announcers: Messrs. Eric Snelling, F. W. Falla and J. J. Eveson.
Recorders: Messrs. H. M. Lihou and T. F. Priaulx.
Clerk of the Course: Mr. E. J. S. Picquet.
Chief Competitors' Steward: Mr. S. Collins.
Assistant Competitors' Stewards: Messrs. E. J. Williams, F. Dorey, F. Damarell and J. Robert.
Hon. Secretary Executive Committee: Mr. T. F. Priaulx.
Hon. Financial-Secretary: Mr. E. Davies.
Marshals: Messrs. G. Lanoe, S. Le Page, E. Ogier, B. Bennett and C. Le Sauvage.
Ground Committee: Messrs. E. J. S. Picquet, T. F. Priaulx and E. J. Williams.

PROGRAMME

LE COURRIER DE L'AIR

APPORTÉ PAR LA R.A.F.   LONDRES, LE 7 OCTOBRE 1943

La Corse est libérée

News from England

For the Channel Islands   DISTRIBUTED BY THE R.A.F.

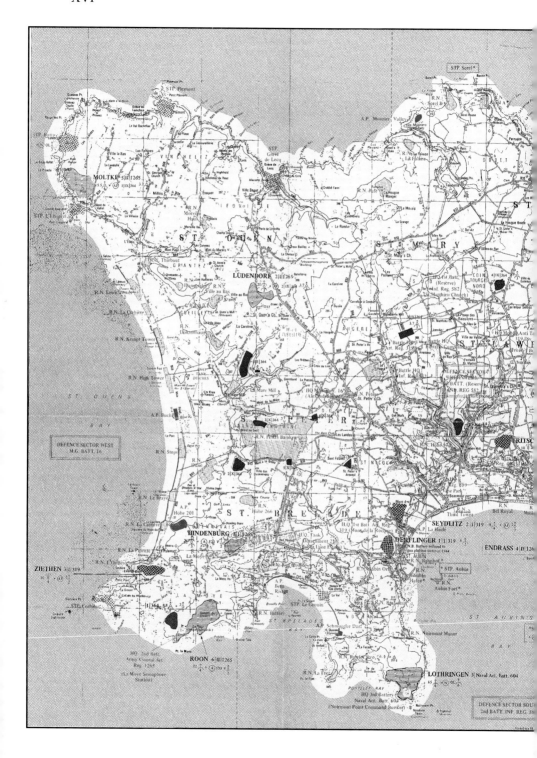

XVII

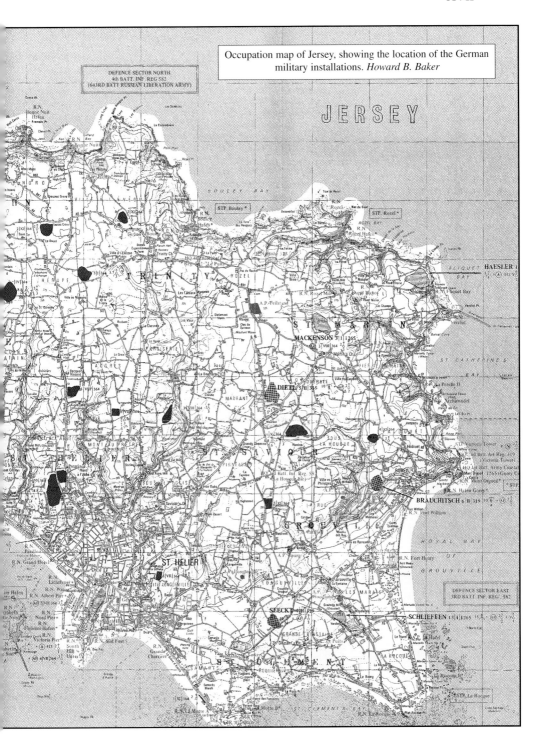

Occupation map of Jersey, showing the location of the German military installations. *Howard B. Baker*

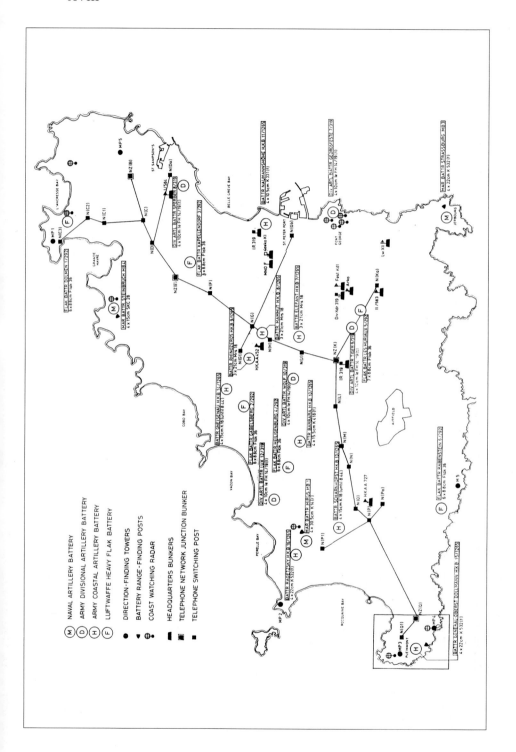

(M) NAVAL ARTILLERY BATTERY

(D) ARMY DIVISIONAL ARTILLERY BATTERY

(H) ARMY COASTAL ARTILLERY BATTERY

(F) LUFTWAFFE HEAVY FLAK BATTERY

DIRECTION-FINDING TOWERS

BATTERY RANGE-FINDING POSTS

COAST WATCHING RADAR

HEADQUARTERS BUNKERS

TELEPHONE NETWORK JUNCTION BUNKER

TELEPHONE SWITCHING POST

Occupation map of Guernsey (*above*) and Alderney (*below*), showing the location of the German military installations. *Colin Partridge*

COAST-DEFENCE GUNS
x3 17cm SK L40 — 360° Traverse
x4 15cm SK C/28 (Turreted) — 360° Traverse
x4 15cm K18 — 360° Traverse
10.5cm K331 (f) (Casemates) — 2 in field positions
10.5cm K331 (f) (uncasemated) — not shown on map
x4 10cm leFH 14/19 (t) — Mobile

ANTI-TANK GUNS (Casemates)
battery Perimeters

ANTI-TANK GUNS (emplaced)
7.5cm Pak40
5cm Pak38
4.7cm Pak (t) — 10 in field positions not shown on map

ANTI-AIRCRAFT GUNS (emplaced)
x6 8.8cm Heavy
x3 3.7cm Light
x3 2cm Light

INFANTRY
Strongpoint
Resistance Nest

MISCELLANEOUS
Headquarters
Searchlight
Defence Sectors
Anti-tank wall
Radar
Hospital bunker
Military Cemetery
Observation post
Tower

NOTE: Strongpoints were codenamed — 1. Turkenberg, 2. Quellenberg, 3. Rosenhof, 4. Ioselberg, 5. Neustadt, 6. Hä-höhe, 7. Schirrhof, 8. Biberkopf, 9. Hummerreste, 10. Steinbruch, 11. Sudhafen, 12. Millionar, 13. Windmuhlenberg.

1 kilometre
1 mile

MINES
Denotes area mined. A total of 30,235 mines were laid, of which 4,669 were anti-tank, 17,147 were anti-personnel and 8,419 were described as "improvised", the siling of which implied use as anti-personnel.

ARTILLERY UNITS

Cat.	Battery	Guns	Type	Range	Unit	
Medium	ELSASS	3	17cm SK L 40	22km (13.7 miles)	MAA 605	(Navy Coastal Artillery)
Medium	ANNES	4	15cm SK C/28	22km (13.7 miles)	MAA 605	(Navy Coastal Artillery)
Light	MARCKS	4	10.5cm K331(f)	8.2km (5.1 miles)	MAA 605	(Navy Harbour blocking battery)
Medium	BLUCHER	4	15cm K18	24.8km (15.5 miles)	IV/HKAR 1265	(Army Coastal Artillery regiment)
Light	FALKE	4	10cm leFH 14/19 (t)	9.6km (6 miles)	IV/AR 319	(Divisional Artillery Regiment)

Cats Bay
Corbiets Bay
Longy Bay
Saye Bay
Brave Bay
Crabby Bay
Platte Saline
Clonque Bay
Hannaine Bay
Telegraph Bay
AIRFIELD (obstructed)

MARCKS
ELSASS
BORKUM
FALKE
BLUCHER
HELGOLAND
ANNES
STLT

Left:
Who is lecturing whom? This photograph of the redoubtable Mrs Sybil Hathaway, the Dame of Sark, was taken towards the end of the Occupation when she weighed around seven stone – a loss of at least four stone in weight which was not noticeably shared by her 'guests'. *Carel Toms collection*

Below:
Major Dr Albrecht Lanz *(right)* chairs a meeting at his headquarters in the Royal Hotel, Guernsey. *Channel Islands Occupation Society*

Left:
The German film *Sieg im Westen* ('Victory in the West') was a popular entertainment at the cinemas in both Islands – but not with the section of the audience who needed subtitles! *Carel Toms collection*

Above:
Daubing 'V' signs was a BBC idea.
Being caught at it brought about serious
consequences. *Jersey Evening Post*

Below:
A firing party salutes the dead from
HMS Charybdis and *Limbourne* at Foulon
Cemetery in Guernsey. *The Ancient Monuments
Committee, Guernsey*

DOPPEL : *Verbleibt bei der Feldkommandantur.*
DUPLICATE : To be retained by the Field Command.

MOTOR TYRES (RESTRICTION ON SALE) (JERSEY) ORDER, 1940.

ANTRAG AUF GENEHMIGUNG ZUM BEZUGE VON REIFEN.
APPLICATION FOR PERMISSION TO BUY TYRES.

An die Feldkommandantur in **VICTORIA COLLEGE, JERSEY.**
To the Field Command at

I. Name und Adresse des Händlers **S. C. S. (1940) Ltd.** **(From own stock)**
   Name and address of dealer

II. Name, Beruf und Adresse des Kraftfahrzeugbesitzers **SAFETY COACH SERVICE (1940)**
    Name, profession and address of owner of motor vehicle **Lt**

OMNIBUS PROPRIETORS, GREEN ST., ST. HELIER, JERSEY.

III. Polizeiliche Kennzeichen, Fabrikmarke und Standort
     Registration No., Make and Situation of Vehicle

A.E.C. OMNIBUS. J.5933. No. 77 A.

IV. Ist das Fahrzeug von der Kommandantur zugelassen ? Nummer
    Has the vehicle a Field Command permit ? **YES.** Number **77**

V. Begründung des Antrages **2 TYRES WORN OUT and 1 TUBE.**
   Reasons for application

VI. Angabe über Grösse (Decke oder Schlauch) **825 X 24**
    Size (Cover or Tube)

VII. Wurde für obiges Fahrzeug schon ein Antrag gestellt ?
     Has an application already been made in respect of the above vehicle ? **No.**

   Beantragt am   Anzahl der Reifen
   Date of application   Number of tyres

   Genehmigt am   Anzahl der Reifen
   Date of Permission   Number of tyres

VIII. Ich versichere, dass die erbetenen Reifen für mich selbst und das oben erwähnte
      Fahrzeug bestimmt sind, und dass alle Angaben der Wahrheit entsprechen.

      I certify that the tyres applied for are for my own use and are intended for use on the
      vehicle mentioned above, and that the particulars mentioned above are correct.

(Ort und Datum)
(Place and Date)
                            p.p. Safety Coach Service (1940) Ltd.
                            (Unterschrift des Antragstellers).
                            (Applicant's Signature)

GENEHMIGT/ABGELEHNT
APPROVED/REFUSED   (Managing Director)
                 den **28 Okt. 1942.**
this

                            Der Feldkommandant.
                            The Field Commandant.

Left:
Motor tyres were a rare enough commodity to require a formal application form giving the reasons why new tyres were needed.
Trevor du Feu collection

Below:
A popular postcard designed by Bert Hill in 1945. The theme is self-explanatory.
Author's collection

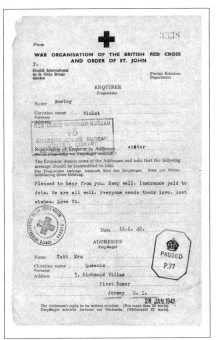

Above:
Lines in praise of SS *Vega*. For many the vessel was a life saver. *Trevor du Feu collection*

Below:
Red Cross parcels from the SS *Vega* being distributed in Guernsey. *Red Cross & St John*

Above:
Red Cross letters were the only means of communication with the outside world. *Author's collection*

Mr Frank Hy Blondel
18 Poplar Avenue
St Saviour.

The Jersey Prison Board would like to interview you with reference to your application for a post of Warder in the Prison. Will you please present yourself at the Prison on Monday the 12th instant at 10.45 a.m.

6th March 1945.

Above:
In March 1945 Jerseyman Frank Blondel applied for the post of warder in Jersey's Public Prison. The response was typed on tissue paper just 2½ inches deep and posted in an envelope headed 'On His Majesty's Service' with a German cancellation. He changed his mind and did not attend the interview. *Author's collection*

WORKERS' REVIEW.

Jersey, January, 1945.   No. 4.

1945!
RETROSPECT AND VISION.

The working-class movement in Jersey has again raised its head in spite of many difficulties. Some workers are still chary of joining up as they are of the opinion that "nothing can be done just yet," forgetting that the workers of 140 years ago organised their Unions under equally as difficult conditions as we are facing today.

In England, 140 years ago, the anti-Combination Laws were enforced with drastic penalties, yet despite this the pioneers of the Trade Union movement battled on until ultimately our Unions became recognised legal organisations.

We are again in the same position as the old pioneers, but we have this advantage over those stalwarts; we now have more than 140 years' experience to guide us in our activities. Such a heritage cannot be ignored.

Let us assume that at the end of the Occupation the local employing class decide to introduce a new anti-Combination Law (and such an assumption is not wholly absurd) then where do we stand?

We shall find ourselves in exactly the same position as we are at the present moment, and we shall still be confronted with the problem of organising in defiance of the law or of remaining as an unorganised rabble at the mercy of the employing class. We must remember that, speaking generally, the employers do NOT like Unionism, unless it is a so-called "Company Union" controlled by themselves.

Remember how quickly our wages and conditions were abolished in the period June, July, August, 1941. We were told "There's no Union now", and 30s. to £2 became the regular weekly rate of pay for many workers.

OUR IMMEDIATE TASK.

Hence the necessity for strong Unionism, in fact, 100% Unionism, not only amongst Dockers, Storemen and Building workers, but amongst the hitherto unorganised workers. At its greatest strength the T. and G.W.U. in Jersey reckoned 6,000 members. We must surpass this number and also raise the level of working class solidarity.

We must work for a combination of all Unions operating in the Island. These various Unions must be welded into a Trades and Labour Council, with a single, unified industrial and political policy.

Finance must be built up and the whole Union organisation got into really good working order. The "WORKERS' REVIEW" must be kept going until the day when it can come out as a proper working-class and T.U. paper covering every phase of workers interests.

All these tasks call for more than passive support, they need active co-operation. We all recognise the necessity for

Left:
In January 1945, the workers of Jersey were uniting – or at least a couple of dozen of them were. *Trevor du Feu collection*

Bescheinigung

Generalmajor **H e i n e** , der stellvertretende Festungs-Kommandant und Kommandeur der Truppen des Heeres der Insel Guernsey ist von mir bevollmächtigt, die Kapitulations-Bedingungen zu unterzeichnen.

-, den 8. Mai 1945

Vizeadmiral und Befehlshaber Kanalinseln.

Above:
The letter of authority to surrender given to his chief of staff by *Vizeadmiral* Hüffmeier. *Author's collection*

Right:
Generalmajor Siegfried Heine and *Kapitänleutnant* Armin Zimmermann hear the terms of unconditional surrender aboard HMS *Bulldog. Société Jersiaise*

Above:
The Union flag flies once again outside the Pomme d'Or Hotel, for five years the headquarters of the *Kriegsmarine* in Jersey. No wonder Mr Seymour was concerned for his balcony! *Channel Islands Occupation Society*

Left:
After the Liberation *Vizeadmiral* Friedrich Hüffmeier and *Generalmajor* Rudolf Wulf are greeted on their arrival at Plymouth en route to interrogation in London. *Western Morning News*

Above:
The liberators of Force 135 handed out
cigarettes, sweets, biscuits and even milk cubes
to the crowds welcoming them.
Jersey Evening Post

Above:
Brigadier Snow reads
the Royal Proclamation
on the steps of
Guernsey's Elizabeth
College. *Carel Toms
collection*

BUCKINGHAM PALACE

To my most loyal people in the Channel Islands, I send my heartfelt greetings.

Ever since my armed forces had to be withdrawn, you have, I know, looked forward with the same confidence as I have to the time of deliverance. We have never been divided in spirit, Our hopes and fears, anxieties and determination have been the same, and we have been bound together by an unshakable conviction that the day would come when the Islands, the oldest possession of the Crown, would be liberated from enemy occupation. That day has now come and, with all my Peoples, I cordially welcome you on your restoration to freedom and to your rightful place with the free nations of the world.

Channel Islanders in their thousands are fighting in my service for the cause of civilisation with their traditional loyalty, courage and devotion. Their task is not yet ended ; but for you a new task begins at once—to re-build the fortunes of your beautiful Islands in anticipation of reunion with relatives, friends and neighbours who have been parted from you by the circumstances of war. In this task you can count on the fullest support of my Government.

It is my desire that your ancient privileges and institutions should be maintained and that you should resume as soon as possible your accustomed system of government. Meantime, the immediate situation requires that responsibility for the safety of the Islands and the well-being of the inhabitants should rest upon the Commander of the Armed Forces stationed in the Islands. I feel confident that the Civil Authorities, who have carried so heavy a burden during the past years, will gladly co-operate with him in maintaining good government and securing the distribution of the supplies which he is bringing with him.

It is my earnest hope that the Islands, reinstated in their ancestral relationship to the Crown, will soon regain their former happiness and prosperity,

(Signed) GEORGE R. I.

Right:
The King's message to
Channel Islanders at the
Liberation.
Author's collection

Left:
Jaws of plenty. A US Navy LST prepares to disgorge its precious contents on the sands of Jersey's St Aubin's Bay. *Jersey Evening Post*

Left:
This Russian youth was the youngest of the occupiers. He was, supposedly, the mascot of his unit. *Jersey Evening Post*

Above:
After the Liberation, Islanders queue up at the
St Helier branch of the Midland Bank to convert
their accumulated *Reichsmark* back to Sterling.
Jersey Evening Post

Right:
Most of the non-lethal artefacts left behind by
the occupiers were sold by public auction.
Trevor du Feu collection

BY ORDER OF THE M.O. COMPETENT MILITARY AUTHORITIES

G.  R.

O.H.M.S.

A CATALOGUE OF

CAPTURED GERMAN

GROUND MATERIAL

TRUCKS, CARS, & MOTOR CYCLES (CIVILIAN & GERMAN
ARMY TYPE)

Which will be sold by Public Auction at

CAR PARK, NORTH SIDE, ST. SAMPSON'S HARBOUR,

ON THURSDAY, APRIL 11, 1946, AT 2 P.M. PROMPT

C. FRAMPTON, Auctioneer to H.M. Government,
Meuilpied, St. Martin's, Guernsey.   Telephone 5673

This Catalogue will admit to Private View on Wednesday, April
10th, 1946, from 10 a.m. to 4 p.m. and morning of the Sale.

Wardleys.

Left:
The original German occupant has long since departed for a prison camp but his effigy attracts some youthful attention at Faldouet crossroads in Jersey. *Jersey Evening Post*

Below:
The German cemetery at St Brelade in Jersey. Later the Rector used the crosses for firewood. *Trevor du Feu collection*

Above:
Sword into a ploughshare: Ho1, a tunnel complex in Jersey's St Peter's Valley that once housed 6,000 tonnes of ammunition, is now a mushroom farm. *Author's collection*

Above:
The Jersey War Tunnels, formerly known as the German Underground Hospital, deep under a Jersey hillside. *Author's collection*

Left:
Bunkers decaying in the sunshine in the present day. *Author's collection*

Above:
Jersey's memorial to the Islanders who endured five years of enemy occupation is overlooked by a mouldering gun site that was once part of Batterie Lothringen. *Author's collection*

More discreetly, of necessity, there were also 'Jerryboys', youths who formed liaisons with homosexuals amongst the Occupation forces, in those days a doubly dangerous deviation given the Nazi Party's views on homosexuality and the savage penalties for being caught.

There were those for whom the Occupation was not a nightmare but a business opportunity. As goods usually commonplace became in short supply a thriving black market soon developed. Goods bought cheaply were hoarded to be sold later at vast profits. Those with substantial resources could buy almost anything at any time, provided they were prepared to pay the price demanded. Guernsey businessman Gerrit Timmer's defence to the charge of collaboration that hung over him after the Liberation was that he had seen a business opportunity and exploited it, something Channel Islanders had been very adept at down the centuries.

However, the black market was not just something for the locals. The Germans, especially the *OT* and the sailors of the *Kriegsmarine* and merchant ships' crews with access to goods in France, were active in the black market themselves, goods intended exclusively for the military often finding their way, at a price, into civilian hands.

There were grave risks. The official *FK515* line was that the black market was something to be stamped out and woe betide the black marketeer who tried to sell the wrong product to the wrong person. Black marketeers were regularly denounced and, unlike a crystal set, illicit stocks of food, drink or bicycle tyres could not easily be moved or hidden. Punishments usually involved fines and imprisonment and one exponent, a Jersey doctor, had his confiscated hoard of foodstuffs and spirits put on display in Burton's window for all his fellow Islanders to see.

There were those who openly collaborated, acting as spies on their neighbours and workmates, relying on the protection of their new friends to guard them against the loathing of their fellow Islanders. Among the most notorious in Jersey was one we've already met: Alexandrine Baudains, and her son George. At the Liberation another infamous Jersey informer, Marjorie Robins, was dragged from her home in Midvale Road, her hands and feet were bound and she was about to be lynched from a lamppost when the police arrived.

Islanders themselves were very unsure how far to go in their dealings with the occupiers. They were everywhere and could not be ignored. Thus did exchanging a greeting with a German soldier proud to show off how well he spoke English constitute some sort of treason? What about the mother who, in the very early days of occupation, accepted from a German officer an ice-cream he had just bought from a man with a tricycle urging all and sundry to 'Stop Me and Buy One' to give to her child? Could that very human interaction be deemed dealing with the enemy? And what if a housewife took in a German sailor's washing and received extra rations or cigarettes for so doing? Was that giving aid and comfort to the enemy?

Did those who actually worked voluntarily for the Germans in order to provide for their family when no one else could or would, commit an awful crime?

How should we judge Pearl Vardon, the Jerseywoman dubbed 'Lady Haw Haw'?

Pearl Joyce Vardon was 25 when the Germans invaded and was employed as a teacher at Halkett Place Primary School and for a time at the Jersey Ladies College. In June 1941 she met and became the mistress of *Oberleutnant* Siegfried Schwatlo. In August she later claimed that she was summoned to the British Hotel in St Helier — the hotel was still fulfilling its original function but now catering for visiting German dignitaries, the highest ranking of whom was *Generalfeldmarschall* Erwin von Witzleben (much, much later it would play host to the Beatles) — where she met building contractor Theodor Elsche who told her he needed someone who could act as an interpreter between the local men on the firm and his German-speaking staff. She began working for him the following day, having been told, she claimed, that she had no choice in the matter. She stayed with the firm until the end of 1943, acting as a secretary, translating and paying the accounts the firm had with local tradespeople. According to the statement she made to MI5 in May 1945, when, early in 1944 Schwatlo (now promoted to *Hauptmann*) was due to be posted back to Germany, she applied to accompany him. In the event her lover stayed in Jersey and by 1945 he had been promoted to *Major* and was a battalion commander.

Once arrived in Germany, Pearl (presumably believing her lover was following her) was offered the position of announcer on Radio Luxembourg (her statement implies that this was a condition of her being allowed to travel to Germany in the first place) on which she presented a music programme and spoke on daily broadcasts 'For the Forces and their Kin' which featured letters written by British prisoners of war in German camps to their relatives and friends at home. Her broadcasts were full of Nazi propaganda and her colleagues formed the impression that she was 'a keen Nazi'. As the Allies advanced she was transferred to Apen near Wilhelmshaven to continue her broadcasts, then to Berlin and then back to Apen in October 1944 where she remained until April 1945. She was detained by Allied troops in Wilhelmshaven on 1 May.

Pearl Vardon was tried at the Old Bailey on 27 February 1946 and sentenced to nine months in prison. Upon her release she moved to Wales to be with her lover who was in a Welsh prison camp. When he was repatriated to Germany she went with him. Since Lord Haw Haw ended his life at the end of a rope in Wandsworth Prison, Pearl Vardon should well have counted herself very fortunate that her interrogators, and ultimately her judges, considered that her labours on behalf of the German war effort were of little consequence and what she did was done for love.

Curiously the German reaction to the activities of those who were dubbed 'friends of the German Reich' was ambiguous. Liaisons with local girls were discouraged since there were a number of instances where the attachments led to dereliction of duty and several young Lotharios found themselves facing harsh disciplinary penalties, even the firing squad. Venereal diseases were rife and other Lotharios found themselves gazing down upon a very different penalty.

Even the German administrators were sometimes shocked by the stream of denunciations pouring into College House, Grange Lodge and the *GFP* and in one instance, when a list of those in Sark concealing wireless sets was posted on a tree on The Avenue, Sark's major (and only) street, the Germans dismissed it, reasoning that it must be the work of a sick mind. The unfortunate oak has had the sad sobriquet of 'Traitor's Tree' attached to it ever since. But in the main the Germans' task of maintaining their version of law and order was made easier by those Islanders who were prepared, for whatever motives, to denounce their neighbours. The occasional practice of the Islands' police forces in passing information to the German military police either directly or via the Crown Officers, for offences against the occupiers' rules and regulations (such as concealing wireless sets), aids the cause of those who believe the local authorities were too willing to carry out the Germans' orders and that they should have refused or just done nothing and let the Germans do their own dirty work. It was difficult then and is still difficult today to find ready justification for such actions and the rigid adherence to the rule of law — which was probably the motivation — seems a poor excuse when held up to the same scrutiny that identifies those who resisted as heroes willing to risk their lives (and, in some cases, losing them).

There is no doubt that there were many instances when the authorities certainly did seem to be too compliant. Offering a reward for information leading to the conviction of the daubers of the 'V' signs is perhaps one example. The acceptance without demur (except for the honourable exception of Sir Abraham Lainé of Guernsey's Controlling Committee) of the German anti-Semitic legislation is another, although there was little local knowledge or comprehension of what might be the consequences. That there appeared to be little protest when three Jewish women were deported from Guernsey just for being Jewish may today look weak-willed and unduly co-operative but, since their initial deportation was to France, it is likely that even the *Nebenstelle* were unaware of their ultimate fate.

It is easy to be wise (and even belligerent) with hindsight but the reality is that the Island authorities had very little choice. If they wished, as indeed they did, to maintain their ability to govern, then they had to comply with German demands. Failure to do so would have simply led to direct rule by the occupiers. That was made very clear. What's more, as we have seen in the Nicolle/Symes saga, the Germans were quite prepared to threaten deadly reprisals against the civil population if their will was thwarted. It would take a very brave man to be prepared to test just how far the Germans were bluffing, largely because they weren't. That hostages were only ever taken on very rare occasions does not mean that had the local authorities failed to co-operate, the practices of terror that were routine in other occupied territories, would not have also become commonplace in the Islands. In Jersey in June 1942 10 well-known Islanders were taken as hostages and threatened with internment on the Continent unless the people who were distributing leaflets exhorting Islanders not to give up their wireless sets owned up. Just a week or so later five teachers from Victoria College were also held until the distributors of more leaflets gave themselves up. They duly did and all the hostages were released within 10 days.

Perhaps the most telling feature of the authorities' compliance is that both Island administrations were headed by long-serving lawyers who were unwilling to act outside the law since the Germans' occupation of the Channel Islands was not an illegal act. Perhaps where the two authorities differed was that Victor Carey's age and particular experience more often than not led him to accept the legality of the actions, such as the 'V' sign rewards notice, that were forced upon him, whereas Alexander Coutanche's wily legal mind led him to use the same legal processes to frustrate them. This respect for the rule of law led to all sorts of other problems, including not acceding to the assumption that what would be a criminal act in peacetime was an act of resistance in war. Several young men found themselves being arrested and charged by the local police forces and sentenced by local courts for what they perceived as striking blows for freedom and the courts perceived as misdemeanours. An understandable sense of injustice still rankles today.

On 24 February 1942 Guernsey's Bailiff wrote to the *Feldkommandantur* complaining about the number of thefts that were taking place after curfew since the arrival of so many, apparently light-fingered, foreign workers. He concluded his letter with, as events would prove, the rather unfortunate phrase: 'I have no doubt that the local police are doing their best.' The phrase was especially unfortunate since many of the thefts were being carried out by members of the Island's police force! Altogether 18 members of Guernsey's 30-strong force (unlike Jersey there were no honorary policemen although there were 12 Auxiliary Constables) were arrested and charged with various offences involving thefts from military and civilian stores. Four civilians, including three women, were charged with them. In the view of many of the accused, they had merely been pursuing activities prejudicial to the German war effort but the Germans sought to use their forthcoming trial to the maximum propaganda advantage. Furthermore *Rittmeister* von Oettingen, Military Commandant of the *Nebenstelle*, wrote to Jurat John Leale advising that henceforth the Island's police force would come under direct German control.

The accused were all mistreated during interrogation, several losing teeth and sustaining other injuries from beatings from the *GFP*. Perhaps being policemen led their interrogators to be particularly harsh with them although the *GFP* was just as likely to beat its own people if they fell from grace.

The trial lasted two and a half days and 17 of the 18 were found guilty and sentenced to up to four and a half years' hard labour. All but one served their sentence on the Continent, often being treated brutally by their jailers. One died in custody. The others returned home bringing with them a justifiable (to them) sense of grievance.

One factor which many postwar commentators have overlooked is the ratio of occupiers to occupied. In occupied Norway there were approximately 1,200 Norwegians (albeit including a proportion of Quislings) for every German occupier. In France that ratio was one German for every 120 Frenchmen although many parts of France never ever saw a German during the entire occupation. What made the massacre at Oradour-sur-Glâne (where more than 600 men, women and children were shot, bombed and burned by the *SS Das Reich Panzer Division* on 10 June 1944) an even greater atrocity was that it occurred at a place which, until that appalling Saturday, had not seen a German soldier and life had gone on for the past four years almost as though the occupation of France was happening somewhere else to someone else. In Jersey the ratio was three local civilians for every German and in Guernsey the ratio was almost one to one. Nowhere else in the Reich, including Germany itself, saw such a concentration of German military might. Is it no wonder that resistance was well-nigh impossible and compliance was well-nigh inevitable? In the early months of the occupation, the Germans regarded their tenure of the Islands as a rehearsal for the real event — the invasion and occupation of Britain. In fact they already had a tenth of one per cent of Great Britain's population within their hegemony. But that was all they were ever going to get.

Active resistance was far from most Islanders' minds. Surviving and living from day to day were not.

Islanders became used to coping with shortages and were becoming increasingly resourceful. Shoes were soled and re-heeled with pieces of wood or old car tyres. A type of clog with a wooden sole and a simple leather upper became popular (we've already noted that 45,000 pairs were made). They were said to be very comfortable although Islanders had to shuffle rather than walk when wearing them. Clothes were tailored from curtains and blankets, and hemlines rose. Collars were turned, turned again and finally discarded. Buttons were replaced with string. Stockings were rare and in Jersey in particular Islanders rediscovered the skills of knitting hose. For the ladies there was little or nothing in the way of cosmetics and lipsticks but enterprising chemists made mixtures from oil and dyes. Old tins were remodelled into kitchen utensils and lengths of hosepipe and rope replaced irreplaceable rubber bicycle tyres.

And as 1943 turned into 1944 major changes in the fortunes of war and life in the Channel Islands were afoot.

Chapter 9
D-Day: freedom for some

D-Day brings the prospect of freedom to Western Europe and starvation to the beleaguered Channel Islands yet the Germans' will to resist remains as strong as ever as a 'Nazi' becomes Commander-in-Chief. The Channel Islands as stepping stones to Europe? Operation 'Subordinate', the invasion that never was. Winston Churchill says 'Let them starve!' but who does he mean? Shortages and near starvation. The Vega, *13 million cigarettes and diarrhoea!*

Early in 1944, the German High Command became certain that an Allied invasion of Europe would come some time that year. At the express order of Adolf Hitler combat zones were established under the overall command of *Generalfeldmarschall* von Rundstedt and 15 *Festungen* (fortresses) were designated covering the coastline from the Gironde Estuary in France to Den Helder in Holland. In February Jersey, Guernsey and Alderney were similarly designated as the 16th fortress, to be strengthened and then defended against invasion to the last man and the last bullet. *Generalmajor* Graf von Schmettow was confirmed as *Festungkommandant* in Guernsey, *Oberst* Siegfried Heine in Jersey and *Major* Schwalm in Alderney.

Despite the advice of his generals, Adolf Hitler was convinced that the Allies would invade in the region of the Pas de Calais because of its proximity to the English coast but *General der Artillerie* Erich Marcks predicted accurately that the invasion, when it came, would occur on the wide beaches of Normandy. His view was supported by *Generalfeldmarschall* Erwin Rommel, who on New Year's Eve 1943 had been appointed Commander of Army Group B, and who, over the next few months, began reinforcing the defences of Normandy by installing thousands of beach obstacles and laying down four million mines. To help with this task, most of the *OT* workers in the Channel Islands were withdrawn to work on these defences, as well as fulfilling Hitler's determination to fortify the Pas de Calais.

Just a few hundred *OT* workers remained in the Channel Islands although their numbers were boosted by Italian *Hilfswillige* (auxiliaries) as the garrison steeled itself for invasion. Would the Allies use the Islands as practice for the real thing or as stepping stones into mainland Europe? Even were this to be the case it was made clear to the fortress commanders that there would be no further manpower made available to them. They would have to defend their *Festungen* with the forces they had.

In mid-May *Feldkommandantur 515* was downgraded to *Platzkommandantur 1*, a change intended to reflect the change in circumstances brought about by the threat of an Allied invasion of Europe.

Whereas the role of *FK515* had been to manage the peaceful co-existence of occupier and occupied, the role of *PK1* was to manage a resumption of hostilities. In practice, apart from the change of name (and thus dozens of direction signs), Islanders would see little difference. *Oberst* Knackfuss had already been posted in February to the Balkans (where he would die in a Yugoslav prison camp in September 1945) and *Major* Willi Heider had taken charge, being formally titled *Platzkommandant* on 19 May.

The garrisons on the Islands practised their anti-invasion strategies over and over, expending thousands of rounds of ammunition and causing much annoyance to local residents as they were evacuated from defence zones time and time again and suffered hailstorms of shrapnel that clattered on to their rooftops and concussion from gunfire that shattered their windows.

In 1943 Mountbatten wrote to the Secretary of the Chiefs of Staff Committee. In a letter marked 'MOST SECRET' he gave details of Operation 'Constellation', an offensive against the Channel Islands, Operation 'Concertina', an offensive against Alderney, Operation 'Coverlet', an offensive against Guernsey and Operation 'Condor', an offensive against Jersey. In the preamble to his report Mountbatten suggested that 'the assumption has been made that, in order to further our Mediterranean strategy, a well timed offensive operation in N.W. Europe will be required during the summer of 1943'. The report went on:

'The geographical position of the Channel Islands shows that prior to an assault on the N.W. beaches of the Cherbourg Peninsula the assault and capture:

of Alderney would be essential.

of Guernsey would be highly desirable, and essential if large forces were to use those beaches, but impracticable unless Alderney were already in our hands.

of Jersey would be desirable but by no means essential and, in any event, not possible without the prior capture of Guernsey.

'There is no doubt that the enemy has fully appreciated the value of the Channel Islands and the potential threat those Islands would offer if re-occupied by our forces.

'Consequently, each Island has been turned into a veritable fortress the assault against which cannot be contemplated unless the defences are neutralised or reduced to a very considerable extent by prior action.'

In this context 'prior action' would have meant either a naval bombardment or aerial bombing. However, if the bombarding vessels or aircraft were to stay safely out of range of the artillery that could be ranged against *them*, an accuracy greater than a mile on either side of any particular target could not be guaranteed. Although the majority of the Islands' defences were on or near the coast, such an accuracy (or inaccuracy!) had the potential of laying waste more than two-thirds of Guernsey's land surface and half of Jersey's. Just where the 65,000 or so local residents would have taken refuge while all this was going on (on the assumption that the Germans would have been snug in their bunkers and tunnels) is not answered in Lord Louis' paper although the existence of the civilian population was acknowledged, as was the potential for civilian casualties. An assault without a 'softening-up' beforehand (such as was subsequently employed at Arnhem) was, in 1943, when 'Constellation' and its satellites were planned, unheard of.

It was not only the main Islands that came under Combined Operations' scrutiny, for minor raids were planned on Brecqhou (Operation 'Catswhiskers') and Herm (Operation 'Pussyfoot'), while Operation 'Bunbury' was intended to kill or capture the entire garrison on Sark. None was ever carried out.

In the event the operations were shelved and Lord Louis moved on to other glories in south-east Asia.

However, one incursion that did take place, Operation 'Basalt', which preceded all these, was to have consequences out of all proportion to its effect.

At 11.30pm on Saturday, 3 October 1942, a party of 12 commandos, under the command of Major J. G. Appleyard, was landed from a Royal Navy motor torpedo boat between Dixcart Bay and Derrible Bay on Sark. By moonlight the commandos negotiated the stiff climb up the Hog's Back. From a householder (who must have been surprised to see them) they learned that there were Germans billeted in the Dixcart Hotel. In his official history, Cruickshank relates that the party's informant, a widow, gave the raiding party a copy of a newspaper reporting the recent deportations and they also learned that the Islanders were upset that they had not been mentioned in the King's Christmas broadcast some 10 months earlier! According to the commandos' report they went to the hotel where they encountered five Germans and in the subsequent fire fight killed four and captured one. They met no other opposition and safely re-embarked at 3.45am.

The German report of the events of that night was rather different.

According to the official report four men of a pioneer unit working at the harbour were overpowered, trussed and led away. Near their quarters they attempted to escape and in the mêlée a German soldier was both shot and stabbed to death, two others, although wounded, did manage to escape but one later died of his injuries, a third escaped unharmed and the fourth remained captured and was taken to England. The man who got away, *Obergefreiter* Klotz, was subsequently presented with a watch in recognition of his action in escaping after having been 'cold-bloodedly tied up by the English'.

The incident, which caused Sark's Commandant, *Oberleutnant* Stefan Herdt, and that evening's duty officer to be threatened with being court-martialled (although they never were) was serious enough to be reported to Berlin where *Generalmajor* Walther Warlimont, deputy to *General* Alfred

Jodl, head of the *Wehrmachtführungsstab* (the armed forces Operations Staff) endorsed an estimate of 16 raiders and the improbable comment that the success of the raid had been aided by communications with agents on Sark by carrier pigeon! Hitler himself took note of the fact that the prisoners had been bound and on 8 October he ordered that 1,400 Allied prisoners taken at Dieppe should be shackled in retaliation.

So began a period of blast and counterblast. The British published their own report of the raid which revealed that large-scale deportations had taken place from the Islands to labour camps in Germany, evidenced by the newspaper and the captured German soldier (who was obviously well informed!). The Germans were also advised that unless the Dieppe prisoners were unshackled, a similar number of German POWs would receive the same treatment. The German response was that should that happen, then three times as many British POWs would be shackled. The Canadian government joined in by putting an equivalent number of German prisoners there in chains. If this was not enough, another consequence of 'Basalt' and other raids against his empire was Hitler's notorious *Kommandobefehl* (Commando Order) of 18 October which stated: 'In future, all terror and sabotage troops of the British and their accomplices, who do not act like soldiers but rather like bandits, will be treated as such by the German troops and will be ruthlessly eliminated in battle wherever they appear.' Thereafter this order was often followed to the letter.

'Basalt' also led to further deportations from the Channel Islands although one idea of deporting the entire population of Sark was shelved after the widow who had given the British commandos the information that there were Germans billeted in the Dixcart Hotel volunteered the information (the German who subsequently interrogated her thought her 'a helpless and somewhat simple-minded woman'). She was promised that she would not be punished but Hitler thought otherwise and she was amongst the Sarkees deported to Germany in February 1943.

No less a personage than *Generalfeldmarschall* von Rundstedt studied the evidence and decided that although Sark was not actually riddled with enemy agents communicating with Britain by pigeon, the deportations would go ahead and a plan to return some of the earlier deportees was dropped 'because the behaviour of a woman in one of the Channel Islands has made necessary an extension of the evacuation on military grounds'.

A year later Operation 'Hardtack 7' took place on Christmas night 1943. A Lieutenant A. J. McGonigal with four commandos tried to climb the cliffs at Sark's Derrible Bay. They failed but tried again two days later and this time stumbled into a minefield (which Appleyard and his party had somehow managed to avoid) where four of the five men were injured when they triggered off two mines. Trying to find their way back they set off more mines and two of the party — both Frenchmen — were killed and their bodies abandoned. Flares showed that the incursion had been discovered and the remainder of the party hurried back to the rendezvous where they were taken off without further casualties.

Somehow the word 'shambles' comes to mind.

Operation 'Hardtack 28' took place at the same time although its target was Jersey. Ten men, four of them French, led by Captain P. A. Ayton, landed at Petit Port in the parish of Trinity. They passed by a minefield whose warning signs were displayed in both German and English and found a farm but the occupant refused either to let them in or give them any information other than pointing them towards another farmstead. There two brothers, almost too petrified by this Noeltide apparition of British forces to speak, eventually told them that there was no resistance movement in the Island and everyone got on really rather well together. The uninvited guests were sent on their way with a glass of milk, still looking for Germans to interrogate. A strongpoint at Les Platons was unmanned and the empty-handed party decided to return to its starting point where Captain Ayton stepped on a mine and, sadly, later died of his injuries in hospital. Today there is a monument at Petit Port to the Captain whose courage was never in doubt but once again the expedition had as many elements of farce as tragedy.

Plans to invade Europe had first been drawn up in 1943 following the Washington Conference and a draft of Operation 'Overlord' was first produced on 1 August that year and discussed at the Quebec Conference later that month when President Franklin Roosevelt and Premier Winston Churchill decided on 1 May 1944 for D-Day. The planners considered three invasion areas: the Pas de Calais, Normandy and Brittany. The last was ruled out by distance, both from Britain and Allied objectives in Europe, and the Pas de Calais was too obvious. It was decided that Normandy to the west of the Seine estuary, with its long sandy beaches and the large port of Cherbourg, was a better choice.

In December 1943 US Army General Dwight D. Eisenhower was appointed Supreme Commander, Allied Expeditionary Force, and on 12 February 1944 was directed to 'enter the Continent of Europe and, in conjunction with other United Nations, undertake operations aimed at the heart of Germany and the destruction of her armed forces'. His deputy was Britain's Air Chief Marshal Sir Arthur Tedder and all three component commanders were also British: General Sir Bernard Montgomery would command the ground forces, Admiral Sir Bertram Ramsey the naval forces and Air Chief Marshal Sir Trafford Leigh-Mallory the air forces.

It was, of course, noted that only a few miles to the west of Normandy's Cotentin peninsula were the German-occupied Channel Islands. Frequent aerial photo reconnaissance showed the Islands to be heavily defended out of all proportion to their strategic worth but that same reconnaissance was also revealing there to be few *Luftwaffe* units on the Islands other than one or two Junkers transports and some visiting Dornier 'Flying Pencils', probably reconnaissance aircraft themselves. There were no fighters. Similarly the only units disposed by the *Kriegsmarine* appeared to be several minesweepers, a number of *Artillerieträger* (barges with low freeboard to minimise their radar reflection but armed with a variety of weapons), several transports, many of which appeared to be former Rhine barges, and some armed fishing boats. Furthermore there had been recent movements of men and materials away from the Islands, the vessels being so harried by darting attacks by the RAF that all shipping movements now took place only in the hours of darkness.

* * *

What follows is another what if? Operation 'Subordinate' is a fictional title for a fictional event (with some fictional characters) but such plans, as we have seen, were conceived at the instigation of the energetic Lord Louis Mountbatten, Chief of Combined Operations, albeit a year earlier.

Let us imagine then that the Prime Minister, who in 1940 had initially insisted that a German invasion should be resisted, sent one of his famous minutes.

'I want to reclaim the Channel Islands. Tell me how this can be done.'

There were immediate objections from his military advisers. There was no strategic value in recapturing the Channel Islands. Despite the lack of *Luftwaffe* and *Kriegsmarine* units, the Islands were well defended with more than 150 gun sites on Jersey alone. Whether an assault came from the air or the sea, it would be stoutly resisted. There would be considerable loss of life. Besides, on Jersey there were still 45,000 non-combatant civilians, half that number on Guernsey. There were no known resistance movements in either Island, since resisters had nowhere to hide and the most recent covert incursion, 'Operation Hardtack 8' on Jersey on Christmas Day 1943, had yielded no intelligence of any worth whatever and the leader, Captain P. A. Ayton, had stepped on a mine and died of his injuries.

Yet the Prime Minister persisted and Operation 'Condor', proposed by Mountbatten in 1943 and rejected because of the likely high loss of life, military and civilian, was retrieved from the archives and dusted off.

'The holding of the Channel Islands gives Germany a constant propaganda victory,' the Prime Minister insisted. 'We plan to invade Europe in the late spring, how better to start than by freeing our British kin from Nazi bondage. Besides the Islands will be valuable stepping stones to Europe and even more valuable practice!' And his advisers knew him well enough to know when the Prime Minister had made up his mind.

General Eisenhower was not convinced. So much so that he vetoed the use of American personnel although he was prepared, grudgingly, to allow the use of US Navy landing ships and craft provided the Navy had no other use for them at the time. He justified this agreement by accepting that the invasion of one of the Channel Islands would indeed be valuable practice and if Jersey were chosen, and the landing were to succeed, it would prevent the Island being a platform for heavy guns capable of firing on Allied troops as they fought their way down the Cotentin peninsula. Whereas in 1943 Alderney had been perceived to be the prime target, with the invasion of Europe now planned, Jersey's proximity to the French coast rendered it a much more worthwhile objective. Alderney, with a minimal civilian population, would be subdued by intensive naval and aerial bombardment as and when the Allies advanced upon Cherbourg. This Island's defences were well photographed and estimates of the quantity of high-explosive bombs and large-calibre naval shells required to reduce the fortifications to rubble and destroy the will to resist of the garrison were carefully worked out.

'There won't be much of Alderney left . . .'

'Anything is better than what is there now!'

In contrast to his Commander-in-Chief, General Montgomery was enthusiastic. Unlike the Normandy beaches, whose defenders could be reinforced within hours by Panzer divisions known to be held in reserve in the Pas de Calais region, reinforcing the Channel Islands would take a logistic exercise that even his old adversary Erwin Rommel would baulk at.

By the end of February a plan was agreed and given the title Operation 'Subordinate'.

There would be a full-scale invasion of Jersey and it would take place approximately two weeks before the projected invasion of Normandy. However, unlike Operation 'Overlord' or Operation 'Condor' there would be no preliminary bombardment either by air or sea. The intention was to take the German garrison completely by surprise.

But first there would need to be more intelligence and it was arranged that two serving soldiers, both Jersey-born and trained commandos, would be landed by submarine on the Island's north coast and hopefully, this time, not where the Germans had planted a minefield. Their role would be twofold: to estimate the Germans' strength and to reconnoitre suitable sites for paratroops to land.

Captain Eric Blanchard and Sergeant Albert Cartwright had both served in the Royal Jersey Militia and had joined up in 1939. Although known to each other, Eric Blanchard's service in the Victoria College OTC had earned him an immediate commission in the Hampshire Regiment while Albert Cartwright had joined as a private soldier and been promoted to sergeant in December 1943. Both had their homes in St Helier and were advised to contact their families only if they were certain it was safe to do so. They would be provided with forged papers (although their own identities would be retained) based on papers brought out of Jersey by Denis Vibert.

Since both would be wearing civilian clothes they were advised that, if caught, they could be shot. None the less both volunteered without hesitation.

The submarine surfaced at 01.00hrs on Saturday, 1 April 1944, off Bouley Bay on Jersey's north coast where there was a considerable depth of water

close inshore. There was a German gun position at the end of the short pier
and another in a fortification dating back to Napoleonic times at the foot of
the long, twisting hill that was the bay's only access on the land side. But
neither position was manned although there was a small German detachment
billeted in the Water's Edge Hotel at the bottom of the hill.

Blanchard and Cartwright were landed without being seen and scaled the
slopes of the bay that in gentler times would provide natural grandstands for
watching cars and motorcycles racing against the clock up the long hill. They
passed close enough to the hotel to hear the occupants talking amongst
themselves and Blanchard, who spoke French, German and Jersey-French,
realised he could not understand what they were saying for they were
speaking in Russian since this sector was *Abschnitt Nord* — Defence Sector
North — manned by the 643rd Battalion of the *Russiskaya Osvoboditelnaya
Armiya*, the Russian Liberation Army.

Both commandos made contact with their families although Sergeant
Cartwright was surprised to discover that his parents had moved into a much
larger house once lived in by a wealthy uncle who had evacuated in 1940.
Despite their families having little detailed knowledge of German
dispositions, they were able, from their own observations, to assess the
strength of the enemy forces and even their likely ability to respond to a
surprise attack. They were able to note that although the occupiers had tanks,
they were pre-war Renault *Char B1*s, slow and no match for more modern
machinery and anti-tank weaponry. There were few vehicles, military or
otherwise, on the roads and there seemed to be a significant shortage of fuel.
Petrol stations were mostly boarded up, as were many shops. The German
garrison seemed disciplined but consisted of many old soldiers and youths.
However, they were everywhere, not only mingling with the locals on the
streets but also living amongst them.

Four days later Blanchard and Cartwright — who despite moving about
openly in broad daylight had never been challenged since it was actually much
riskier to be out after curfew when there were many more German patrols —
descended to Bouley Bay at midnight and, as arranged, sent a signal by
shaded torch out to sea at 10-minute intervals. At just after 02.00hrs they were
taken off in the submarine's rubber dinghy.

The planners were pleased and three weeks later the plans, still largely based
on Operation 'Condor', were approved by General Montgomery and, with his
recommendation, by the Prime Minister. General Eisenhower, although still
expressing grave reservations, nevertheless abided by his agreement to release
the necessary landing vessels and the personnel to work them.

The date picked would require to be moonless and with a high tide at or
near dawn. The airborne landing would be made by men of the 1st Parachute
Brigade who had earned their spurs during the invasion of Sicily and latterly
in southern Italy. The seaborne invasion would be made at or just before dawn
on the high tide, in St Aubin's Bay on the south coast. While less ideal than

the five-mile-wide sweep of sand that stretched along the Island's west coast, it was apparently less well defended and towards the western end the anti-tank seawall had not yet been completed although, it had been noted by Blanchard and Cartwright, the stretch of beach was mined and also covered by *Batterie Derfflinger,* four 10cm Czech guns in open pits on the hillside above the bay. Rendering the battery inoperative would be an early priority once pathfinders had found a route through the minefield which would be opened by M4 Sherman tanks fitted with flails, the so-called Hobart's 'Funnies', which would be tested for the first time under battle conditions.

The invasion force would comprise men from 69 Brigade of the 50th Division and the 8th Armoured Brigade who, some weeks later, would also land on Gold Beach on D-Day. Two hours before the arrival of the main force of infantry and tanks, a detachment of Royal Marine Commandos would storm Noirmont Point on the south coast, to the south-west of the intended landing beach, where the Germans had mounted *Batterie Lothringen* which comprised four 15cm naval guns, two 7.5cm field guns and one 2.5cm anti-tank gun, six 2cm Oerlikon anti-aircraft guns, two mortars, 13 machine guns, some mounted in tank turrets, no fewer than 16 flamethrowers and three searchlights manned by the *Kriegsmarine*, the whole sited behind defensive fields of 'S' anti-personnel mines. Another detachment would land at the base of cliffs at Les Landes, at the Island's north-western extremity, where the Germans had a *Gema Seetakt* radar array on the *Kriegsmarine* direction and range-finding tower defended by machine guns, flamethrowers and anti-personnel mines.

It was estimated that a force of 5,000 men could be landed in the space of two hours and they, supported by three companies (circa 360 men) of 1st Para who would land in the sector guarded by the Russian Liberation Army, would be sufficient to deal with the German defenders. Although they were believed to number around 12,000, they were a mix of defensive troops and civilian administrators in uniform and thus no match for the hardened soldiers whose battle honours had been well earned in North Africa and Italy. Provided, of course, they could achieve a landing without too many casualties. The Royal Air Force would provide continuous air cover for 24 hours after the initial landings to deter any interference by *Luftwaffe* incursions from French airfields while, at sea beyond the range of *Mirus* and other batteries in Guernsey and Jersey, HMS *Rodney* with escorting destroyers and minesweepers would ensure that the landing ships would have a clear run to the beach and pursue and sink any units of the *Kriegsmarine* that attempted to involve themselves. These same units were to stand by to provide close cover for any withdrawal and, in that event, RAF rocket-equipped Typhoons would harry the German ground forces.

There was one overriding consideration, however, which once again caused much discussion and heart-searching. How many civilian casualties would be acceptable?

Blanchard and Cartwright had been able to identify the principal German headquarters, several of which, such as College House and the Metropole Hotel, were in populated areas. Others, such as the battle headquarters bunkers in St Peter, were in open country with only isolated farms nearby. An attack by rocket-equipped Hawker Typhoons or precision bombing by de Havilland Mosquitos with 500lb high-explosive bombs — both aircraft types being fast enough to confound the anti-aircraft batteries — would destroy these headquarters or render them inoperable.

It was agreed that the airborne assault would take place in the relatively lightly populated area in the Island's north-eastern corner at the dead of night at 02.00hrs (British time) and the seaborne landing in the two-hour period before dawn. Within six hours (it was estimated) Jersey should be secured. It was assumed, at first, that with Jersey recaptured, Guernsey and the other Channel Islands were likely to surrender. General Alan Brooke and his own advisers demurred. There was no evidence that in any similar situations, the Germans had done that, he suggested. Each Island was a separate and independent fortress and indeed all the available evidence so far showed that German forces would cling on ferociously to any territory they held until forcibly removed, and the fighting quality of the ordinary German soldier should never be underestimated. He also pointed out that Jersey was within range of *Batterie Mirus* on Guernsey with its radar-guided 30.5cm guns.

But in this instance, Brooke was overruled. The Islands, the planners insisted, although heavily fortified were ruled by the *Feldkommandantur* who were mostly civilians in uniform and the regular military units were untried in battle. The distance between the Islands themselves and between them and the French coast meant that, with the English Channel dominated by the Royal Air Force and the Royal Navy, there was little likelihood that forces from either Guernsey or the other Islands would be able to intervene. Likewise, it was agreed that there was little likelihood of retaliation from the German forces on the Cotentin because of the Allied domination of sea and air.

There were concerns about 'Subordinate' because of its impact on 'Overlord'. The landings on the European mainland had originally been planned for the beginning of May but had already been put back to the first week in June. Advisers were divided. If the Channel Islands were to be stepping stones into Europe, sufficient time should be allowed for the lessons learned from Operation 'Subordinate' to be incorporated into the detail of the D-Day plans. However, it was pointed out, a successful invasion of Jersey would also require sufficient forces to be diverted from Operation 'Overlord' to the Channel Islands to ensure that any German surrender was maintained and a major evacuation of the German forces in Jersey (who it was presumed would have surrendered) to cages in the United Kingdom would be required. That the Island authorities would co-operate was taken for granted.

Nevertheless, the decision was taken. Operation 'Subordinate' would go ahead. The successful capture of Jersey would be the first chime of the bell of freedom from Nazi tyranny in Europe. Even if it failed, as many still feared it might, valuable lessons would be learned.

The date was fixed as two weeks before D-Day, Saturday, 20 May, long enough in advance for lessons to be learned and acted upon, too short a period for the Germans to mount any viable operation to recapture the Islands before the landings in Normandy.

On the night of Friday, 19 May, the people of Jersey knew that at last something momentous was afoot as they heard the drone of aircraft overhead flying lower than ever before and the unfamiliar sound of anti-aircraft fire in anger and the clatter of falling shrapnel.

On the north-western tip of the Island at Les Landes technicians of the *Kriegsmarine* garrison of the lookout tower were warming up the *Gema Seetakt* radar when a company of Royal Marines came swarming up the cliffs, having paddled ashore from three silenced Motor Launches of Coastal Forces. Amongst them was Corporal Edwin Vibert who, as a boy, had played amongst the ruins of nearby Grosnez Castle, a medieval structure that had once sealed off the headland and provided shelter for Islanders from marauders from France. Corporal Vibert was one of the pathfinders who picked their way carefully through the minefield that stretched down the cliffs, reeling out white guidance tapes for the Marines following behind.

Most of the garrison were still pulling on their uniforms in the adjoining personnel bunker which, like the tower, was well designed and equipped to beat off attackers, when the Marines burst in through armoured entrances obligingly left open for them. There was little active resistance although *Leutnant* Holgar Givensius was shot dead as he cranked the bunker's only telephone. There were no other casualties on either side. The Germans were secured in their own mess and the tower itself stormed. Three technicians were wounded — one would succumb to his wounds an hour later — and all surrendered with only a brief struggle. The radar array was destroyed with clumps of plastic explosive.

In the north-east of the Island the 400-strong Russian Liberation Army and its German officers were taken completely by surprise as the advance guard of the 1st Parachute Brigade, under the command of Lieutenant-Colonel Alan Streatham MC, descended amongst them and resistance to the landing was sporadic and disorganised. Casualties on both sides were light as the Russians laid down their arms and although their officers fought bravely they were easily overcome without any fatalities. No alarm was given and no other German units intervened. Lieutenant-Colonel Streatham mustered his troops, detailed parties to guard the Russians and studied his Island maps before making his next move.

The storming of *Batterie Lothringen* at Noirmont Point was rather more eventful. Here the *Kriegsmarine* personnel were much more alert and, as the 96 Marines scaled the loose granite of the cliffs and sought to skirt the minefields, they were detected and the *Oberleutnant* in charge ordered several flares to be fired to illuminate the attackers for the defenders who then directed accurate and deadly machine gun and mortar fire towards them. Casualties were heavy since cover on the bare cliffs was minimal. The officer leading the assault, Major Miles Penberthy DSO MC, was killed outright by a burst of machine-gun fire and his second-in-command, Captain John Arkwright, was severely wounded in the same burst. Altogether the Marines sustained more than 50% casualties without securing any of the German positions. Pinned down at the bottom of the cliff, Lieutenant Brian Eastham called down a naval bombardment well aware that the nearest RN ship was still some 10 miles distant, within range of Island batteries which would certainly respond and that, although he was able to give very precise co-ordinates, the likelihood of the naval bombardment silencing the machine gun nests that had his men scrabbling for cover almost at the water's edge was negligible. Nevertheless, knowing he might well be signing his own death warrant, Lieutenant Eastham gave the order for the bombardment to begin.

In battle headquarters at the *Kernwerk* near the centre of the Island, the officer in charge, an *Oberstleutnant* who had lost his right eye and right arm on the Eastern Front listened with incredulity as frenzied reports of the raids were received by telephone and messenger. Reports from the remaining *Freya* radar arrays indicated an invasion fleet to the south of the Island and approaching rapidly. He ordered a General Alarm, putting the garrison at battle stations and spoke personally to *Befehlshaber* Graf von Schmettow in Guernsey, *Oberst* Heine, the *Festungkommandant* at Government House and *Major* Heider at the *Platzkommandantur*. He contacted *Batteries Lothringen* and *Derfflinger* to direct their barrage towards the targets at sea and learned that *Lothringen* was under attack but successfully beating off the attackers.

Although the majority of the men of *ID319* had yet to fight a battle, they were led by commanders many of whom had had hard battle experience on the Eastern Front and although most had been invalided out to a non-combative posting, lessons once learned were not forgotten. Being aware that his erstwhile Russian allies had most likely laid down their arms since no contact could be made with them, within an hour of being wakened *Oberst* Heine had established a defence line that isolated the north-eastern corner of the Island where the insurgents had landed and sent in a squadron of tanks supported by several companies of infantry to find them.

'The invaders must be thrown back into the sea,' had been von Schmettow's terse order. The *Befehlshaber* had not long returned from an anti-invasion briefing in Rennes and was due to attend war games for senior officers there at the beginning of June.

The Germans fought fiercely, harrying the men of 1st Para across fields and isolated farms, giving no quarter unless the parachutists surrendered with their hands up. Hours and hours of practice bore fruit as the British force was surrounded. There were heavy casualties on both sides and several furious exchanges of fire as the invaders sought cover in barns, pig-sties and abandoned farmhouses. The Germans sent in tanks armed with flamethrowers and soon a pall of acrid smoke was drifting across the battlefield. Despite the planners' assessment, the Germans proved to be capable opponents and as dawn began to streak the eastern sky, the last remnants of 1st Para were rounded up. Of the 360 men who had parachuted on to the Island more than 100 had been killed or wounded in the fire fights and more than 200 were taken prisoner. A small number escaped capture by hiding out in buildings and the still quite heavily wooded valley that led down to Rozel Bay. Most would either be captured or surrender themselves the following day although a few, very few, would remain hidden by Islanders despite rigorous searches until Liberation.

Meanwhile Lieutenant Eastham's call had been answered and HMS *Rodney,* at a range of eight miles, commenced a radar-guided bombardment of the gun positions of *Batterie Lothringen,* with her secondary armament of 6in guns. The first salvo fell short, crashing harmlessly into the sea. In *Batterie Lothringen's* command bunker *Oberleutnant* Hans Bliesener saw the battleship's gun flashes and directed the large range-finder in their direction. In a minute *Batterie Lothringen* was roaring its response. The gun duel lasted 15 minutes, at the end of which HMS *Rodney* withdrew having received just one hit on the port side causing slight injuries amongst the crew of one of its 4.7in gun turrets. No hits were recorded on the guns or installations of the battery but several 6in high-explosive rounds fell amongst the buildings beyond the battery including the former Portelet Hotel which had been taken over by the *Luftwaffe* as a military hospital, causing several deaths and severe injuries amongst the patients and staff. Many of the Marines, retreating towards the water's edge, blundered into the minefield and suffered a dozen or more casualties. The Motor Launches that had brought them came under sustained machine gun and mortar fire as they pulled the shaken and battered Marines from the water. ML335 was severely damaged enough to be abandoned and sank within minutes. Its crew and the Marines already embarked were rescued by other boats with only slight casualties.

At 06.15am Rear-Admiral Lindsey-Scott, officer commanding Operation 'Subordinate' in HMS *Rodney*, gave the order for those units already landed to withdraw as indicated in the operational orders and stood down the main invasion force which had hove to some 20 miles to the south-west of Jersey, out of range of the shore batteries.

Operation 'Subordinate' was over with the loss of almost 200 casualties and a similar number taken prisoner. Lieutenant Eastham, wounded by splinters during HMS *Rodney's* bombardment and evacuated by motor launch, was awarded the Military Cross and Sergeant-Major Gerald Atkinson who had led the successful assault on the *Kriegsmarine* radar tower at Les Landes was awarded the Military Medal.

* * *

The foregoing is fiction and readers might well ask in that case why include it and why invent characters and even awards? Is this just the historian showing off and trying to prove that he can also write fiction?

Operations 'Constellation', 'Concertina', 'Coverlet' and 'Condor' did exist and were planned in great detail. The recapture of the Channel Islands was a serious consideration. Russian leader Joseph Stalin was continuously urging the Western Allies to open a second front to relieve the pressure on the one in the East and specifically mentioned the recapture of the Channel Islands as an obvious objective. The attempt at Dieppe had already proved a disaster but once recaptured the Channel Islands could be held with all the propaganda advantages of being able to announce to the oppressed peoples of Europe, 'You're next!'

Thus what we have just witnessed might have happened had a version of Operation 'Condor' been put into effect. Operations similar in concept to 'Condor' *were* put into effect — at Cherbourg, Caen, St Malo and Brest after D-Day, operations where hundreds or even thousands of civilian casualties could well have been sustained except, unlike the Channel Islands, the civilians in the firing line had somewhere to run to. True, these were land encirclements and not the same type of assault envisaged for Condor but the targets were not dissimilar — supposedly impregnable fortresses commanded by men who had taken an oath to defend them to the last man and the last bullet.

However, during the night of Monday, 5 June, Channel Islanders were aware that at last something truly momentous was afoot. The drone of aircraft over the French coast was almost continuous once darkness fell. Even Guernsey, more than 30 miles from the nearest French coast, trembled slightly to the rumble of distant aero engines.

In all the Islands the German forces were put on full alert and several anti-aircraft batteries found illusory targets and opened fire, showering their neighbourhoods with shrapnel and rattling window panes.

The next morning, on the BBC, John Snagge announced that 'D-Day has come!' The landings in Normandy had taken place precisely where General Marcks had predicted. His judgement was vindicated although he himself was killed in an air strike on his headquarters just a few days later.

The *Befehlshaber* Graf von Schmettow was attending the war games in Rennes and hurried back although, before embarking for Guernsey at Granville, he took the time to examine the nearby fortifications, deciding they were inferior to his own. A telephone call to his headquarters quickly established that no landings had taken place on the Islands and he returned on Thursday, 8 June. The day before, the London *Daily Telegraph* had actually quoted German sources as claiming that 'Allied airborne formations landed on Guernsey and Jersey' and that they were 'at once engaged in exhausting, costly battles'. In someone's dreams but nowhere else.

Initial euphoria at an early liberation for the Islanders soon dissipated. Although the occasional sounds and smoke of battle could be detected on the eastern horizon, the expected invasion fleets did not materialise and it soon became obvious that no one appeared to be giving the beleaguered Channel Islands a second glance. The Germans remained on high alert and, the anti-aircraft batteries in particular, were ready to open fire at anything that came within range. But little did except high-flying bombers returning to their East Anglian bases after bombing the U-boat pens at Brest, Lorient or La Pallice.

Although D-Day was something happening somewhere else, within a matter of days there were sporadic raids around the Islands with aerial attacks on patrol boats and escort vessels. On 14 June Jersey airport was bombed and the following day a bomb was dropped on Elizabeth Castle.

Within three weeks of D-Day it was obvious to the German High Command that the Channel Islands were to be bypassed. There were no plans to invade, rather the Allies would simply isolate the garrisons and allow them to starve. The Islands were already suffering supply problems which were manifesting themselves before D-Day thanks to the vulnerability of the sea links between the Islands and mainland France. Those links were made even more tenuous as a result of the loss of several of the regular transport vessels in the invasion but more so due to the lack of fuel. While former Rhine barges operating at night with their low freeboard presented smaller radar silhouettes, their use was limited to fine weather and even in summer that could not be guaranteed — D-Day itself had been delayed by unseasonal gales.

Baron Hans Max von Aufsess, head of the Civil Affairs branch of the Military Administration in Jersey, in his *Occupation Diary* (translated by Kathleen J. Nowlan and published by Phillimore, 1985) wrote: 'The dogs of war have passed us by. We joke at the forgetfulness of the British at leaving us behind.'

Although the *Luftwaffe* maintained fortnightly transports to the Islands (principally for mail and personnel) until April 1945 shortage of fuel meant that each increasingly hazardous flight could be the last. Consideration was even given to supplying the Islands by U-boat. A U-boat could bring in up to 25 tonnes of supplies and Graf von Schmettow even went as far as preparing a shopping list per U-boat — 10 tonnes of sugar, 11 tonnes of fats, 3 tonnes of soap, half a tonne of razor blades, grape sugar, dextrose and as much diesel oil as could be spared without prejudicing the craft's return journey to its base in Germany. But, as had been the case when the Islands' suitability as U-boat bases was assessed, the shallowness of the seas around the Channel Islands made operations for submarines particularly hazardous and nothing came of the idea.

However, U-boats had attempted to become involved in the D-Day landings and at least five were reported as operating in Channel Islands waters. One, *U-275*, under the command of *Oberleutnant zur See der Reserve* Helmut Bork, put into St Peter Port for repairs having sustained damage in a depth-charge attack in the Channel. While in St Peter Port, *U-275* came under attack from the Royal Air Force but managed to avoid any further damage. Being unable to be repaired because of Guernsey's limited facilities, the disabled *U-275* sailed for Brest. The U-boat was eventually sunk off Newhaven by a mine on 10 March 1945.

Although the British and Canadian forces had become bogged down outside Caen, General George Patton's US 3rd Army was mopping up the German forces on the Cotentin, although reducing the fortress at Cherbourg would take some time since its commander *Generalleutnant* von Schlieben decided to take the order to fight to the last man and last round almost literally (although Hitler was disappointed how quickly the fortress fell). Thus, while there was still time, most of the remaining *OT* workers were shipped out to St Malo, as were the *SS* penal construction brigade on Alderney and all the concentration camp prisoners. Apparently Hitler himself commanded that 'in no circumstances must they fall into enemy hands'. On 17 July, Rommel himself suggested to Hitler that most of the troops be removed from the Channel Islands in order to play a much more worthwhile role in resisting the Allied advance. Hitler refused, flying into one of his rages and forbidding Rommel from ever raising the subject again.

In July *Marinegruppe West* believed that the garrisons in the Channel Islands could no longer be supplied since with the Cotentin ports in Allied hands and St Malo about to fall, the supply routes from further afield were hazardous in the extreme such was the Allies' domination of the English Channel. It was considered, therefore, that the civilian population, except for those active in the production of foodstuffs, should be evacuated to France since Jersey and Guernsey were self-sufficient enough to feed the garrisons if the provisions and fuel destined for the Islanders were diverted to the troops. By international convention the occupying force had an obligation to feed the civilian population, but such an obligation would go if the civilians went too. Were the Allies to be advised that 'English' civilians were aboard the evacuation ships then they should be assured of a safe passage. However, Hitler decreed that he alone would determine the fate of the civilian population and the military authorities would have to wait for his decision.

While Hitler vacillated no further supplies were being received and, although not yet two months after D-Day, the Islands were already running short of essentials. On 31 July, *Vizeadmiral zur See* Friedrich Hüffmeier, the newly appointed *Seekommandant* (*Seeko*) of the Channel Islands (which put him in charge of the harbour commanders of Jersey, Guernsey and Alderney and all coastal defence artillery on the Islands), pointed out that not only had nothing been done following the *Führer's* order to strengthen the Islands to enhance their *Festung* status, they were running dangerously low on vital supplies such as coal, sugar, salt and diesel oil, the last particularly essential for the maintaining of Guernsey's waterworks, without which the Island would be vulnerable to disease. At the same time consideration was also being given to evacuating the elderly and the sick. But no decision had yet been taken about evacuating civilians even though once they went the amount of food available for the troops would dramatically increase and the amount of crime, most of it involving the theft of foodstuffs by civilians, the remaining workers and even the troops themselves, would reduce. The same day more than 500 tonnes of food was transported safely from St Malo to Guernsey but it was abundantly clear that if Hitler didn't make up his mind promptly about what to do with the civilian population, the garrison would be stuck with them because very soon there would be nowhere for them to go and no ships to take them.

By 3 August the leading edge of the American advance was 20 miles from Dol-de-Bretagne, a town just a few miles from St Malo, the major French port at the mouth of the River Rance dominated by the walled city known as the Intramuros. It had been Patton's plan to bypass St Malo — his ultimate targets were the much more significant ports of Brest and Lorient — but VIII Corps commander Major General Troy Middleton decided that the advance could not leave a large concentration of German forces in its rear which would ultimately pose a threat to Patton's lines of communication. He ordered Brigadier General Herbert Earnest with his armoured columns to take the port. Patton agreed with the strategy and made more troops available to Earnest's forces although he believed that once by-passed, the Germans would make only a token defence of St Malo.

The defences of the port were under the command of *Oberst* Andreas von Aulock, a veteran of Stalingrad who, like the other *Festung* commanders, had sworn an oath to defend his to the last man, or as he put it, 'the last stone'.

On the same 3 August, von Aulock, aware of how close the Americans were, summoned town officials and told them that, since he wished to spare the civilian population harm from the coming battle, they would have to be evacuated. To French requests that St Malo, the historic walled city from which Jacques Cartier had set out to colonise Canada, should be declared an 'open town' to save it from inevitable destruction, von Aulock replied that he had already put the question to *Generalfeldmarschall* Günther von Kluge (who had replaced von Rundstedt as German C-in-C West) who had referred the matter to Hitler whose response was that in warfare there was no such thing as an historic city.

Two days later, during the early evening of 5 August, almost the entire civilian population exited the town walking under white flags, pushing carts and carrying suitcases with their belongings to the American lines.

The battle for St Malo began the next day with the walled city coming under shellfire from both the Americans and the German-held island of Cézambre, 4,000 metres offshore in the mouth of the River Rance. Fires started and, thanks to the Americans cutting the town's water supplies to hasten a German surrender, raged on unabated. The Germans added to the conflagration by setting off demolition charges that destroyed the port facilities entirely.

After 10 days of fierce bombardment which reduced the ancient walled city to little more than piles of rubble, the German resistance was concentrated on the island of Cézambre and the *Fort de la Cité*, a fortress built by Vauban at the instigation of Napoléon Bonaparte and subsequently heavily fortified by the Germans. Artillery fire from these two redoubts was causing heavy casualties and it seemed that von Aulock was determined to fulfil his oath to his *Führer*. However, despite an abundance of food, water and ammunition and relatively little damage (the citadel was riddled with tunnels just like the Channel Islands), after 40 minutes of a massive air attack which featured for the first time the use of bombs containing 'gasoline jell' (which today we know as napalm), a white flag indicated that von Aulock was prepared to surrender, a decision taken, despite his oath, because, he claimed, of the low morale of his troops due to the ferocity of the American attacks.

Reducing Cézambre took rather longer — the garrison did not surrender until 2 September, almost a month after the start of the assault on St Malo. Despite almost continuous bombardment from land, air and sea, the end came only when the 15in guns of HMS *Malaya* were brought to bear, and then only because the island's water supplies had finally run out as the sea water distillation plant was destroyed. During the siege the island — just half a mile long and a quarter of a mile wide — was supplied with food and ammunition from the Channel Islands, a very risky enterprise given the Allies' domination of the seas but one which was carried out with courage and daring and instigated by the *Seeko*, *Vizeadmiral* Hüffmeier.

Why I have dwelt at some length on the siege of St Malo is that it serves as a model for what might have occurred in the Channel Islands had a full-scale assault been planned and executed. Furthermore *Vizeadmiral* Hüffmeier, although at that time in command only of the Islands' sea defences, played a key role in maintaining St Malo and Cézambre's resistance. The Islands' *Festungkommandanten* had taken the same oath as von Aulock and although *Oberleutnant* Richard Seuss was only acting *Kommandant* of Cézambre (a relatively junior officer, he had already been awarded the Knight's Cross with Oak Leaves for distinguishing himself in the fighting around St Malo), he would not surrender until given the appropriate permission from his superiors to do so. At the end, unable because of bad weather to take further supplies to the island, Hüffmeier gave the necessary permission. Clearly the Admiral's experience would have a material effect on how he himself would behave when in a similar position, as we will see.

What is most frightening about the defence of St Malo is the degree to which ordinary German soldiers were prepared to demonstrate so convincingly the value of military discipline in pursuing their leader's will. These were not élite paratroops, nor were they fanatical *Waffen-SS*, both of whom were to demonstrate as the war progressed into Germany itself that they were prepared to fight to the last man. These were instead the same ordinary German soldiers who made up the garrisons of the Channel Islands.

In a similar situation would they behave in the same way? A little later we will
be examining a scenario where they might just have done so.

By the end of August the adjacent French coast was in Allied hands
(although Patton would not achieve his objective of capturing Brest until 18
September and the garrison of Lorient would not surrender until the day
after VE-Day) and this meant that no more fuel, food or medical supplies
could be imported to the Channel Islands from France.

Due to Hitler's vacillation the projected evacuation of civilians had not
taken place, so the occupiers were faced with many thousands of mouths to
feed as well as their own. In Jersey Bailiff Coutanche produced a detailed
report which gave precise predictions of just how long various commodities
would last without replenishment. In mid-August it was estimated that the
garrisons had provisions for three months, perhaps less. Orders were received
that food supplies must be strictly controlled to extend the survival of the
garrisons as long as possible and that the rations to the civilian population be
cut accordingly. Supplying the Islands by air was contemplated but the
Islands' airports were unsuitable for the ideal transport aircraft — long-range
Focke-Wulf *Condor* aircraft capable of flying from Germany — to land and
the equipment needed for drops by parachute was generally no longer
available. Nevertheless some flights to Guernsey were tried using much
smaller Heinkel *He111* bombers and some parachute drops did take place at
Jersey airport.

As early as the end of August a revised estimate reduced the food supply to
just 45 days and it was clear that if starvation was to be avoided, something
had to be done. Once again the military authorities considered evacuating the
civilian population, although the original intent to use their own vessels to
evacuate the population to France was now quite out of the question. So if
the Germans couldn't do it, the British would have to. Since this would
involve an approach to the British government, Hitler had to be informed and
his permission sought. It was given reluctantly — it was an admission of
defeat — but since Hitler was still determined to retain the Islands within the
dwindling German Empire, it was an acceptable stratagem. Britain would be
advised that rations to civilians would be stopped since foodstocks were
exhausted and therefore she should remove all her citizens except those who
were essential for the German war effort.

By mid-September the Channel Islands' isolation was complete and what
the Germans would refer to as *Die Grosse Hungerzeit* (The Time of Great
Hunger) began in earnest.

At the same time, on 10 September, a member of Jersey's Superior Council,
Deputy Edward Le Quesne, whose portfolio was Labour, was arrested by the
GFP for having a concealed wireless set and at his trial a fortnight later was
sentenced to seven months' imprisonment, a sentence he could not begin until
Monday, 9 October because the prison was full. However he was released on
Sunday, 22 October, principally because he was of greater value to the

Germans fulfilling his Superior Council function. He was later to describe his brief incarceration as a 'welcome rest'.

To hasten the capitulation of the German garrison, Britain's Psychological Warfare Department, never short of ideas on how to upset German troops and undermine their morale (leaflets filled with pornographic pictures of their wives at home entertaining non-combatant Party officials being just one example), had been already been active and at the end of August RAF Albemarles began dropping thousands of leaflets on the Islands, a nightly exercise during the first weeks of September. The leaflets were printed in German and titled *Nachrichten für die Truppen* (News for the Troops). They set out in considerable detail the Allied successes on all battlefronts which made it clear that it was only a matter of time before a total German collapse. Why not surrender now?

On 1 September, the day after the first leaflet drop, another message was dropped by parachute suggesting that the telephone line between Guernsey and France be reconnected to allow a German general (only ever referred to as 'Mr John Black' but actually *Afrika Korps* veteran General Bassinger) who was already a prisoner of war to speak directly to von Schmettow and urge him to surrender the garrisons.

This particular suggestion was ignored but a further attempt was made on 22 September by a Major Alan Chambers of the Supreme Headquarters Allied Expeditionary Force accompanying 'Mr Black' on a hazardous voyage on a high-speed launch, *HSL2632*, under a white flag from Carteret on the Cotentin coast to St Peter Port. Letters to von Schmettow had once again been dropped by parachute but no one knew whether or not he had received them. Contact was made at around 1.30pm (Chambers having transferred to a dinghy in which he attempted to row ashore) but the German naval *Oberleutnant* in command of the E-boat *S112* that met the dinghy advised Major Chambers, through an Army interpreter, that if he had come about a surrender he was wasting his time. Bravely, given that the German craft was both heavily armed and fully manned, Chambers insisted on hearing that from von Schmettow himself and wished to discuss the military situation with him. The *Oberleutnant* (who could well have blown Chambers out of the water for his impertinence) did pass the message on and almost two hours later von Schmettow replied that he was well aware of the military situation, thank you very much, and therefore 'declines any discussion'. Major Chambers (who, if he didn't get an award for this, certainly should have done) had one last try and asked the *Oberleutnant* and his Army interpreter if they were aware of the consequences of this action. Chambers later reported that, judging by their expressions, these two Germans at least probably were.

Chambers' adventures that day were not quite over for as *HSL2632* was passing Alderney on the way home to Cherbourg it was fired on by a *Luftwaffe* flak battery and had to take violent evasive measures.

A little earlier, on 19 September, the German Foreign Ministry made an approach to Switzerland, the so-called 'protecting power', to inform Britain that food supplies for the civilian population on the British Channel Islands were exhausted. The German government was prepared to allow civilians, except those fit to bear arms against Germany, to be evacuated or alternatively Britain could supply the Islands with foodstuffs and other essentials.

In Whitehall, after much discussion, the German proposal for Britain to supply provisions was accepted as being the more acceptable of the two alternatives. The Home Secretary agreed on the grounds that it was likely that many Islanders would refuse to leave and it would be 'unseemly' if Britain were to be seen to force such an evacuation, particularly after the Islanders had suffered the privations of occupation for so many years.

Unfortunately Prime Minister Winston Churchill did not agree. A fortnight earlier he had already scrawled in the margin of a paper that proposed that the Islands' garrisons be starved out, 'Let 'em starve. No fighting. They can rot at their leisure.' Clearly he was referring to the Germans but the reality was that if the garrisons starved, so would the Islanders. Nevertheless he wrote in a minute dated 27 September: 'I am totally opposed to our sending any rations to the Channel Islands ostensibly for the civil population but in fact enabling the German garrison to prolong their resistance.' What's more, the Germans were to be reminded that it was their responsibility to feed the people and if they couldn't do that, they should surrender.

With the benefit of hindsight Churchill's typically robust response may well have been right in the circumstances but there was little evidence elsewhere in Europe that German garrisons were prepared to be 'starved out'. There was another factor that perhaps Churchill, who often described himself as 'a former Naval person' (recalling his days as First Lord of the Admiralty), might also have considered. After the Bomb Plot of July 1944, Adolf Hitler had lost whatever faith he had ever had in the German Army and the responsibility for defending his *Festungen* was increasingly being put into the hands of officers of the fervently patriotic and highly disciplined *Kriegsmarine*. Few, if any, of the German personnel in the Channel Islands played a part in the plot itself (although von Aufsess's wife was suspected of being peripherally involved and was arrested but ultimately released). Nevertheless, *Seeko* Hüffmeier used the opportunity to advance his own position by consistently reporting on the failures of his army superiors in their dealings with the local authorities and their questionable enthusiasm for continuing the struggle until final victory. Eventually Hüffmeier, when he achieved his objective of overall command, would contemplate 'eating grass' rather than surrender.

The British government's response was passed to the German Foreign Ministry who cabled von Schmettow to find out the true position, particularly with regard to the numbers involved and whether or not civilian evacuation, however it might be achieved, was still an option.

Von Schmettow reported that, as at the beginning of October, there were 28,500 troops in the Channel Islands, 12,000 of them in Jersey, 13,000 in Guernsey and 3,500 in Alderney. The numbers had been augmented with the arrival, in August, of hundreds more Germans, particularly naval personnel, who had fled the Allied advance down the Cotentin. The garrison was supplemented by 39,000 civilians in Jersey and 23,000 in Guernsey. Current food supplies could be eked out until January, although certain items were already in very short supply and medicines were virtually non-existent. Quite apart from the practical difficulties, evacuation was now out of the question since the garrison could not maintain the Islands' infrastructure — agriculture, generation of electricity, running the waterworks, etc — without employing a large section of the local population. In short, without the civilian population, the garrison was doomed anyway. However, were the Red Cross to supply the needs of the civilians, current food stocks could last until May 1945 although certain essentials, medicines, cereals, soap and even tobacco, were required straight away.

The Islands' authorities decided that they would not be left out. In Guernsey Bailiff Carey wrote a long letter to von Schmettow pointing out to him his responsibilities. Von Schmettow wrote an even longer letter back pointing out the limitations he faced in meeting those responsibilities, even if he agreed that he had those responsibilities, which was not necessarily the case. Furthermore, there was no question of him contacting the protecting power. It was decided therefore that there was no alternative but to send someone to England with a letter advising the British government of the state of the civilian population. Carey was wary about agreeing to this, maintaining Sherwill's earlier view that escapers created problems for the Islanders left behind. However, a group of Islanders who thought that the Controlling Committee was being too easy on the Germans (for not continually reminding them of their responsibilities to feed the population, for instance) pointed out that the Island's administration would come under scrutiny after the war and it would be in his interest and that of the members of the Controlling Committee to show that the Islanders' plight was the fault of the Germans, not their own maladministration.

Fred Noyon, a retired merchant navy captain, left Guernsey with a companion 'on a normal afternoon's fishing expedition' and just kept going. His vessel was spotted by an American warship which towed them to Cherbourg (where it was damaged) and Noyon, with ample evidence of the state of affairs in Guernsey, eventually arrived in England on 12 November. After the Liberation, when Fred Noyon returned to Guernsey, he was presented with a cheque for £19 15s 3d (£19.76) by the Bailiff to cover the cost of repairs to his boat in Cherbourg. Louis Guillemette, who had been Carey's secretary throughout the Occupation, suggested that the cheque might be accompanied by a letter of thanks for his public-spirited action.

In Jersey Bailiff Coutanche had prepared a very detailed memorandum on the food situation at the end of August and this was taken to England by an escaper (the number of successful escapes to the nearby French coast now in American hands dramatically increased — there were 81 successful escapes between September 1944 and January 1945) and was in the hands of the British government by 23 September. Coutanche was not aware of this and prepared another, updated, memorandum which another successful escaper, former member of the purchasing commission in Granville, Norman Rumball, took with him and was delivered to the British government in mid-November.

As it happened, as we shall see, the War Cabinet had decided to arrange for the Red Cross to supply the Islands before either appeal arrived.

In October, faced with a bleak and hungry winter, the Bailiffs of both Islands appealed to the International Committee of the Red Cross (ICRC) for help. Once again the British government blocked the appeal. Food supplies would simply prolong the Germans' will to resist, it maintained (almost as though it had read von Schmettow's report which, in fact, it might well have done) and, indeed, overtures to the German commander to surrender now that the Islands were isolated had been curtly rebuffed. However, it was clear that if the Germans *were* to be starved out, then inevitably the Islanders would starve with them. Furthermore, if the garrison were to requisition all the foodstuffs and leave the civilians to survive on minimum subsistence, despite this flying in the face of international conventions who could actually stop the garrison if its commanders chose that course of action? Threats of postwar retribution would be of little succour to the starving Islanders.

Opinions in Whitehall were divided. The Home Office (who managed the Crown's responsibility towards its 'peculiars') was in favour of allowing the Red Cross to visit the Islands to see for itself what the situation was for the civilian population. However, the War Cabinet persisted with the view that sending provisions to the civilian population would bolster the garrison's will to resist, although it would not object to medical supplies and soap. There were even differences of opinion as to how long current supplies would last, the Home Secretary taking the view that the people could not hold out beyond mid-November and the War Cabinet believing that the end of the year was a more realistic estimate. For the time being, the view of the War Cabinet prevailed but it was agreed that the German commander should be reminded of his obligations under international law.

However, Brendan Bracken, Minister of Information and confidante of Winston Churchill, felt that reminding the Germans of their obligations was a pointless exercise if they had no means of fulfilling them. Instead, the privations and misery of the civilian population should be used to encourage the Germans to surrender although, it had to be admitted, there was little sign of this. The German garrison, despite its own obvious privations, was well armed, stubbornly sitting in virtually impregnable fortresses and gave every indication of remaining belligerent.

Members of Parliament began asking questions. The Channel Islands were now well behind the war fronts and yet were still hosting some very stubborn Germans whose presence was causing acute physical distress to subjects of His Majesty. Something had to be done.

The War Cabinet looked at three options.

Evacuating the civilians was still a possibility but that would leave the Germans with probably enough supplies for several months and look what happened at St Malo. And the Channel Islands were much more fortified than ever St Malo was. Retaking them would be a bloody affair. Not on.

Relief supplies could be sent. This was another option but it would simply prolong the Germans' will to resist even if it salved Britain's conscience that it did not let these subjects of His Majesty starve. So this was not really on either.

The third option was to do nothing except promise dire consequences for the garrison commander if his failure to surrender led to civilian deaths from malnutrition and disease. The prospect of such retribution might just cause the garrison commander to throw in the towel. Although it was recognised that there had been no indication whatever that this coincided with any German thinking, as late as 6 November Winston Churchill was holding this particular line. 'I am entirely opposed to our feeding the German garrison in the Channel Islands and thus prolonging its resistance.' So there!

However, just a day later, Churchill changed his mind. Perhaps someone pointed out the political consequences of visiting starvation on the Islanders to bring about the capitulation of a garrison which, while it was an irritation because it existed, actually posed no threat to the Allied advance into Germany and the ultimate destruction of the German Reich. How little effect the Islands could have on the outcome of the war had been illustrated when German batteries on Alderney had fired on the Americans advancing down the Cotentin. The Americans had merely moved out of range without slowing down but military depots and ammunition dumps were damaged or destroyed as a result of the intelligence gained during the German raid on the peninsula in April 1945. Anti-aircraft gunners on the Islands were still occasionally bringing down Allied aircraft but this could be avoided if the aircraft (mostly those returning from bombing the submarine pens on the Biscay coast) flew around the Channel Islands instead of over them, where the Islands' 'flak umbrella' with its 88mm guns extended up to 14,000 metres (over 45,000ft).

Churchill's change of heart was notified to the German government who responded on 23 November to the effect that it would allow the Red Cross to provide food parcels and other essentials to the civilian population.

If we were looking for winners out of this confrontation then it would be the Germans who could claim the laurels — the feeding of the civilian population would allow them to continue to resist until beyond the war's end.

Thanks to Winston Churchill's intransigence, Islanders had undergone two months of deprivation and uncertainty that might have been avoided. In the end the other guy blinked — that guy being Churchill because von Schmettow hadn't.

As real hunger and the onset of winter exerted their iron grip, the cargo vessel *Vega* (which had, since 1941, been chartered by the Red Cross from the Swedish shipping company Stockholms Rederi Aktiebolag Svea to carry parcels from Lisbon to French Mediterranean ports) sailed from the Portuguese capital loaded with more than 750 tonnes of New Zealand and Canadian Red Cross supplies comprising 100,000 food parcels, 4,000 invalid diet parcels, soap, salt, medical supplies and 13 million cigarettes!

Put into a modern context, the contents of each parcel (meant to last a month) would have barely filled a supermarket basket, let alone a supermarket trolley. A typical food parcel contained 6oz of chocolate, 20oz of biscuits, 4oz of tea, 20oz of butter, 6oz of sugar, a 20oz tin of milk powder, a 16oz tin of marmalade, a 14oz tin of corned beef, a 13oz tin of ham or pork, a 10oz tin of salmon, a 5oz tin of sardines, an 8oz tin of raisins, a 6oz tin of prunes, a 4oz tin of cheese, a 3oz tablet of soap and 1oz of pepper and salt.

The *Vega* arrived first in Guernsey, docking in St Peter Port at 6.00pm on Wednesday, 27 December. Unloading of the parcels began immediately. However much the Germans might have envied the contents of the parcels, they were scrupulous in ensuring that they went exclusively to civilians but, with the civilian population now being fed, they requisitioned anything else even remotely edible and despite Islanders keeping their dogs and cats under lock and key as best they could, many family pets ended up in the cooking pot.

In order to stretch the garrison's food stocks as far as possible, the ration scale was continually reduced and as a result all training was curtailed. Those troops not actually on duty were ordered to rest every afternoon in order to conserve their energy.

Meanwhile Islanders used to significantly less than 1,500 calories a day and unused to such 'luxuries' as 'Klim' powdered milk, Spam, prunes, powdered eggs, jam and chocolate found themselves suffering all sorts of stomach upsets varying from painful constipation to rampant diarrhoea!

However, alongside any euphoria that these 'luxuries' might have engendered, there was the reality that indeed the Germans' will to resist had been strengthened and there were emerging changes at the top which showed that any thoughts that the Germans, although reduced to dining on limpets, rats, domestic pets and even seagulls, were about to surrender were very wide of the mark.

Chapter 10
We will eat grass

'Mr Bailiff, you and I will be eating grass before we surrender!' The raid whose success was foiled by a falling tide, but what would have happened had the raid been successful? 'German forces retake Granville! United Nations personnel captured!' The mutiny that fizzled out. The spectre of the real Gestapo

Despite the advances of the Allies into Germany itself the first three months of that bitterly cold and hungry winter of early 1945 brought no quick end to the siege of the Channel Islands where electricity and gas supplies became increasingly sporadic and the constant quest for firewood resulted in hundreds of trees, and even wooden buildings, disappearing, sometimes overnight. Permits to cut firewood were mandatory and anyone found gathering firewood without a permit faced arrest and imprisonment.

In February the newly appointed German Commander-in-Chief, *Vizeadmiral zur See* Friedrich Hüffmeier, told Bailiff Coutanche in Jersey: 'We will never surrender even if, at the end, you and I are eating grass.'

So let us spend a few moments examining this Admiral who would rather eat grass than surrender.

In May 1944, a week after *Vizeadmiral* Hüffmeier's 46th birthday, he was detached from the *Wehrgeistiger Führungsstab* (literally the Military Spiritual Leadership Staff, the *Kriegsmarine's* branch of the Armed Forces National Socialist Leadership Staff) to Navy Group Command West in France. The office he had left oversaw the co-ordination and assignment of National Socialist Leadership officers to naval units, ships and submarines. These officers disseminated propaganda and issued political and ideological instructions to keep the men properly motivated. This was a blatant example of overt Nazi ideological infiltration of the German armed forces and these officers were very similar, in their role, to Soviet political commissars.

After the eventual German surrender many commentators would dub Hüffmeier 'a fanatical Nazi', proof of his ideology being that he would not surrender when all other German forces had laid down their arms, and that his trusted emissary to the British liberating forces, *Kapitänleutnant* Armin Zimmermann, who was talking of an armistice rather than asking where he signed the surrender documents, gave the Nazi Party salute rather than the Navy salute still favoured by the vast majority of his fellow officers (despite Hitler's instruction after July 1944 that the rigid raised arm should replace conventional military salutes).

Friedrich Hüffmeier joined the *Kriegsmarine* as a War Volunteer in September 1914 with the intention of making the Navy his career. He served in several surface vessels of the High Seas Fleet until undertaking submarine training in March 1918. He was a watch officer aboard *U19* when the Armistice was concluded. He was awarded the Prussian Iron Cross in 1914 and the Cross of Honour for Combatants in 1918.

Hüffmeier spent many of the interwar years in training establishments and when World War 2 broke out he was Naval Liaison Officer to the General Staff of the Army. He took command of the light cruiser *Köln* in May 1941 and on 29 March 1942 he was appointed as commanding officer of the mighty battlecruiser *Scharnhorst*, at that time Germany's most successful warship.

Although he commanded *Scharnhorst* until 17 October 1943, when researching his book *Death of the Scharnhorst* (Antony Bird, UK, 1983) author John Winton discovered that it took only a short time for *Scharnhorst's* company to decide, to a man, that 'Poldi' Hüffmeier was a walking disaster area who owed his appointment more to social (or was it political?) influence than to ability. There was obviously something in what they thought since the raiding activities of *Scharnhorst* and her sister ship *Gneisenau* had, until Hüffmeier's plodding captaincy, been one of the few success stories of Germany's surface fleet. He was in command when *Scharnhorst* and *Gneisenau* made their famous 'Channel Dash' and although given some credit for the operation's outcome, the planning of the operation and its success were due to the vision and capability of *Admiral* Otto Ciliax. Hüffmeier quickly proved to be a poor seaman and ship handler, once running *Scharnhorst* aground at 26 knots, wrapping a wire around a screw leaving harbour and colliding with *U-523* while on manoeuvres in the Baltic.

In the manner of these things, instead of being reduced to the ranks Hüffmeier was promoted to *Konteradmiral* and posted to the *Wehrgeistiger Führungsstab.*

This was the man who, in July 1944, was appointed *Seekommandant Kanalinseln* (*Seeko KI*) of the Channel Islands, a role which had been fulfilled since its inception in July 1942 by the highly competent and much respected *Kapitän zur See* Julius Steinbach, which put him in charge of the *Hafenkommandanten* (Harbour Commanders) of Jersey, Guernsey and Alderney and all coastal defence artillery on the Islands. Although regarded by many of his contemporaries as a Nazi zealot, he was popular with the naval personnel who thought highly of him. Theo Krausen, *Marineartillerie-Obermaat* (Naval Artillery Chief Petty Officer) at *Batterie Lothringen* in Jersey, remembers him greeting the battery's personnel with 'Good morning, soldiers of *Batterie Lothringen!*' rather than the more usual 'Heil Hitler'. At the same time he was also appointed as deputy to the *Festungkommandant* in Guernsey. In October 1944 he was promoted to being Chief of Staff to *Befehlshaber* von Schmettow who had been promoted to *Generalleutnant* the previous April. He eventually succeeded von Schmettow as Commander-in-Chief on 27 February 1945 after a prolonged campaign to undermine his superior officer and, colleagues noted, there were times when the *Befehlshaber* and his new Chief of Staff were frequently not on speaking terms. In radio messages to Germany Hüffmeier had frequently complained of von Schmettow's 'soft' attitude towards the Islanders. He was aided in this by the fact that only the *Kriegsmarine* wireless station at St Jacques in Guernsey had the necessary power to reach Germany. It is most likely that Adolf Hitler, since the July Bomb Plot which had involved so many senior Army officers, now only trusted the Navy. The service's loyalty (albeit to the Fatherland as much as to its leader despite the indoctrination) had never wavered, and he would have been pleased that his flagship conquests now had somebody truly 'on message' in command. In any event the Channel Islands had been removed from the control of Army Group West (whose Commander-in-Chief [C-in-C] *Generalfeldmarschall* Günther von Kluge, implicated in the Bomb Plot, had committed suicide and been replaced first by *Generalfeldmarschall* Walther Model then by the erstwhile C-in-C, *Generalfeldmarschall* Gerd von Rundstedt) and placed under the overall command of *Admiral* Theodor Krancke of *Marineoberkommando (MOK) West* (Naval High Command West) whose headquarters were at Friedrichshafen.

However, it would be a mistake to believe that Hüffmeier's opinion that von Schmettow was 'too soft' on the Islanders implied a weakness on the latter's part. Von Schmettow's relations with the Island authorities had always, as far as his remit would allow, been correct and, like the Islands' leaders themselves, revealed a respect for the rule of law that his masters in Berlin often lacked. Moreover when Major Alan Chambers (he of the abortive surrender initiative) reported on his failed mission he came to a number of conclusions about *Generalmajor* Graf von Schmettow and his command, even without meeting him. For instance, that von Schmettow was toeing the party line of 'no surrender' (like other remaining German commanders still holding out in the West) because of the consequences to his family at home in Germany if he hadn't. In Germany the principle of *Sippenhaft* (family guilt) was widespread and after the July Bomb Plot the *Gestapo* was knocking on the doors all over Germany of thousands of relatives of those directly involved, often their only link being that they had shared grandparents. Alternatively, the communications with the shore had been intercepted by the *SS* and Graf von Schmettow had not actually been consulted. Another remarkable conclusion was that force would be needed to bring about the Germans' surrender, but not much!

There is no evidence that any pressure was ever exerted on von Schmettow's family, there were no *SS* personnel in Guernsey then or at any other time and Chambers' supposition that not much force would be needed to get the Germans to surrender seemed to be based on his reading of the reactions of the two German officers he actually met. What seems not to have occurred to anyone exposed to Major Chambers' report is that von Schmettow was quite simply a loyal officer of the old school, brought up on the traditions of the Imperial German Army, who would never contemplate surrendering until convinced that all was lost or specifically ordered to do so.

In September 1944, in the opinion of the German High Command, all was certainly not lost and no one was going to order von Schmettow to surrender. Indeed, not only did von Schmettow not contemplate surrender, after D-Day he established an Officers' School at the Palace Hotel in Jersey where senior non-commissioned officers studied for promotion to commissioned rank. On achieving their commissions, these newly promoted officers were given the opportunity of putting their studies into practice with postings to the German fortresses holding out on the French Biscay coast. These transfers were carried out by transport aircraft making the extremely hazardous supply and mail flights to the Islands across newly liberated France every 10 days or so. Their *alma mater* was later destroyed in a mystery explosion on 7 March 1945 which was subsequently claimed to be deliberate sabotage by dissident German troops. What evidence there was implied that the explosion was accidental.

Nothing in von Schmettow's actions during that bleak mid-winter gave any indication that he was about to give up.

Christmas 1944 proved to be a desolate and isolated celebration for occupier and occupied alike. There was little traditional Christmas fare although farming families would have looked forward to a chicken or a rabbit, while those living in the town might make do with turnip soup and potatoes, the 'trimmings' being decorative strips of 'Window', the aluminium foil dropped by Allied aircraft, particularly in the run-up to D-Day, to confuse German radar. Most would have been cheered by the thought that this *must* be the last Christmas under enemy occupation.

In Jersey the Germans had requisitioned more than 2,000 chickens and in his diary Baron von Aufsess commented that the meals served were as 'opulent as in times of peace'. In the evening the Baron was invited to a party in the Officers' Club where Sister Marie of the *Deutsches Rote Kreuz* (German Red Cross) had set up 'a toy electric railway and, clad in an unsuitably youthful ballgown and tall paper hat, appeared as a fairy'. Despite what von Aufsess clearly considered as a somewhat bizarre entertainment he noted in his diary that 'we all recognise her goodwill and appreciate her good cooking'. A goodwill Christmas message was also received from *Admiral* Krancke.

Leslie Sinel described Christmas Day in Jersey as being cold and frosty but with bright sunshine. The electrical supply was on all day until midnight without any blackouts and the curfew too was extended until midnight so that friends and relatives could visit each other. Many a sigh of relief, he wrote, was heard when at last the rabbit, fowl or duck made its appearance on the table for, with robberies every night, either by civilians or Germans, one could not be sure what would happen. The bakehouses, he reported, also had a bumper day and carried out their task of being communal cookhouses to everyone's satisfaction.

On Boxing Day Leslie Sinel noted that a large crowd attended a football match in the afternoon and in the evening the Jersey Green Room Club presented the pantomime *Aladdin* at the Opera House (which had been opened by the Jersey-born actress Lillie Langtry in 1900). On a sadder note he also reported that a Miss Waddell had been admitted to hospital with a bullet wound in the thigh after being shot at her house in Portelet. She had disturbed a uniformed German intruder and, grabbing his rifle, suffered a bullet wound from which she later died in hospital. A murder enquiry was initiated.

New Year was celebrated in the Islands by the arrival of SS *Vega* with her cargo of foodstuffs, medicines and, above all, cigarettes. When the *Vega* docked in Guernsey, Bailiff Coutanche travelled to that Island (having been given just 50 minutes' notice) to meet with Bailiff Carey, the president of the Controlling Committee Jurat Leale and the Red Cross representatives, Colonel Iselin and Monsieur André Callias. However, an invitation extended to the two Bailiffs to lunch aboard the *Vega* with Captain Gösta Wideberg was withdrawn by the Germans. There would be no meeting with the Red Cross representatives unless the Germans were present. After all, who knew what these wretched Channel Islanders, particularly the 'vulpine-visaged' Coutanche, would confide?

The meeting was held on the afternoon of 28 December (but not on the *Vega*) and was attended by the two Bailiffs, the two Red Cross representatives, *Vizeadmiral* Hüffmeier, by now Chief of Staff to von Schmettow, *Oberst* von Helldorff, the former Chief of Staff, Baron von Aufsess, Counsellor Zachau Schneeberger, the head of Guernsey's *Nebenstelle*, Jurat Leale, Sir Abraham Lainé, Guernsey's medical officer of health Dr Symons and Dr Collings, Guernsey representative of the British Red Cross. Iselin and Callias asked after the health of the Islanders and were informed that their health was deteriorating through undernourishment and an unbalanced diet. It was discovered that the number of parcels intended for Guernsey (at the rate of two per head of population) was more than 1,700 short while Jersey had 20 to spare. After some hasty calculations it was confirmed that the population of Guernsey was 22,806 and Jersey 39,840. One point that was also confirmed was that there would be no charge to the Islands for the parcels since the cost was being met in entirety by the British Red Cross.

The parcels were unloaded on Saturday, 30 December and delivered to shops so that Islanders could get one each. There were parcels for everyone including babies, the sick and even prison inmates. Later that day the *Vega* sailed for Jersey although Hüffmeier had expressly forbidden Coutanche to return to Jersey in her and, despite the Islands' chronic shortage of fuel, laid on a German patrol boat for him instead. In the event Coutanche arrived in Jersey before the *Vega* and was on the quayside to welcome her. By the time the *Vega* departed on 4 January she had unloaded 77,384 Canadian Red Cross parcels, 2,700 diet parcels from the British Red Cross, almost four tons of salt, 27,000 tablets of soap and 52 cases of medical supplies. The New Zealand

Red Cross sent 15 cases of tobacco (88lb in 2oz packets). A collection amongst Islanders for the Red Cross had already raised more than £2,000.

In his New Year message to the garrisons von Schmettow reminded the troops that they had had a hard year and that they must be ready for more sacrifices in 1945. They were now entirely dependent on their own resources and what mattered now was comradeship, self-discipline, belief in ultimate victory and a will to fight to the last. Von Schmettow repeated these sentiments in response to a broadcast greeting from Propaganda Minister Josef Goebbels thanking the Channel Islands garrisons for collecting more than a million *Reichsmark* for the German Red Cross. This splendid sum had caused much pleasure at home since it showed confidence in victory and solidarity with the Fatherland. Cruickshank gives von Schmettow's response in full: 'In our complete isolation on British soil for many months past we particularly appreciate the broadcast as well as your personal greetings. The three Island fortresses, conscious of their strength, and following the example of other fortresses, will faithfully hold out to the last. With this in mind we salute our Führer and Fatherland.' While von Schmettow's intent is quite evident, his choice of words, 'British soil' rather than 'former British soil' and 'to the last' rather than 'until final victory' were not following the party line.

On 8 January a Lightning P-38, the distinctive twin-boom fighter of the United States Army Air Force, crashed on Jersey's Beauport headland. The pilot, Lieutenant Kelly Moultrie, had baled out and splashed down in Beauport Bay where he was in danger of drowning. John de la Haye, despite being ordered not to by a German coastguard (who presumably thought he was trying to escape to France), paddled out on a flimsy pre-war pleasure float to help the casualty. Unfortunately the float was unable to cope with the two of them and broke up, leaving the airman clinging to a rock while John de la Haye swam to the shore for help. A boat was launched and Moultrie was rescued along with a German soldier who had also plunged into the sea in a rescue attempt and had got into difficulties himself. After the war John de la Haye was awarded the American Medal of Freedom and the medal of the Jersey Humane Society as well as a commendation from the Bailiff. Lieutenant Moultrie was conveyed to a cage created out of a group of former *OT* huts surrounded by barbed-wire and situated behind the South Hill gymnasium where he would soon find he was joined by other American guests.

The *Vega* made her second voyage to the Islands at the beginning of February. Although she once again carried a large quantity of Red Cross parcels, she brought no flour, which was desperately needed, and eight tonnes of soap, intended for the Islands, were left behind in Lisbon because the Portuguese would not grant an export licence for it. The Germans allowed the Bailiffs to contact the ICRC by radio to request that flour be sent at once. The possibility of bringing in coal and of evacuating sick Islanders and German wounded was also considered but no suitable hospital ship was available.

On 27 February, Hüffmeier's machinations came to fruition and he was appointed *Befehlshaber der britischen Kanalinseln* as part of a radical shake-up of the Channel Islands' command structure. *Generalleutnant* von Schmettow was being replaced on health grounds, it was announced. Although the man himself had not needed to see a doctor for more than 15 months, he was ordered to return to Germany by the first available transport aircraft without waiting for his successor as commanding officer of *Infanterie Division 319*. As it happened, von Schmettow kicked his heels for two weeks since no such transport was available and he eventually returned to Germany on the aircraft that brought in his successor, *Generalmajor* Rudolf Wulf.

The change in leadership also meant that many of the important positions were transferred to naval officers with *Korvettenkapitän* Kurt von Cleve replacing *Major* Heider at the *Platzkommandantur*. Von Cleve was of the opinion that Heider had been so soft on the Islanders that his behaviour was worthy of him being shot! Not all the appointments were naval since *Oberst* Siegfried Heine, Jersey's *Festungkommandant*, was promoted to *Generalmajor* and appointed as Military Adviser to Hüffmeier while the *Luftwaffe's Generalmajor* Alexander Dini was appointed Hüffmeier's Chief of Staff. Within days of his appointment *Generalmajor* Wulf had transferred the headquarters of *ID319* to Jersey, a move which had been suggested as long ago as 1942.

What was obvious was that, with the new regime in place, any talk of surrender was tantamount to an act of treason. At an early meeting with Bailiff Coutanche Hüffmeier made his famous statement that they would be eating grass before any such action could be contemplated. (As a matter of interest, although grass may be very nutritional for cows and other domestic animals, human beings would derive more nutritional value from the soil in which it grew.)

He also set out to raise the morale of the garrison by instituting a daily guard of honour outside Staff Headquarters and decreed that any slovenly behaviour by of the troops (which included fraternisation with local women) would be punishable by cuts in the already meagre rations or, in really serious breaches, death by firing squad.

By March 1945 things were going badly for the Germans everywhere. The Allies were on the west bank of the Rhine, the Russians were preparing for the final assault on Berlin, German cities were subject day and night to devastation from the Allied air forces. The *Luftwaffe*, despite the advent of jet-powered fighters, was powerless to stop the bombers and Hitler's high-tech V-weapons had failed in their primary mission of destroying London or the Allies' will to strive towards Germany's unconditional surrender. German jet aircraft never made it to the Channel Islands although a Messerschmitt *Me262A* did land at Jersey airport on 29 June when, flown by Lieutenant Robert Anspach of the United States Army Air Force en route eventually to the USA, it got lost! Similarly there is no evidence of any V-weapons being deployed in the Channel Islands although in his fictional work *The Occupation* (Headline, 2004) author Guy Walters not only places a V-3 'supergun' site in Alderney, he equips the weapons with uranium warheads!

Yet on 9 March, the day that American forces captured intact the bridge over the Rhine at Remagen, came news of a German victory! A force of German commandos, operating more than 500 miles behind the front line, had raided the port of Granville on the French Cotentin peninsula, destroying the port facilities that had been re-established after being fired by the retreating Germans in July 1944, capturing Allied personnel and releasing (probably to their dismay) German prisoners from American custody. The purpose of the raid was to capture supplies, particularly coal, destined for distribution throughout France, Granville being one of the few ports that, although skilfully sabotaged by the retreating Germans, required less work to render it operable than ports like St Malo, Le Havre, Dieppe and Brest. Granville would act as a welcome relief to Cherbourg which, once in Allied hands and cleared of obstacles, became the second busiest port in the world after New York.

The plan to raid Granville had been initiated while von Schmettow was still in command. The Allies had been shipping coal into Granville for some time, the Germans only becoming aware of this after setting up an observation post on Maître Ile on Les Minquiers reef, 14 miles south of Jersey and a similar distance from Granville itself. From this post sightings of Allied shipping were radioed to Naval Headquarters at St Jacques in Guernsey and thence to *MOK West* in Germany. On 21 December 1944 the outpost radioed that it was under attack by the Royal Navy until it was discovered that the attacking vessel was a landing craft that had been captured by escaping German prisoners of war who had been employed unloading coal at Granville. The escapees were able to give full details of the working of the port and the minimal American defences. Following liberation by the Americans the formidable German defences had been abandoned and the port's defences were limited to one 57mm gun and a patrol boat whose prime role was shepherding the coal boats safely into port.

An operation was planned, under *Kriegsmarine* command, the purpose of which was threefold: the capture of as many supply ships as possible, the destruction of the port facilities and the capture of staff officers for interrogation. A large-scale model of Granville was created for briefing the assault force.

The first assault on Granville took place on the night of Tuesday, 6 February, comprising a strike force of nine officers and 140 men, and 15 sundry naval vessels, all of which had been allocated specific tasks including a tug whose role it was to take in tow any prizes. Unluckily for the Germans, what had started as an evening of calm seas changed rapidly (as the weather and sea conditions can do in the Bay of St Malo) and the raid had to be abandoned since the assault troops could not be transferred to the craft designated for the landings due to the rough seas. However, the German craft were able to approach to within a few hundred metres of the shore, close enough to note the lack of sentries. The raiders returned to Jersey safely, still under the cover of darkness (and by now also in thick fog), although the captured landing craft whose personnel had played a key intelligence role in the operation struck a rock and was abandoned without loss.

Until the Channel Islands' isolation, most communications with higher authority had been either by telephone or teleprinter, but with telephone lines now in Allied hands, the only means of communication was by radio and this was where a factor that the Germans had never considered came into play — Ultra.

All radio signals between German positions were routinely intercepted by listening posts in Britain and deciphered at one of the outstations of the Government Code and Cipher School at Bletchley Park, the whole operated in conditions of extreme secrecy under the code name 'Ultra'. Since the capture of Enigma coding machines and the code books to break their ciphers, the Allies had been able to decipher German radio communications almost as soon as they were sent. In a series of signals to *MOK West*, Hüffmeier spelt out his plans for a further raid 'in approximately four weeks' time' when tidal conditions would be right. At 6.35am on 27 February *MOK West* sent the signal to the Islands that confirmed von Schmettow's replacement by Hüffmeier, a signal that was duly read by Bletchley Park.

At 9.00pm on Thursday, 8 March the strike force, under the command of *Kapitänleutnant* Mohr in minesweeper *M412*, sailed from St Helier with eight Army assault detachments, three naval assault groups and one *Luftwaffe* flak crew, a total of 12 officers and 188 men.

That the Americans in Granville were taken completely by surprise is almost an understatement, even though it is highly likely that, Hüffmeier having confided his plans in detail by radio to *MOK West*, Bletchley Park were well aware of what was afoot and when and why. In order to protect Ultra (whose veil of secrecy was not lifted until well into the 1970s), the Americans were warned 'in general terms' to be on the alert for a raid but they took no notice.

Although some commentators have since opined that the raid was a failure because the state of the tide meant that most of the vessels carrying coal and other supplies were sitting on the mud in the inner harbour (something the Germans might have foreseen since they were aware of the tidal range in the Bay of St Malo, with even Mohr's command vessel running aground and having to be abandoned and blown up), many of von Schmettow's originally stated objectives were achieved. Altogether four of the stranded ships were damaged and most of the dockside cranes were put out of action. A planned assault on the radar station overlooking the port was beaten off, with the leader of the naval commandos, *Leutnant zur See* Scheufel, being killed and his body abandoned.

One British vessel was captured, the SS *Eskwood*, a collier which was still afloat. Her master, Captain Wright, had been killed in the indiscriminate firing that preceded the German landings but, under German supervision, the crew were able to make the vessel ready for sea. Unfortunately the *Eskwood* had already been unloaded of her cargo of coal from Swansea and had only 112 tons of bunker coal aboard. Nevertheless the Germans did find charts and convoy routeing instructions for all the coastal waters around Britain.

Altogether there were three Germans killed, 15 wounded and one missing (subsequently taken prisoner by the Americans). Casualties on the Allied side were somewhat higher, with 15 Americans killed, 13 wounded and 19 missing (subsequently confirmed as prisoners of war). British casualties were confined to the personnel on the ships in the harbour and here eight were killed and nine wounded with eight missing (also subsequently found to be prisoners of war). Amongst the latter was John Alexander, an official of the United Nations Relief and Rehabilitation Administration (UNRRA), who had the dubious distinction of being the only UNRRA official to be made a prisoner of war during World War 2. Six French civilians were killed and eight wounded. The Germans also released 67 of their own people who had been held as POWs by the Americans but 12 managed to 'escape' and, in due course, were recaptured. This dozen clearly did not relish exchanging the hard and dirty work of unloading coal boats (but with comfortable billets and plenty of food) for active duty in the cold and hungry Channel Islands where the staple diet was often reduced to limpets and swedes enhanced by the occasional cat!

The two Germans killed in the assault were buried with full military honours in St Brelade's cemetery in Jersey alongside their colleagues from this conflict and the Great War. *Oberleutnant zur See* Otto Carl, the officer commanding a group of *Artillerieträger* (barges bristling with a variety of multi-barrelled weaponry that were so low in the water they could not be picked up on radar) tasked with drawing off the Granville guardship and extinguishing the lighthouse on Grande Ile de Chausey (both of which he achieved), was awarded the Knight's Cross.

The captured Americans were incarcerated for the six weeks left of the war in the group of former *OT* huts where they provided welcome company for Lieutenant Kelly Moultrie.

Despite the efforts Hüffmeier had expended in seeking to replace von Schmettow as *Befehlshaber*, in his signal to *MOK West* he gave the General credit for devising the plan which he believed had been so successfully carried out and, if nothing else, had caused huge embarrassment to the Americans, so much so that they strongly recommended the obliteration of all German naval forces in Channel Islands harbours by saturation bombing. Fortunately wiser counsels prevailed since the end of the war was clearly only weeks away and the inevitable loss of civilian life would have been totally unacceptable regardless of how much American pride had been hurt. However, *Vizeadmiral*

Hüffmeier seemed not to be aware of the war's imminent end and not only sought to follow up the success of his Granville raid with another (planned for 7 May!) but also had plans to bar the ports of Granville and St Malo to traffic with blockships, one being the newly acquired *Eskwood*, which would be filled with concrete blocks and sunk in the harbour mouth at the port where she had been captured. These plans came to nothing and following the Liberation *Eskwood* was towed from St Helier to Swansea where, refitted, she was renamed *Kilworth* in 1946. In 1951 she was sold and renamed *Fenchurch* and in the same year sold again when she was renamed *Holdernoll.* She visited the Channel Islands many times before being broken up at Gateshead in 1956.

A further raid did take place on 5 April when a small German force of commandos landed by small boats on the French coast at Vauville intent on sabotaging strategic targets in and around Cherbourg. The plan was that their success would be followed up by a naval assault on the port of Cherbourg itself. Hüffmeier was nothing if not an optimist.

However, things went wrong from the start. Since the Granville raid, the Americans were much more alert and the Germans' boats were discovered by a patrol that sent a warning to Cherbourg. Then a sentry on the railway line to Paris was attacked but managed to raise the alarm and report that a group of German soldiers was proceeding in the direction of Cherbourg. This group was intercepted at Martinvast as the Germans were attempting to mine a bridge and a brief firefight ensued. Three Germans were injured and taken prisoner; the rest fled. In Cherbourg another group was intercepted but managed to escape. By 7 April all Cherbourg was alerted. More explosives were discovered but the Germans who had placed them were never found. Overall the raid had been a failure and the intended naval assault never took place. However, intelligence gained from the raid allowed the gunners in Alderney to pinpoint Allied munitions and fuel storage areas for bombardment and right up to early May 1945 the villages of Jobourg, Herqueville and Auderville on the Cotentin coast were regularly subjected to long-range fire from the Island.

What we have just read is what actually happened but what if the Germans *had* succeeded in capturing the ships loaded with coal and other supplies? *Vizeadmiral* Hüffmeier was determined to hold out, in his words, 'until final victory' and the Germans' shows of aggression suggested their inevitable surrender was still a long way off. The raids proved that the Germans, as hungry as they might have been, were still a potent and aggressive force.

Supplies of food and coal would have both sustained the garrisons and provided the necessary power for the massive array of armament Hüffmeier had at his disposal. On the Channel Islands there were 67 guns of 15cm (6in) calibre or more, sited in 16 different batteries. The largest — *Batterie Mirus* on Guernsey — had four guns of 30.5cm (12in) calibre with a range of 23 miles. On Jersey *Batterie Schlieffen*, *Batterie Haesler* and *Batterie Lothringen* mounted 15cm guns with a range of more than 15 miles and *Batterie Blücher* on Alderney was similarly equipped. Much of the nearby French coast was in range and, following the Granville raid, batteries on Jersey and Alderney had opened fire on the lighthouse at Carteret (40 miles to the north of Granville), in the belief that it would help guide Allied reinforcements, and put it out.

Thus any force approaching the Channel Islands would run enormous risks unless these batteries could be silenced and to do so would involve unacceptable civilian losses. What's more, these same civilians, already in the firing line, also provided Hüffmeier with a significant bargaining counter. Unlike the other fortresses holding out in western France, Hüffmeier could not evacuate his civilian populations even had he wanted to. The Granville raid had seriously depleted his fuel stocks and although he had ships aplenty, most were laid up and the small quantity of coal he had acquired from the *Eskwood* would be too little, too late. There was no likelihood that the British government, with the war's end so evidently near, would agree to hospital ships or other similar vessels being made available to evacuate the population, and any overt threats to the civil population would have ensured dire consequences for the perpetrators had they ever been carried out. But Hüffmeier was a Nazi zealot and at other places in the diminishing German empire, zealots were proving that they and rationality could still be wide apart. It is intriguing to speculate what would have been the reaction of the garrisons which were still largely German army personnel under army commanders had they been ordered to make a last-minute war on civilians. There is also little doubt that Hüffmeier regarded the Island authorities as enemies of the German state and, unlike von Schmettow, kept them at a distance.

One of the enduring myths to emerge from the German Occupation is that the tunnels that riddled the Islands' valleys were to be used for the extermination of the civilian populations. That it was, for instance, no coincidence that the wards of the underground casualty clearing stations created in both Islands from existing storage facilities were of similar dimensions to the brick-built 'shower rooms' that were the gas chambers at the extermination camps! Quite how the gas was going to be administered has not really been answered, although in *From Auschwitz to Alderney* (Seek Publishing, 1995) author Tom Freeman-Keel suggests that cyanide pellets would have been dropped down the escape shafts. Given the configurations of the complexes, each cyanide pellet would have had to find its way down more than 40 metres of twisting stairway, through boiler rooms, and then along corridors (turning left or right once or twice) before ending up in the wards Tom suggests would have been the gas chambers themselves.

At the end of March Hüffmeier visited Jersey where he addressed a mass meeting of officers and men held at the Forum Cinema where *Sieg im Westen* (Victory in the West) had once been shown. His address was reported in the garrison's newspaper *Deutsche Inselzeitung*, which was still being published whenever power and newsprint were available. He explained why holding on to the Channel Islands was so important and that there could be an attack by the Allies at any time. The garrison must be prepared and conditions were being created to allow them to hold out indefinitely. He concluded by stating: 'I shall hold out here with you until final victory... we cannot be shamed before the Fatherland which bears unendingly a much heavier burden than any one of us.' According to the report the *Befehlshaber's* address was 'permeated with true National Socialist feeling and with a clarity of thought and purpose which admits no compromise. We stand by him, officers and men of the fortress of Jersey!'

But not everyone agreed and the spectre of a mutiny amongst the troops almost became a reality.

Despite Hüffmeier's fortitude a memorandum issued at the beginning of 1945 by an army doctor gives an indication of the extent to which the garrison's morale had sunk. It was noted that the basic rations were now barely at subsistence level and even such 'luxuries' as the minuscule weekly issue of sardines had been withdrawn. Supplies of new razor blades had run out at the end of 1944 but, much more seriously, there was a desperate shortage of soap for the troops and skin diseases were already manifesting themselves. Stocks of medicines were exhausted. Theft had become commonplace amongst the garrison and a grenadier caught red-handed was sentenced to death on 5 February.

Nevertheless, despite the privations they were suffering, the discipline of the men of *ID319* was largely maintained. What news they had from home — the weekly Heinkel *He111* bringing mail and a few supplies from Germany was becoming an increasingly vulnerable link — was almost always bad, with German cities being razed day and night by Allied bombing and the Russians advancing inexorably on Berlin, raping and pillaging like the barbarian hordes of Tamerlane. The German garrisons were isolated in the Channel Islands as helpless as if they were already in Allied prison camps. If ever there was a time for the garrison to mutiny against its 'Nazi' officers, the first months of that bitter winter of 1945 were it.

In fact some incitements to mutiny had begun earlier, following D-Day, when two middle-aged French women, who had retired to Jersey in 1937, began a campaign of typing notes which they left in public places to be found by members of the garrison, or casually dropped them into Germans' coat pockets. These notes, almost always attributed to a German 'soldier with no name', encouraged the troops to overthrow their officers.

Lucille Schwob and Suzanne Malherbe were wealthy Jewish step half-sisters from Nantes who had been, under the male pseudonyms Claude Cohun and Marcel Moore, well known in Parisian art circles in the 1930s as a photographer and graphic designer respectively. Today, no doubt, they would be the subjects of all sorts of lurid speculations (with considerable justification), but in those days they were simply regarded as 'bohemian'; that they were Jewish seems to have passed everyone by. The two ladies were arrested in July 1944 and spent six months in solitary confinement. A search of their house revealed works of art by Picasso and Miró and much that was condemned, even by the urbane and worldly Baron von Aufsess, as obscene and subsequently destroyed. Early in 1945 they were sentenced to death for their subversive activities but, at Bailiff Coutanche's pleading that their execution would cause major civilian unrest, their sentences were commuted to life imprisonment. They were released at the Liberation to resume their bohemian existence in the Island, Lucille Schwob, who became ill in prison and never really recovered, dying in 1954. Suzanne Malherbe died in Jersey in 1972.

The prime mover behind what was to be the only true mutiny planned in the Channel Islands (albeit that it never quite took place) was Paul Mülbach, a deserter from the German garrison in Jersey, a member of a so-called 'Soldiers Committee', and a Marxist and a fervent anti-Nazi whose father had been Social Democratic mayor of Koblenz until 1933 when he was incarcerated in Dachau concentration camp, where he died. Mülbach had fought with the International Brigade in Spain, been captured and repatriated to Germany where he was given a harsh choice: be sent to Dachau or join the army. He joined the army determined to undermine the Nazis wherever and however he could. Posted to Jersey he eventually deserted in April 1945 and, in the weeks leading up to liberation, managed to evade capture. He was helped in his venture of stirring up a mutiny, particularly among army and air force personnel (the naval personnel, although not overtly Nazi, were fiercely loyal to the Fatherland), by members of the Jersey Democratic Movement (JDM) and the Jersey Communist Party.

To the minds of many, even today, these two bodies were indistinguishable but although several members of the former were also members of the latter, and the two 'political parties' shared the agenda of radical post-Occupation change, the Communist Party members (effectively an inner circle of the JDM) were, it has been alleged, actually planning the bloody overthrow of the established order, with several members of the Jersey administration, including the Crown Officers, targeted for liquidation. Their objective was the setting up of a 'People's Democracy' on the lines of those being established in Eastern Europe in the wake of the Russian advance. Leaders of the JDM were Leslie Huelin and Norman Le Brocq, both avowed Communists, but few of the JDM membership, who were mostly men and women who were either socialists or possessed of a social conscience, were aware of their Communist colleagues' alleged grisly intentions.

Mülbach's plan was for a successful mutiny leading to an immediate surrender. He had the support, he claimed, of sympathetic officers and men in Jersey and Guernsey, although quite how he communicated with the latter has not been revealed. Hüffmeier would be replaced by someone who would surrender. This was no mad ideal, but a very plausible scenario, evidenced by the thoughts Baron von Aufsess confided to his private diary, with the morale of the garrisons at an all-time low.

The date of the mutiny was set for 1 May.

However, before Mülbach and his potentially murderous local colleagues could put their plans into action, dramatic changes were afoot in Germany's fortunes. On 26 April it was learned in the Islands that Hitler had moved his headquarters to the *Führerbunker* in the Chancellery garden in Berlin to lead the final defiance of the Reich. In fact he had moved there some weeks earlier and had been playing soldiers with divisions that had long since ceased to exist as effective fighting forces. Four days later he was dead, Berlin had fallen to the Russians and it was recognised that final Allied victory could only be days away. A mutiny that would lead to inevitable civilian casualties as units loyal to Hüffmeier fought back would be pointless. Despite the higher purpose (if that is how it might be described) the mutiny scheduled for 1 May was cancelled.

On 30 April, the *Deutsche Guernsey Zeitung* published a message from the *Führer* addressed to the *Festungkommandanten* of the Channel Islands and the other outposts around the French coast, Crete and the East Aegean Islands. The message read: 'In the serious hour of fight for the fate of Germany, the *Führer* remembers his soldiers in the Atlantic Fortresses and the advanced bastions of the Aegean Sea and expects of them that they will continue to fulfil their duties with an exemplary soldierly attitude.'

Hüffmeier signalled back: 'On behalf of my officers and men I thank the *Führer* for his remembrance even at this hour. We shall be as faithful to him as he is always to us. Our way is clear. Only our *Führer's* Germany. *Heil* to our beloved *Führer*.'

On 3 May, the *Evening Post* in Jersey reported that: 'Adolf Hitler falls at his post, fighting to the last breath. He has met a hero's death in the capital of the German Reich.' In the same article, his successor, *Grossadmiral* Karl Dönitz, stated: 'My first task is to save German men from annihilation by the advancing Bolshevist enemy. Only to this end will military fighting continue. As long as this objective is hindered by the British and Americans, we shall all defend ourselves against them and must go on fighting.'

Dönitz's statement would have given Admiral Hüffmeier considerable heart in that the lonely stance he had adopted had now surely been endorsed by his own Commander-in-Chief who was now also his country's leader. Although a further raid on Granville had already been planned for 7 May and approved by *MOK West,* Hüffmeier received a radio message late on 5 May, addressed to all Fortress Commanders and Naval Commanders, headed MOST IMMEDIATE and commanding that all actions against the British and Americans cease forthwith. This instruction applied only to offensive operations at or by sea against these powers such as U-boat warfare or the operations planned against Granville and St Malo. The order did not apply to the defence of the land or sea fronts.

So while Hüffmeier was free to continue to defend the Channel Islands he should not attempt to repeat his foray on to the Continental mainland.

Nevertheless he radioed his disagreement on the grounds that an assault on Granville was not an offensive operation against the British or Americans, it was an offensive against the French! He got a chilly response which stated quite baldly that the Admiral of the Fleet had ordered that the operation planned for 7 May should *not* be carried out.

Despite the obvious proximity of the end of hostilities, the Germans complained to Guernsey's Controlling Committee that Islanders working for the forces 'were showing an increasing disinclination to work'. This could lead, they said, to the *Festungkommandant* being forced to consider putting into effect measures which would lead greatly to the disadvantage of the population!

Even the arrival of the *Vega* on 3 May caused an issue when Hüffmeier reprimanded Captain Wideberg for failing to fly his ensign at half-mast as a mark of respect for Hitler's death.

A few years ago papers released into the National Archives suggested that the German authorities were well aware of the activities of the Jersey Communist Party and their fellow traveller(s) amongst the garrison. It has been suggested that within the group was an informer who kept the Germans continually advised of what was going on. If this was the case, why then did the Germans tolerate this nest of Bolshevik vipers in their midst?

The Jersey Democratic Movement and the Jersey Communist Party had both been formed early in 1943. The Communist Party began with a group of seven which, by 1945, had grown to 18 and from the outset they were active in helping the Russian and Ukrainian slave workers, assisting them to escape their *OT* guards and hiding them when they did. They produced news sheets from BBC bulletins, printed in Cyrillic characters (laboriously translated and transcribed by an escaped Russian), which were distributed amongst the inmates of the *OT* camps. Naturally they tended to major on the valiant endeavours on the Eastern Front! They also produced leaflets in German, ostensibly from a group calling itself *Es Leben des freies Deutschland*, the Free Germany Movement, encouraging the garrison to mutiny. They managed to set fire to a small shed at the main German bakery at Georgetown on the eastern outskirts of St Helier with stolen explosives although in fact there was nothing in the store worth blowing up! It was also thought that the destruction of the Palace Hotel, the site of von Schmettow's erstwhile Officers' School, early in 1945 with the loss of nine lives and many more injured, was the work of politically motivated saboteurs but all the evidence points to it having been an accident. In his diary Leslie Sinel records a serious fire at an ammunition store in New St John's Road, St Helier, a few days after the explosion at the Palace Hotel, which may also have been sabotage but no one has ever claimed the credit.

Yet the Germans seemed to tolerate all this. Why?

The main Islands had always been spared the excesses of National Socialism whose principal manifestations were the *Sicherheitsdienst* (Security

Service) and the *Gestapo,* the Secret State Police, between them the cumbersome but deadly home security apparatus under the sinister overlordship of *Reichsführer-SS* Heinrich Himmler. The Germans were well aware that any report of Bolsheviks, sabotage, mutiny or sedition to their superiors in Rennes or St Lô would result in the baleful presence of really nasty Nazis who would not be answerable to anyone but their master in *Prinz Albrecht Strasse* in Berlin and who the Germans governing the Channel Islands would distrust and fear every bit as much as the captive Islanders. Thus, while the local Communists and their allies amongst the garrison could be observed and monitored, action would only need to be taken against them if they really got out of line. The mutiny of 1 May could well have been that occasion. Fortunately (probably for all concerned) it never happened.

Paul Mülbach remained at liberty for the last few days of the Occupation, emerging from his hiding place when the Islands were liberated. A graduate of Hanover University and by training an industrial chemist, he spoke five languages including Russian and was employed by the liberating forces as an interpreter. He was shipped with other German POWs to England where he was attached to a unit dealing with their repatriation to Germany and he himself returned to Koblenz in 1946. In 1950, presumably still a convinced Marxist, he moved to the German Democratic Republic and was never heard of again.

Norman Le Brocq, a skilled stone mason, never renounced his Communist philosophy but nevertheless went on to become a member of the States of Jersey. After many attempts, he was elected in 1972 as a Deputy for St Helier's Number 3 District on a Jersey Democratic Movement ticket, making up lost wages (since in those days States members were not paid) with half-crowns (12½p) donated by his constituents. He served for nine years, being re-elected twice, and although the States tried to tame him by making a troublemaker a corporal, Norman remained entirely his own man, adhering to what to most Islanders was an alien creed but nevertheless managing to top the poll when re-elected and chairing a major States committee.

In Jersey, at a meeting held on Sunday, 6 May, Hüffmeier had advised Bailiff Coutanche that Britain and America were going to join forces with Germany to fight the Russians. Although this was nonsense, there were those much higher up in the Nazi hierarchy who really believed that this was a genuine possibility; that the Allies would, even at this eleventh hour, recognise that they shared a common enemy, the Russian bear rampaging across Germany from the East who would not stop until he was at the Bay of Biscay. Nobody, least of all Bailiff Coutanche, was listening. Instead he asked the *Befehlshaber* for his co-operation in ensuring that his troops did not cause confrontations with Islanders who might be celebrating prematurely. We don't know how Hüffmeier responded but when the admiral had returned to Guernsey later that afternoon, *Platzkommandant* von Cleve, who had been at the meeting, opined that he was glad *Grossadmiral* Dönitz had succeeded since the *Befehlshaber* was more likely to obey orders from his own superior. Von Cleve, who had initially behaved like a clone of his master, seems to have ingested a dose of reality.

By 7 May, most people in the Channel Islands, with the significant exception of the man in charge, realised the war was over. Those listening to the BBC on their previously hidden radio sets, now without fear of discovery, heard everywhere the fanfares of victory. At 6.00pm that evening, Bailiff Coutanche went to the Public Prison and oversaw the release of 30 'political' prisoners: Islanders who had been imprisoned by the Germans for offences against the occupying forces that might, prior to mid-1944, have seen them transferred to camps on the Continent. Further 'politicals' were released the following day as were the British and American prisoners of war held in the camp at South Hill and the French North African prisoners of war held in the old Military Prison in Pier Road, originally built to house miscreant members of the British garrison in Victorian times. Also released were Germans held in custody for a variety of military offences. These men were returned to their units. Thus, for some, liberation came a day early.

Chapter 11
Liberation

A day after Winston Churchill declares that 'our dear Channel Islands are also to be freed today', the Germans reluctantly relax their grip. Why a day late? The Channel Islands were the most fortified and heavily armed section of the much-vaunted Atlantic Wall. The Commander-in-Chief threatened to fire upon the British destroyer bringing the liberators. What would have happened had he done so? Force 135 and Operation 'Nestegg'

At 3.00pm on Tuesday, 8 May 1945 Winston Churchill broadcast from London that, as from the previous midnight, Germany had unconditionally surrendered, the ceasefire had taken effect all along the front and that 'our dear Channel Islands are also to be freed today...' And Force 135, specially formed to bring about the Islands' liberation, was already on the way. His speech, relayed over loudspeakers in Trafalgar Square in London, drew cheers from the gathered crowds. Meanwhile in Jersey, unnoticed, SS *Vega*, the vessel to whose cargoes so many Islanders owed their lives, slipped into St Helier harbour on her fifth visit.

In Jersey, at the conclusion of the speech, Bailiff Coutanche raised the Union Jack over the Royal Court building and, from a window in the courthouse overlooking the Royal Square, led the cheering crowds in singing the National Anthem. Earlier he had published in *The Evening Post* a notice calling for 'calm and dignity in the hours ahead' and for Islanders 'to refrain from all forms of demonstration'.

The broadcast was conveyed over loudspeakers to delirious crowds in Jersey's Royal Square and outside Guernsey's Royal Court but the reality was still slightly different. The German forces, hungry but still at full strength and fully armed, were under the command of a single-minded naval officer for whom unconditional surrender was not yet on *his* agenda. Winston Churchill might say that 'our dear Channel Islands are to be freed today' but Friedrich Hüffmeier was still in charge and did not agree. He wanted an armistice, apparently believing that the civilian population under his control gave him a significant bargaining counter.

Indeed, just a little over three weeks earlier, on Hitler's 56th birthday, *Vizeadmiral* Hüffmeier had addressed *Kriegsmarine* personnel at Guernsey's Regal cinema and told his men that he would not surrender in the event of an armistice (forgetting, perhaps, that the Allies had insisted that there could be no alternative to unconditional surrender) and that the lives of the 70,000 and more British civilians in the Islands would be used as a lever to obtain better terms for a peace settlement for Germany. Was the man dangerously deluded?

Let us examine this scenario in a little more detail and attempt to explore what might have happened had this unlikely state of affairs been enacted.

It had always been assumed that when the High Command ordered the surrender of all German land, sea and air forces, the forces on the Channel Islands would follow suit.

Undoubtedly, the Channel Islands had been created *Festungen*, along with the U-boat bases on the Biscay coast, and some of the other *Festungen* had been devilish hard nuts to crack, but that had been while the war in Europe was still raging, not once the Germans had surrendered.

Plans had been laid as early as 1943 for the re-occupation of the Channel Islands and were known as Operation 'Rankin'. These were divided into three 'cases': Case A assumed an assault on the Channel Islands before D-Day, Case B assumed the withdrawal of the German occupiers to the mainland of Europe, while Case C assumed the surrender of Germany and the cessation of hostilities.

On 10 May 1944 General Walter Bedell Smith, the US Chief of Staff at the Supreme Headquarters Allied Expeditionary Force (SHAEF), sent a report to the General Officer Commanding-in-Chief Southern Command advising that it had been agreed that in the event of the German forces in the Channel Islands capitulating during the forthcoming Operation 'Overlord', he and his staff would be responsible for re-occupying the Islands and dealing with the German garrisons.

By August 1944, it became obvious that the Germans were not going to capitulate and therefore 'Rankin' Case A and Case B were redundant. Case C became Operation 'Nestegg', for which unconditional surrender was a prerequisite, since to avoid unacceptable casualties amongst the civilian populations and widespread destruction the Channel Islands would not be taken by assault.

As we have seen, various attempts were made to induce the garrisons to surrender, all without success. It would require the fall of Germany itself to bring about any change in the occupiers' attitude. By the beginning of May, the Germans' unconditional surrender was only hours away.

On Saturday, 5 May 1945 a signal was sent to Guernsey from the General Officer Commanding-in-Chief Southern Command advising *Vizeadmiral* Hüffmeier that he had been authorised to receive the German garrisons' unconditional surrender and gave the frequency on which the admiral should reply. When the signal was received Hüffmeier was in Jersey, preparing to supervise the planned second raid on Granville, and when he returned to his headquarters he responded by telling the GOC-in-C Southern Command that the 'Commander-in-Chief Channel Islands, receives orders only from his own government'. He didn't add 'so there' but he might just as well have done.

Late on Monday, 7 May GOC-in-C Southern Command tried again. This time the signal was rather more comprehensive.

'You must now be aware that a representative of the German High Command signed the unconditional surrender of all German land, sea and air forces in Europe to the Allied Expeditionary Forces earlier today. As the authority appointed by the Supreme Allied Commander to receive your surrender I require you or your representative to meet British representatives at a position four miles true South from Les Hanois light. British representatives will arrive in two British destroyers flying the British naval ensign at the masthead approaching Guernsey on a course East true. You or your representative will be required to sign a document containing terms of surrender applicable to the forces under your Command. He is to bring with him written details of the safe channel to St Peter Port and a pilot. Acknowledge this signal by giving the name and rank of the Commander of the German Force Channel Islands, and confirm that British ships will not be fired on and will in all respects be given a safe passage. The time for the meeting will be signalled.'

Hüffmeier replied promptly stating that he had received the wireless message and that a representative would be at the rendezvous (Les Hanois lighthouse is on a reef at Guernsey's south-west corner) to receive the terms. He also confirmed that the British ships would not be fired upon 'if I am informed of their arrival in good time'. He added that he would be responsible for their safe passage 'up to this point'.

When the Royal Navy destroyers HMS *Bulldog* and *Beagle* arrived off Guernsey at 14.00hrs (Double British Summer Time) on 8 May with a party under the command of Brigadier A. E. Snow OBE, expecting an unconditional German surrender, Hüffmeier's representative, *Kapitänleutnant* Armin Zimmermann (conveyed to the rendezvous by a battered and rusting minesweeper and who gave the Nazi salute when boarding *Bulldog*), advised that he was empowered only to discuss terms for an armistice that would commence at 00.01hrs the following day, not sign any unconditional surrender. Zimmermann was confined to a cabin where he waited for an hour while Snow and his colleagues prepared a document for him to take back to Hüffmeier demanding that the Admiral arrange a rendezvous which would be attended by a German representative empowered to sign the instrument of unconditional surrender. Zimmermann agreed to do so but also advised that the safe conduct extended to the RN destroyers applied only to the rendezvous and did not constitute permission to remain there. He added that the presence of British warships so close to the Islands was 'a provocative act' and if they lingered they would be fired upon. An angry Brigadier Snow pointed out that such an attack would be in direct contravention of the arrangements already concluded between the German and Allied High Commands and any such action would brand Hüffmeier 'an outlaw'. Apparently he also added that were the admiral to authorise such an attack 'we will hang him tomorrow'. Nevertheless orders were given to move the destroyers rather rapidly out of range just as soon as Zimmermann had clambered back to his rusty minesweeper.

Zimmermann's stance that, as far as he was concerned, a State of War still existed between these particular pieces of the German Empire and the Allies until an armistice was concluded between them was obviously also the view of his Commander-in-Chief, notwithstanding that a formal unconditional surrender had already been signed on behalf of all German land, sea and air forces.

So let us fantasise for a moment and imagine that Rear-Admiral G. C. Stuart DSO DSC RN, who had accompanied Brigadier Snow in *Bulldog* as Naval Force Commander, had given the order to his two captains that they should call the Germans' bluff and stay where they were, hove to, well within range of the mighty *Batterie Mirus* whose 30.5cm guns had the easy capability of blowing the thin-skinned *Bulldog* and *Beagle* right out of the water with a single shot and within range of every other battery on Guernsey's south coast. By comparison, the 4.7in (12cm) guns of the destroyers' main armament were mere pea-shooters. It would have been a most uneven contest were the Germans' bluff to be called.

* * *

The first salvo from the four guns of *Batterie Mirus* fell between the two destroyers at 16.25hrs and were clearly ranging shots directed by the battery's own *Würzburg* radar. Nevertheless the spray from the explosions drenched the officers and ratings on the vessels' upper decks and left the captains in little doubt that the next shots could well be right on target and even with the destroyers' top speed of well in excess of 30 knots there was no time to escape. As if to emphasise the point, a further salvo exploded ahead of the two destroyers before the engine room orders for full power could be translated into movement. As 'Action Stations' was sounded and urgent signals dispatched to the Admiralty, both vessels sustained slight damage from the explosive shells' blast.

Admiral Stuart, on the bridge of HMS *Bulldog,* conferred with the ship's captain, Lieutenant-Commander D. B. G. Dumas RN, and then with Brigadier Snow. 'We have little choice, Brigadier. It is hardly in the tradition of Nelson, but we must seek a truce. Failure to do so will call down further salvoes on us before any intervention by the RAF to silence the battery whose accuracy is not in doubt.'

Brigadier Snow, looking forward to what was to have been the pinnacle of a distinguished military career that had begun with him as a Sandhurst-trained subaltern at the Battle of the Somme, was about to endure the soldier's worst nightmare — surrender.

'Can't we escape under cover of a smokescreen or something?'

The Admiral shook his head. 'The guns are directed by radar and I suspect the Germans have had several years' practice . . .'

'Is there truly nothing we can do? What about calling in a battleship?' Beneath the Brigadier's feet *Bulldog's* deckplates trembled as the destroyer's turbines built up speed. 'HMS *Malaya* was brought in to shell Cézambre, if I recall . . .'

Admiral Stuart and Lieutenant-Commander Dumas exchanged glances. 'We have insufficient time, Brigadier. No reinforcements, either by sea or air, are likely to be with us before we are sunk,' the admiral replied drily. 'Our only option is to heave to and fly a white flag. Surely whatever humiliation we endure cannot last long. Germany is defeated. Hüffmeier is now an outlaw. He cannot survive. It would be bloody silly to be killed on the first day of peace, don't you agree? The Islands will surely be taken within hours rather than days . . .' In fact, he was thinking that if the Germans really dug in their heels, it could be weeks before their defences were neutralised. His thoughts and words were interrupted by the scream of another salvo and *Beagle*, curving away from her consort to disperse the target, was bracketed by towering pinnacles of spray. Damage to her superstructure was immediately evident and the lean destroyer staggered in the water as shrapnel raked her decks. 'We, however, cannot last more than minutes . . .'

'Send the signal then. And raise a white flag. Before they sink us . . .'

The two destroyers hove to, rolling in the swell, white flags fluttering from their mastheads.

In the *Leitstand* (command bunker) which controlled the four 30.5cm guns and anti-aircraft batteries at *Batterie Mirus*, battery commander *Oberleutnant der Marineartillerie* Werner Neumann, newly promoted and posted from the *Kriegsmarine's Batterie Lothringen* in Jersey, removed his earphones and gave the order to cease firing. 'The enemy has signalled requesting a truce,' he reported to the 25 members of the *Leitstand's* duty crew. 'They have surrendered.'

In Plymouth where the main body of Force 135 was preparing to embark on US Navy LSTs (Landing Ship, Tank) the signal from *Bulldog* that the two destroyers were hove to under a flag of truce was greeted with incredulity.

'He's done what? Is Stuart mad? The war is over!' The GOC-in-C Southern Command had been summoned from a victory celebration in the Officers' Mess at The Citadel overlooking Plymouth Sound and Drake's Island.

'Not it seems for Admiral Hüffmeier, sir. He wishes to parley and his bargaining chips are 70,000 or so civilians and two Royal Navy destroyers!'

'What the devil does he expect?'

'He is seeking an armistice with honour, sir. He will not countenance an unconditional surrender and he will resist any attempt at armed invasion.'

'Has his act of banditry caused any casualties so far?'

'*Beagle* reports several flesh wounds from flying shrapnel, sir, and superficial damage to the vessel itself. *Bulldog* and her complement are unharmed.'

'Thank God for that.'

At 22.00hrs a signal was sent to Admiral Hüffmeier. 'Following the unconditional surrender of all German land, sea and air forces in Europe on 7 May, it is impossible to grant your request for a conditional armistice. The Acting Chancellor of Germany and Commander-in-Chief of the German Navy has been requested to issue the appropriate order to you to sign the instrument of unconditional surrender. Until such instruction is acted upon, no military action will be undertaken against the German forces in the Channel Islands. Any further action taken against the vessels of the Royal Navy will result in summary retaliation and extreme personal consequences for those officers involved in persisting with this futile gesture.' The signal concluded by giving the German Commander-in-Chief until 02.00hrs local time (midnight GMT) to respond. The signal was copied to *Bulldog* with a supplementary that the ships should remain hove to (now approximately six nautical miles to the south-west of Les Hanois light).

The instruction from *Grossadmiral* Karl Dönitz, who had established his 'government' at Flensburg in Schleswig-Holstein, arrived at 22.30hrs. It gave clear and unequivocal orders for *Vizeadmiral* Hüffmeier to offer the immediate unconditional surrender of all the German forces in the Channel Islands. This signal ended with a commendation for the garrisons' loyalty and fortitude.

In Plymouth anxious eyes watched the clocks creeping towards midnight GMT. Although a copy of Dönitz's signal had been received, nevertheless planners in the Citadel had also been poring over details of the locations of the principal German headquarters provided by escapers and highly detailed aerial photographs of Guernsey. These showed quite clearly the German defences including the sites, despite camouflage netting, of *Batterie Mirus*, the divisional command bunker in the grounds of The Oberlands and La Corbinerie, the mansion (in Island terms) that was the *Befehlshaber's* headquarters, the *Kriegsmarine* radio station at St Jacques and the nearby La Collinette Hotel, believed to be Hüffmeier's own centre of operations and the *Hafenkommandantur* (Harbour Commander's Office), at the Crown Hotel on The Quay at St Peter Port.

The GOC-in-C turned to the Air Commodore commanding the RAF detachment at nearby Harrowbeer Airfield. 'What do you think?'

'An attack on *Mirus* to silence the battery will require earthquake bombs and they need to be dropped from a considerable height. Besides there are other batteries, each one of which will require being neutralised. There is a grave risk of substantial civilian casualties.' And at the GOC's raised eyebrow, 'These are suburban locations. Likewise with the divisional command and signals bunkers.' He gestured towards the aerial photographs and smiled humourlessly. 'They are in suburban areas. Lots of likely civilian casualties, General, and two days after the war is ended . . .'

The point was not lost on the GOC-in-C. 'What about this man Hüffmeier's headquarters?'

'On the assumption that he is in one of three places . . .' He pointed to the aerial photographs of the Islands that took up most of one wall '. . . rather than down some underground rat hole, then Mosquitos with 500lb bombs or rocket-equipped Typhoons should do the trick. The buildings are pretty flimsy. And these boys are deadly accurate.'

No response having been received by 03.00 GMT, the order was given for a squadron of rocket-equipped Hawker Typhoons to destroy all of Admiral Hüffmeier's known headquarters. At 04.30 GMT (6.30am local time) the attackers swooped in low, almost at sea level, from the south-east, out of the dawn, catching the Germans, although still at uneasy Action Stations, completely unawares. Anti-aircraft gunners on the pierhead ducked as the Typhoons roared over the harbours but not a shot was fired against them. Within moments highly explosive rockets had destroyed the Crown Hotel and severely damaged the buildings on either side of it. A few moments later the same treatment was meted out to La Collinette Hotel. In the smoking ruins lay 38 dead Germans, mostly desk-bound operations staff and clerks and three German Red Cross nurses. Amongst the dead was the Chief Naval Staff Officer, *Kapitänleutnant* Armin Zimmermann. Since the curfew was still in force there were no civilian casualties.

Vizeadmiral Hüffmeier was not in his headquarters. He was leaving the Naval Signals Headquarters bunker at St Jacques on the western outskirts of St Peter Port, by the underground tunnel that linked it with La Collinette Hotel, having composed a response to *Grossadmiral* Dönitz seeking clarification and permission to continue the struggle, when the Typhoons roared overhead, their deadly work partly done. Rockets streaked into the camouflage netting, setting it ablaze and impacting against the massive walls of the Signals bunker, causing little external damage but wrecking the aerial arrays. The concussion cracked the roof and wooden wall panelling, splinters causing slight injuries amongst the personnel. Smoke and debris billowed down the tunnel, enveloping the Admiral and the staff officers with him, but causing no injuries. When he returned to the bunker he received telephone reports that enemy aircraft had destroyed the *Kriegsmarine* headquarters, killing, amongst others, his Chief Staff Officer. Further reports showed that the intruders had escaped unscathed since no defender had opened fire despite the aircraft flying low and being tracked by radar.

At first Hüffmeier raged, threatening to court-martial the gunners involved, but after a telephone consultation with *Generalmajor* Heine at La Corbinerie and then *Generalmajor* Wulf in Jersey, he accepted the inevitable.

A shaken Hüffmeier did not wait for a response to his signal to the *Grossadmiral*. At 05.14hrs a signal was received aboard HMS *Bulldog* advising that *Vizeadmiral* Hüffmeier's representative, *Generalmajor* Heine, would be sent to the same rendezvous at 07.00hrs GMT, fully authorised to sign the unconditional surrender.

At precisely 07.14hrs GMT, *Generalmajor* Heine signed nine copies of the Instrument of Surrender on behalf of the Commander-in-Chief of the German forces in the Channel Islands, seven copies in English and two in German.

* * *

Much of the foregoing is, of course, fantasy. Truly a 'what if . . ?'

Kapitänleutnant Armin Zimmermann did indeed threaten *Bulldog* and *Beagle* but the destroyers sailed away out of range without any threat being carried out. No air assault with the intent of killing or disabling the German Commander-in-Chief took place or was contemplated. At 22.00hrs local time a signal was received by *Bulldog* informing Brigadier Snow that *Generalmajor* Siegfried Heine, second-in-command to the *Befehlshaber der britischen Kanalinseln* and Guernsey's *Festungkommandant*, the authorised representative of *Vizeadmiral* Hüffmeier, would meet them at midnight at the same rendezvous. The signal also guaranteed a safe passage to the vessels and the services of a German pilot.

At midnight *Generalmajor* Heine was piped aboard *Bulldog* accompanied by a subdued *Kapitänleutnant* Zimmermann. He presented Brigadier Snow with a letter from *Vizeadmiral* Hüffmeier authorising him to sign the instrument of surrender.

Preparation of the surrender documents took two hours, and a further four hours, fortified by mugs of Royal Navy coffee, were spent with General Staff Officer II Major J. E. Margesson and Captain H. Herzmark of the Intelligence Corps making sure that there were no points in the surrender document that were not understood. When the preparations were complete, Southern Command was informed and ordered that Operation 'Omelet' be put into effect. 'Omelet' was a 'mini' version of 'Nestegg' designed to establish whether or not there was likely to be any German resistance and calling only for token forces to 'occupy' Guernsey and Jersey ahead of the full force of 'Nestegg' which numbered 6,000 men with their vehicles and thousands of tons of equipment.

It was at 07.14hrs local time (05.14hrs GMT) on Wednesday, 9 May when Brigadier Snow read the terms of surrender and *Generalmajor* Heine duly signed all nine copies, on a table top resting on *Bulldog's* rum cask which, in accordance with Royal Navy practice, was inscribed with the words 'God Save the King'. When Heine had signed, Brigadier Snow announced that he was signing for General Eisenhower, the Allied Supreme Commander, whose representative he was. Clutching two copies of the surrender document, one in English and one in German, *Generalmajor* Heine bowed to Brigadier Snow and left *Bulldog*.

The first British troops ashore in Guernsey were Lieutenant Rex Ferbrache RNVR, a Guernseyman, Colonel H. R. Power, Chief Civil Affairs Officer,

Lieutenant-Colonel E. G. Stoneman, officer-in-command, and Captain Herzmark of the Intelligence Corps, accompanied by a group of 21 Royal Artillerymen under the command of Captain R. H. Hill.

Meanwhile Brigadier Snow had transferred to HMS *Beagle* for passage to Jersey where they arrived in St Aubin's Bay at 10.00hrs. Although ostensibly the Channel Islands were covered by one instrument of surrender, someone with knowledge of the Bailiwicks' traditional independence of each other, had prepared individual documents for each *Inselkommandant* to sign.

Bailiff Coutanche was asked to go to the *Platzkommandantur* at College House to take a telephone call from Colonel Power already in Guernsey. There he was advised of *Beagle's* imminent arrival. He returned to his Chambers to await events while on St Helier's Albert Quay German naval ratings paraded and officers on the ships in the harbour hauled down their German ensigns and afterwards burned them.

At noon the Bailiff was ordered to the harbour where he joined *Generalmajor* Wulf to proceed to *Beagle* for the signing of the surrender. He remarked later that he had never received an order that gave him so much pleasure to obey.

Later that same day the British relief force (Force 135) finally arrived in the Islands amid heart-felt cheering, flag-waving and welcoming kisses. A five-year nightmare was over and the Islands were free again. The first men ashore in Jersey were Surgeon-Lt Ronald MacDonald RN and Sub-Lt David Milne RN, both of whom spoke German, accompanied by four naval ratings whose first act was to drape a Union Jack from the window of the Harbourmaster's office.

At 3.00pm, Lieutenant-Colonel W. P. A. Robinson, Jersey's new Island Commander, stood on the balcony of the Pomme d'Or Hotel, the erstwhile headquarters of the *Kriegsmarine*, overlooking the harbour. In front of cheering crowds he saluted as Harbourmaster Harry Richmond raised the Union Jack on the hotel's flagpole, from which the *Kriegsmarine's* battle ensign had so recently fluttered. Initially they were accompanied only by PC Bill Rowe of the Jersey Paid Police but within a matter of minutes they were joined by dozens of other uniformed liberators, so much so that the Pomme d'Or's owner, George Seymour, who had seen all four of his family's hotels taken over and largely trashed by the occupying forces, feared the balcony might collapse under their weight!

Just how the Islands were liberated is covered in great detail by local historian Mark Lamerton in *Liberated by Force 135*, (ELSP in conjunction with Nestegg Enterprises, 2000). It is a stirring tale but one which, without the benefit of hindsight, might have gone awfully wrong. Had Hüffmeier really decided that he would defy all odds, how long would it have been before other than incisive strikes to kill or disable him would have turned into all-out invasion? Operation 'Nestegg' was conceived to allow for the re-occupation of the Channel Islands with no loss of civilian life. How long would this altruistic view have held had Hüffmeier's batteries been shooting at anything which approached nearer than 10 miles or so? Thank God we never had to find out.

However, as in France and the other occupied countries, following the exhilaration and happiness of liberation were darker, more violent, emotions.

Chapter 12
After liberation, now what?

Joy and Jerrybags, heroes and black marketeers, courage and collaborators. The inquests begin. The Dame and 275 Germans. Do laws passed during the German Occupation still apply? What about war crimes?

There has probably never been such an outpouring of emotion on the Islands as that seen on Wednesday, 9 May 1945, when the first British troops came ashore bearing cigarettes, sweets and freedom. When, at the turn of the century, the *Jersey Evening Post* asked its readers to nominate a picture from its archives to be 'Picture of the 20th Century', the photograph chosen was one of widely grinning local girls and just as widely grinning liberating Tommies standing on the bodywork of a US Army amphibious DUKW on the evening of Liberation Day.

There are thousands of individual memories of that day, each one having its own slant on the events. In both main Islands the rituals were similar — the hauling down of the German ensigns and their replacement with the Union Jack. In Jersey one such pleasing duty fell to Jerseymen Captain Hugh Le Brocq and his batman, Private Raymond Marquis, both of the 11th Battalion (Royal Militia Island of Jersey) of the Hampshire Regiment, who removed the German ensign from Fort Regent overlooking the town and hoisted high the Union Jack.

In Guernsey the liberators were met at the Court House by the Bailiff and Jurats, and the Union Jack was ceremonially hoisted with a Royal Artillery Guard of Honour.

There were speeches in the States Chambers and joyful loyal addresses to the King and the Prime Minister. The King himself broadcast to the Empire at 9.00pm on Liberation Day. He concluded the broadcast by saying: 'Let us turn to this lasting day of just triumph and proud honour. Then let us take up our work with the resolve to do nothing unworthy of those who died for us, for their children and loved ones.' Union Jacks and red, white and blue bunting that had been hoarded and concealed throughout the Occupation were waved triumphantly from windows and hoisted on poles. The Germans had sought to confiscate such manifestations of loyalty to Britain but one enterprising family in Jersey had placed a full-sized Union flag on a wall and papered over it until the day it could be revealed and flown in celebration of victory.

In St Helier, a group of German officers got riotously drunk on hoarded champagne. Whether they were celebrating or drowning their sorrows, they were too intoxicated to tell.

In the euphoria of liberating the main Islands, Sark and Alderney were easy
to overlook and a report was received that there was 'unrest' amongst the
Sark garrison since there had been reports of a large fire on the evening of 8
May. It was feared that the Germans might have embarked upon a last minute
'scorched earth' policy, particularly since all efforts to contact them by
telephone had failed. However, when a British detachment of just 20 men
under the command of Lieutenant-Colonel K. Allen of the Royal Berkshires
was dispatched to the Island (Operation 'Marble') and landed at Creux
harbour on the afternoon of 10 May, there was not a German in sight. They
were greeted by the Dame who explained that the fire had been their own
'victory' celebration and that the Germans had locked themselves in their own
quarters. However, they were persuaded to come out and a formal surrender
was signed by the *Kommandant*, *Hauptmann* Magsam. Lieutenant-Colonel
Allen also gave Mrs Hathaway a letter from Home Secretary Herbert
Morrison MP which recorded the Home Office's appreciation of how she and
the Sarkees had faced the trials and privations of enemy occupation. The
letter concluded: 'We have been very glad to receive in the Home Office some
news of you, both from yourself and from your husband in Germany, and I
hope you will soon be reunited.' Lieutenant-Colonel Allen advised the Dame
that he could spare no troops to guard the Germans and was told by the
formidable lady that he need not bother. She would look after all 275 of them!

On the morning of Saturday, 12 May, at the Crown Hotel, St Peter Port,
Brigadier Snow formally accepted the surrender of all the German forces in
the Channel Islands from Admiral Hüffmeier although the latter, in a final
show of pique, refused to salute the British officer. Neither could he hand
over his sword, as custom demanded, since he had already broken it on being
ordered to surrender. Hüffmeier and his ADC were marched
unceremoniously to HMS *Faulknor* which took them to Plymouth and
captivity. Later more than 2,000 Islanders gathered in the quadrangle of
Guernsey's Elizabeth College to hear Brigadier Snow read a proclamation
vesting in him, by Order in Council, full powers as the officer commanding
the military forces.

Within days the full complement of Force 135 had transferred from Plumer
Barracks in Plymouth to the Islands, the only resistance the men encountering
being a difficulty in marching while surrounded by cheering crowds. Many of
the serving men were returning to their Island homes after five or six long
years of waging war.

The Islands they had left behind had changed beyond belief. Not only was
there the tangible evidence of the conquerors in the grim concrete edifices that
fouled headlands and heartlands and the miles of tangled barbed-wire that
had turned each Island into a cruel prison for occupier and occupied alike,
there was also the change in the people. Relatives and friends had aged more
than the five years — the toll of captivity and the deprivation of the recent
months in particular had made people thin and drawn. Relationships had

changed too. Children had grown up, dear relatives had died. Islanders were often strangely wary and defensive towards their liberators and each other.

The German troops were concentrated in their own camps while they awaited transportation to the United Kingdom and a new status as prisoners of war. In Jersey, many of the troops were confined in the near derelict St Peter's Barracks sufficiently refurbished by the Royal Army Ordnance Corps to make the old buildings wind and watertight and also at Blanches Banques, the site of the Great War POW camp, until arrangements could be made for them to be transferred to Britain. When it happened, few felt any pangs of sorrow at seeing the long queues of Germans being marched to the giant LSTs that would take them to captivity. It was also clear that for many Germans the prospect of captivity also held the prospect of a square meal! But some observers did rue their passing.

There was an awful lot of German ordnance just lying about, particularly mines. At L'Ancresse in Guernsey German officers had insisted that the beach was not mined but a sceptical British officer decided that a lorryload of those officers being driven around the beach would determine whether or not they had been speaking with forked tongue. Luckily for them, and whoever was driving, they had been telling the truth. Although the clearance of mines began right after the day of liberation, it was on 29 May that Captain H. E. Beckingham of the Royal Engineers took over the responsibility for minefield clearance in Guernsey. In his book *Living with Danger, Memoirs of a Bomb Disposal Officer* (Countryvise, 1997) Captain Beckingham tells how, working with *Hauptmann* Kias, the German Engineering Officer responsible for laying the mines in the first place, sappers from No 24 Bomb Disposal Platoon and 300 POWs from the German Engineering Unit, 66,456 mines were lifted by 25 July at the cost of six POWs killed and a further 14 wounded, some seriously. In Jersey the Royal Engineers (with, as the report adds, the co-operation of German POWs) in the 90 days after the Liberation lifted 65,982 mines, removed 5,689 beach obstacles and 100,000 metres of barbed-wire.

Not everything went smoothly. In Guernsey a Royal Army Ordnance Corps NCO was severely burned while supervising the burning of cordite and in Jersey a fire started in a large stack of artillery cartridges. In all, a hundred tons of explosives detonated, fortunately without causing any injuries.

Those who were known to have been too friendly or co-operative with the occupiers came in for denunciation, abuse and occasionally physical violence. Local girls who had consorted with the Germans (the notorious 'Jerrybags') were identified and chased through the streets of St Helier and St Peter Port. When they were caught some had their heads shaved and, in Jersey, two girls were threatened with being thrown in the harbour. Retribution was not long in coming for the notorious Jersey collaborator, Alexandrine Baudains (aka 'Mimi the Spy' and 'Ginger Lou'). Joe Mière remembered her as someone who 'listened on the streets and the cafés and would report what she heard to the Germans', and would-be escaper Peter Hassell's brother Bernard described her as wearing 'a fox fur around her neck with a silver end on the tail. We kept well out of her way — she was lethal'. At the Liberation, her house in Devonshire Place in St Helier was trashed and she surrendered herself with her son to the authorities who locked her up for her own safety in the Public Prison from which a large number of her fellow-Islanders had not long been released.

The couple were still incarcerated in March 1946 when *Sunday Pictorial* journalist Rex North, investigating a story that Islanders were living rather better than their counterparts in Britain (and who discovered that the better rations were approved by Whitehall), heard about Alexandrine Baudains locked up in the Newgate Street Public Prison. He managed to talk his way into the prison with a photographer and her 'story' and photograph duly appeared in the *Sunday Pictorial*. The public was outraged and that barometer of public opinion, the Letters page of *The Evening Post*, condemned 'the poisonous woman' who was now living at the public's expense. In the States, questions were asked as to how a reporter and photographer were able to get into the gaol and, presumably, out again! Baudains and her son were ejected from the prison forthwith and were taken in by the Little Sisters of the Poor, a Catholic order of nuns who cared for old people (and still do) at their nursing home in New St John's Road on the edge of St Helier. An oft-published photograph shows her and her son being escorted a few days later by a warder from the prison to the harbour to begin a banishment for life in Bristol.

The *GFP* personnel in Jersey, also fearing reprisals, similarly turned up at the Public Prison, wearing their Army uniforms (as they were entitled to do) and asking to be locked up for their own protection. We have also earlier mentioned the Jersey informer, Marjorie Robins, who was dragged from her home in Midvale Road, St Helier, and was about to be hanged from a lamppost when the police arrived in the nick of time and carted her too off to the Public Prison. In Guernsey Gerrit Timmer had stones thrown at his windows and 'Timmer is a Quisling' was written on a wall. He appealed for police protection.

Inevitably, particularly in Guernsey, who had collaborated became a matter for public debate and letters to the press. An office was established at the Channel Islands Hotel in St Peter Port and Islanders were invited to report any acts of collaboration they were aware of. Claims and accusations were submitted but no public record has been discovered of what was said or done. There were, however, a number of representations made to the Home Office regarding the conduct of the Island's administration, which were summarised as follows:

1. Did not show a bold enough front to the Germans.
2. Did not adequately protect the interests of Islanders in resisting the German demands for local supplies.

3. Assisted the Germans with the deportations.
4. Encouraged Islanders to denounce fellow subjects for infringements of German Laws.

Pretty strong stuff.

The Home Office, probably to the disappointment of many, seemed unwilling to pursue matters and to accept that the authorities (without any guidance from the Home Office itself, of course) acted as they saw fit in the circumstances. While it was acknowledged that some of the public pronouncements, particularly by Bailiff Carey, were ill-chosen and unwise, they stemmed more from his inability to cope with the circumstances than any real favouring of the occupiers against the occupied.

There was the problem of what to do with the *OT* labourers still in the Islands, particularly those, mostly the Russians and Ukrainians in Jersey, who were disinclined to return to their homelands. With good reason. The Soviet authorities were intensely suspicious of any of their citizens who might have collaborated with the Germans (and they numbered hundreds of thousands). They were also fearful of the exposure of their citizens to the alien western culture and that they might have been recruited by western intelligence agencies. Repatriated Soviet citizens could look forward to nothing much more than constant surveillance for the next 20 years at best and at worst incarceration in a *gulag* until they no longer posed even an imaginary threat to the Soviet system.

At the Liberation the number of foreign workers left in Jersey was actually rather small. This eclectic mix comprised some 65 Russians (of whom 16 had escaped and been in hiding for some time), 85 Frenchmen, 56 Spaniards, 36 Dutchmen, eight Poles, three Algerians, three Italians, a Belgian, an Arab, a Swiss, a Hungarian and an Estonian. Not included in this number were the 115 North African prisoners of war and Italian *Hilfswillige*. Most of the French and Dutch were voluntary workers and the Russians had long been concentrated at Fort Regent while, six weeks before the Liberation, all the Spaniards had been turned loose by the *OT* and been obliged to survive by scrounging and hand-outs from sympathetic Islanders. The soldiers amongst the Russians were issued by the British with khaki battledress with USSR shoulderflashes. In Guernsey the *OT* workers (about 150 of them) were housed in *Lager Ursula* at St Sampson.

Reprisals against German personnel were almost non-existent and within days, by mid-May, the bulk of the occupiers, still numbering almost 30,000 men and a small number of women, were transferred in the American tank landing ships to prison camps in Britain. As they marched along Guernsey's White Rock quay they were booed. Several hundred sappers remained to assist British bomb disposal experts in tracing the thousands of mines that had been laid down, dig them up and render them safe. Unfortunately plans for the minefields, as was the case with most German defences, particularly in

Guernsey, had been destroyed shortly before the Liberation and, as we have
seen, many Germans found to their cost just how lethal their own weapons
were. In Jersey the situation was slightly different for, as related by former
engineers Hans Kegelmann and Ernst Kämpfer many years later to the
Channel Islands Occupation Society's Jersey president, Michael Ginns MBE,
when ordered to destroy the plans they hid them instead since 'we knew that
the British would make us clear the mines!'

Following the British soldiers and the American sailors who made up the
liberating force, came an army of Whitehall 'warriors' to assess the damage
done by the occupiers and to instigate measures for restoring the Islands'
commerce and everyday life. The only currency in use was the German
Reichsmark and, after an initial hesitation, these were redeemed by the British
Exchequer at face value. Unfortunately (for them) many Islanders failed to
exploit the situation and one farmer, offered two suitcases full of *Reichsmark*
by a German officer just before the Liberation, promptly burnt them!

As early as 13 April 1944 a memorandum was issued by the five clearing
banks operating in the Channel Islands 'respecting points for reference to
HM Treasury (through the Bank of England) upon questions which may arise
respecting banking and currency in the Channel Islands upon the re-
occupation of the Islands'. The interested banks were Barclays, with branches
in Guernsey and Jersey; Lloyds, with branches in Alderney, Guernsey and
Jersey; Midland, with branches in Guernsey, Jersey and Sark; National
Provincial, with branches in Alderney, Guernsey, Jersey and Sark; and
Westminster, with branches in Alderney, Guernsey and Jersey. The preamble
to the memorandum stated that 'liberation of the Channel Islands may or
may not be long delayed but in any event may be sudden'. It was further noted
that contact between the branches and the respective head offices had ceased
on 28 June 1940 and thereafter the Islands were deemed enemy territory —
under the Trading with the Enemy Act 1939 — as from 1 July 1940. There had
been no correspondence with the now 'enemy' branches and such information
as had been received had been culled from Red Cross messages and the
evidence of evacuees. The memorandum also gave the names of all the
individual branch managers, noting, however, that a Mr de la Rue, the
National Provincial's senior officer in charge, was only an Accountant-in-
Charge. In Jersey the largest banking business was probably that of the
Midland, and in Guernsey that of the Westminster. The amount of currency
left in the Islands, as at 30 June 1940, including Bank of England and State
notes, was £384,043, notes to the value of £2,500 having been destroyed. The
memorandum went on to address how the banks would treat the quantities of
Reichsmark their branches would have been likely to accumulate. It was
agreed to issue further memoranda once the situation of the Islands was
better known.

A further memorandum of 17 June 1944 (following a meeting held at the
British Treasury on 8 June) laid more elaborate plans, it being noted that on

the Islands 'banks' staffs were depleted and over-tired and, while some were transported to Germany some two years ago, it may be that further staff will be found to have been removed prior to re-occupation'.

On Saturday, 12 May a nondescript Army lorry bumped down the ramp of an LST in Jersey's St Aubin's Bay. Privates John Ward and Fred Chapman belonged to the Army Pay Corps and had been sent to Jersey with their three-tonner loaded with cash (more than £1 million and worth many times that today) for the Island's banks. Presumably it was perceived that the very anonymity of the three-tonner was security enough. Once their cargo was in safe custody Privates Ward and Chapman explored St Helier where they met local carpenter John Buesnel and in an act of friendship he invited them to his home to meet his wife Mollie and their daughter Marjorie. So began a friendship between Mr Buesnel's family, his children and grandchildren and John Ward in particular which has lasted for these 60 years.

On Monday, 14 May the Channel Islands received a visit from the Home Secretary, the Rt Hon Herbert Morrison MP, who, alighting first in Guernsey, assured Bailiff Carey that the Islands had never been absent from his mind, nor from that of the British government, especially after D-Day. Jurat John Leale, still head of the Controlling Committee, reported that the German troops had 'behaved well' and that, when a case of rape had been proved (by a drunken German soldier against a 72-year-old woman) the soldier had been executed. Thereafter there had been no further such incidents. The formal minutes of the meeting also recorded that 'The Home Secretary stated that he was grateful to the Bailiff and Administration for the way they had carried on during the Occupation. He thanked them for acting on the assumption that deliverance would come and thought they had done their job very well.'

At 7.15pm the Home Secretary and his party, which included Guernseyman Major W. Le Patourel VC (won in North Africa in 1942), arrived in Jersey and the following morning attended a specially convened meeting of the States. Bailiff Coutanche presided and Brigadier Snow occupied the seat on his right (a few inches lower) usually occupied by the Lieutenant-Governor. In his address to the States, Herbert Morrison reiterated that 'never were the Channel Islands far from our thoughts'. In conclusion he thanked the Islanders for their welcome and on behalf of His Majesty's Cabinet offered the Islands its 'warmest wishes for the future happiness of these prize possessions of the British Commonwealth'.

Later Herbert Morrison addressed crowds in the Royal Square and once again praised the Islanders for their fortitude and their 'loyalty and grit in the Occupation'.

On 17 May, in answer to a question in the House of Commons, the Home Secretary responded:

'I found the situation very much better than might have been expected. I explained fully to the States the necessity, in the interests of the Islands themselves, of withdrawing the British forces in 1940 and the reasons for refraining, after D-Day, from retaking the Islands by force in order to spare them the destruction which such operation would inevitably have involved. It was clear that these courses were both understood and approved. As regards the material conditions, the health and physique of the population are on the whole better than I, at least, had dared to hope and I was particularly impressed by the healthy appearance of the children whom I saw. While there seems to have been a gratifying absence of the grosser and cruder atrocities associated with the Nazis, I saw plenty of evidence of the wanton damage which the Germans did to houses and other property.' He concluded: 'I am sure that the House will join me in expressing our admiration for the fortitude and the loyalty which, with creditably few exceptions, our kinsfolk in the Channel Islands have shown during these long and hard years and for the courage and devotion to duty with which the Bailiffs and other Crown Officers have discharged their arduous and sometimes dangerous responsibilities during every phase of the Nazi occupation.'

Morrison's comment about Island children was an interesting one since Jersey's Medical Officer of Health, Dr McKinstry, had reported in 1943 that medical checks in the schools had revealed that the weight and height figures of children were below normal by an average of seven pounds in weight and one inch in height. However, the Dental Consultant, a Mr Price, also noted that dental caries were considerably reduced and as few as 13% of children required dental treatment. He put this down to a more natural, albeit restricted, diet together with an absence of sugar and sweets!

One slightly ticklish problem raised during the Home Secretary's visit to the Islands was just how legal were the laws and regulations passed by the States during the German Occupation. The Occupation itself had been a legal act since the Islands had surrendered and the procedures that applied before the occupation had been followed. Nevertheless it was agreed with the Home Office that all legislation passed during the Occupation would lapse with the end of the German administration but any measure that had been introduced that it was desired to keep in force would be submitted in the usual way to the Home Office for Royal Assent.

On 24 May Herbert Morrison reported to the War Cabinet on his visit to the Channel Islands. His report is worth repeating in full.

'Everything I heard led me to the conclusion that the Island officials had discharged their difficult responsibilities during the occupation in exemplary fashion and had succeeded to a remarkable extent in getting the best possible treatment from the Germans commensurate with the avoidance of any semblance of collaboration.

'There appears to be no evidence of anything which could be regarded as a war crime as far as the Germans were concerned. The two deportations of

1942 and 1943, which involved the removal of more than 2,000 men of United Kingdom origin, were not the responsibility of the occupying forces.

'As regards Islanders themselves, with very few exceptions, their conduct seems to have been exemplary. We were told of no cases of collaboration involving active disloyalty. On the other hand, there were a certain number of women who consorted with the Germans and the Germans were able to induce Island labour to work for them by offering very much higher wages than the Island authorities could pay.'

Alderney was the last Island to be liberated, a week later than all the others. Since it was known to be heavily fortified, indeed the most heavily fortified of the Channel Islands, and with very few civilians, the decision had been taken to bypass Alderney until the main Islands were secured. Thus on 16 May Operation 'Merit' went into effect when Brigadier Snow, accompanied by Lieutenant-Colonel E. J. Jones OBE RA and a senior German officer from Guernsey, supported by troops of Force 135 in an armed trawler and two landing craft, landed at Braye harbour to be greeted by a group of German officers led by the *Kommandant, Oberstleutnant* Schwalm. The party proceeded to the *Kriegsmarine* headquarters (a bungalow now known as Peacehaven) to complete the surrender. At the time the German garrison numbered just under 3,000 with just 18 British subjects on the Island. Due to the stories of atrocities committed against the inmates of the camps and the *OT* workforce, a Military Intelligence officer, Major 'Bunny' Pantcheff, began an enquiry into the allegations. That atrocities similar to those that had been revealed as Allied forces had advanced into Germany and overrun concentration camps such as Belsen, Buchenwald and Dachau might have taken place on British soil was the potential stuff of headlines. Major Pantcheff's investigations would confirm the horror stories but the principal perpetrators, Maximilian List and his deputies Klebeck and Braun, who had long since returned to Germany, were never brought to justice.

On 17 May the Channel Islands lighthouses operated by Trinity House (the Islands' most famous lighthouse, La Corbière in Jersey, was operated by the States of Jersey) were inspected by that body and found to be in good order and reactivated. The lighthouse on the Casquets reef to the west of Alderney had had its own German garrison since not long after the invasion whose role it had been to maintain the light and to report on Allied air and shipping movements. On 2 September 1942 the reef was raided by 10 officers and men of a Small Scale Raiding Force and the garrison taken prisoner, its equipment smashed (although not the light) and its code books removed. On 5 September the reef was re-occupied and on 17 May 1945, almost three years later, the German garrison of two officers and 20 other ranks was transferred to Guernsey, the men becoming prisoners of war.

Life began to get back to normal — euphoria can last only so long.

The rule of the road with driving on the left was restored and compulsory

German lessons in schools ceased altogether. By 17 May the telephone links with mainland Britain were reinstated. Daily deliveries of newspapers and mail were resumed as the airports reopened to civilian traffic and on 26 June the SS *Isle of Guernsey*, still in her wartime grey livery, reopened the Southampton to the Islands mail steamer service, arriving proudly flying the house flags of both the Southern and the Great Western railways. Shops that had been boarded up for years reopened as stocks began to arrive, albeit at wholesale prices rather different from those they had last paid, and strict rationing was maintained, as it was in Britain, until the early 1950s.

On 12 June there was another memorandum from the five clearing banks operating in the Channel Islands arising from their liberation. Amongst laying down guidelines for the resumption of normal business with their customers in the Islands, it was noted that the total of the obligations of the States of Guernsey and Jersey to the five banks, after the calling in of *Reichsmark* currency and local notes (for which the States had assumed liability) was not accurately known but it appeared to have reached, if not exceeded, £10 million. In fact the figures were £5,960,000 for Jersey and £4,232,000 for Guernsey. The States, it was also noted, were anxious to liquidate the indebtedness to the banks (and were concerned about what rate of interest they might be charged since June 1940) and, in any case, were hoping for assistance from the British Treasury.

A conference was convened involving HM Government, the States of Guernsey and Jersey and the five creditor banks to resolve the situation, whereby the banks agreed to refund the interest which had accrued on loans to the States during the Occupation. The British government agreed to provide a capital sum of £4,200,000 to Jersey and £3,300,000 to Guernsey on the understanding that these sums be used to liquidate the debts to the banks and that the strictest economy be exerted with plans for rehabilitation. To cover the balance of the debts, circa £3,000,000, the banks agreed to accept States' bonds.

In later years, when decimalisation of Britain's currency came about, Islanders from the Occupation era commented that it was tried on them first and they hadn't liked it much then!

In the months after the Liberation many who had been evacuated in 1940 returned from their exile as strangers, their children speaking in the strange accents of London, Liverpool and Glasgow. Some found their homes as they left them, carefully preserved by friends and relations. Equally many returned to find their homes stripped of everything, in many cases having been requisitioned by the German garrisons but as often emptied by those same friends and relations. Others found that their homes had been demolished as the Germans had laid their railways or cleared their field of fire. They would have noticed the dearth of trees, for so many had been given up to firewood, and also how overgrown coastal areas and headlands, cleared of habitation and animals, had become.

Young men in demob suits returned from the services, sometimes to find pre-war girlfriends still waiting for them but, as often, that the girls had fallen for and even married someone else.

Weeks after the Liberation deportees also returned but there were gaps in their ranks. Of the 2,190 deported from the Channel Islands as a whole, 46 died while in internment. A few — very, very few — returned from Germany's horrific concentration camps, among them Jersey school-teacher Harold Le Druillenec, who, when released from Belsen, required long hospitalisation to restore him to health. He was subsequently an impressive witness at the Belsen trials at Lüneburg in September 1945 when camp commandant Joseph Kramer and 10 of the guards, including three women, were convicted of the responsibility for ill treatment and death of prisoners and hanged at Hameln jail in December.

However, some form of official recognition of his suffering was a long time coming. There was a feeling, commonplace in both Islands, that those who by their acts had upset the Germans had put their whole communities at risk. The dividing line between the moderate rule of a Graf von Schmettow and the organisational tyranny that was routine in other parts of occupied Europe was a very fine one. The humanitarian considerations of Harold Le Druillenec and his sisters, and particularly the savagery of their punishments, illustrated just how very fine that line was. Harold Le Druillenec was awarded the French *Ordre de la Libération* and eventually the MBE on his retirement from teaching. In March 1966 20 Jersey people had been honoured by the Soviet government with gifts of inscribed gold watches. Among them were Harold Le Druillenec and his sisters Ivy Forster and Louisa Gould (posthumously).

Harold Le Druillenec died in 1985.

On 5 June the *Vega* paid her last visit to the Islands with her cargo of Red Cross parcels, and departed for London where the ICRC insignia were removed and the vessel resumed her long mercantile career. On a previous visit Bailiff Coutanche had presented Captain Wideberg with a set of silver milk cans as a gesture of appreciation of the vessel's crucial role in maintaining the Islanders' morale and physical well-being.

Altogether the *Vega* delivered almost 460,000 Red Cross food parcels as well as supplies of yeast, flour, soap and cigarettes. A few months after the Liberation the Islanders expressed their gratitude to the Red Cross by donating more than £170,000 raised entirely by voluntary subscription.

On Thursday, 7 June King George VI and Queen Elizabeth visited the Channel Islands in the 'Colony' class cruiser HMS *Jamaica*, calling first at Jersey and then Guernsey, their first excursion out of Britain since the beginning of the war. In Jersey they attended a meeting of the States where Bailiff Coutanche delivered a Loyal Address, to which His Majesty graciously responded. In Guernsey the Loyal Address was delivered in the open air before cheering crowds. Again His Majesty responded by saying that it gave him great joy that the Channel Islands, the oldest possessions of the Crown, were once again restored to freedom. While in St Peter Port, two midshipmen from *Jamaica* managed to get ashore and returned with souvenirs including a Schmeisser sub-machine gun, a notice in German saying 'Flying Officers' Mess' and a copy of the official Proclamation announcing that the occupation of the Islands was over.

A few days later a conference was held at the Home Office to determine what should be done about collaborators in the Islands. Jersey was represented by Attorney-General Charles Duret-Aubin and Guernsey by Acting Procureur, J. E. L. Martel. Also present was the United Kingdom's Director of Public Prosecutions, Theobald Matthew.

The conference agreed that collaboration fell into five categories:

a) Women who associated with the Germans;
b) People who had entertained Germans or who generally had had unduly friendly social contacts with them;
c) Profiteers;
d) Information givers; and
e) Persons, whether contractors or workmen, who had carried out work for Germans. In this class there were a number of Irish citizens who had volunteered for work on arms production in Germany.

Regarding a) and b) it was agreed that no official action could be taken and rather that such persons should be 'dealt with by social sanction'. Persons who fell into category c) could be dealt with by appropriate legislation that would tax the profits they had made during the Occupation. It was felt that categories d) and e) would come within the ambit of the Treason Act, the Treachery Act or Defence Regulation 2A. Conviction under the first two carried a mandatory death sentence and conviction under DR 2A carried a sentence of penal servitude for life. It was also agreed that any such trials would take place in the United Kingdom. Notices were placed in the local press to this effect. At the same time the War Crimes Branch of the Treasury Solicitor's department was taking an interest in the Islands, particularly with regard to the deportations of 1942 and 1943 and who was responsible for them, as well as other actions by the occupiers such as the cut in the bread ration as a reprisal for an RAF raid and the air raids of June 1940. It was decided that no war crimes had been committed by the officers or men of the garrisons of Jersey, Guernsey or Sark although the same might not be true of Alderney.

In a report to the States shortly after the Liberation, Jurat John Leale, president of the Controlling Committee since December 1940, stated: 'Ours has been an occupation in which neither side went to spectacular extremes. When one hears, in other places, of war criminals and quislings and the Gestapo as being the chief actors, one rather heaves a sigh of relief that ours wasn't that sort of an occupation. We shall associate the occupation with hunger and cold and homelessness rather than with dramatic arrests and sensational sentences.'

On Saturday, 19 May, the *Evening Post* published the following leader:

'WE PAY TRIBUTE TO
the many who, in a variety of ways, have helped to make things easier for their fellow-citizens during the Occupation. We refer, for instance, to the Post Office officials, who, at considerable, personal risk, opened letters addressed to the German Secret Police and, whenever they found the letters were from informers, took the trouble to call on the persons informed against and warn them. They saved many a resident from gaol. Those who, by keeping their wireless sets and distributing the news, helped to keep up the morale of the people. And to the many who helped the boys to escape from the island, together with the plucky lads themselves who 'made it' and took away much valuable information. And last, but not least, those loyal folk who helped the escaped prisoners of war, whether Americans or Russians. Everyone referred to is deserving of the highest praise, for they helped to brighten a page of local history which unfortunately bears many blots.

'WE DENOUNCE
and we despise those others, the informers, collaborators and quislings, the black marketeers, and the farmers who sold to the Germans food which should have gone to civilians, and thereby helped to sustain the morale and physical well-being of the enemy troops. These traitors played a dishonourable part, and we trust they will be tracked down and brought to justice, together with those others, among them some of our better-known residents, whose subversive activities against our own authorities is another shameful story and deserving of the strongest condemnation.'

And so say all of us.

Chapter 13
Nazis, what Nazis?

Today's commentators often refer to the Nazi occupation of the Channel Islands. But was it? Were all the Germans Nazis and were all the Nazis Germans? Babies for the Reich. The Germanisation that didn't happen. The men from Jersey who fought for the Reich. The biter bit. Just so much scrap

In later years some commentators would remark on a lack of organised resistance and even active co-operation with the occupiers. What they forgot is that unlike most of the occupied countries of Europe, where there were several hundred of the occupied to every single occupier, in the Channel Islands that ratio was never less than one to three. Also there was no *maquis* or mountains in which to hide. Furthermore there was no history within the Channel Islands of anti-authoritarianism or even the political groupings that would have focused organised revolt. Those political bodies that did exist — for instance, the Jersey Communist Party and the Jersey Democratic Movement — had the established local authorities in their sights just as much as the occupiers. When asked how he resisted, Jersey's wartime Bailiff Alexander Coutanche maintained that he 'protested' and kept on protesting. Jurat Leale in Guernsey stated equally simply: 'Against their might we pitted our wits.' Other, more overt, resistance would have been futile.

Nevertheless Islanders did resist, some methodically, some with almost careless disregard for their lives.

Acts of rebellion and sabotage, printing and distributing news sheets from the BBC broadcasts, concealing radios, harbouring escaped forced labourers and slave workers, were commonplace and subject to savage reprisal — imprisonment and even death — if the perpetrators were caught. There was even an institutional snook cocked at the occupiers when stonemasons re-laying granite slabs in Jersey's Royal Square incorporated a large 'V' into the design, later modified into a memorial to the *Vega* and, at the 50th anniversary of the Liberation, a commemoration to the stonemasons themselves.

By the end of the Occupation in Jersey more than two and a half thousand Islanders had served time in the local Public Prison for activities against the occupiers, more than 6% of the population. At one time, once there was no longer the option of sending the convicted to France, there was even a waiting list, those convicted being advised that they would be notified just as soon as there was room in the prison for them! Nevertheless only one person was shot by firing squad actually in the Islands: the fleeing paroled French soldier who, with a number of comrades, had fled from France and, landing in Guernsey, believed that a landfall had been made in Britain. Since breaking parole was an offence all sides recognised, despite the severity of the penalty imposed on the group's leader, no action was taken against the perpetrators after the Liberation. Indeed there is every likelihood that, had the situation been reversed, and the escapers been paroled German soldiers, all might well have found themselves in front of a British firing squad! The Germans did, however, execute a number of their own personnel for military offences such as desertion, theft, drunkenness on duty and one case of rape.

After the adjacent coast of France came under Allied domination in mid-1944, 225 Channel Islanders attempted to escape, always at risk of their lives, not just from the fickle tides and currents but also because the German coastal patrols tended to shoot first and ask questions afterwards. Although the shore patrols usually aimed at the boats rather than their occupants, many would-be escapers drowned when their often flimsy craft sank beneath them. The ability to swim, even in the sea-girt Islands, was by no means universal. Those who did escape provided valuable information to Allied intelligence, particularly with regard to the morale of the occupiers and the hungry state of the occupied.

Today the German Occupation of the Channel Islands is mostly dim memory, the numbers of those who endured it dwindling year by year. Yet interest in the period is undiminished; indeed it grows as more and more information from those grim years becomes available. Distance lends enchantment, they say, but the distance from the German Occupation, in a more cynical age when professing national pride seems archaic and jingoistic, also lends distortion.

There has been a tendency of late, particularly in the media, to refer to the *Nazi* occupation of the Channel Islands. It is all too easy to brand the Germans of 1940 to 1945 as Nazis, since the *Nationalsozialistische Deutsche Arbeiterpartei* had ruled Germany absolutely since shortly after being democratically elected in 1933. However, membership of the Party was never compulsory (a little over three million in a population 20 times that) although from 1939 membership for young people of either the Hitler Youth or the League of German Maidens was. It was the Nazi Party's agenda for European domination and retribution for the humiliation of the Treaty of Versailles that led to World War 2 and the occupation of the Channel Islands. The Nazis regarded the Versailles Treaty as a deliberate Carthaginian peace to destroy Germany. For Party Leader Adolf Hitler the treaty was '*eine Schande und eine Gräueltat*' (a shame and an outrage), a dictated peace imposed on an undefeated Germany. This was a humiliation to be expunged for all time. Occupying the British Channel Islands gave Hitler a little compensation against one of the principal architects of that detested Versailles Treaty.

Yet it is clear that the Channel Islands, with the unhappy exception of Alderney, were spared the extreme manifestations of Nazism. Although

Hitler took a personal interest in the Islands — the propaganda value of conquering British soil (although the Islands had surrendered without putting up any sort of a fight) was too good not to exploit and at times his interest amounted almost to a mania — he never visited in person or sent special envoys to inspect his prized possessions on his behalf. Instead he was content to leave their management to military men, most of whom eschewed Nazi party political ideals.

Despite the importance Hitler attached to his new possessions, the instruments of Nazi rule so manifest elsewhere in occupied Europe, *Reichsführer-SS* Heinrich Himmler's security apparatus of the *Reichssicherheitshauptamt* (RHSA; State Central Security Office), the *Sicherheitdienst* (SD; Security Service) and the *Geheimestaatspolizei* (*Gestapo*) were never deployed to the Islands. The members of the *Geheimefeldpolizei* were branded *Gestapo* but in reality, although the *GFP* often adopted the visual appearance of secret policemen — the trilby hats, the long trenchcoats and the Citroën *Onze Légère* — at the war's end they donned the army uniforms that they were entitled to and one oft-published picture shows one of the 'hated' *GFP* leaving Jersey's New North Quay in his army uniform, guarded by Gunner Morgans of the Royal Artillery and carrying on his back his version of the kitchen sink.

High-ranking members of the *Wehrmacht did* visit the Islands: *Generalfeldmarschälle* Erwin von Witzleben and Walther von Reichenau, the latter when he was commanding an army group in France in 1941, the former as *Oberbefehlshaber West* (Commander-in-Chief Army West) early in 1942. Both were shown how well the Islands were being fortified. Visiting the Channel Islands brought neither of these warriors any notable benefit, von Reichenau being killed in an air crash on 17 January 1942, and von Witzleben being executed in Plötzensee Prison in Berlin for his part in the July 1944 Bomb Plot against Adolf Hitler. Other notables were *Generaloberst* Friedrich Dollmann, Commander-in-Chief of the 7th Army and *Generalleutnant* Erich Marcks, Commanding General of *LXXXIV Armee Korps* (84th Army Corps) of which *319 Infanterie Division* was part.

The only true Nazi of note to visit the Islands was Reich Minister for Armament and Munitions, *Dr Ing* Fritz Todt (he of the *Organisation*), who made a flying visit in November 1941 and once again he seems to have spent his brief visit inspecting plans for fortifications. An uncaptioned photograph on display in the Jersey War Tunnels implies that Todt's successor, Albert Speer, might also have visited the Islands but there is no firm evidence that he actually did so although, when interviewed by Channel Television in 1965, former *Befehlshaber* Graf von Schmettow hinted that such a visit did take place.

There is no doubt that towards the end of the German occupation the Islands did come under a form of local Nazi domination in the person of *Vizeadmiral* Friedrich Hüffmeier, with his devotion to the Party's cause, his veneration for his Leader and his belief in 'ultimate victory', even as Germany was collapsing into ruins. Yet Hüffmeier relied on the steadfastness of the *Kriegsmarine* and its loyalty to the Fatherland to maintain discipline and morale rather than calling on those dark forces that would have been available to him. Although a mutiny was planned to bring about the Islands' surrender, it is likely that, knowing its protagonists, it would have still been planned had Graf von Schmettow been in charge since even he had pledged to hold out 'to the last cartridge'.

'The last cartridge' for all the *Festungen* along the French coast occurred on 9 May when their *Kriegsmarine Festungkommandanten* laid down their arms on the orders of their own Commander-in-Chief, *Grossadmiral* Dönitz, who had enjoyed (not the right word) the role of *Führer* for just seven days. That a few isolated posts (such as Sark and Alderney) actually held out for a few days longer had nothing to do with an extended German resistance and everything to do with the liberators taking that much extra time to get around to dealing with them.

So what did the liberators find, particularly those who had left to join the forces in 1939 and 1940?

Despite five years' occupation and the obvious and ubiquitous evidence of the enemy's presence, changes were not those they might have imagined. Contemporary photographs show the Islanders looking pale and drawn but comparatively well fed (they had suffered more from malnourishment than starvation) and they were even comparatively well dressed, albeit that the celebratory nature of the Islands' liberation probably meant that best suits and posh frocks were dusted off and worn for the first time for years. They had also had the benefit of Red Cross parcels for five months which had provided the necessities of a basic nutrition denied to the occupiers.

But the people *were* different. Even loved ones were a little wary. Five years of looking over shoulders and avoiding eye contact had taken their toll.

There were some oddities. Bailiff Coutanche almost managed to clear the wardroom of HMS *Beagle* by puffing on a pipe of home-grown tobacco (tins of Royal Navy issue tobacco were showered on him, presumably in self-defence) and soldiers of Force 135 invited into Islanders' homes for a celebratory drink found themselves choking on spirits home-distilled from sugar beet to whose violent alcoholic content Islanders had long since become accustomed.

Several well-known landmarks had disappeared, notably the Doyle Monument on Guernsey's southern tip, the Palace and Abergeldie Hotels in Jersey and on both Islands an 18th century Conway tower or two. The Channel Islands had rediscovered the railways, albeit not for long since German engineer POWs were soon busily tearing the tracks up again. Seawalls and harbours were festooned with miles of coiled barbed-wire and almost every valley had a mysterious tunnel or two leading off it. On the roads where, for the first few days at least and until petrol supplies were restored, only military vehicles trundled, there was a plethora of German military directional signs, many of which were torn down as souvenirs.

What those returning from Britain or overseas did not find, apart from those ubiquitous direction signs, was any other evidence of 'Germanisation'.

Compared with what the Nazis sought to achieve in other parts of the Greater German Reich, particularly Poland, where, by decree what had once been Polish became German overnight, there were few manifestations of German culture. Even those who had had to endure the German lessons in school made a point of forgetting however much they had learned almost immediately (although perhaps they might now regret that understandable impetuosity!). German lessons had largely ceased anyway as school hours were restricted because of lack of heat and light during that long, hard winter.

While metric units had had to be used when dealing with the Germans, Imperial units continued to be used by Islanders. Although the Germans had introduced their own names for places — in Guernsey they 'Germanised' local place names, eg Grandes Rocques became *Grossen Fels* — this did not happen in Jersey where almost all the strongpoints took their name from the 1933 Ordnance Survey map. In effect, they did no more than was already the case in the Islands where French and English differing place names existed side by side, and the Islanders never used the new names anyway.

Although the sheer numbers of the occupiers meant that they were truly ubiquitous, integration between the two strands of the Island communities (occupiers and occupied) was very limited. There were the inevitable personal relationships detailed elsewhere, but in the main the Islanders chose to ignore the strangers in their midst and managed to keep their distance, despite tripping over them at every turn.

The long-term German plan may well have been to turn the Islands into 'Strength through Joy' holiday centres with Germanic names (the *OT* had already renamed the Islands *Julius*, *Gustav* and *Adolf*) but nothing had been done to bring this idyllic scenario about. Apart from the hideous architecture of war, the kinfolk of Walter Adolph Gropius, founder of the Bauhaus school, created nothing that did not have a gun sticking out of it. Similarly the countrymen of Bach and Beethoven played only the instruments of the marching band and the descendants of Goethe confined themselves to penning a mass of orders and diktats in what even they dubbed as *Der Papierkrieg*, the paper war.

In the same way, German installations, once stripped of armaments and ammunition by teams from the Royal Engineers and the Royal Army Ordnance Corps (with the assistance of those who had put the arms and ammunition there in the first place), were systematically looted by avid souvenir hunters who as often wore the uniforms of British soldiers and American sailors as they did the well-worn attire of inquisitive and acquisitive Islanders. Nevertheless, in the main, the souvenir hunters were visitors in one guise or another, since, apart from farmers whose canny eyes could tell that a wooden container that once held a German field telephone would make an excellent nesting box for chickens, or the clamps that held together central heating ducts in bunkers were an ideal size for filling with soil and propagating tomato plants, and portable flamethrowers, with a little adaptation, could be used for spraying potato and tomato plants with insecticide, the reaction of most Islanders to all things German and reminiscent of German military occupation was to get rid of every last vestige of them. What today we would regard as priceless artefacts were piled on rubbish heaps, burnt or otherwise destroyed.

However, for one Jersey schoolboy, the debris of war would become a treasure trove. Richard Mayne began a formidable collection of Occupation memorabilia in the 1960s when most Islanders were still seeking to rid themselves of such unwelcome mementoes and later put his collection on display in a bunker turned museum. He came across an Enigma Model C encoding machine (one suggestion was that it had been thrown on a rubbish heap outside the Hotel Metropole, the German Army's headquarters in Jersey) but believed it to be no more than a rather complicated typewriter. It was to be 30 years and more before the significance of this machine was recognised and some time after Richard's sadly early death that the secrets of Ultra in breaking the ciphers scrambled by the Enigmas became common knowledge and the subject of books and films. Today, this particular Enigma is on display in the Jersey War Tunnels.

In Guernsey, a child born in 1944, became, at the age of 12, one of the founders of an embryo 'Occupation Society', having collected Occupation relics almost as soon as he was old enough to learn what the Occupation was. Ten years later, Richard Heaume put his considerable collection of artefacts on public display and today his Guernsey Occupation Museum, situated adjacent to the Forest parish church, houses in two cottages one of the finest displays of materials from that era in the Islands.

Amongst the trophies of war in Guernsey were the 600 draught horses which were sold off. Half went into the cooking pot (although the Islands have never really subscribed to the French taste for horsemeat) while the others resumed their labours, this time for the Island's farmers.

In Sark, where, before the war, the Dame had banned motor vehicles, were discovered two cars, a Morris and a Ford, two vans and a three-ton truck!

In Guernsey almost two-thirds of the mines had been cleared by the end of June 1945. By October it was estimated that only 492 (someone being very precise) POWs would be needed to complete the clearance of ordnance, of whom 250 would be needed to dispose of the vast quantities of barbed-wire. In Sark 120 POWs were employed tidying up until the end of November.

Huge piles of ordnance were gathered together at various locations, revealing for the first time just how heavily armed and lavishly equipped these German forces had been. Jersey's Springfield stadium, venue for the annual battle of footballing wits between Jersey and Guernsey, was filled with motor cars awaiting disposal by the War Department by auction. Many of them had been captured from the British Expeditionary Force in France in 1940 or had been commandeered locally. Much German military equipment, particularly vehicles and mobile guns and limbers, merely changed sides, while many installations were stripped of valuable parts (such as gunsights, range-finders and searchlights) which could be recycled into British military stores. Redundant or damaged vehicles were stripped of tyres and other parts. Hundred of tons of small arms, machine guns, anti-aircraft guns, field guns, tanks and munitions were loaded into landing craft which proceeded to Hurd's Deep, the deepest part of the English Channel to the north of Alderney, where their cargoes were unceremoniously tipped over the side to join the junk of the ages on the sea's bottom. Some gun barrels were tipped over the Islands' tall cliffs into the sea in the fond belief perhaps that there, pounded by the tides, they would rot and never be recovered. However, such is our curiosity today, and so well built were they, that many have been hauled back up the cliffs in recent years and seven of these barrels once again decorate the bunkers and gun positions whose teeth they once were. The massive 30.5cm guns of *Batterie Mirus* were cut up on site by the Evans Welding Company of Croydon into 5-ton pieces for ultimate melting down. A thin section of a barrel — a circle of steel — in the Guernsey Occupation Museum is all that remains. In Jersey two batteries of German searchlights were used for many years to illuminate Mont Orgueil Castle, their intense but misty blue light bathing the ancient walls in an ethereal glow that the modern devices that finally replaced them in the 1980s have never quite matched.

There was a curious sequel to the convictions of the Guernsey policemen for theft in 1942. Inspector Sculpher (he who had played a significant role in Guernsey's surrender) had been, with his wife, amongst the deportees of September 1942 and, on his return to Guernsey from Biberach, wished to be reinstated. On 7 August 1945 he was allowed to 'resume duty', his absence for almost three years being attributed to 'German action'. Others, who had been convicted by the German military courts, were not treated so benignly and were not offered their jobs back, their German convictions counting against them. Furthermore a Committee of Investigation, set up to sort out the matter, found that at the time of the offences the Police Force was demoralised, the cause being inadequate training, poor organisation as well as defective supervision and control. And who had been responsible for that? Step forward Inspector Sculpher. The Committee recorded that allowing the Inspector to resume his duties had been 'imprudent'. On 22 January 1946, the newly reconstituted Board of Administration agreed and terminated Inspector Sculpher's contract forthwith. He and his wife left the Island believing he had been made a scapegoat for the faults and maladministration of others. Many, including Ambrose Sherwill, felt the Inspector had been unfairly treated. Encouraged by the support he received, Mr Sculpher petitioned the Home Secretary for a fresh enquiry which was duly held and from which the Board of Administration resolved, on 19 December 1946, that Mr Sculpher's career could be deemed to have been terminated by 'notice properly given to him, expiring on 30 September 1946' which rendered him eligible to receive a pension. Although the former inspector might have wished for a result which exonerated him rather more fulsomely, he was nevertheless very appreciative of the support he had had from Islanders.

On 29 June, a Messerschmitt *Me262A* landed at Jersey airport piloted by Lieutenant Robert Anspach of the US Air Force, becoming the first jet-powered aircraft to do so. This aircraft was a twin-jet fighter which had proved to be a formidable combatant in the latter stages of the war in the hands of such aces as *Generalleutnant* Adolf Galland. This particular aircraft was being flown from Melun in eastern France to Cherbourg with an ultimate destination in the USA where it was to be evaluated but Lieutenant Anspach made a minor navigational error and found himself in Jersey where sufficient kerosene was found to allow the aircraft to reach Cherbourg.

However, there were many disturbing sights too, particularly the remains of the camps in which the forced and slave labourers had been confined although many of the huts had disappeared, having been torn down and used for firewood in the bitter winter of 1944/5. Some of the remaining camp buildings — most were the ubiquitous German equivalent of the Nissen hut — were burned since they were filthy, verminous and, laden with germs, potential breeding grounds for disease. Some remained, once fumigated, to be used as accommodation for farmworkers. One, formerly a hut of *Lager Schepke* on Jersey's Goose Green Marsh, stayed in use until the 1980s as the headquarters of the Pegasus table tennis club. Much of *Lager Schepke* itself was levelled and for years provided a playing field for the Jersey Rugby Club. Today, despite a tendency to flood in winter, the area is likely to become the site of more than a hundred houses.

Inevitably salacious attention was focused on a group of innocents, the babies born to local girls of German fathers. Although fraternisation with local women was prohibited by their military commanders, it would have taken more than written orders to prevent intercourse and intimacies of all varieties taking place between the victorious young men who arrived in 1940 and the women whose menfolk had left them behind. These babies could well have been absorbed into Himmler's *Lebensborn* but, in the event, this never happened because the Islands were cut off by the Allied invasion of Europe. The evidence is that liaisons between local girls and German soldiers, where they were true love-matches, were rather more tolerated in the Bailiwick of Guernsey than they were in Jersey. In Guernsey several Germans, once freed from their prison camps in Britain, returned to the Island and were able to resume their relationships, marry and become part of the community, in one instance, in Sark, eventually assuming public office. In Jersey only one such relationship is known.

In May 1975, to coincide with the 30th anniversary of the Liberation and an exhibition at the Imperial War Museum opened by HM the Queen Mother, Dr Charles Cruickshank launched his definitive work *The German Occupation of the Channel Islands*, commissioned by the Islands' governments and originally published for the Trustees of the Imperial War Museum by the Oxford University Press. In response a certain Mr Peter Tombs emerged from the woodwork rubbishing the work as a 'whitewash' of the alleged collaboration of the Islands' wartime authorities. Mr Tombs' claimed his own seminal work, *The Traitor Isles*, was also about to be published and at the ceremony he produced a leaflet promoting the work co-signed by Messrs Eric Pleasants and John Leister, both of whom alleged that they had been handed over by the civil authorities in Jersey to the Germans early in the Occupation for being in possession of stolen German petrol. Just who Mr Tombs was or is (it is alleged that in 1976 he claimed to have found Martin Bormann working on a farm in Norfolk) is now rather academic but who Messrs Pleasants and Leister were bears a little closer examination.

These two gentlemen came to Jersey with members of the Peace Pledge Union Scheme in the spring of 1940 as agricultural labourers. The Peace Pledge Union had been founded in 1936 as a pacifist movement opposed to the Spanish Civil War and was especially opposed to the view that fascism in Europe could be stopped only by war. John Leister was of German descent, had lived in Germany and spoke the language. In July 1940 he became an interpreter for the German forces although German court records list him as a baker.

Eric Pleasants was born in Norfolk and had a diploma in physical education which he put to effect by joining Oswald Mosley's British Union of Fascists as a bouncer. In company with safe-breaker Eddie Chapman (who was to become the British double agent known as Zig-Zag) he made a living from looting abandoned properties. Eddie Chapman was to achieve fame (or is that infamy?) by offering his services to the Germans who had him parachuted into England in 1942 with orders to blow up the de Havilland aircraft factory. Chapman immediately gave himself up and became a double agent, returning to Germany and back to England for a second time in 1944. He was the only Englishman to be awarded a medal by both sides! His exploits were turned into the film 'Triple Cross' starring Christopher Plummer and Trevor Howard. He died in 1997.

Late in 1940, along with Keith Barnes, another Englishman, Leister and Pleasants found a boat capable of taking them to England and proceeded to steal petrol for the attempt. Despite their claims 35 years later, they were caught at it by the German *Feldgendarmerie*, and although they exonerated Barnes of any blame, they were tried, convicted and sentenced to serve time in Dijon in France. Released from gaol, they were interned at the civilian camp at Kreuzberg and then seemed to transfer from incarceration to incarceration until, having claimed they were actually merchant seamen (hearing that rations were better in *Marlags* — the camps run by the *Kriegsmarine* for naval and merchant seamen) they were transferred to Marlag/Milag, a special camp for naval personnel at Westertimke near Bremen. There they were recruited into the British Free Corps, the smallest of the foreign contingents of the *Waffen-SS*. Their reasons, they claimed, were that rations would be better, they had ready access to the opposite sex, they did not like the discipline of camp life (they obviously had little idea of the discipline exerted by the *Waffen-SS*) and they had no intention of fighting anybody anyway.

The British Free Corps (BFC) had been founded by John Amery, renegade son of British Cabinet Minister Leopold Amery, initially as the British Legion of St George, to fight Bolshevism, alongside Germany. Amery was hanged for treason in Wandsworth Prison on 29 December 1945.

The BFC rarely numbered more than two dozen and had little impact on Germany's fortunes since most of the recruits seemed to display the same attitude to warfare as Pleasants and Leister who, inevitably, ended up in an *SS* punishment camp where they were put to repairing roads — poor rations, no women and guarded by trigger-happy Eastern European *SS* auxiliaries. Drafted back into the BFC in November 1944 and based in Dresden for training as *SS* pioneers, Pleasants was selected to box for the Pioneers against the *SS* Police in Prague and spent most of November and December in training. He won his bout and later boxed German champion Max Schmeling in exhibition bouts. At the same time he began courting Dresdner Annaliese Nietschner, whom he married in February 1945.

In January 1945 the British Free Corps reached its peak strength of 27 members and on 11 February, at the home of his in-laws a few miles from the city, Eric Pleasants watched the destruction of Dresden by firestorm. He was in the city when it was overrun by the Russian advance and for a time he entertained Russian troops with a strongman act. In 1946 the couple were arrested as spies and he was sentenced to 25 years in the Siberian *gulag*. He never saw his wife again and was repatriated to Britain in 1952 where no charges were ever laid against him. His life story was sensationalised in the *News of the World* and his autobiography is titled 'Hitler's Bastard — Through Hell and Back in Nazi Germany and Stalin's Russia'. He died in 1998.

John Leister also married his German sweetheart Lena Jurgens and fled with her before the Russian advance, making it to Milan where he surrendered to the Americans. He was repatriated to England in June 1945, arrested with four other members of the BFC and eventually convicted of treason at the Old Bailey in January 1946. He served just three years' penal servitude.

Vizeadmiral Hüffmeier, along with *Generalmajor* Wulf, was taken to Plymouth (where the duo were offered a meal of a Cornish pasty) and then to the London District Prisoner-of-War Cage at 8 Kensington Palace Gardens for interrogation. Their ultimate destination was Special Camp 11, the Island Farm prison camp near Bridgend in South Wales, from where, in March 1945, no fewer than 70 German prisoners had tunnelled their way to temporary freedom. All were eventually rounded up.

In Special Camp 11 Hüffmeier was in exalted company since his fellow POWs included *Generalfeldmarschälle* Gerd von Rundstedt, Ewald von Kleist, Walter von Brauchitsch and Erich von Manstein, and *Generalmajor* Walter Dornberger, who had been in charge of Germany's V-weapons programme. Despite the appalling suffering inflicted on those building the V-weapons, Dornberger was spirited out of the camp by the Americans and would later be instrumental, with Professor Wernher von Braun, in putting Americans on the moon in 1969.

Hüffmeier was released from the camp on 9 October 1947 and repatriated to Germany on 2 April 1948, where he became a Lutheran pastor. He died in Münster in Westphalia in January 1972. Wulf was released from the camp on 17 May 1948. He also died in 1972, in November.

The bulk of the German forces in the Channel Islands were held in Le Marchant Camp at Devizes in Wiltshire where, in December 1944, *Waffen-SS* and *Fallschirmjäger* prisoners had planned to break out, seize weapons and even tanks from a local Army depot and march on London. The enterprise was planned to coincide with the Battle of the Bulge which, at the time, was going in the Germans' favour. The escape was thwarted by alert guards and the ringleaders of the escape plot were sent to maximum security Camp 21 in Comrie, Perthshire. Unfortunately a *Feldwebel* Rostberg was sent to the same camp in error. He was believed to have informed the British authorities of the plot and after a severe beating he was hanged in a latrine. The five prisoners responsible were caught, tried and hanged in Pentonville Prison on 6 October 1946, just 10 days before most of the leaders of Nazi Germany went to the scaffold in Nuremberg.

Most troops from the Channel Islands were repatriated to Germany within three years although a number did stay in Britain, having formed lasting liaisons with local girls. One or two even returned to the Islands for the same romantic reasons but, as we have seen, the welcome in Guernsey was likely to have been rather warmer than in Jersey.

Serious consideration was given in Jersey to maintaining the railways in situ but it was recognised that there was no likelihood of their ever being a paying proposition and the tracks were lifted and the engines and rolling stock broken up or shipped to France. Literally tons of material were auctioned off, while any equipment of use to the military such as radar sets, searchlights and range-finders was shipped to Britain. In Jersey alone some 185,000 items of furniture and barrack room material and more than a thousand tons of stores were disposed of, mostly by public auction. The carcases of Renault *FT17/18* tanks, stripped of their guns, engines and electrical equipment, were sold for scrap for as little as £5 each. In both Islands the larger Renault *Char B*s had their guns removed but languished, quietly rusting, in parking areas until returned to their rightful owners, the French Army, in May 1946.

A buyer from Derby, it is reported, made a substantial profit after buying several thousand scrubbing brushes at just a halfpenny each. In Guernsey a George Dawson offered to purchase from the States all the scrap iron in the Island for £25,000. Although a very considerable sum in those days, one suspects that Dawson, known for some reason as 'Orange Juice', made a good profit from his enterprise since there was, at the time, an acute steel shortage in Britain. The steel shortage persisted until the early 1950s and this warranted a further scrap metal drive in the Islands. One imagines that there were certain regrets that so much scrap had been dumped in Hurd's Deep.

On 12 December 1945 a list of 'Occupation Honours' was published. Victor Carey, Alexander Coutanche and John Leale were knighted and there were CBEs and OBEs for various members of Jersey's Superior Council and Guernsey's Controlling Committee as well as a CBE for Ambrose Sherwill who, on 1 March 1946, would take up the office of Bailiff on Victor Carey's resignation, tabled just five days after he was awarded his knighthood.

However, hotelier George Seymour discovered that he would be receiving no compensation for having his four hotels taken over by the Germans, with most of his stocks of furniture, beds and other fitments either dispersed or damaged beyond repair.

In Jersey auctioneer Harold Benest, acting for the War Department, was still offering German goods for sale. There were many bargains: a box containing 500 pairs of scissors fetched £2 15s (£2.75), 49 wooden chairs realised 1s 3d (6p) each and 300 assorted plates, cups and saucers fetched 16s (80p).

Life was returning to normal.

Chapter 14
Aftermath

The scars and the heritage — some reminiscences of those who lived through Occupation — those for whom the Occupation is distant history — the swords of war into the ploughshares of peace. How we remember — was it victory or peace?
A reconciliation

There have been many successful attempts to ensure that memories of the Occupation do not fade. Liberation Day remains, in all Channel Islands, a public holiday and attempts to 'merge' it with May Day have rightly been treated by the Islands' governments with contempt.

BBC Radio, in particular, has captured on tape the memories of hundreds of Islanders and to commemorate the 50th anniversary of the Liberation the Jersey Heritage Trust mobilised the seamstresses of the Island's parishes to produce a series of 12 atmospheric and evocative tapestries. These capture in a uniquely involving form the lives of those who endured five years of enemy occupation. The Occupation Tapestry now has a gallery of its own alongside Jersey's Maritime Museum on St Helier's New North Quay. Adjacent to the entrance of the Maritime Museum is a memorial to those who were sentenced to imprisonment in Germany and did not survive. The memorial itself is a cast-iron lighthouse that once stood on the end of St Cathcrine's Breakwater on the Island's north-eastern corner.

Memory is often as frail as the body in which it lives but concrete, while it may weather, does not pass away and the Islands are still littered with the enduring detritus of those bitter years.

The German garrisons in the Channel Islands never had to defend their fortifications against any direct assault yet for several hundred of the occupiers the Islands were their last resting place.

Jersey had played host to German prisoners in World War 1 and some had died while in custody (mostly from Spanish flu), being buried in the Strangers' section of St Brelade's parish churchyard, that parish being where the prison camp was sited. Their numbers were considerably swelled in World War 2 (the first burial actually took place only 10 days after the German invasion) and the Strangers' section of the cemetery was elevated, in March 1942, to the status of a *Heldenfriedhof* (Heroes' Cemetery).

On the night of 4/5 January 1943, the SS *Schokland,* a Dutch-built 1,100-ton freighter used since 1941 to carry coal and general cargo between the Channel Islands and St Malo, struck a rock off Jersey's south coast while en route to St Malo. On board were more than 200 German troops going on leave as well as a number of female entertainers who had been with a concert party entertaining the troops at the Forum cinema until 31 December. The ship sank with a large loss of life (although the girls managed to clamber into a lifeboat and survived) and 28 bodies were washed up (including a Virginie Hacx, a clerk with the *OT* contractors of Heilmann & Littmann) and subsequently buried in the cemetery.

Altogether 214 Germans were interred in this particular cemetery, each grave marked with an oak Iron Cross. One of the first steps taken after the Liberation was to replace the Iron Crosses with standard British military white crosses. A few crosses were preserved in Richard Mayne's collection of Occupation memorabilia but the rest were used by the Rector of St Brelade, the Reverend William George Tabb, this author's uncle, for firewood.

In Guernsey, 113 German dead were buried in the military cemetery inside Fort George and a further 150 were buried in other Island cemeteries, although the bulk were buried alongside British war dead and foreign workers in St Peter Port's Foulon cemetery. Unlike Jersey, Guernsey does not have a separate cemetery for British war dead.

In 1961, at the request of the *Volksbund Deutsche Kriegsgräberfürsorge* (the German equivalent of the Commonwealth War Graves Commission), all the German military and *Organisation Todt* war dead, except those buried in Fort George, were exhumed and transferred to a new charnel house at Mont-de-Huisnes near Mont St Michel in Normandy. There lie the remains of 11,931 dead from World War 2 previously buried in the Channel Islands and the French Departments of Ile-et-Vilaine, Indre, Indre-et-Loire, Loir-et-Cher, Mayenne, Morbihan, Sarthe and Vienne.

The German fortifications in the Channel Islands never had to prove how strong they were but a visit to the similar bunkers and redoubts built behind the landing beaches in Normandy, which were subject to heavy naval bombardment just prior to the D-Day landings, gives an idea of just how incredibly destructive high-explosive shells up to 16in calibre can be.

So, apart from rising damp, the bunkers, blockhouses and tunnels lie mouldering. Most were sealed once their belligerent contents had been removed. Some were filled by the detritus of occupation, their entrances crammed with barbed-wire and then bricked up. Within a matter of months the War Department (who laid immediate claim to every bunker, tower and tunnel) had handed them back to the States who then promptly sold them to the owners of the land on which they were situated. In most cases these owners were private individuals who found themselves with some unwanted intrusions into their property while others discovered they had a veritable gold mine at the bottom of the garden. Many were put into immediate use as storerooms or even living space while others offered other opportunities.

In a landmark judgement in 1961, Jersey's Royal Court decided that the owners of the land above what had become known as the German Underground Hospital owned what was underneath it and they were free to develop or exploit the complex, which was already a tourist attraction, as they wished. As a result of this judgement, the States had to refund the charges they had levied for all the other bunkers. A landmark indeed!

Notwithstanding, most German defences were on the coast and almost all were in the ownership of the people of the Islands in the person of their governments, the States. The Channel Islands Occupation Society in both Islands has taken on the task of restoring several of these bunkers to the condition they were in when their purpose was still being fulfilled. The skill and dedication of this relatively small band of enthusiasts is amazing to behold. In the opinion of Theo Krausen, the one-time *Marineartillerie-Obermaat* (Naval Artillery Chief Petty Officer), the restoration carried out at *Batterie Lothringen* at Noirmont Point in Jersey, where he served between 1941 and 1944, has created the best preserved fortification of the Atlantic Wall. Some structures on public land, stripped of all their contents even down to the electric wiring, are still open and may be explored with care, not only because of the hazards that such mostly rubbish-filled bunkers possess as a matter of course — they were never supposed to be easy to get into — but also because over the years they have attracted all sorts of wildlife, much of it human, which has not always been too caring as to where it has deposited its waste. Wisely the Channel Islands Occupation Society counsels that it must be assumed that to enter any Occupation structures on private land without first obtaining permission is to commit a trespass, which may render the intruder liable to prosecution.

The Channel Islands have been fortified in some shape or form ever since they cast their lot with King John of England and cocked a snook at King Philippe Auguste of France. No previous fortifier would have claimed the Islands as 'impregnable fortresses' (or been prepared to spend the money to achieve that objective) and while Guernsey's distance from France meant that few French adventurers ventured that far from the coast, Jersey's proximity meant that any Frenchman with his eye on a bit of booty could flit across that strip of sea in the morning and be back by his fireside the same evening. Thus a string of fortified and armed towers were created on the east coast facing the French who were also supposed to be cowed by the glowering presence of Mont Orgueil Castle despite its obsolescence once the cannon had been introduced to the Islands.

Although few fortifications were planned after the conclusion of the Napoleonic Wars, many had been built during those years when the threat was, rightly, perceived to be from the sea. Sark and the other smaller islands were not defended since it was felt that even the French would recognise that it was hardly worth beating themselves on their rocky coasts and sheer cliffs only to find, once they got ashore, there was nothing there except a few wind-blown fields. What were built in the 19th century were barracks for the British garrisons, unlovely structures that in many instances, thankfully, have disappeared under later developments to house the Islands' growing populations. The German fortifications are merely the latest manifestation on the Islands, whatever their military hue, of the desire to keep invaders out. Like it or not, these concrete edifices are as much a part of these Islands' heritage as the castles that stood against Cromwell (and which lost those battles, too).

Nevertheless there are instances where swords have been turned into ploughshares. In Jersey, in the parish of Grouville, the *Organisation Todt's* granite crusher near Les Maltières quarry forms the framework of a block of luxury flats and, less than half a mile away, the building that housed an AC/DC converter now houses seed potatoes. Likewise on St Aubin's Bay in Jersey visitors now buy ice creams and pop from a bunker (the Gunsite Café) where once a 10.5cm gun menaced any invader. Tunnels under Verclut (known erroneously to locals as Gibraltar because it is a large rock) near St Catherine's breakwater on Jersey's east coast are now used to breed turbot, and *Ho1*, a tunnel complex in St Peter's Valley that once housed 6,000 tonnes of ammunition, is a mushroom farm. *Ho5* was located inside a tunnel built by the Jersey Railways & Tramways Company in 1896 and was planned as a fuel store, although its eventual use was for the storage of ammunition. It is the only tunnel complex to be completed and totally lined; it now stores the artefacts for Jersey's annual Battle of Flowers and several small-bore rifle ranges. Not surprisingly several bunkers (most famously *Ho8*) have become the homes of Occupation museums but even the hi-tech exhibition at the Jersey War Tunnels cannot completely eradicate the dank chill that is apparent within minutes of 'going underground'.

In Guernsey the 'underground hospital' (*Ho7/40*) is a much more extensive complex than its Jersey counterpart and, without the expensive trappings of a state-of-the-art exhibition, in many ways offers a much more evocative and unnerving experience. Planned as quarters for a self-propelled armoured unit with an adjacent ammunition store, at the Liberation it was discovered that in *Ho7/40* was stored eight tonnes of drugs and medical supplies. An actual 'underground hospital' had been planned close by the Princess Elizabeth Hospital but work never commenced. *Ho4* and *Ho8* are companion tunnels at the end of the road leading past the Bathing Pools at the southern edge of St Peter Port. *Ho4*, originally intended as a fuel store for the *Luftwaffe* but latterly housing oil made from coal for submarines (removed in 1947 to heat Guernsey's glasshouses), now houses La Valette Underground Military Museum with a comprehensive collection of wartime artefacts, including one of the original oil tanks, as well as depicting Guernsey's long military history. A tunnel driven under St Saviour's Church (*Ho12*) was planned as a ration store although, as with most tunnels, it actually stored ammunition and has had something of a chequered history since. Although the tunnel is privately owned, it passes under the churchyard and the churchwardens have banned any access to their section of the tunnel complex by erecting a formidable barred gate just 50 metres from the tunnel entrance. Before even just those 50 metres of it could be opened to the public, the 2,000 tonnes of gun parts, tanks, accoutrements and general rubbish that had been dumped there by the Royal Army Ordnance Corps after the Liberation had to be sealed off.

In Alderney, although nine tunnels were planned, only four were actually started and none was completed by the time the *OT* workers were withdrawn in October 1943. The Museum of the Alderney Society, housed in the old Town School, contains exhibits from all periods of the Island's history including the German Occupation. One of the most chilling is a striped uniform worn by inmates of *Lager Sylt*. Today there is even a small Occupation museum on Sark.

Although the German occupation of the Channel Islands did not itself bring about political change, it was undoubtedly the catalyst for the changes that took place within three years of the Liberation, reforms of the governments that increased the number of democratically elected representatives to the States (although many thought the processes were still not democratic enough) while largely doing away with those who sat in the Islands' parliaments by virtue of their office (such as the Jurats and Rectors) rather than by any popular writ. The process of democratisation continues to this day.

It is often argued that true heritage lies in the memories of those who were there. Some years ago, at the time of the 50th anniversary of the Liberation of Jersey, my wife Therese was moved to write down her own view of the Occupation. These are her own words.

'I was born three weeks after Pearl Harbor on 28 December 1941 and 18 months into the German Occupation of Jersey so the words 'occupation' and 'liberation' have always been part and parcel of my life.

'I was only three years, four months and 11 days old on 9 May 1945 but I have vague memories of standing in front of the Pomme d'Or Hotel looking up at the British soldiers on the balcony and being delighted when toffees landed at my feet.

'For my parents it had been a long wait from D-Day, when they thought liberation would follow within days or weeks, to hearing those emotional words from prime minister Winston Churchill that "our dear Channel Islands are also to be freed today" which my father was able to pick up on the crystal set he had kept hidden away. From their home in Grouville overlooking the French coast, they had been able to see the smoke from the bombing as the Allies fought their way into France. The next few months were the hardest as produce became scarcer and scarcer only to be relieved by the arrival in Jersey of the Red Cross ship Vega at the end of December 1944. I remember that first taste of chocolate which stayed with me for a long, long time.

'On Liberation Day itself we walked as a family the four miles and more to town, my parents and my 11-month old sister in her pram, calling first to see my grandparents before joining all the jubilation outside the Pomme d'Or Hotel where the Union Jack had just been raised. My mother and we two girls stayed in town overnight but my father had to go home to milk our two cows Katy and Ginger. Although it was very late when he did so he remembers that there were lights on everywhere, so unusual after years of curfew and blackout.

'This Liberation story really begins with the marriage on 22 June 1939 of my parents, three months before the outbreak of war on 3 September. They set up home in Grouville, where my father farmed, growing potatoes, tomatoes and cauliflowers, and settled down to married life.

'As the news from Europe got worse, the word "evacuation" was being discussed amongst the population and amongst my family. This family consisted of my parents, Fred and Joyce Bannier, Joyce's parents John George and Mollie Buesnel and their daughter Marjorie who was then aged 17½. My mother's brother Maurice had joined up in 1938 and was already on active service in France.

'The family's decision was to GO.

'Everyone was packed and ready when my father realised that he just could not leave his valuable crops in the ground. So he decided to stay and my mother, loath to leave him and her new home, decided to stay as well. Her parents did not want to go without her so they decided to stay too.

'Hence they all stayed and subsequently I was born at home on 28 December 1941. My sister was born two and a half years later on 8 June 1944, two days after D-Day.

'Life, although not always easy, was lived in as normal a way as possible. A section of German soldiers were billeted in a big house behind our home. For most of the time our paths never crossed but, of course, there were stories related to me by Mum and Dad involving the occupying forces who were so close by.

'One day I wandered off from the farm with our Alsatian dog in tow. I had walked as far as a granite crusher a few hundred yards down the road near Les Maltières quarry (where the Germans had excavated much of the stone for their bunkers and things) when I was found by a German soldier who brought me safely home. Imagine the shock on my mother's face when she opened the door to be greeted by me hand in hand with the enemy!

'My father can relate lots of stories covering those five years but three in particular I always enjoy hearing again and again.

'The first concerns a bonfire that relit itself in the middle of the night. My father was woken by Germans tapping on the bedroom window. The bonfire he had lit earlier in the day and thought he had damped down had burst into flame again! Since a rigorous black-out was in force Dad had to put it out on his own carrying water in a leaking bucket while the two Germans ostensibly watched the skies for enemy bombers taking advantage of the beacon Dad had unwittingly lit for them!

'One night Dad heard Germans near the house and when he investigated he discovered they were stealing his cauliflowers and, with a lamp hidden under his coat, he went to challenge them but at the critical moment the lamp went out! Fortunately the Germans took fright — theft was a serious offence — and ran off.

'Early in 1945, the winter was bitterly cold and Dad needed firewood. The section's sergeant told Dad that he would allow him to cut down a tree when the Commandant was away for a day or more since cutting down trees for firewood required a special licence from the Feldkommandantur. When next the Commandant was away visiting Guernsey for a couple of days Dad got on with the job but had to call on two friends, Messrs Farcey and Le Chaire from nearby Gorey Village, for help with the crosscut saw. They also had a rope but none of them was capable of climbing the tree so they actually asked a German soldier to help. He agreed provided he could have a share of the firewood. However the Germans did not have a saw so they borrowed Dad's and broke it! They managed to cut down two trees, sharing the wood between them. However Dad had to take the damaged saw into town for repair and hoped that no one would ask him how it came to be broken in the first place.

'Since Dad was a farmer we did not suffer the same food shortages that afflicted many people who lived in town but we all shared the other deprivations and despair the Occupation brought with it. Fortunately Dad had his crystal set and we knew that, sooner or later (we prayed it would be sooner) the Germans would be beaten and go home.'

Not necessarily the stuff of a best-seller nor indeed the scenario for a high-rating television series. Indeed, only two television series have ever majored on the German Occupation of the Channel Islands — *Enemy at the Door* in the 1980s and *Island at War* screened during 2004, both shown on ITV. By coincidence, and it was probably no more than that, both were set in Guernsey although the former was actually filmed in Jersey and the latter in the Isle of Man! In the opinion of many Islanders who were confident they knew better, neither was particularly realistic, and *Island at War* was, according to a report in the *Jersey Evening Post,* described by one local historian (not this one) as rubbish, a judgement which may well be a little harsh given that an authentic portrayal of the Occupation would probably be as about as exciting as the test card.

The media have long held a fascination for the German Occupation of the Channel Islands and as well as numerous newspaper articles (many rather more sensational than the reality), there have also been many film and television documentaries including some made by German and Russian (post-*Glasnost*) television companies. Much wartime newsreel footage has been assembled by Tomahawk Films into *A Living History — Channel Islands Occupied*, a 50-minute documentary largely featuring the islands of the Bailiwick of Guernsey produced to commemorate the 50th anniversary of the

Liberation in 1995. The most recent version also includes considerable footage of the restoration work carried out by the members of the Channel Islands Occupation Society and is suitably titled *Stars on the Landscape*.

The Channel Islands featured peripherally in the film version, starring Michael Caine and Jenny Agutter, of Jersey resident Jack Higgins' best-seller *The Eagle Has Landed*, although scenes supposedly set in Alderney were filmed in Yugoslavia. Islanders in Jersey had a chilling experience of *déjà vu* when, in the 1970s, Messerschmitt *Bf109* fighters of the Spanish Air Force landed at Jersey airport in *Luftwaffe* livery for the filming of *The Battle of Britain*.

But what does the Occupation mean to someone whose own parents were only months old at the time of the Liberation?

Natalie Guegan was born in Jersey in 1980. This is her view of the Occupation and Liberation:

'To me the occupation represents a vital part of our Island's history. It is a unique time, which Jersey should be keen to promote. I have been lucky to have first hand accounts of the occupation from my grandparents but I am aware that many of the remainder of this generation will not live to see the liberation celebrations beyond their 60th anniversary. Initiatives such as the Liberation tapestry and the restoration of the war tunnels are important in order to keep the memory alive.

'Watching the ITV drama *Island at War* provided a good talking point through which to discuss the events of the occupation with my parents. Their commendable annual display of regalia and loyal presence at the re-enactment in Liberation Square highlights the importance of these events to them. I believe it becomes harder for each new generation to relate to such events and embrace them with quite as much enthusiasm. That being said I do have a school friend who still makes a special effort to go out for lunch and celebrate Liberation Day even though he has now lived away from the island for several years.

'Dramatisations of the liberation such as the Jersey Youth Music Theatre's *"And our dear Channel Islands . . ."* bring the events to life and have an important educational and historical role. Having heard Winston Churchill's speech replayed countless times I still feel a sense of pride when he mentions "our dear Channel Islands". The fact that we have our very own Liberation Day just goes to show how unique and special we really are!'

Her sister Kim (two years older) agrees:

'For me, the Occupation of Jersey is an important part of our history and makes me respect the older generation who lived through it. The bravery that was shown in very difficult times is an inspiration. It also helps me to appreciate what we have and how lucky we really are.

'I think it is important that we are still taught about it at school, although most of what I know about the Occupation I have learnt from my family who actually lived through it. However, I do feel that future generations may not be as well informed as they won't be able to talk to the people who have first-hand experience, and this is a shame.

'I think that is why the Liberation celebrations are so important. The same goes for the many tourist attractions in Jersey which I have visited both through school trips and through my own curiosity. I have found them very moving and informative and a mine of information. We must make sure that people don't forget, and that the memories live on.'

Extracting humour from the Occupation is difficult although the *Jersey Evening Post* was moved to try on 1 April 1977 when it reported that a 54-year-old German soldier had been caught by a Trinity housewife in the act of 'pinching her broccoli'. The German, whose name was given as Hans Gruber, was living nearby in a tiny air raid shelter and, the newspaper reported, believed the war was still being fought, a belief strengthened by the constant roars overhead which he believed to be V-2s on their way to London instead of the incoming British Airways jets they really were. The newspaper even published a picture of a hunched 'Hans' giving an interview to a *JEP* reporter. Thanks to the coarse 65-line screen the picture concealed the fact that 'Hans' was wearing modern flared check trousers with his uniform jacket and a helmet decorated with *SS* runes. The date, of course, gave the game away since the newspaper shares with the rest of the media a delight in running spoof stories on All Fools' Day, just to see how many of its readers believe them.

In his collection of Occupation stories (published by La Haule Books, Jersey, in 1995), Luke Le Moignan mentions the spoof and suggests that the soldier was played by 'no doubt a member of the local Occupation Society'. In fact Hans was played by *Jersey Evening Post* staff photographer Ron Mayne who had been deported with his parents and younger brother to Biberach in September 1942.

The Channel Islands Occupation Society's bulletins consistently incorporate a feature called 'Do they come back?' devoted to the stories of German occupiers who have, over the years, returned to the Islands and frequently added to the sum of knowledge about that momentous period in the Channel Islands' history.

Without any doubt the most notable of the 'returnees' was the former *Befehlshaber der britische Kanalinseln* Rudolf Graf von Schmettow who visited the Islands in 1965. While he was in Jersey (he visited all the Islands he had once so omnipotently ruled) he gave an interview to the then *Jersey Topic* magazine which, in its introduction, described him as 'a man of high honour and of great kindness and compassion, a Prussian soldier of the old school who believed passionately in correct behaviour towards people, a man who had risked his career and, indeed his life, to plead constantly for the people of the Channel Islands . . .' During the interview Graf von Schmettow revealed that his pleas for favoured attention for the Channel Islands became something of a joke. He was quoted as saying: 'I remember when I was visited by General Obert, head of the 16th Army, he opened his talks with me by saying 'Don't tell me — we are going to hear more about your special circumstances!' I was able to reply that conditions certainly were special in comparison with all the sabotage, resistance and trouble he was having in France.' He was asked about the rumours of gas chambers, deportations and the ultimate intentions for the Islands had Germany won the war. His response was that no plans had been made for that eventuality other than, as we have already learned, to be the venue for Strength through Joy holidays. There were, he confided, abortive attempts to evacuate the civil populations, particularly when food became short but he had fought against them, calling them ludicrous since '90% of the population were employed in keeping vital services going'. Asked why he did not surrender earlier, especially when it was evident that Germany must lose the war, he replied, 'You are asking a soldier of many years why he did not turn traitor and commit treason on his country. That is very difficult for a professional soldier to do. It was impossible for me.'

The interview concluded with the former Commander-in-Chief being asked what was his outstanding memory of the Occupation. His reply is worth repeating in full. 'More than anything, I think of the outstanding leadership in both Islands by the officials who found themselves in almost impossible positions. Their handling of the situation was quite exemplary. I remember too the intense loyalty of the people of the Channel Islands to their country and their King. I am firm in my belief that the occupation of the Channel Islands will go down in military history as unique in which mutual respect of the population and the occupying forces for each other was the ruling factor. It is my sincere hope that one of the pleasant memories of the population of the Islands in what was an unpleasant five years for them was the high standard of behaviour by troops who were, in effect, the conquerors for that long period of five years.'

An occasional curious choice of words, perhaps, since while the generally correct behaviour of the troops belied the reputation of the army that had rampaged across France and the Low Countries, 'pleasant' was hardly how any of the occupied would have described it. Unexpected might have been more appropriate and the cynics might also surmise that when he praised the local authorities, given where he was when he did it, he would, wouldn't he?

To commemorate the 50th anniversary of the Liberation of the Channel Islands, each Bailiwick chose to express its remembrance in a different way. What a surprise!

Guernsey chose to inscribe a length of curving granite wall near the harbour where many of the deaths had occurred in the air raid of 28 June 1940 and erect a granite column, designed by local sculptor Eric Snell, to act as a sun dial, casting its perpetual shadow on the wall whereon were chiselled the names of those who died in the raid.

Jersey chose to commemorate the anniversary by creating Liberation Square, adjacent to the old Harbour Office and the Pomme d'Or Hotel, the erstwhile *Kriegsmarine* headquarters, where the Union Jack had first been hoisted with such jubilation on 9 May 1945. As a further touch, a bronze sculpture was commissioned from Philip Jackson which was probably the most controversial work of public art put up in Jersey in the 20th century. When the design was unveiled, public opinion was generally one of astonishment that the intended life-sized figures representing the beleaguered people of Jersey were shown releasing doves of peace. The Committee set up for the purpose explained that it had decided to change the brief from commemorating the Liberation to commemorating 50 years of peace. The public disagreed, while pointing out that had there been any doves around at the end of the Occupation they would have been eaten! What the public were expecting was a commemoration of victory, not of peace. And that is what they got — instead of releasing doves, the figures are now holding aloft a fluttering Union Jack.

Near the sculpture a plaque records:

'At this place on 9th May, 1945
advance parties from the Royal Navy
and the British Army liberated Jersey
from nearly five years of occupation
by German forces. They and the return
of the British flag were greeted by
thousands of Islanders with intense relief,
joy and gratitude.
'On the 50th Anniversary of that day,
the States and people of Jersey dedicate
this new Liberation Square to commemorate
that historic event and all those whose
efforts and sacrifices made it possible.
'This Sculpture by Philip Jackson F.R.S.S.
was commissioned by the Jersey Public
Sculpture Trust and unveiled by His
Royal Highness The Prince of Wales
On 9th May 1995.'

In London the Imperial War Museum dedicated its 50th anniversary of the war's end to a special commemorative exhibition of the occupation and liberation of the Channel Islands.

For the remembrance celebrations of Liberation Day, 9 May 2002, the Bailiff of Jersey, Sir Philip Bailhache, took the bold decision to invite the mayor of Bad Wurzach, *Herr* Helmut Morczinietz and his wife to be present. Not long afterwards, an assembly of the people of the Parish of St Helier overwhelmingly approved a proposition that St Helier should be 'twinned' with Bad Wurzach, where one of the Islands' internment camps had been located, and on 27 July a service of reconciliation was held in St Helier's Parish Church where the new mayor of Bad Wurzach *Herr* Roland Bürkle, gave an address wherein he asked for forgiveness and extended the hand of friendship to the people of Jersey. In September, a party of 27, led by the Bailiff, visited Bad Wurzach where a wreath was laid at the town war memorial upon which are engraved the names of all those who had died while interned in the Schloss.

As the result of the visit, which has been repeated annually since, lasting friendships are being forged and the furtherance of closer ties between the two communities is being accomplished.

Although the Germans did occasionally take hostages in the Channel Islands (but always released them), the large number of Islanders, all non-combatant civilians, who were imprisoned, suffered and died during the five years of enemy occupation is a tribute to the courage and rugged, obstinate distinctiveness that the people of the Islands have shown for a thousand years of proud, and still undefeated, independence.

And, once more, so say all of us.

Appendices

Appendix I

ORDERS OF THE COMMANDANT
OF THE GERMAN FORCES
IN OCCUPATION
OF THE
ISLAND OF GUERNSEY

(1) — ALL INHABITANTS MUST BE INDOORS BY 11PM AND MUST NOT LEAVE THEIR HOMES BEFORE 6AM.

(2) — WE WILL RESPECT THE POPULATION IN GUERNSEY; BUT, SHOULD ANYONE ATTEMPT TO CAUSE THE LEAST TROUBLE, SERIOUS MEASURES WILL BE TAKEN AND THE TOWN WILL BE BOMBED.

(3) — ALL ORDERS GIVEN BY THE MILITARY AUTHORITY ARE TO BE STRICTLY OBEYED.

(4) — ALL SPIRITS MUST BE LOCKED UP IMMEDIATELY, AND NO SPIRITS MAY BE SUPPLIED, OBTAINED OR CONSUMED HENCEFORTH. THIS PROHIBITION DOES NOT APPLY TO STOCKS IN PRIVATE HOUSES.

(5) — NO PERSON SHALL ENTER THE AIRPORT AT LA VILLIAZE.

(6) — ALL RIFLES, AIRGUNS, PISTOLS, REVOLVERS, DAGGERS, SPORTING GUNS, AND ALL OTHER WEAPONS WHATSOEVER, EXCEPT SOUVENIRS, MUST, TOGETHER WITH ALL AMMUNITION, BE DELIVERED AT THE ROYAL HOTEL BY 12 NOON TODAY, JULY 1.

(7) — ALL BRITISH SAILORS, AIRMEN AND SOLDIERS ON LEAVE IN THIS ISLAND MUST REPORT AT THE POLICE STATION AT 9AM TODAY, AND MUST THEN REPORT AT THE ROYAL HOTEL.

(8) — NO BOAT OR VESSEL OF ANY DESCRIPTION, INCLUDING ANY FISHING BOAT, SHALL LEAVE THE HARBOURS OR ANY OTHER PLACE WHERE THE SAME IS MOORED, WITHOUT AN ORDER FROM THE MILITARY AUTHORITY, TO BE OBTAINED AT THE ROYAL HOTEL. ALL BOATS ARRIVING FROM JERSEY, FROM SARK OR FROM HERM, OR ELSEWHERE, MUST REMAIN IN HARBOUR UNTIL PERMITTED BY THE MILITARY TO LEAVE.

THE CREWS WILL REMAIN ON BOARD. THE MASTER WILL REPORT TO THE HARBOURMASTER, ST PETER-PORT, AND WILL OBEY HIS INSTRUCTIONS.

(9) — THE SALE OF MOTOR SPIRIT IS PROHIBITED, EXCEPT FOR USE ON ESSENTIAL SERVICES, SUCH AS DOCTORS' VEHICLES, THE DELIVERY OF FOODSTUFFS, AND SANITARY SERVICES WHERE SUCH VEHICLES ARE IN POSSESSION OF A PERMIT FROM THE MILITARY AUTHORITY TO OBTAIN SUPPLIES.

THESE VEHICLES MUST BE BROUGHT TO THE ROYAL HOTEL BY 12 NOON TO-DAY TO RECEIVE THE NECESSARY PERMISSION.

THE USE OF CARS FOR PRIVATE PURPOSES IS FORBIDDEN.

(10) — THE BLACK-OUT REGULATIONS ALREADY IN FORCE MUST BE OBSERVED AS BEFORE.

(11) — BANKS AND SHOPS WILL BE OPEN AS USUAL.

(Signed) **THE GERMAN COMMANDANT OF THE ISLAND OF GUERNSEY JULY 1, 1940**

Appendix II

Orders of the Commandant of the German Forces in Occupation of the Island of Jersey

1. All inhabitants must be indoors by 11 p.m. and must not leave their homes before 6 a.m.

2. We will respect the population of Jersey; but, should anyone attempt to cause the least trouble, serious measures will be taken.

3. All orders given by the military authority are to be strictly obeyed.

4. All spirits must be locked up immediately, and no spirits may be supplied, obtained or consumed henceforth. this prohibition does not apply to stocks in private houses.

5. No person shall enter the Aerodrome at St Peter's.

6. All Rifles, Airguns, Revolvers, Daggers, Sporting Guns, and all other Weapons whatsoever, except Souvenirs, must, together with all Ammunition, be delivered to the Town Arsenal by 12 noon tomorrow, July 3rd.

7. All British Sailors, Airmen and Soldiers on leave, including Officers, in the Island must report at the Commandant's Office, Town Hall, at 10 a.m. tomorrow, July 3rd.

8. No Boat or Vessel of any description, including any Fishing Boat, shall leave the harbours or any other place where the same is moored, without an Order from the Military Authority, to be obtained at the Commandant's Office. All boats arriving in Jersey must remain in harbour until permitted by the Military to leave.
   The crews will remain on board. The Master will report to the Harbourmaster, St. Helier, and will obey his instructions.

9. The sale of Motor Spirit is Prohibited, except for use on Essential Services, such as Doctors' vehicles, the Delivery of Foodstuffs and Sanitary Services where such vehicles are in possession of a permit from the Military Authority to obtain supplies.

   The use of cars for private purposes is forbidden.

10. The black-out regulations already in force must be obeyed as before.

11. Banks and shops will remain open as usual.

12. In order to conform to Central European Time, all watches and clocks must be advanced one Hour at 11 p.m. TO-NIGHT.

13. It is forbidden to listen to any wireless transmitting station except German and German Controlled Stations

14. The Raising of Prices of Commodities is forbidden.

(Signed) **THE GERMAN COMMANDANT OF THE ISLAND OF JERSEY**

JULY 2nd, 1940

Appendix III

ORDERS OF THE COMMANDANT OF THE GERMAN FORCES IN OCCUPATION OF THE BAILIWICK OF GUERNSEY
DATED THE 2ⁿᵈ DAY OF JULY 1940

(1) – THE GERMAN COMMANDANT HAS TAKEN OVER THE MILITARY POWERS IN THE ISLANDS OF GUERNSEY AND JERSEY.
THE POPULATION IS HEREBY REQUIRED TO RETAIN CALMNESS, ORDER AND DISCIPLINE.
IF THIS IS ASSURED, THE LIFE AND PROPERTY OF THE POPULATION WILL BE RESPECTED AND GUARANTEED.
THE GERMAN COMMANDANT IS IN CLOSE TOUCH WITH THE CIVIL AUTHORITIES AND ACKNOWLEDGES THEIR LOYAL CO-OPERATION.
THE GERMAN COMMANDANT EXPECTS THAT EVERY EFFPRT WILL BE MADE TO ADJUST THE ECONOMIC LIFE OF THE ISLAND TO THE CHANGED CIRCUMSTANCES ARISING OUT OF THE EVACUATION AND OCCUPATION AND TO PRESERVE ITS ECONOMIC STRUCTURE AND LIFE.

(2) – THE CIVIL GOVERNMENT AND COURTS OF THE ISLAND WILL CONTINUE TO FUNCTION AS HERETOFORE, SAVE THAT ALL LAWS, ORDINANCES, REGULATIONS AND ORDERS WILL BE SUBMITTED TO THE GERMAN COMMANDANT BEFORE BEING ENACTED.

(3) – SUCH LEGISLATION AS, IN THE PAST, REQUIRED THE SANCTION OF HIS BRITANNIC MAJESTY IN COUNCIL FOR ITS VALIDITY SHALL HENCEFORTH BE VALID ON BEING APPROVED BY THE GERMAN COMMANDANT AND THEREAFTER SANCTIONED BY THE BRITISH CIVIL LIEUTENANT GOVERNOR OF THE ISLAND OF GUERNSEY.

(4) – THE ORDERS OF THE GERMAN COMMANDANT WILL AUTOMATICALLY HAVE EFFECT IN THE ISLAND OF SARK ON PROMULGATION THEREIN BY THE GERMAN MILITARY AUTHORITIES.

(5) – THE ORDERS OF THE GERMAN COMMANDANT HERETOFORE, NOW AND HEREAFTER ISSUED SHALL IN DUE COURSE BE REGISTERED ON THE RECORDS OF THE ISLAND OF GUERNSEY IN ORDER THAT NO PERSON MAY PLEAD IGNORANCE THEREOF. OFFENCES AGAINST THE SAME, SAVING THOSE PUNISHABLE UNDER GERMAN MILITARY LAW, SHALL BE PUNISHABLE BY THE CIVIL COURTS AND THE ROYAL COURT SHALL, WITH THE APPROVAL OF THE GERMAN COMMANDANT, ENACT SUITABLE PENALTIES IN RESPECT OF SUCH OFFENCES.

(6) – ALL CLOCKS AND WATCHES ARE TO BE ADVANCED ONE HOUR FROM MIDNIGHT OF THE 2/3 JULY 1940 TO ACCORD WITH GERMAN TIME.

(7) – ASSEMBLES (sic) IN CHURCHES AND CHAPELS FOR THE PURPOSE OF DIVINE WORSHIP ARE PERMITTED. PRAYERS FOR THE BRITISH ROYAL FAMILY AND FOR THE WELFARE OF THE BRITISH EMPIRE MAY BE SAID. SUCH ASSEMBLES SHALL NOT BE MADE THE VEHICLE FOR ANY PROPAGANDA OR UTTERENCES AGAINST THE HONOUR OR INTERESTS OF OR OFFENSIVE TO THE GERMAN GOVERNMENT OR FORCES.

(8) – CINEMAS, CONCERTS AND OTHER ENTERTAINMENTS ARE PERMITTED SUBJECT TO THE CONDITIONS SET OUT IN ORDER NO 7 ABOVE.

(9) – THE BRITISH NATIONAL ANTHEM SHALL NOT BE PLAYED OR SUNG WITHOUT THE WRITTEN PERMISSION OF THE GERMAN COMMANDANT. THIS DOES NOT APPLY IN PRIVATE HOUSES IN RESPECT OF A BRITISH BROADCAST PROGRAMME RECEIVED THEREIN.

(10) – THE USE OF WIRELESS RECEIVING SETS IN PERMITTED.

(11) – NO INCREASE IN THE PRICE OF ANY COMMODITY SHALL BE MADE WITHOUT THE PREVIOUS ASSENT OF THE GERMAN COMMANDANT. ON ANY CONTRAVENTION OF THOS ORDER TAKING PLACE, THAN, WITHOUT PREJUDICE TO ANY CIVIL PENALTIES THEREBY INCURRED, THE BUSINESS PREMISES CONCERNED WILL BE CLOSED BY THE MILITARY AUTHORITIES.

(12) – FOR THE PURPOSE OF REMOVING DOUBTS, IT IS HEREBY DECLARED THAT THE PROHIBITION OF THE SUPPLY AND CONSUMPTION OF SPIRITS APPLIES TO ALL CLUBS.

(13) – THE SALE AND CONSUMPTION OF WINES, BEER, AND CIDER IS PERMITTED IN SUCH PREMISES AS ARE LICENSED IN THAT BEHALF BY THE CIVIL AUTHORITIES.

(14) – HOLDERS OF LICENCES FOR THE SALE OF INTOXICATING LIQUORS SHALL TAKE THE MOST RIGID PRECAUTIONS FOR THE PREVENTION OF DRUNKENNESS. IF DRUNKENNESS TAKES PLACE ON LICENSED PREMISES THE, WITHOUT PREJUDICE TO ANY OTHER CIVIL PENALTY, THE ISLAND POLICE SHALL, AND ARE HEREBY EMPOWERED TO, CLOSE THE PREMISES.

(15) – ALL TRAFFIC BETWEEN JERSEY AND GUERNSEY, WHETHER DIRECT OR INDIRECT, IS PROHIBITED.

(16) – THE RATE OF EXCHANGE BETWEEN THE REICHMARK AND THE GUERNSEY POUND HAS BEEN PROVISIONALLY FIXED AT 5 MARKS TO THE £. A DEFINITE RATE WILL SHORTLY BE FIXED.

(17) – THE CONTINUANCE OF THE PRIVILEGES GRANTED TO THE CIVILIAN POPULATION IS DEPENDANT UPON THEIR GOOD BEHAVIOUR. MILITARY NECESSITY MAY FROM TIME TO TIME REQUIRE THE ORDERS NOW IN FORCE TO BE MADE MORE STRINGENT.

(Signed) THE GERMAN COMMANDANT OF THE ISLAND OF GUERNSEY

JULY 2, 1940

Appendix IV

NOTICE

FROM to-day, the 9th August, 1940, I have taken over the Command of the Channel Islands, so far as there are no military objects concerned.

For military purposes the Island Commandants remain.

The assurances previously given in regard to the lives and property of the inhabitants of the Islands will be observed in the future by myself.

I expect from the local Authorities, and from the whole population, the same loyalty which they have shown up till now to the Island Commandants.

All orders already issued by the Island Commandants in relation to administration and commerce in civil life are to remain in force, until further notice.

Jersey, 9th August, 1940

THE FIELD COMMANDANT OF THE
BRITISH CHANNEL ISLANDS

Schumacher,
Col.

Appendix V

SUPERIOR COUNCIL OF THE STATES OF JERSEY 1940–5

President	A. M. Coutanche Esq., Bailiff
Attorney-General	C. W. Duret-Aubin Esq.
Solicitor-General	C. S. Harrison Esq.
Essential Commodities	Jurat E. P. Le Masurier
Transport and Communications	Jurat J. M. Norman
Finance and Economics	Jurat E. A. Dorey
Agriculture	Jurat T. J. Brée
Public Health	Jurat P. M. Baudains
Essential Services	Deputy W. S. Le Masurier
Public Instruction	Jurat P. E. Brée
Labour	Deputy E. Le Quesne

Appendix VI

CONTROLLING COMMITTEE — STATES OF GUERNSEY 1940–5

President — Major A. J. Sherwill (HM Procureur) to Oct 1940
Jurat Rev. J. Leale Oct 1940
Vice President and in charge of Essential Commodities — Jurat Sir A. Lainé, KCIE

Health Services Officer	Dr A. N. Symons
Horticulture	Jurat A. M. Drake to May 1941
	P. Dorey Esq. to May 1945
Agriculture	R. O. Falla Esq.
	W. Sayer Esq. from Jan 1941 to his deportation in 1942
Labour	Deputy R. H. Johns
Information	Deputy S. Raffles (died Jan 1942)
H.M. Comptroller	G. J. P. Ridgway Esq. from Dec 1940 (died Sept 1942)
Acting Attorney-General	J. E. L. Martel from Mar 1943

Appendix VII

MESSAGE FROM THE ISLAND OF GUERNSEY

Invited by the German Commandant of the Island of Guernsey to write a short message from the people of that Island to their relatives and friends in the United Kingdom for transmission over the German Radio, we gratefully avail ourselves of that opportunity.

To all who are dear to us and from whom we are separated temporarily, we send our loving greetings and good wishes.

The German occupation took place without a single person being harmed.

As loyal British subjects we do not pretend that we are happy at being in German occupation but it is the fact that we are being treated with courtesy and consideration.

The Civil Government of the Island functions as before the occupation and the Churches and Chapels are freely open for public worship. Every Island official is at his post, not a single civilian has been deprived of his or her liberty and the utmost correctness characterises the relations between the German Forces and the Civil Population.

We ask that this message, when received in the United Kingdom, may be retransmitted by the B.B.C. and published in the English newspapers so that the natural anxiety of our relatives and friends may be relieved.

Once again, our love and good wishes

....

VICTOR G. CAREY
Civil Lieutenant-Governor and Bailiff of Guernsey

....

A. J. SHERWILL
His Majesty's Attorney-General.

....

G. J. P. RIDGWAY
His Majesty's Solicitor-General.
Guernsey,
July 6th 1940

Appendix VIII

THE FORTIFICATION DIRECTIVE OF 20 OCTOBER 1941

The Führer and Supreme Commander of the Armed Forces
High Command of the Armed Forces/Armed Forces Operations Staff
Department L (I Op) no. 441760/41
SECRET
HQ of the Führer, 20 October 1941

Fortification and Defence of the British Channel Islands

British raids against those areas in the West occupied by us unlikely on a large scale. But the situation in the East, and for propaganda reasons, may cause small British raids at any time; especially the British may attempt to reconquer the Channel Islands which are important for our convoys.

Defence measures on the Channel Islands must guarantee that a British attack will be repulsed before reaching the islands irrespective of whether the attacks are by air, by sea, or a combination of both. It must be taken into account that the enemy may use bad weather for a surprise attack. Immediate steps to strengthen the defence measures have already been ordered.

For the permanent fortification of the Channel Islands, which must be pressed forward energetically in order to create an impregnable fortress, I therefore order the following:

High Command of the Army is responsible for the overall fortification and will integrate the installations for the Navy and the Air Force into the overall programme. The strength and sequence of the programme will be based on the principles and experiences learnt during the consolidation of the West Wall.

For the Army the most important constructions are close-meshed flanking installations spacious enough to contain guns with a calibre sufficient to penetrate armour 100mm thick, and for defence against tanks which may have been landed from barges; accommodation for reserve groups and tanks; accommodation for plenty of ammunition (this also applies to the Navy and the Air Force); the integration of minefields into the defence system. The number of installations planned must be reported.

The Navy must install three of the most heavy batteries (one on Guernsey and two on the Continent) to protect the area with artillery; also, with the aid of the Army, additional light and medium batteries suitable to shell sea targets. These batteries must be deployed in such a manner on the islands and on the Continent that the whole Bay of St Malo is protected.

For the Air Force buildings must be erected for anti-aircraft positions, including searchlights, which are necessary to protect all important installations.

Foreign workers, especially Russians, Spaniards, but also Frenchmen, can be employed.

4] Orders will follow concerning the evacuation of those English to the Continent who do not belong to the purely local population of the islands.

5] C-in-C of the Army will report the progress of work on the first of each month via High Command of the Armed Forces/Armed Forces Operations Staff/Department L.

(Signed)
Adolf Hitler

Bibliography

A selected list of publications relating to the German Occupation of the Channel Islands

Occupation Diary by **Leslie Sinel** (Jersey Evening Post, 1945, and La Haule Books, 1984) is a most comprehensive record of the Occupation, having been compiled on a day-by-day basis during the Occupation itself. Leslie Sinel was a proof-reader at *The Evening Post* and had a unique insight into the daily goings-on. The diary was published 'unexpurgated' within weeks of the Liberation.

Jersey Under the Swastika by **R. Mollet** (Hyperion Press, 1945), *Jersey in Jail* by **H. Wyatt** (Ernest Huelin, 1945), *Smiling Through* by **R. Grandin** (Jersey Evening Post, 1946), *Jersey Under the Jackboot* by **R. C. F. Maugham** (W. H. Allen, 1946) and *Islands in Danger* by **A. and M. S. Woods** (Evans Brothers, 1955). These were the first Occupation 'histories' to be published while memories were still fresh but obviously they do not include material subsequently available to later authors, eg, Cruickshank et al. Nevertheless they provide a useful insight into immediate postwar attitudes to the Occupation and the occupiers.

Swastika over Guernsey by **Victor Coysh** (Guernsey Press, 1955). This is a history of the German occupation of Guernsey written by a Guernsey journalist and is a valuable source of reference.

Swastika over Jersey by **Leslie Sinel** (Guernsey Press, 1958). This is essentially a condensation of his Occupation Diary into a brief but readable history.

Hitler's Fortress Islands by **Carel Toms** (New English Library, 1967). This is a largely photographic essay compiled by a Guernsey photographic journalist and is another valuable source of reference albeit from a largely Guernsey viewpoint.

The German Occupation of the Channel Islands by **Charles Cruickshank**, (Alan Sutton and Guernsey Press, 1975). This is the official history commissioned jointly by the States of Jersey and Guernsey. It is generally accepted as the definitive work since Cruickshank was given access to wartime documents that were not yet in the public domain. Nevertheless Professor Cruickshank went on to publish a work of fiction — *The V-Mann Papers* — which revealed that, despite the research facilities available to him, he too was subject to indulging in a certain amount of fantasy when writing fiction rather than fact.

The German Occupation of Jersey 1940-1945 Reference Maps with supporting text and comprehensive history compiled by **Howard Butlin Baker.** A highly detailed map of the German fortifications of Jersey supported by a brief but informative occupation history. A must for anyone who wishes to study the defensive plan evolved by the occupiers in its entirety.

A Doctor's Occupation by **Dr John Lewis** (Corgi 1982) recounts the story of the German Occupation from the point of view of a local doctor. The newly married Dr Lewis moved to Jersey in 1939 and was enjoying a successful practice until the Germans invaded. His story gives an unusual insight of five years of hardship, particularly as medical supplies dwindled and even such items as babies' nappies became almost impossible to obtain although his accuracy as an historian must, on occasion, be called into question.

The von Aufsess Occupation Diary, edited and translated by **K. J. Nowlan** (Phillimore, 1985), covers the last 18 months or so of the German Occupation. Baron von Aufsess was the German Civilian Affairs Administrator and his diary is more of a personal record of his time in Jersey (his wife was peripherally involved in the July 1944 plot against Hitler and his concern for her is evident throughout) than a definitive history of the Islands in that period. His comments on many of the local officials with whom he had dealings and the local people with whom he made friends (some intimately) make interesting reading.

The War on the Channel Islands — Then and Now by **Winston Ramsey** (Battle of Britain Prints International, 1985) lives up to its title. Lavishly illustrated with 'then and now' photographs, despite being published almost 20 years ago, it is probably still the most useful publication from the point of view of the visitor seeing Occupation sites today and wishing to put them into their wartime context.

Jersey, Occupation Remembered, compiled by **Sonia Hillsden** (Jarrold, 1986) features the personal reminiscences of Islanders and illustrates just how varied viewpoints and memories can be of the same events.

German Tunnels in the Channel Islands by **Michael Ginns MBE**, is the Channel Islands Occupation Society's Archive Book No 7 (published 1993). With detailed plans by Paul Burnal, this A4-sized guide features the major excavations in Jersey and Guernsey and, although written for the serious military historian rather than those with only a casual interest, this work is undoubtedly the most comprehensive guide of these fortifications published to date.

The Organisation Todt and the Fortress Engineers in the Channel Islands, the Channel Islands Occupation Society's Archive Book No 8 (published 1994) is a definitive guide to the German and French civilian contractors who built the fortifications and the organisation that provided the workforce of forced and slave labourers.

The Channel Islands Occupation and Liberation 1940-1945 by **Professor Asa Briggs** (Batsford, in association with the Imperial War Museum, 1995). This was the IWM's 'official' publication commemorating the 50th anniversary of the Liberation of the Channel Islands and its own concurrent exhibition in London. Well illustrated, concise yet comprehensive, unfortunately this publication is marred by several common errors of detail and some careless captioning.

A Model Occupation by **Madeline Bunting** (Harper Collins, 1995) is probably one of the most controversial of the recent publications on the Occupation. Ms Bunting does no favours for her hypothesis that the Islands' authorities were unduly co-operative with the German occupiers with a multitude of easily avoided errors of detail and fact.

The Channel Islands at War — A German Perspective by **George Forty** (Ian Allan Publishing Ltd, 1999, paperback edition 2005). This is a photographic essay as well as an account of the Occupation. It contains a lot of interesting, and much previously unpublished, detail of the German forces that occupied the Channel Islands and a useful illustrated directory of wartime sites that can be visited today.

Jersey's German Bunkers, the Channel Islands Occupation Society's Archive Book No 9 (published 1999) is an invaluable guide to the design and construction of the bunkers, towers and blockhouses built by the Occupation forces between 1941 and 1944. Although once again a publication for the historian rather than the merely curious, this publication answers the frequent questions as to why there were so many different types of bunker (among several reasons was that different building contractors used different architects) and why they still litter the Island's landscape.

The Occupation of Jersey Day by Day — The Personal Diary of Deputy Edward Le Quesne (La Haule Books, 1999). Edward Le Quesne was a member of the States of Jersey Superior Council from 1940 until 1945 with the responsibility for organising labour. His diary records how he agonised over decisions he had to take over providing labour for the occupiers to work on their fortifications. When food became short he organised communal kitchens and ultimately spent some weeks in Jersey's Public Prison for illegally possessing a radio. An intriguing insight into how an 'amateur' politician dealt with the most bureaucratic military machine the world to date had ever known.

Liberated by Force 135 by **Mark Lamerton** (ELSP in association with Nestegg Enterprises, 2000). A detailed history of the Liberation of the Channel Islands in May 1945 from planning to execution, containing much previously unpublished material.

A Boy Remembers by **Leo Harris** (Apache Guides 2000). The personal memories of a schoolboy's Occupation, combining wit and not a little pathos, with the benefit of half a century's hindsight.

A Boy Remembers More by **Leo Harris** (Apache Guides 2002). More of the same memories of schooldays spent under enemy occupation.

Battleground Europe — Atlantic Wall Channel Islands by **George Forty** (Leo Cooper, Pen & Sword Books, 2002). One of a series which currently comprises 17 volumes, each with a different perspective on 'Battleground Europe'. This volume features the German occupation and the liberation of the Channel Islands told mostly from the point of view of the occupying forces. A complementary volume to his earlier publication ***The Channel Islands at War — A German Perspective*** *(Ian Allan Publishing Ltd, 1999, paperback edition 2005)*, it is well illustrated with many new photographs and includes a useful illustrated directory of wartime sites that can be visited today.

Batterie Lothringen by **Paul Burnal**, the Channel Islands Occupation Society's Archive Book No 10 (published 2002), is the fully illustrated story of the only naval coastal battery to be established in Jersey during the Occupation and the foreword of the book has been provided by one of its original personnel. The command bunker of the battery has been comprehensively restored by the CIOS and this is yet another authoritative and definitive work.

Guernsey Occupied But Never Conquered by **William M. Bell** (2002). Probably the most definitive and detailed history of the German Occupation of Guernsey published to date. The book proclaims itself as a factual portrayal of the Occupation period based upon thousands of Occupation files, both German and civilian, and personal reminiscences recorded at the time. And it is.

Bulletins of the C.I.O.S., published by the Channel Islands Occupation Society. These publications are produced on a regular basis and focus on different aspects of the German Occupation of the Channel Islands. Bulletins tend to be published by the Guernsey and Jersey branches in alternate editions and are a vital and valuable source of detailed information about the German Occupation of the Channel Islands compiled by a dedicated group of enthusiasts who have no agenda other than to reveal the German Occupation in every facet. Details are available from the **Hon Secretary, Michael Ginns MBE, Les Geonnais de Bas, La Rue des Geonnais, St Ouen, Jersey JE3 2BS.**

Websites with content relating to the Channel Islands

www.ciosjersey.fsnet.co.uk — The official site of the CI Occupation Society

www.jersey.co.uk — The official Jersey Tourism site. Contains references to the German Occupation

www.jerseyheritagetrust.org — This site features many aspects of the German Occupation of the Channel Islands including matters relating to Jews in the Channel Islands and is also the official site of the Jersey Archive Centre

www.jerseywartunnels.com — The official site of the Jersey War Tunnels (German Underground Hospital)

www.occupied.guernsey.net — The site of the CI Occupation Society (Guernsey)

www.societe-jersiase.org — This site features the German Occupation of Jersey and is a valuable source of photographs and illustrations

www.societe.org.gg — This site features the German Occupation of the Bailiwick of Guernsey

www.thisisguernsey.com — The site of the *Guernsey Evening Press & Star.* Contains many references to the German Occupation

www.thisisjersey.com — The site of the *Jersey Evening Post.* Contains references to the German Occupation

www.tomahawkfilms.com — The site features German newsreel footage of the Occupation of the Channel Islands (mostly filmed in Guernsey)

Glossary

Artillerieträger — barge equipped with a variety of artillery pieces

Bailiff — the chief citizen of the Bailiwicks of Jersey and Guernsey, uniquely combining the head of the judiciary with the president of the legislature

Bailiwick of Guernsey — Guernsey, Alderney, Sark, Herm, Jethou, Brecqhou, Burhou and Lihou

Bailiwick of Jersey — Jersey and Les Minquiers and Les Ecréhous reefs

Befehlshaber der britischen Kanalinseln (BdbK) — Commander-in-Chief of the Channel Islands

Blitzkrieg — lightning war

British Free Corps — section of British renegades with the *Waffen-SS*

British Union of Fascists — Overseas Department — the Jersey branch of Sir Oswald Mosley's 'Blackshirts'

Centenier — an honorary policeman (or woman) unique to Jersey responsible for charging miscreants and prosecuting them at the Police Court (Magistrates' Court)

Chausey — French Channel Island eight miles west of Granville

clameur de haro — ancient right of Channel Islanders to seek the intercession of their Duke in a dispute

Connétable — in Jersey the 'mayor' of a parish, in Guernsey the parish's senior citizen

Constable's Officer — the lowest ranking honorary policeman (or woman) in Jersey

Controlling Committee — wartime governing body of the States of Guernsey

das Rathaus — Town Hall

die Grosse Hungerzeit — The Time of Great Hunger

der Papierkrieg — the paper war

Deutsche Guernsey Zeitung — German Guernsey News

Deutsche Inselzeitung — German Island News

Douzaine — parish council in Guernsey

Douzenier — parish representative in Guernsey in the States of Deliberation

ein Insel Wahnsinn — an island madness

Elizabeth College — Guernsey's boys' public school

Enigma — German encoding machine

Es lebe des freies Deutschland — the Free Germany Movement

Fahnengesetz — the Flag Law which replaced the Kaiser's black, red and white striped ensign with the swastika as Germany's official symbol

Feldgendarmerie — Field Gendarmerie

Feldkommandant — Field Commander

Feldkommandantur 515 — Field Command 515
Festungen — fortresses
Festungkommandant — Fortress Commander
Festungkommandantur — Fortress Command
Freya — German radar
Führerbefehl — An order from Adolf Hitler
Führerbunker — Hitler's underground headquarters in the Chancellery
  garden in Berlin
Gazette Officielle — Official notices section in the local press
Generalfeldmarschall — Field Marshal
Generalleutnant — Lieutenant-General
Generalmajor — Major-General
Generaloberst — Colonel-General
Generaloberst der Flieger — Colonel-General of Flyers
Gestapo (Geheimestaatspolizei) — Secret State Police
GFP (Geheimefeldpolizei) — Secret Field Police
Grossadmiral — Admiral of the Fleet
GUNS — Guernsey Underground News Service
Hafenkommandant — Harbourmaster
Hafenkommandantur — Harbourmaster's Office
Hauptmann — Captain
Heer — German Army
Heldenfriedhof — Heroes' Cemetery
HM Attorney-General — the senior Crown Officer in Jersey
HM Comptroller — Guernsey's Solicitor-General
HM *Prevôt* — the Royal Court official in Guernsey responsible for carrying
  out Court procedures, collecting fines, etc
HM Procureur — Guernsey's Attorney-General
HM Receiver-General — a title common to both Islands, the junior ranking
  Crown Officer
HM Solicitor-General — the second-ranking Crown Officer in Jersey
HM *Vicomte* — the Royal Court official in Jersey responsible for carrying
  out Court procedures, collecting fines, etc
Ho (Hohlgangsanlage) — cave passage installation, designation of German
  tunnels in the Channel Islands
Jerrybags — local women and girls who consorted with Germans
Jersey Democratic Movement — Jersey political party
Jurat — a title unique to the Channel Islands, a 'judge of fact' elected for
  life and, until 1948, with a seat in the States
Kampfgeschwader — *Luftwaffe* squadron
Kanalinselnmilitärischegericht — the Channel Islands Military Tribunal
Kapitänleutnant — German Naval rank equivalent to Lieutenant-
  Commander in the Royal Navy
Kapitän zur See — Navy captain

Kapo — concentration camp overseer drawn from the inmates
Kernwerken — Battlefield command headquarters
Kommandierender Admiral Frankreich — Commanding Admiral France
Kommandobefehl — Commando Order
Konteradmiral — Rear Admiral
Korvettenkapitän — German naval rank equivalent to Commander in the
    Royal Navy
Kraft durch Freude — Strength through Joy movement
Kriegsmarine — the German Navy
Kriegsverwaltungsrat — War administrator
Lager Norderney — a punishment camp in Alderney
Lager Schepke — OT workers' camp in St Lawrence, Jersey
Lager Sylt — SS concentration camp on Alderney
La Service Travail Obligatoire — Compulsory Work Service in France
Lebensborn — Fountain of Life
Légion d'Honneur — France's highest award
Les Chroniques de Jersey — French-language newspaper in Jersey
Leutnant — Lieutenant
Liberation Day — Wednesday, 9 May 1945
Lieutenant-Governor — the Sovereign's representative in each Bailiwick
Lord Haw Haw (William Joyce) — British traitor who broadcast for the
    Germans
LST — Landing Ship, Tank
Luftwaffe — German Air Force
Luftwaffe Feldbauamt Kanalinseln — Air Force Field Works Office Channel
    Islands
Major — Major
Marinebefehlshaber Nordfrankreich — Naval Commander North France
Marinegruppe West — Navy Group West
Marinehafenbauamt Kanalinseln — Navy Port Works Office Channel Islands
Marine Oberkommando West (MOK West) — Naval Headquarters West
Marinestosstruppabteilung — German Marines
Nationalsozialistische Deutsche Arbeiterpartei (Nazi) — National Socialist
    German Workers Party
Nationalsozialistische Kraftfahrerkorps (NSKK) — the National Socialist
    Motor Transport Corps
Nebenstelle — Subordinate Authority branch
Oberfeldwebel — Senior sergeant-major
Obergefreiter — Senior corporal
Oberkommando der Kriegsmarine (OKM) — German Naval High
    Command
Oberkommando der Wehrmacht (OKW) — German High Command
Oberleutnant — Senior Lieutenant
Oberst — Colonel

Oberstleutnant — Lieutenant-Colonel

Occupation *Reichsmark* — Wartime unit of currency in the Channel Islands worth approximately 10p

Organisation Todt (OT) — German workforce comprising forced and slave labourers

OT Heim(e) — club(s) for *OT* officers

Platzkommandant — Area Commander

Platzkommandantur — Area Command

Prinzalbrechtstrasse — street in Berlin, site of *Reichsführer-SS* Himmler's headquarters

Procureur du Bien Public — public trustees of each Parish whose principal role was to oversee the parish accounts

Rasse und Siedlungshauptamt — Race and Settlement Head Office

Reichsarbeitsdienst — State Labour Service

Reichssicherheitshauptamt (RSHA) — State Central Security Office

Rittmeister — Cavalry captain

Royal Guernsey Militia and **Royal Jersey Militia** — form of compulsory territorial army service in the Channel Islands

Russiskaya Osvoboditelnaya Armiya — Russian Liberation Army

Seekommandant (*Seeko*) — Sea Commander

Sicherheitsdienst (SD) — Security Service

Sippenhaft — family guilt (by association)

Soldatenheim — a facility providing recreation for German officers and other ranks alike

Sonderführer — Special leader, a quasi-military rank for civilian affairs officers

SS (Schutz Staffel) — Elite guard, formed in 1933 as a group of bodyguards for Adolf Hitler

SS Baubrigade — SS Work Brigade

SS Hauptsturmführer — SS rank equivalent to Army Captain

SS Obersturmführer — SS rank equivalent to Army First Lieutenant

States of Guernsey — Guernsey's parliament also known as the States of Deliberation

States of Jersey — Jersey's parliament

Superior Council — wartime governing body of the States of Jersey

The Evening Post — then and now Jersey's only daily newspaper, renamed *Jersey Evening Post* in the mid-1960s

The Evening Press — Guernsey's daily evening newspaper

The Star — Guernsey's morning daily newspaper, eventually merged with the *Evening Press*

U-boat (*Unterseeboot*) — German submarine

Ultra — code name of deciphering service of the Government Code and Cipher School at Bletchley Park

Unternehmung — Operation

Verteidigung Sektor Norden — Defence Sector North in Jersey

Victoria College — Jersey's boys' public school

Vingtenier — an honorary policeman (or woman) in Jersey whose role is also to collect the parish rate

Volksbund Deutsche Kriegsgräberfürsorge — the German equivalent of the Commonwealth War Graves Commission

Waffen-SS — Fighting SS

Wehrgeistiger Führungsstab — Military Spiritual Leadership Staff

Wehrmacht — the German armed forces

Wehrmachtführungsstab — German Armed Forces Operations Staff

Würzburg — German radar

Index